CARLISLE
VS.
ARMY

CARLISLE

vs.

ARMY

JIM THORPE, DWIGHT EISENHOWER, POP WARNER, AND THE FORGOTTEN STORY OF FOOTBALL'S GREATEST BATTLE

LARS ANDERSON

RANDOM HOUSE   NEW YORK

Published in the United States by Random House, an imprint of The Random House
Publishing Group, a division of Random House, Inc., New York.

RANDOM HOUSE and colophon are registered trademarks of Random House, Inc.

LIBRARY OF CONGRESS CATALOGING-IN-PUBLICATION DATA

Anderson, Lars.
Carlisle versus Army: Jim Thorpe, Dwight Eisenhower, Pop Warner, and the forgotten
story of football's greatest battle / Lars Anderson.
p. cm.
Includes bibliographical references.
ISBN 978-1-4000-6600-1
1. United States Indian School (Carlisle, Pa.)—Football. 2. Football—History. I. Title.
GV958.U33A53 2007
796.332'630973—dc22   2007008410

Printed in the United States of America on acid-free paper

www.atrandom.com

246897531

First Edition

Book design by Susan Turner

For Sara Jane Anderson,
my sublime wife

"After thirty-six years of coaching at such widely separated and differing schools as Iowa State, Cornell, University of Georgia, Carlisle, University of Pittsburgh and Stanford, the experiences that stand out most vividly in my memory are those connected with the Indian lads."

—GLENN "POP" WARNER, *1931*

CONTENTS

CARLISLE
VS.
ARMY

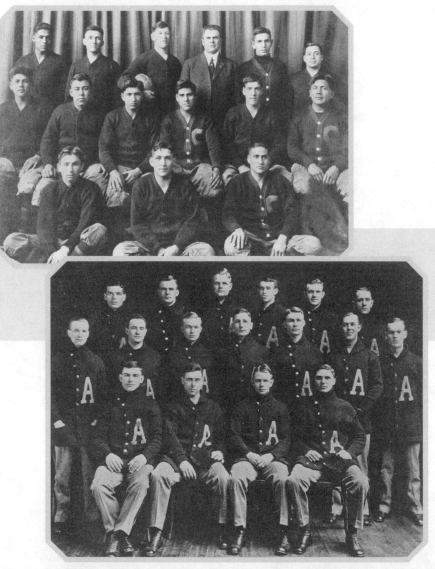

Top: *The 1912 Carlisle Indian football team. James Francis Thorpe, twenty-four (back row, third from left), and Coach Glenn "Pop" Warner, forty-one (back row, fourth from left), are standing side by side.* (Courtesy Cumberland County Historical Society)

Bottom: *The 1912 Army football team in their lettermen sweaters. Dwight David Eisenhower, twenty-two, is standing third from the left in the center row; Omar Bradley, nineteen, is in the back row, third from the left.* (Courtesy the Dwight D. Eisenhower Library)

1

THE THRILL OF POSSIBILITY

The hand-rolled cigarette dangled from his lips, and a string of smoke drifted up around his brown eyes as he nervously paced through the locker room at West Point. Dressed in a bowler hat and dark gray suit, Glenn "Pop" Warner was buried deep in his own thoughts. Out on Army's football field five thousand fans filled the wooden bleachers and hundreds of others sat in folding chairs along the sidelines. Warner could hear the crowd murmur with expectation as he took another drag from his usual pregame cigarette, releasing more smoke from the orange glow of the burning tip. Time was running out before kickoff, and he was still searching for just the right words to spark a fire in the hearts of his Carlisle Indian School football players.

He moved between the benches in the small, musty locker room, striding past his players as they pulled on their red jerseys with the letter *C* emblazoned on the front, tightened the laces on their black cleats, and strapped on their leather helmets. The forty-two-year-old coach, with his bushy dark hair and barrel chest, had been daydreaming for months of this moment: the game against Army. On this autumn afternoon in 1912 he planned to unveil his latest offensive creation—the double wing—for

the first time. The Indians had been practicing the complicated formation since the middle of the summer, and Warner hoped it would confuse
the bigger, brawnier, stronger Cadets.

It was late in the season and, for Carlisle, the national championship
was tantalizingly close: If the Indians beat Army, just three opponents
stood between them and an undefeated season. Warner looked around at
his twenty-two boys. They ranged in age from eighteen to twenty-four.
Most of them had close-cropped dark hair, copper skin, and coffee-
colored eyes, and were as thin as blades of prairie grass. They had come
from reservations that dotted the plains of Middle America and as far
west as Arizona to attend the Carlisle Indian Industrial School, a boarding
school in Carlisle, Pennsylvania, for Indian boys and girls.

At Carlisle, the Indians were assimilated into white culture and
forced to abandon every last trace of their heritage. The white teachers cut
the Indians' shiny black hair that reached down to their shoulders. They
took their clothing, which was made from animal hides, and handed the
boys blue military uniforms and the girls Victorian dresses. From the
moment they first rode through the school gate in a horse-drawn covered
wagon, the kids were not allowed to speak in their native languages. It
would be English only from this point on.

The football team at Carlisle played all the powerhouses of the day—
Harvard, Yale, Princeton—and now, on November 9, 1912, at West Point,
Warner narrowed his eyes into a liquid gleam of intensity and began to
speak in his gravelly voice, hoping to prepare his boys for a battle with another of those top-ranked teams. With the fervor of a tent-revival
preacher, the coach told his players that this was the time and the place
for the Indians to finally prove that they could play the white man's game
better than the white man himself could. In graphic language, he explained that this was a chance to exact revenge for all the cold-blooded
horrors that the white man had inflicted on their people in the past. It was
the ancestors of these Army boys, Warner forcefully stated, who had killed
and raped the ancestors of the Carlisle players.

*On every play I want all of you to remember one thing. Remember that it was
the fathers and grandfathers of these Army players who fought your fathers
and grandfathers in the Indian Wars. Remember it was their fathers and
grandfathers who killed your fathers and grandfathers. Remember it was*

their fathers and grandfathers who destroyed your way of life. Remember Wounded Knee. Remember all of this on every play. Let's go!

Nothing could cause the emotional temperature of the Indians to rise like the mention of the massacre at Wounded Knee, and after Warner's speech was over the players stormed out of the locker room and into the cool November air, filled with primal rage. Outside, the maples, elms, and oak trees that towered throughout the sixteen-thousand-acre West Point campus were tinted red and gold—the colors of the northeastern autumn—and a breeze strummed the branches. Above the Indians as they jogged onto Cullum Field, the cold sky was heavy with an underbelly of clouds that threatened to flood the ground with sleet. It was the kind of football weather that Warner loved: raw and foreboding, perfect for the most important game of his career.

Located forty-five miles north of New York City, the field at West Point was laid out on the granite cliffs high above the Hudson River. Hundreds of feet below the grassy field, scores of boats that had ferried fans from Manhattan and other ports along the Hudson were docked on the rocky shoreline. Late-arriving fans streamed out of the tiny West Point train depot. Once they stepped off the coal-driven locomotive, they climbed the steep hill that led to the broad green plain of the United States Military Academy, anxious to see the battle between Carlisle, the most famous underdogs of the early twentieth century, and the Cadets of Army.

While the Carlisle players warmed up, halfback Jim Thorpe loped around the field in his easy, graceful gait. Every movement he made to prepare for the game looked effortless. He kicked forty-yard field goals that cleaved the uprights, he flung beautiful passes that spiraled sixty yards through the air, he sprinted up the field with the ball in his hands and faked out imaginary defenders with feet as light as a ballroom dancer's. The twenty-four-year-old Thorpe had participated in the decathlon and pentathlon at the Fifth Olympic Games in Stockholm, Sweden, just four months earlier, and had generated more newspaper stories than any other athlete in the summer and fall of 1912—more than Ty Cobb of the Detroit Tigers, Shoeless Joe Jackson of the Chicago White Sox, or the Kentucky Derby winner, Worth. At this moment Thorpe was operating at the height of his athletic powers, and a stadium full of onlookers followed his every step, his every kick, his every snap of the wrist.

On the other side of the field a twenty-two-year-old Cadet player with blond hair and penetrating, icy blue eyes loosened up. Jogging in his gold leather helmet, black jersey, gold knickers, white socks, and black cleats, Dwight David Eisenhower didn't look intimidating—he stood five feet, ten inches and weighed 180 pounds—and he wasn't as fast as Thorpe nor as muscular. But Eisenhower possessed something that Army coach Ernest Graves couldn't teach: determination as strong as the gray granite of the Cadet barracks. Ike charged around the field like no one else on Graves's roster, and though he was only in his first year as a starter, Eisenhower had already established himself as Army's hardest hitter and toughest runner. Like every other player warming up on the field, Eisenhower played full-time on both sides of the ball—halfback on offense, linebacker on defense. Now, as he stretched and prepared for the game, his mind was focused on two things: stampeding over Thorpe and the other Carlisle defenders when he had the ball in his hands on offense, and punishing Thorpe with vicious hits on defense.

Ever since Eisenhower and his Cadet teammates found out that Carlisle and Jim Thorpe would be coming to West Point, a day rarely passed at the Academy when the Army players didn't talk about how they were going to "stop Thorpe." A Cadet would become famous, the Army players believed, if he knocked Thorpe out of the game with a hit so powerful it kidnapped Thorpe from consciousness. Eisenhower especially had been looking forward to this game for months. Finally, he would come head-to-head with the great Jim Thorpe on the football field.

As Eisenhower continued to warm up on this chilly afternoon, he had nearly as many eyes locked on him as Thorpe did. Ike, as his friends called him, had been prominently featured in *The New York Times* a few weeks earlier. The paper ran a two-column photo of Eisenhower and called him "one of the most promising backs in Eastern football." Ike was a bruising inside runner who had a knack for dragging tacklers along with him for five, ten, even fifteen yards. And on defense, from his linebacker position, the rough kid from Abilene, Kansas, fully expected to be the chosen one—the player who was going to deliver the knockout blow that would send Thorpe out of the game and into a hospital bed.

Minutes before kickoff, the bleachers on each side of Cullum Field were full. A cluster of sportswriters from New York City stood on the sidelines with pencils and notebooks in their hands. Walter Camp, the former Yale player and coach known as the "Father of American Football," also was on the sideline. Wearing an overcoat and top hat, Camp wondered the same thing that every other fan did: Could Thorpe and the Carlisle Indians keep their national title hopes alive by beating Army, a team that Camp ranked as one of the best in the East?

Just then, the field shook and the air rumbled: A cannon on the north end of the field had fired a thunderous salute to the crowd. The fans erupted in applause. The team captains—Thorpe for Carlisle, Leland Devore for Army—met at midfield and shook hands. The coin spiked upward—Thorpe won the flip and elected to defend the north goal. Devore told the referee that Army would kick off. Thorpe walked back to the sideline, where Warner gave his players a few last-second instructions and then ordered them onto the field. Thorpe was the team's deep return man, and he cantered onto the field with the cool of a confident Thoroughbred approaching the starting gate. With a bitter wind feathering his cheeks, Thorpe buckled his helmet strap tightly under his movie-star chin. He was ready to play.

Eisenhower lined up with the other defenders on the kicking team. Warner glowered and paced the sideline, another cig pinched between his lips. Standing on the opposite sideline, Omar Bradley, a reserve Army player, surveyed the field. The Army kicker, Devore, booted the ball high into the gray sky. It landed in Thorpe's arms at the Carlisle fifteen-yard line. Warner yelled for Thorpe to run. Eisenhower sprinted as fast as he could toward Thorpe as the Indian slashed up the field.

The thrill of possibility now pumped in the hearts of everyone on the field. Just twenty-two years after the battle of Wounded Knee ended the Indian Wars, whites and Indians were at it again.

The last death of the Plains Indian Wars occurred when Plenty Horses (under guard in center), a former student at the Carlisle Indian School, gunned down Edward Casey, a former West Point cadet, in January 1891. Twenty-one years later, Indians and soldiers would square off again—on the football field at West Point.
(Courtesy Library of Congress)

2

SHOT LIKE BUFFALO

The end came at dawn on December 29, 1890, in a remote valley in South Dakota next to a creek the Indians called Wounded Knee. As the first blush of sunlight spread across the endless Dakota sky, a bank of storm clouds grew larger on the western horizon. About 450 Sioux Indians had set up camp along the winding creek, and as the last whispers of smoke from the previous night's campfire drifted through the frosty winter air, they shook off the heavy sluggishness of sleep. They could see that on the bluffs all around them stood four troops of the U.S. Seventh Cavalry, outfitted in long blue woolen coats and muskrat hats. Each soldier carried a Winchester rifle slung over his shoulder. Each troop had a small-caliber Hotchkiss cannon. These instruments of death were mounted on light carriages with two wooden wheels, and all the barrels were pointed directly at the camp.

The Indians had a few old rabbit guns and a handful of knives, bows and arrows, and hatchets. At around 8 A.M., five Indian men emerged from their teepees and sat down in a semicircle. The colonel of the cavalry troops, James W. Forsyth, cautiously approached and told an interpreter to shout an order to the Indian leaders: *Return to your lodges immediately and bring me all of your weapons.*

Reluctantly, the Indian men stood up and walked toward their teepees. In their limited English, they told Forsyth that they didn't want to fight. The cavalry troops ignored them. Pointing their rifles at the Indians, they quickly moved within fifty feet of the camp. A few Indian women inside the teepees peeked through the slits of the entryway, and what they saw left them cold with fear: The bluecoats were so close the women could see the scuffs on their black boots and the brass buttons on their uniforms gleaming in the morning sun.

On the instructions of President Benjamin Harrison, the cavalry's mission was to eradicate the Native American practice known as the "Ghost Dance." The dance, which was performed over four or five days, combined singing and chanting with slow, shuffling movements that followed the sun's course. Many Indians believed that if they danced the Ghost Dance, a new springtime of bountiful green grass and cool running water would come. The buffalo would reappear, and the white man would vanish. They thought they'd be lifted into the air and transported to a place as perfect as a garden full of fruits, plants, and flowers as far as the eye could see. Here their ancestors would greet them with bright smiles and open arms. The Ghost Dance would take the Indians back to a happier time, and its seduction was so powerful that in the early 1890s it was prevalent in Montana, Wyoming, Nebraska, the Dakotas, Texas, and Oklahoma. Hundreds or sometimes thousands of dancers shuffled around a pole staked in the earth, or "tree of life." They wore Ghost Dance shirts, which were blue around the neck and adorned with brightly colored birds, suns, and moons. They believed that these shirts were magical and made them invulnerable to bullets—a belief similar to that of the Boxers in China's 1900 rebellion.

Settlers had reacted with alarm. A federal agent on the reservation at Pine Ridge, South Dakota, in the southwestern corner of the state, panicked at the sight of these Ghost Dances and asked that troops be sent in for reinforcement. "Indians are dancing in the snow and are wild and crazy," the agent wrote to his superiors. "We need protection and we need it now. The leaders should be arrested and confined at some military post until the matter is quieted, and this should be done now." The agent's request was ultimately granted, and within days the cavalry was galloping into Indian country.

General Nelson Miles, the head of the cavalry, suspected that the movement was fomented by the Sioux chief, Sitting Bull, and so he ordered his arrest. The fifty-six-year-old Sioux warrior and holy man was working as a farmer at the Grand River on the Standing Rock Reservation. The federal agent there, James McLaughlin, wasn't as fearful of Indians as the agent in Pine Ridge who asked for reinforcements. McLaughlin regarded Sitting Bull as an obstructionist, but he would have preferred not to intervene. Hoping to avoid a clash, McLaughlin arranged for the arrest to be carried out by Indian police with the cavalry as backup. Before sunup on December 15, 1890, a group of forty-four Indian police rode on horseback to Sitting Bull's log cabin. They were under the command of a former Sioux chief, Lieutenant Bull Head, who had been at Sitting Bull's side in the fights against the cavalry at Rosebud and Little Bighorn.

Along with sergeants Red Tomahawk and Shave Head, Lieutenant Bull Head entered Sitting Bull's cabin and roused the chief, who was still in his bed.

"What do you want here?" asked Sitting Bull as he pushed away the blur of sleep.

"You are my prisoner," explained Bull Head. "You must go to the agency."

After Sitting Bull put on his clothes, the three Indian police escorted him out the door and into the freezing darkness of the early morning. What they found outside amazed them all: A crowd of Ghost Dancers had gathered, demanding to know why the Indian police had stormed the chief's cabin. As soon as Sitting Bull saw that he had the full support of his people, his demeanor changed. No longer willing to go peacefully to the agency, he stopped walking, forcing the Indian police to drag him toward his horse. The police officers didn't let go of their firm grip on the chief, and tension escalated as quickly as a spark turns gas into a fire. One of Sitting Bull's most faithful followers, Catch-the-Bear, called out, "Let us protect our Chief!"

Catch-the-Bear pulled a rifle from underneath a blanket that was wrapped around him. He aimed at Bull Head and pulled the trigger. The bullet hit Bull Head in his left side and spun him backward violently. As he fell to the ground, Bull Head drew his pistol and fired into the chest of Sitting Bull. The chief was dead, instantly. To make absolutely sure, Sergeant Red Tomahawk shot Sitting Bull in the back of the head.

A storm of chaos then rained down. As Sitting Bull's followers scuf-

fled with the Indian police, the chief's horse started neighing and snorting and bucking. The chestnut-colored horse had been a gift from Buffalo
Bill Cody. For a brief time Sitting Bull had been an actor in Buffalo Bill's
Wild West Show, a traveling outdoor spectacle that depicted life on the
frontier. The interactive performance featured a ride on a look-alike
Pony Express, gun battles between cowboys and Indians, and rodeo
events such as calf roping and riding wild bucking broncos. Sitting Bull
joined the show in 1885. Along with other Indians, he acted out make-
believe scenes of wild and screaming Indians attacking stagecoaches and
raiding the homes of white settlers. In every town where the show
stopped, the image of Indians as heathens and savages was drilled into the
minds of increasingly large audiences.

Buffalo Bill and Sitting Bull grew close. As a gesture of this friend-
ship, Cody presented him with a horse that had been part of the show.
While the angry Indian police officers outside of Sitting Bull's cabin were
ripping off the dead chief's scalp, Sitting Bull's horse began to perform
his circus tricks just a few feet away.

Many local newspapermen applauded Sitting Bull's death. "With Sitting
Bull's fall, the nobility of the Redskin is exterminated, and what few are left
are a pack of whining curs who lick the hand that smites them," wrote
L. Frank Baum, in the December 20, 1890, issue of the *Aberdeen Saturday
Pioneer*. "The Whites, by law of conquest, by justice of civilization, are masters of the American continent, and the best safety of the frontier settlements will be secured by the total annihilation of the few remaining Indians.
Why annihilation? Their glory has fled, their spirit broken, their manhood
effaced; better they die than live the miserable wretches they are."

News of Sitting Bull's death blew like a cyclone across the plains.
Many Indians fled their reservations in fear, believing that the cavalry was
trying to exterminate their entire race. The biggest band was the 450 en-
camped at Wounded Knee Creek. Fifteen days after Sitting Bull had been
murdered, they were surrounded by cavalry.

The troops were a part of the biggest military deployment since the
Civil War. From the Dakota bluffs, they continued to advance, slowly.
When they stood within twenty feet of the camp's perimeter, the Indians
still hadn't emerged from their teepees with their weapons. Colonel

Forsyth then issued an order to a handful of his men: *Enter the teepees and conduct the search yourselves.* Guns drawn, the soldiers cautiously stepped into the teepees. They overturned blankets, scattered bed clothing, and pawed through everything in sight. Women inside the lodges screamed; children wailed and clung to their mothers.

Outside the teepees, a medicine man named Yellow Bird blew an eagle-bone whistle, signaling his people to resist and fight. Yellow Bird began dancing the Ghost Dance around the fire pit and reminded his tribe that their sacred garments would make them safe from the white man's bullets. Between praying and crying, he picked up some dirt from the ground and threw it in the air. "This is the way I want to go back," Yellow Bird shouted, "to the dust!" Forsyth ordered more soldiers into the teepees. He told the troops to search the Indians from head to toe.

A light snow fell, dusting the trees. Soon a second wave of soldiers ran into the teepees, fingers firmly pressed up against the triggers of their carbines. One young Indian, Black Coyote, refused to turn over his rifle. The soldiers ripped off his blanket, yanking him around. Black Coyote then held his gun above his head and told the white cavalrymen that he had paid good money for it, and wanted to be compensated. Seconds later, as a brawl erupted, the gun discharged—perhaps an accident, perhaps not. The shot echoed across the frozen plain and scaled up the valley walls. A cavalryman collapsed. Before anyone really understood what had happened, the bluecoat was on the ground, dead, blood leaking out of him like water out of a cracked wooden bucket.

It took only a moment for the soldiers to retaliate. Lieutenant James Mann yelled, "Fire! Fire on them!" then several rifles blasted all at once. Nearly half the Indian warriors were instantly cut down. The ones who survived the initial volley drew concealed weapons—knives and hatchets mostly—and charged the soldiers. At close range, it was a murderous, blind rage. Screaming war chants, the Indians clubbed the soldiers, who frantically tried to hold the Indians at bay while they reloaded their Winchesters. A few Indians drove their hatchets into the flesh of the bluecoats, who howled in agony and fell to the ground. It all happened so fast—just minutes earlier, the Indian leaders had been sitting in a circle and talking quietly among themselves—but now order and any chance of a peaceful negotiation had slipped away. The hopeless shrieks of dying men pierced the icy winter air as both Indians and soldiers fought with all their strength to stay alive.

The fight didn't last long. Seeing the Indians advance, the soldiers who were manning the Hotchkiss guns on the hilltop overlooking the camp opened fire, blasting nearly a shell a second at the men, women, and even the children who poured out of the teepees, hysterical with fear. Within seconds, many of the teepees were ablaze. A wave of thick black smoke rushed into the sky, rising like a devilish ghost to haunt the scene. The shells hammered the ground where the Indian fighters were frantically swinging their knives and hatchets at the cavalrymen, sending chunks of earth and chunks of man flying through the frigid air.

A stumbling mass of Indian women and children and a few surviving men escaped down into a ravine that led away from the encampment. The soldiers reloaded their Hotchkiss guns and began sweeping the ravine with fire, mowing down anything that moved. Within minutes, corpses dotted the snow-sprinkled plain.

"They had four troops dismounted and formed a square around the Indians, and they were so close they could touch the Indians with their guns," wrote Private Eugene Caldwell in a letter to his father. "At the first volley we fired, there were about twenty or thirty Indians dropped, and we kept it up until we cleaned out the whole band."

The firing finally stopped. For a moment, everything in the valley of Wounded Knee Creek was silent and absolutely still.

"Everyone was shouting and shooting, and there was no more order than in a bar-room scrimmage," wrote one private in the Seventh Cavalry in a letter to his brother in Philadelphia. "I shot one buck [Indian] running, and when I examined him, he had neither gun nor cartridge belt."

"We tried to run," recalled Louise Weasel Bear, who was a child at the time of the Wounded Knee massacre, "but they shot us like we were buffalo."

Some of the Indians managed to run as far as two miles from the camp before they died of their wounds. Others made it only a few feet. A total of twenty-five white men were killed—most had likely died as a result of friendly fire. Because the Indians were equipped only with knives, hatchets, and a few guns, more than 180 had lost their lives on this bloody winter morning. For three days, the dead were left to lie where they had fallen while a blizzard swept over them, freezing their skin solid.

A burial committee was sent to the scene on New Year's Day, 1891. One by one the frozen bodies were dragged from under the snow and heaved into a single pit. One baby girl, about a year old, was discovered still alive, wrapped in her dead mother's shawl. She was wearing a cap that bore an American flag made of beads. Almost all of the other children were dead. "It was a thing to melt the heart of a man if it was of stone," said a member of the burial task force, "to see those little children, with their bodies shot to pieces, thrown naked into the pit."

"Fully three miles from the scene of the massacre we found the body of a woman completely covered in a blanket of snow," wrote Dr. Charles Eastman, a local physician who helped retrieve the bodies, "and from this point on we found them scattered along as they had been relentlessly hunted down and slaughtered while fleeing for their lives."

The burial committee dug a pit sixty feet long and six feet deep. They threw more than 180 Lakota bodies into the mass grave, stripping jewelry, clothing, and ghost shirts from many of the bodies. A few weeks later eighteen Medals of Honor—awards the military gave for uncommon valor and bravery on the battlefield—were bestowed to officers and enlisted men for their actions at Wounded Knee. Corporal Paul H. Weinert, who fired two shells from his Hotchkiss gun that exploded on a group that included delirious women and children, was awarded the Congressional Medal of Honor, the highest military accolade in the United States.

A few days after all the bodies were buried, a twenty-two-year-old Lakota Indian named Plenty Horses crept up behind Edward Casey, a lieutenant in the cavalry. Tall with wide shoulders and his face colored with war paint, Plenty Horses looked like a classic Sioux warrior. His long dark hair was braided and he wore tan-colored buckskin and moccasins—the traditional Indian dress. He looked far different on this cold January day than he had just a year earlier, when he attended the Carlisle Indian School in Carlisle, Pennsylvania. For five years at the boarding school, he donned a military uniform and his black hair was only a few inches long. Now, as he approached the unsuspecting lieutenant, and with a Winchester rifle hidden under a blanket that he had wrapped around himself, his experience at Carlisle was fresh in his mind—and motivating him.

Lieutenant Casey, an 1873 graduate of West Point, was at the Pine

Ridge agency with other soldiers trying to convince the Indians to lay down their arms. On the morning of January 7, 1891, he was riding on the back of his towering black horse alongside two Indian scouts—both of whom had enlisted in the cavalry six months earlier—when they encountered about forty Sioux Indians who were also galloping across the wide-open prairie. The two groups met and, while still on horseback, spoke peacefully in a circle for several minutes. Casey extended his hand to Plenty Horses, who had been at the Pine Ridge reservation on the morning of the Wounded Knee massacre.

"Hau, kola"—hello, friend—Casey said to Plenty Horses. The two shook hands. The two groups then talked in English for several minutes as they slowly rode their horses for a mile or two. Casey told Plenty Horses that he wanted to visit a nearby Lakota camp. The Indians halted. Plenty Horses warned Casey that he should not move a step closer to the camp. For a few minutes, the two groups continued their dialogue. Everyone appeared calm. But then, in the middle of the conversation, Plenty Horses leisurely withdrew from the circle, backing his horse away. He quietly positioned himself about four feet behind Casey.

The discussion ended. Casey agreed that he wouldn't move any closer to the Lakota camp. As Casey was saying goodbye to the Indians, Plenty Horses raised the Winchester from his blanket, positioned it on his shoulder, and aimed it at Casey. Just as Casey started to ride off, Plenty Horses calmly pulled the trigger. The piece of hot lead sank into the back of Casey's head and tore out just under his right eye. Casey's horse reared and threw him onto the ground. The lieutenant was dead before he landed on the frozen ground. A Carlisle Indian had killed a West Point officer, and this death would be one of the last ones in the bloody Indian Wars that had raged for decades on the plains of America.

Plenty Horses was soon arrested. At his trial he explained his actions by pointing at one place: the Carlisle Indian School. "Five years I attended Carlisle and was educated in the ways of the white man," Plenty Horses said. "When I returned to my people, I was an outcast among them. I was no longer an Indian. I was not a white man. I was lonely. I shot the lieutenant so I might make a place for myself among my people. I am now one of them. I shall be hung, and the Indians will bury me as a warrior."

The murder of Edward Casey put Carlisle on the front pages of newspapers from New York to Los Angeles for the first time. It wouldn't be the last.

The massacre at Wounded Knee was the final major armed encounter between Indians and whites in North America, marking the end of the Plains Indian Wars. But profound distrust—and hostility—between whites and Indians would continue as the nineteenth century gave way to the twentieth. Most whites viewed Indians as savages who needed to be "civilized" if they were ever going to fit into proper society. Dime-store novels, Wild West shows, and silent movies all reinforced the "savage" image of Indian people.

It was in this racially charged environment that three young Indian boys—Jim Thorpe, Albert Exendine, and Gus Welch—were raised in the late 1800s. Almost every day of their youth they were reminded of their lowly status in society, from stories about how bounties were being offered for the scalps of Indian men and women to how Indians were being sequestered onto parcels of land the government called "reservations." The families of Thorpe and Exendine, who both lived in the Oklahoma Territory, had little money and little hope for the future. It was the same for Welch, who grew up in the woods of northern Wisconsin. But soon all three of these boys would be lured to the first boarding school for Indian children in America that didn't sit on Indian land. Located in the thick of Pennsylvania coal country, the Carlisle Indian School was founded in 1879 by Henry Pratt, a cavalryman who had fought in the Civil War and hoped to "kill the Indian and save the man" with his experimental school. At Carlisle, Thorpe, Exendine, and Welch would wear the clothes of whites, receive the education of whites, speak the language of whites, and play the games of whites—basketball, baseball, and football.

Soon, these three young boys—plus a coach with an imagination as wild as a child's—would lead the Carlisle Indian School football team to national prominence. Many of the Indian players had the same blood pumping through their veins as the men, women, and children who fell at Wounded Knee, and the brutal massacre would stay vividly alive in all the players' minds for years. But the Indians of Carlisle couldn't exact revenge on the battlefield. They would seek it instead on the football field.

Big-boned and jolly, Glenn Warner was viewed as an uncle-like figure by his team-mates at Cornell, who started calling him "Pop" during the fall of 1892. Dressed in his familiar Carlisle sweater and football knickers, Warner (far right) enjoyed lin-ing up and practicing with his Indian players. Warner had been a star lineman at Cornell from 1892 to 1894. Here Warner is pictured with (left to right) Captain Emil Wauseka, Jimmie Johnson, and Albert Exendine. (Courtesy Cumberland County Historical Society)

3

POP LEARNS FROM MA

The chubby boy dressed in his thick winter coat waddled down a snow-covered sidewalk in Springville, New York, passing two-story houses and trying to avoid the other kids walking home from school. Ten-year-old Glenn Scobey Warner was big for his age and overweight, which made him a bull's-eye for the playground bullies who ruled the middle school in that town of 2,500. The kids teased Warner by calling him "Butter," a nickname that would stick for years. During recess they flung rocks at Glenn with their slingshots and during lunch period they blew beans through their straws at him as he ate. The boy quietly accepted his fate as the picked-on kid until one winter day, as he was walking home from school, when he decided he'd had enough.

A classmate approached Warner on the sidewalk. He taunted Glenn with a few words, then plucked the youngster's stocking cap off his head and tossed it into an icy mud puddle. To up the humiliation ante, he stomped on the cap like he was trying to put out a fire. The other boys laughed while the schoolyard bully jumped up and down on the cap, expecting Butter to melt in the face of the challenge and slink away like he always did. But as suddenly as a shift in the wind, Warner's comportment stiffened. For the first time in his life, he raised his fists and charged forward like a Yankee after a Confederate.

Warner's father, William, had been a captain for the Union in the Civil War. On many occasions William would sit in the Warners' parlor and have a heart-to-heart with his boy. While stroking his long dark beard, William would tell his son that he should fear no one, just as he himself hadn't, even when the guns were firing in battle. It was William's tough-guy demeanor that had helped him survive the terrors and the hardships of the Civil War, and he tried to pass on this same attitude to his boy, who already possessed his father's menacing dark eyes, iron jaw, and steely gaze.

Now, facing his tormentor, Glenn fought back just like his father had taught him. With a crowd of boys watching, Warner balled his fists and swung wildly at the classmate who had tossed his hat into the puddle. Butter was only ten years old, but years later he would recall this moment as a significant one in his life, as the day he learned that he could assert his will on others. After bloodying the schoolyard bully on this winter afternoon in 1881 and winning his first fistfight, Warner gained more confidence and self-assuredness. He began to shed his cocoon of shyness, and he never backed down from another bare-knuckled brawl. By the time he was sixteen, the big-boned Warner had slugged his way to elite status: one of the toughest kids in school.

When he wasn't in the classroom, Warner was usually out in the fields of his family's wheat farm, which was located just outside of town. Every September, Warner and his younger brothers, Fred and Bill, helped their father plant the wheat seeds, and every June the Warners harvested the plants with a horse-drawn combine. The work was strenuous, and as Warner gained inches in height, all the hours he spent in the fields transformed his flabby, pear-shaped body. At age sixteen he had developed a thick, sturdy build, and when he played games with his classmates, Butter was the one kid everyone wanted on their team.

One of the most popular games that Warner played with his friends in the mid-1880s was a crude mix of soccer and baseball. On a field that measured about one hundred yards long, with two cross streets serving as the goal lines, two teams of boys pushed and shoved each other around as they tried to get an oblong-shaped ball—actually, a blown-up cow's bladder—across the goal line. Throwing and kicking the ball to their teammates, each squad tried to maintain possession and keep the cow's bladder away from the opposition, which gave the game a faint resemblance to a new sport that had been created only a decade earlier and only a few of the kids were familiar with: football. But Warner's favorite game in high school was baseball. At six feet tall and 190 pounds as an eighteen-year-old, Warner was an oversized right-handed pitcher blessed with a blistering fastball. And when he gripped a bat with his big hands and strode to the plate, he had a knack for crushing balls over the head of the left fielder.

When Warner graduated in 1889 from Springville's Griffith Institute, a combined elementary and secondary school, a teacher persuaded him to take the entrance exam for the U.S. Military Academy at West Point, 350 miles to the southeast of Springville. Warner wanted to follow in the footsteps of his father and become a soldier. In addition, he could play baseball at West Point, which made the school even more appealing.

On the day of the entrance test Warner brimmed with optimism. But then he looked around the exam room and did the rough math. There were forty other young men sitting down for the test, which meant that the odds were stacked against him to win one of the handful of appointments that were going to be awarded to this group of applicants. In the end, four of the students won appointments—but not Warner.

This disappointment would stay lodged in Warner's mind for years to come. He would always be fascinated by the military and he sometimes wondered how his life would have been different if he had earned his way into West Point. But one day Warner would finally walk onto the tree-covered campus that sat on the granite cliffs along the Hudson River. He had failed to impress the military men of West Point once; he didn't plan on letting that happen twice.

His options limited after graduating from Griffith, Warner moved with his mother, father, and younger brothers to the tiny town of Wichita Falls, Texas, northwest of Fort Worth near the Texas-Oklahoma border. There the family purchased a cattle and wheat ranch spread over hundreds of acres.

Shortly after arriving in Wichita Falls, the men in the family mounted horses and spent ten hours inspecting their vast swath of land, riding over pastures and streams that wound through their property. Warner had never seen so much wildlife—quail and antelope drank from the Red River, fat-bellied wild turkeys scooted across the dusty terrain, prairie chickens scurried through the brown tallgrass. Warner was excited to become a cowboy, which was what he did. He planted wheat, built and fixed windmills that pumped water, cleared large areas for grazing, and herded cattle. For ten months he rarely stopped working other than to sleep and eat.

Then, in the summer of 1890, he was offered a job he couldn't refuse: For fifteen dollars a week, he became an assistant to a local tinsmith. Even as a boy, he had been fascinated by art and using his hands to create things. In his free time he liked to sit in front of an easel and, with a brush in his right hand and a palette of watercolors in his left, paint landscapes. This was his escape, and it revealed a softness of character that was hard for others to fathom when he was wearing his cowboy hat and herding cattle under the brutal Texas sun.

Warner also enjoyed using shears, hammers, punches, and stakes to build objects out of tin. Working at the tin shop, he used his tools to fashion cups, baking pans, milk pails, teapots, and lanterns, which were used by the local night watchmen. The handcrafting also fired his creativity, and years later he would apply all that he learned at the tin shop to football, developing gadgets such as shoulder pads, thigh pads, cleats, blocking sleds, tackling dummies, and even lightweight uniforms.

A few days after receiving one of his first paychecks from his boss at the tin shop, Warner tried to make some easy money. He owned a little cow pony that he believed was one of the fastest four-legged creatures in all of the Lone Star State. One of his friends owned a much larger mustang, and Warner bragged that he thought his cow pony could beat the mustang in a race. To make matters interesting, he backed up his belief by wagering twenty dollars. His friend gladly accepted the bet. Warner, even though he weighed about two hundred pounds, decided that he would ride his own horse. His friend would also play jockey—only he tipped the scale at 140 pounds.

At the appointed hour, the two horses stood at the starting line. A signal was given, the horses flared their nostrils, and then stamped their feet into the Texas afternoon. The race wasn't even close: The cow pony struggled to gain speed because of all the weight on its back, while the mustang and its jockey blazed effortlessly across the finish line. Warner lost his twenty dollars—not to mention a sizable chunk of pride.

Warner went back to work in the tin shop, and soon became so proficient at the art form that he was placed in charge of the entire store. Wearing an apron and using an anvil made of a block of steel, Warner could lose himself for hours as he hammered out different objects. His one reprieve from his tinwork came on the weekends, when he'd camp out with his brothers on the ranch under a sky speckled with stars. Over the next two years Warner was so content that time could have frozen and he wouldn't have cared.

In June 1892, Warner rode the train to Springville to spend the summer there with his childhood friends. While in his hometown he pursued his two loves: he played amateur baseball for the local team and he wagered on the horses. In the middle of summer Warner pitched and hit in a bitterly contested five-game amateur series against the nearby town of Gowanda. Afterward, he took a train thirty miles north to Buffalo. He'd heard that the Grand Circuit harness races were coming to the eastern shore of Lake Erie, and he wanted to see if he could turn some of the cash he had earned back in the tin shop into big money with some calculated bets.

Warner considered himself an astute judge of equines and, after spending one week at the track, he was up fifty dollars. Pressing his luck, he followed the circuit to its next stop—Rochester, New York—where he thought he could double his money. Then, he'd be able to proudly walk onto his dad's ranch at the end of the summer, pockets bulging with bills. It all seemed effortless, as easy as stealing second on a wild pitch.

But then the odds caught up with Warner and his luck stole out the back door. He went on a long cold streak, and within days he'd lost not only all of the money he'd made at the track in Buffalo, but also all the cash he'd earned at the tin shop except for the few dollars he would need for his train ticket back to Texas.

With his wallet empty, he traveled by rail from Rochester to Springville. As he gazed out the window at the lush hills of upstate New York, his mind raced to find a way out of his financial pit. He considered coming clean with his father and telling him about how he'd blown all his money at the harness races, but that would send the old man into the kind of rage that Warner didn't want to face. He also tried to think of ways he could make money fast, but nothing came to him.

This was another key moment in Warner's life: He had to come up with a plan to make up for his lapse in judgment at the races. During the past few years, his father had urged him to go to law school, but Warner had demurred, saying he liked working in the tin shop and camping out in the moonlight on the Texas range. But now, as the locomotive clanked and sputtered to a halt in the Springville station, his situation had changed. He was penniless and desperate. He decided to write his father a letter explaining that he had changed his mind and that he now wanted to attend Cornell Law School, which at the time didn't require an undergraduate degree for admission. To prove he was serious, Warner included with the letter the law school's catalog, which listed all the classes at the Ithaca, New York, school. He also mentioned that he didn't have money to cover the tuition and the costs for room and board. He needed financial help.

A few weeks later, while Warner was still staying with friends in Springville, he received a reply from his father. When he opened the letter, he saw exactly what he was hoping for: a check for one hundred dollars. His father also wrote that he was as proud as he'd ever been that his son was becoming a lawyer and would make a difference in the world. But the father wasn't as happy as Warner himself. Now he could keep his secret from his parents. As penance for his sin of gambling he would have to go to law school, but at least he had been spared the embarrassment of telling his father the truth.

Shortly after receiving the check, Warner applied to Cornell Law and was promptly accepted. Near the end of the summer of 1892 he packed his suitcase and boarded a train in Springville. Lugging his bag on board, he took a seat. As the steam engine cranked up and the wheels churned forward, Warner looked around at the other passengers. He spotted a boyhood friend who also was traveling to Ithaca for school. The two chatted. The buddy mentioned that there was someone else on board that he wanted Warner to meet. His name was Carl Johanson, and he was the captain and coach of the Cornell football team.

After the introduction was made and the two shook hands, they struck up a conversation. Johanson told Warner all about the relatively new game of football. As the miles ticked off, Johanson detailed the rules and strategies of football. Warner leaned in close, rapt. This new game sounded incredibly intriguing.

Warner didn't know that twenty-three years earlier, on November 6, 1869, the first official intercollegiate football game was played in New Brunswick, New Jersey, between Rutgers and Princeton. The sport was slow to catch on, but gradually football gained popularity at several East Coast colleges, especially Yale, Harvard, and Princeton—schools that came to be referred to as the "Big Three." In the early days of college football, opposing teams rarely even scored on the Big Three, but one team that routinely gave them a good fight was Williams College, a small school in Williamstown, Massachusetts. Johanson told Warner that he had played at Williams for several seasons, and now he was the head coach of Cornell, which had begun playing the sport two years earlier, in 1887.

As the train swayed and lurched closer to Ithaca, Johanson took a hard look at Warner. The young man appeared to be about six feet tall, two hundred pounds. He had bushy dark hair that stuck up from his forehead in unruly waves, as if he had just come in from a long run, and thick, expressive eyebrows. His arms had the rounded, muscular shape of a lumberjack's. He had a thick chest and a torso as stout and solid as a fire hydrant. And there was something about the look on his face, about the intense way his eyes zeroed in on whatever was in front of him, that seemed to indicate he was about to discover a secret that would save the world. This Warner guy, Johanson concluded, might just have what it takes to become a heck of a football player, the kind who could rip open holes on the offensive line, and on defense be able to flatten ballcarriers like bugs.

Before the train reached Ithaca, Johanson asked Warner if he'd ever played any organized sports; Warner said sure, that he'd swung a lot of bats and caught plenty of baseballs growing up. Johanson kept pressing. He needed bodies to fill out his roster, so he asked Warner if he'd be interested in coming out to the football field the next afternoon to join the team for a practice. There might be a spot for you, Johanson said. As the train slowed on its approach into the station, Warner accepted the invitation.

The next day Warner wandered out to Percy Field, where the team practiced on a patchy expanse next to splintering wooden grandstands. "Get on your stuff right away," Johanson told Warner. "We need a left guard."

"Wait a minute," replied Warner. "I don't know anything about the game at all."

"Never mind," insisted Johanson. "All you've got to do is to keep 'em from going through you and spoiling the play when we've got the ball, and when they've got the ball, knock the tar out of your man and tackle the runner. Perfectly simple."

Protect my man on offense, tackle the runner on defense. Warner wasn't sure about this strange game, but there were few things in life he liked more than being thrown into competition, and so he bounded onto the field for a team scrimmage, ready for a rumble. Like a stranger in a foreign country, it didn't take long for Warner's naïveté to surface. When his team punted, Warner sprinted down the field, hoping to make a crushing tackle—and a positive first impression on Coach Johanson. But the deep safety, instead of catching the punt, let it hit the ground. The ball thumped on the grass and bounced high into the air. Warner, not knowing any better, leapt after it and swatted the ball into the end zone. He had broken two rules—he wasn't allowed to touch the ball during the play (this was the rule at the time) and he wasn't allowed to push it forward. But he succeeded in drawing the attention of Johanson. In his first moments on the gridiron, Warner played with passion and intensity, as if the game really meant something to him, and that was precisely the kind of player Johanson wanted on his roster. After the scrimmage Johanson told his team to jog around the track. Johanson informed Warner that he didn't have to run because it was his first day and he didn't want him to overdo it, but Warner insisted. He joined the other players on the track for four laps, completing a mile.

The next day, Cornell played the opening game of their 1892 season, hosting the Syracuse Athletic Club. Playing the entire game at left guard, Warner helped Cornell—called the Red Men—to a 16–0 win. He'd been playing football for only two days, but he was already obsessed. The face-to-face fighting within the game, the athletic tests it presented, the endless chess game of strategies, the camaraderie that came with being on a team—Warner couldn't get enough of it.

They called him "Pop."

The nickname was tattooed on Warner soon after he made the Cornell football team in the fall of 1892. He had spent most of the previous three years of his life out in the wide-open spaces of Texas, which meant he was older than most of his teammates. The younger players considered Warner, who was big-boned and jolly, to be a father-like figure, and on one of the first days of practice Johanson at one point called out, "Good work, Pop!" Immediately, the sobriquet stuck to Warner as if it were sewn onto his shirt. Soon, everywhere he went—to class, to practice, to the dining hall—everyone called him Pop. Warner didn't mind the nickname; it neatly portrayed a few of his most endearing qualities—his friendliness, his maturity, and his leadership, which was rapidly developing on the football field.

Cornell rolled to a 6-0 record to begin their 1892 season, outscoring their six opponents 286 to 12. In early November the team rode the train to Cambridge, Massachusetts, to take on Harvard, one of the top teams in the early dawn of the sport. The interest in the matchup was so great that about ten thousand fans paid one dollar apiece to sit in the bleachers on the sidelines of the field. It wasn't just men who were fascinated by the game; many well-heeled women in large, billowing hats rode onto the Harvard campus in horse-drawn carriages.

As soon as the ball was kicked off to start the game, the fans were treated to a festival of violence. At the time, the forward pass was outlawed and most plays featured a rugby-style scrum as the offensive and defensive lines tried to push each other back. When Harvard had the ball, they often employed the flying wedge formation, in which the center was the only player on the line of scrimmage. The other ten offensive players leaned forward in a gaggle about ten yards behind the line of scrimmage. After the captain gave a signal, nine of the ten players then took off for the line, grunting and running as fast as they could. Just before they crossed the line, the center snapped the ball back to the lone remaining player in the backfield.

From the bleachers, the collision of offensive and defensive players looked like two rival clans engaged in hand-to-hand combat. After the initial push, the ballcarrier put his head down and barreled ahead. As the play unfolded, punches were thrown and, in the tangled pile of arms and legs, it wasn't unusual for players to bite each other. Harvard won the game 20-14, but Warner learned two important lessons: To play with the elite teams, you had to be as tough as a back-alley street fighter; and, to win, you needed a detailed plan of attack in which all eleven men operate in perfect synchronization.

Cornell finished the 1892 season with a 10-1 record. Warner, a starting lineman, was having more fun playing football by the day.

Dressed in his football knickers and a thick red-and-white sweater, Warner played again in the '93 season. The team was so popular that Campbell's, a relatively new company that sold soup, was inspired by the Cornell football uniforms to make its labels red and white. And Warner improved with each game. From his position on the line, he could usually push around the opponent because of his superior size and strength. But his blossoming talent didn't prevent the Red Men from struggling to a 3-6-1 record. After the season, Warner prepared to enter the nine-to-five world as an attorney.

In the spring of 1894 Warner finished his two years of law school, but before he left campus the football manager asked him to return to the team for the '94 season. He told Warner that, to maintain his eligibility, all he needed to do was sign up for a few postgraduate courses. After pondering his two options—football or work—Warner agreed to play one more season for the Red Men. In his spare time, when he wasn't on the field or in class, he'd make some money by waiting tables at a local restaurant. He'd also try to sell his watercolors, which he painted whenever he could—although after games he was often so sore he barely could lift his brush.

When the team gathered at Percy Field for the first fall practice, the players elected Warner as their captain. The coach was Marshall Newell, who had been an All-American tackle at Harvard. When he played for the Crimson his teammates called him "Ma," for two reasons: It was a shortened form of his first name, and he enjoyed taking younger players under his wing and teaching them the game. Ma was the perfect mentor for Pop. Newell constantly drilled his players in the fundamentals of the game—blocking and tackling—and taught them proper techniques. He put his players on a no-dessert diet. On Sunday afternoons, to bring his boys closer together, he led the team on hikes through the Redbud Woods, located on a wooded slope near campus. As the team walked through the thicket of yellow oaks, hackberry trees, and the dense stands of redbuds, Newell pointed out different flowers and talked to his boys about sportsmanship and the need to trust your teammates like they were your blood brothers. Out there in the quiet of nature, as the team trampled over sticks and shrubs, Newell had his players visualize playing football and what each of them needed to do to win games. These Sunday walks some-times lasted over an hour. Like Thoreau at nearby Walden Pond, Newell used Redbud Woods to inspire his players and make them as mentally strong as any team in the nation.

Warner soaked it all in, absorbing every word that came out of Newell's mouth as if it came directly from the Gospels. Late in the season Newell was summoned back to Harvard for two weeks to help the Crimson prepare for their upcoming game against Yale—the biggest game of the 1894 college football season. There was only one player who Newell thought was up to the task of taking over while he was away. That player was Warner.

The night before his first practice as substitute head coach, Warner excitedly sketched out a trick play. This was his first dabble in coaching, and it charged his imagination in the same way that painting did. Warner thought he could bamboozle Cornell's next opponent with his new play. So the next day, after he walked onto the practice field in charge for the first time, he told his players to gather around. He had an idea he wanted to share with them—and he hoped it would be a doozy.

On a small chalkboard, Warner diagrammed play "Number 39," as he called it. The play was based on an aspect of football strategy that in-trigued Warner the most—deception. Earlier in the season he had sat in the stands of the Yale-Princeton game and closely watched both teams use the "flying interference" offense, in which the offensive players charged straight ahead at the opposing defense with as much force as possible. This got Warner thinking: What if you faked running straight ahead but then bolted to the outside?

Warner outlined the basics of "Number 39" to his players: After the ball was hiked to the quarterback, all the backs and linemen would run to the left. This would look like a sweep, and the quarterback would take a few steps to his left and fake a toss to one of the backs, who would also run left. At that precise moment, the left guard would curl back and receive a sleight-of-hand pitch from the quarterback. The guard would then run around the right end without any blockers. The defense, Warner told his players, would believe that the back had received the toss from the quarterback and that he still had the ball. Meanwhile, the guard would have nothing but open field in front of him once he received the pitch. It was a revolutionary concept—teams ran only straight-ahead plays; none ran this kind of reverse—and Warner believed it would shock Williams College, the next team on their schedule.

A few days later Williams traveled to Ithaca for Warner's head-coaching debut. In the closing minutes of the fourth quarter, with the score tied 0–0, Warner decided the time was right for his trick play. Cornell had the ball around midfield and Warner, who was playing left guard, grabbed his quarterback and whispered into his ear, "Number 39." The quarterback relayed the play call to everyone else in the huddle, and then the Cornell offense walked to the line of scrimmage.

The ball was hiked to the quarterback. The line and backs surged to the left. The quarterback took a few steps to his left, then faked a pitch to the back. Warner, from his position of left guard, took a step back, pivoted, then ran to his right as fast as he could. The quarterback, barely moving his arms, handed him the ball. Warner sprinted around the right end and looked up the field. There were no defenders in sight.

Warner ran hard. Five yards, ten yards—still no one on the Williams team even seemed to know that he had the ball. Warner lumbered on. He had always been one of the slowest players on the team, but now he was exerting all his energy, huffing with every step. He went twenty yards and could see the goal line. For a moment, he thought his trick play was going to win the game.

Warner had never carried the ball before. Wanting desperately not to drop it, he bear-hugged it to his chest, tightly wrapping both arms around the ball like it was the only thing in the world that mattered to him. The crowd was on its feet.

Seconds later, seemingly out of nowhere, a Williams tackler lunged at him. The speedy defender caught Warner from behind and wrapped his arms around his waist. As Warner's knees buckled underneath him, he tried to use the football to cushion his fall. But as soon as the ball smacked the ground, it squirted out of his grasp as if it were slathered with grease. The ball was eventually recovered by a Williams player and, a few minutes later, the game ended 0–0. But after the game Warner felt energized, as if he had uncovered a secret. His trick play had worked. What if, he thought, I called all the plays?

Shortly after the final whistle blew on the 1894 football season, Warner reluctantly accepted a job at a law firm in Buffalo. The time for games was over, he supposed. Now he needed to earn some money and make his father proud. Yet his early days in the legal profession were lean. Warner struggled to find casework. As he sat behind his desk with his clean shave and dressed in a coat and tie, Warner wondered how he could earn extra cash. The answer came to him in the form of a letter. The business manager of the Cornell football team wanted to know if he could recommend Warner to be the new head coach at Iowa Agricultural College (now known as Iowa State University) in Ames, Iowa. The school had contacted Cornell, an established eastern power, for help in their job search, and the team's business manager thought Warner would be the ideal hire.

After Warner scanned the letter, he fired off his own missive to the graduate football manager at Iowa expressing his interest in the job. He soon learned that the salary was twenty-five dollars a week, which was more than he was making as a practicing attorney. Warner wrote the manager back and accepted the job. But Warner knew a thing or two about negotiating contracts, so before he traveled to Iowa he sent letters to about a dozen schools in the East and South inquiring if they were in need of a football coach. One school official at Georgia responded, offering Warner thirty-five dollars a week to coach in Athens. Warner told Iowa about the new offer and then cut a deal: He would coach at Iowa from August through the first week of September and be paid $150, then he would take the job in Georgia. It was a win-win situation for Warner, who never thought he could earn so much money in one season of coaching. But cash wasn't the only thing that lured Warner back to football. He was still obsessed with the game, and he wanted more fuel for his hungry fire.

Warner eyed the farm boys and preachers' sons closely, looking at their muscular arms and tree-trunk legs. On the first day of practice in Ames, Warner liked what stood in front of him. Though the thirty or so players who showed up for the first day of practice had virtually no background in football—the popularity of the sport was slowly spreading westward in the summer of 1895—the corn-fed boys were strapping and fit. The majority had worked on farms all of their lives, and their bodies had been sculpted by years of toiling in the cornfields.

After a few days on the job, Warner received an invitation to play the Butte Athletic Club football team in Butte, Montana. The exhibition game would be played in mid-September, which would be Warner's last week on the job. The letter from the Butte coach, whose roster was filled mostly with adults who played simply for the love of the sport, went on to state that the game would be played on a Sunday in order to attract a large crowd—and a large gate. The Butte coach promised Warner a "financial guarantee sufficient to cover the team's expenses" for traveling to Montana. Warner knew that Iowa school officials would never allow his team to play a game on a Sunday—the holy day—so he did what lawyers sometimes must do: He tweaked the truth. He told the school's faculty that he believed the game was scheduled on a Saturday; the faculty, to the delight of Warner and his players, approved the trip.

Mimicking his former Cornell coach, Marshall Newell, Warner schooled his players in the basics of the game—blocking and tackling. He also taught Bert German, a graduate of the Ames, Iowa, school who would take over the head coaching responsibilities when Warner left for Georgia. For about a month, Warner had his boys scrimmage frequently in the blazing midwestern heat, trying to prepare them for the hard-hitting chaos that awaited them in Montana. When they boarded a tourist passenger train destined for Butte after four weeks of intense practice, Warner was confident that his boys were ready to win.

The Iowa team traveled in luxury on a steam-engine train that had a dining car and sleeping cars. Dining cars had recently been added to trains throughout America, and the Iowa team brought along its own chef to prepare eggs in the morning, sandwiches in the afternoon, and steaks at night for the players. The sleeping cars were likely in an open-air section of the train that consisted of a pair of seats—one faced forward, the other backward—on each side of the aisle. The seats could be manipulated to create upper and lower berths, which looked like bunk beds stacked on top of each other. For privacy, the passenger could pull a screen across to separate himself from the aisle.

At night, using the electric lights that had first been wired into trains in 1882, many of the players and other passengers read books to kill time, losing themselves in the most popular books of the day, works such as

Mark Twain's *Adventures of Huckleberry Finn,* and *Ben-Hur* by Lew Wallace. Black porters, mostly former slaves who were dressed in spiffy dinner jackets and spit-shined shoes, walked up and down the aisle offering hot toddies or beers, which sometimes were poured in an elaborate twelve-step process. The train traveled at about forty-five miles per hour and periodically stopped at small depots to pick up and discharge passengers. At most stations a group of wide-eyed locals would be waiting to see the train steam into town and to get the latest national news from the passengers stepping off the "hotel on wheels," as such fancy trains were called in this golden age of rail travel.

As the locomotive carrying Warner's team weaved through the Rocky Mountains, it got stuck in a snowstorm. The food supply was quickly exhausted. After the train finally pushed through the banks of snow, it stopped at the first town to purchase food for the passengers. But the general store in the small Colorado town had sold out nearly all its supplies before the storm hit. There were a few berries on its shelves, so Warner and his players munched on them as the train completed its journey to the hardscrabble mining town of Butte, Montana.

As the teams warmed up on the day of the game, Warner was likely making small talk with a local when the subject of a bet was broached. As soon as the wager was offered, the temptation to Warner proved too great. Warner eventually bet his entire coaching salary—$150—that his squad would win the game.

The Butte Athletic Club, as the team was known, wasn't a bunch of has-beens and out-of-shape shopkeepers, as Warner had thought when he agreed to play the game. Instead, the team was composed of former eastern college players—even a few All-Americans—and several miners who looked like they could single-handedly lift a cow. As the time for kickoff neared and fans showed up at the field, which was covered by a layer of sand, Warner's eyes scanned a crowd of about three thousand. Many of the cowboys in the crowd had pistols at their sides; some even fired them off into the big Montana sky before the game got under way.

After the first snap, it was clear to Warner that his team was no match for Butte. It was rookies against veterans, and the Montana men overpowered the Iowa farm boys at the point of attack on nearly every play. To make matters worse, Warner could see that the fans intimidated his players. Whenever Butte made a positive gain on offense, it sounded like a twenty-one-gun salute was being fired into the air as the cowboys in the stands whooped, hollered, and shot their pistols.

Trailing 10–2 at halftime, Warner pulled a desperate move: He inserted himself into the game as a guard. At first, the sight of their coach inspired the Iowa team. Running plays behind Warner, Iowa began to move the ball. But Butte made an on-the-fly adjustment and began double-teaming Warner with Jim Hopper, who in a few months would go on to star at Michigan, and Jack Monroe, a gritty, scrappy miner who later became a professional boxer. Still, Iowa inched closer late in the third quarter, scoring to make it a 12–10 deficit.

Throughout most of the third quarter Warner and Hopper fought from snap to whistle on every play. They swung fists at each other, they wrestled, they tossed each other down. Warner's frustration grew by the minute—he stood to lose a lot of money, after all—and his emotions exploded the moment Hopper grabbed his jersey and slung him onto the ground while tearing off a large chunk of the jersey in the process. This was clearly a foul, but the referee, who was from the area and may have been influenced by the crowd, refused to throw a flag. Warner was irate. He ordered his team to march off the field. They were quitting.

Warner's coaching inexperience was showing. Caught up in the heat of the moment, he decided that it was better for his team to take flight than to stay and fight. It was an act of poor sportsmanship and even poorer leadership. As Warner's team stormed away, he was told they wouldn't receive a penny in payment if they didn't finish the game. After considering it for a few moments, he relented and sent his boys back onto the field. Warner went with them and Iowa played one more quarter, but it was a lost cause: Butte won 12–10. Warner's record as a head coach now stood at 0-1. His bank account also took a hit as the $150 in salary was gambled away.

Two weeks after the Butte game, Warner rode the train about a thousand miles to Athens, Georgia. A graduate football manager picked him up at the depot on a late September afternoon, the kind of day on which humidity hung in the air so thick you could watch it suffocate the trees. As the southern heat seared the Georgia countryside, the graduate manager gave Warner a tour of the campus in a horse-drawn wagon that bumped and rattled over the dirt roads winding through the thick stand of trees that covered the university. When they reached the football field, Warner stood up and saw it was mostly covered in slick, red clay with only a few patches of weathered grass. He guessed that the rickety bleachers nearby could hold no more than 150 fans. The facilities were so poor that Warner's first instinct was to return to the Hawkeye State, but the graduate manager assured him that the players at Georgia were as talented as any that Warner had ever coached.

Once again emphasizing the fundamentals of blocking and tackling in every practice, Warner led the Bulldogs to a 3-4 record in 1895 and a 4-0 mark in '96. During these two years Warner also acted as a long-distance coach for the Iowa State team. After he had lost his salary in the bet against the Butte Athletic Club, he needed money—and fast. And so he struck a deal with school officials at Iowa State: For thirty dollars, he would review weekly accounts of Iowa State's practices and games that were mailed to him by Bert German. Warner would analyze German's letters and fire a telegram back, dispensing advice on subjects ranging from practice drills to game strategy. Though Warner was more than a thousand miles away, he helped Iowa State beat Northwestern and the Sioux City Athletics in 1895 and his advice helped Iowa State go 8-2 in '96.

During those two years of essentially coaching two universities simultaneously, Warner's confidence rose with every victory. He built Georgia and Iowa State into regional powers, and his reputation as a young, innovative, intense, and successful coach spread to every football outpost in the country, including his alma mater, Cornell.

In the summer of 1897 the Red Men were looking for a coach, and Warner was their first choice. Cornell offered Warner six hundred dollars to coach the entire season. Warner took the job, believing it would be the last of his career.

When Warner arrived in Ithaca in August 1897, the game possessed his thoughts night and day, and he constantly found new ways to make his team better. Warner didn't have the best players in the nation at Cornell, but he believed his team could win every Saturday afternoon as long as they played with intelligence and discipline. The Red Men started the season with victories over Colgate (6–0), Syracuse (16–0), and Tufts

(15–0). Cornell then tied Lafayette (4–4) before hosting Princeton on October 23, 1897—the most important game of Warner's young career.

In the days before kickoff several stories appeared in an Ithaca news-paper that detailed how mighty Princeton was going to steamroll Cornell. Warner compared the undefeated Princeton team to a "human tank" that "crushed every team in its path." Warner's game plan was to keep the score close for the first three quarters and then try to score late to steal the victory.

With two minutes left in the first half, Warner's conservative approach to the game was working: Princeton led only 4–0. Now Cornell had the ball on Princeton's thirty-yard line. It was third down and two yards to go for a first down. (At the time, the offense had only three tries to make ten yards and a first down.) From the sideline, Warner ordered his quarterback to punt the ball. He wanted to pin the Tigers deep in their own territory, making it virtually impossible for Princeton to score again before halftime.

Cornell lined up. But to Warner's astonishment, the Red Men didn't punt the ball. Instead, his boys attempted a running play, which the Princeton defense stuffed for no gain. Before the half was over, Princeton marched down the field to score a touchdown and take a 10–0 lead. That wound up being the final score of the game.

Warner was livid. When the final whistle blew, he stormed back to the locker room, found a small separate room off of it, slammed the door, locked it, sat in a chair, and cried. For several minutes he cried like a boy who was being picked on by the school bully. He cried because his quarterback hadn't listened to him, and he cried because Cornell had lost the game. Warner was never a good loser, and this moment, sitting alone with his hands covering his face, would be one of the low points of his coaching career.

On October 6, 1898, Warner stomped along the sidelines of Cornell's Percy Field, his chocolate eyes scanning the field. Kickoff between Cornell University and the Carlisle Indian School was moments away, and the young Cornell coach was as anxious as he'd ever been on a football field. Warner had scouted the Indians weeks earlier, and their collective team speed and cunning play had made him a nervous wreck. He'd never seen a team quite like this—their players appeared to be as quick as cornered rabbits and as athletic as gymnasts. Now the Carlisle football team was warming up in front of the twenty-seven-year-old Warner, and these Indian kids were just as fast and as shifty as he remembered them from his scouting trip.

Unlike Warner's nerves, the scene around Percy Field was pleasurable: The towering oaks and maples were like fireworks—blazing hues of red, orange, and gold spreading over the peaceful hills and dips of upstate New York. A breeze blew off nearby Cayuga Lake, sending the leaves raining onto the ground. Several hundred fans surrounded the field, drawn to the game by both Cornell's burgeoning reputation and a desire to see if Indians could really be any good at this game of football.

Up to now, football had been a game of pushing and brute force as teams merely ran the ball right, left, and up the middle. Most of the players in the sport were big and slow. But not these Carlisle Indians. Just a few moments into the game, it was clear that the Indians weren't typical football players. They flew around the field with eye-popping speed and spectacular agility, and they treated every play like it would be the one to cinch the game.

Warner's team had its hands full with the Indians. Realizing that his players couldn't match the athleticism of Carlisle, Warner instructed his boys to use the "double pass." This involved a player taking a handoff from the quarterback, sprinting to the left end, and flipping the ball to another player who was running in the opposite direction and around the right end. Warner called the double handoffs trick plays, because few teams in the nation were using these reverses at the time, and the plays consistently fooled the Carlisle boys, whose coach, John Hall, was a former Yale player with little coaching experience. Cornell won the game 23–6, but the referee, who had been Cornell's 1897 team captain, had done his part to assist the Red Men of Cornell. He called back two Carlisle touchdowns, which prompted the *Carlisle Daily Herald* afterward to label him "the twelfth member of the Cornell team." The paper also noted "slugging was indulged in openly by the Ithacans."

Even Warner tacitly acknowledged to reporters after the game that the final score had been artificially inflated by a handful of timely calls by the referee. "We outscored 'em but we didn't defeat 'em," Warner told reporters, "if you follow me."

Nearly everywhere they went, the Indians of Carlisle faced discrimination—from the referees, the fans, and opposing players. But that only enhanced Warner's admiration for them. Long after the game, when Warner thought of the Indians, his mind was like a ticker-tape parade—showering down possibilities, a thousand new, exciting, and colorful ways the game could be played with athletes as versatile as those Carlisle Indians. The Indian boys were fleet, nimble, and astonishingly quick; in other words, they were the ideal players for the new style of football that Warner dreamed of kick-starting to life. If he coached them, football would be like an intriguing plot line in which you never knew what was coming next. If he was at Carlisle, Warner figured, he just might be able to change the fundamental way the game was played.

Maybe one day, he thought, maybe . . .

As football gained popularity on the East Coast in the final years of the nineteenth century, Warner increasingly found himself in the spotlight. People throughout New York now knew his name. He had status and a following of true believers, which made him a marked man. After all, not everyone was thrilled that he was becoming a mini celebrity in Ithaca.

When Warner wrapped up his second season at Cornell on November 24, 1898, with a 12–6 loss at Penn, he expected to return to Ithaca in '99 for a third year as head coach. But soon after the team's final game of the '98 season, Warner's top assistant coach made it known that he'd like to have Warner's job. The players on the team were split. At the time, the captain of the squad had considerable influence picking the head coach, but when the team was scheduled to choose its '99 team captain, Warner postponed the vote. One of the players up for captain backed Warner; the other supported the assistant coach. Warner knew that the issue of who would be the coach for the upcoming 1899 season had divided the team, and he thought there was a good chance that school administrators would intervene and fire him before the situation got out of control. In the meantime, Warner began looking for another job. Without hesitation, his thoughts shifted to Carlisle.

Warner wrote a letter to Captain Richard Pratt, the superintendent of Carlisle, expressing his interest to be the football coach at his school. He asked Walter Camp, the coach at Yale, to pen a letter of recommendation for him and send it to Pratt, which Camp did. Pratt telegrammed back to Warner, asking him to come to Carlisle for a visit. The two could discuss a potential job.

Days later, Warner stepped onto a train that was waiting at the Ithaca depot. He took a seat in his Pullman car. A prolonged whistle pierced the air and soon the wheels started to churn and grind. Warner was now on his way to Pennsylvania coal country, a trip that would set the course of Glenn Warner's life—and shape the future of football.

Surrounded by one of the first classes on the Carlisle grounds, school founder, Richard Pratt, shakes the hand of Spotted Tail, a Brule Sioux chief who sent five of his children to Pratt's school. (Courtesy Cumberland County Historical Society)

4

THE TRICKIEST PLAY

Pop Warner arrived at the depot in Carlisle, walked off the train in his supremely confident gait—arms swaying at his sides like those of a marching toy soldier—and then boarded a trolley headed for the town square. When the trolley eased to its stop on Garrison Street, Warner hopped off. For the first time, his eyes feasted on the campus of the Carlisle Indian School, located on a gently sloping hill on the south side of town.

Sprawled out in front of Warner was a tree-lined parade green that served as Carlisle's central common area and, beyond that, twenty-seven acres of manicured lawns that housed several Federal-period wooden buildings: a hospital, stables, barracks, a dining hall, a coal house, and a guardhouse. A seven-foot white picket fence circled the school and footpaths crisscrossed the grounds. Though it didn't boast the leafy atmosphere or the prestige of an Ivy League school like Cornell, Carlisle had an austere, military-school air. Warner strolled across a small bridge that stretched over a creek called LeTort Springs Run and passed a set of two brick posts at the entrance gate. A sentry stood at each post, and they pointed Warner to the superintendent's quarters, where he eagerly shook the hand of Richard Henry Pratt, the founding father of Carlisle.

Tall, muscular, and wearing his dark-blue cavalry uniform, Pratt was fifty-nine years old and had the rugged, creased face of a man who'd been under the sun most of his life. The most distinguishing feature on Pratt's face was his meaty nose, which looked abnormally large on his rounded, smallish head. Pratt was the son of a missionary, and the notion that anyone could be saved by submitting to a higher power—or a higher authority—was drilled into him at an early age.

Pratt was born in 1840 in Rushford, New York. When he was a young boy, his father was struck with gold fever, and the elder Richard Pratt rushed to the hills of California. Working as a prospector, Pratt made a fortune. But as he was traveling back across the country to reunite with his family, he was robbed by another prospector and murdered. The younger Pratt was forced to drop out of school at age thirteen and find work as a printer's devil to support his mother and two younger brothers. Five years later he became an apprentice to a tinsmith. Pratt hoped to one day became a full-fledged tinsmith, but then, on April 12, 1861, Confederate soldiers in Charleston, South Carolina, bombed the Union garrison at Fort Sumter, igniting the Civil War. Pratt enlisted eight days later to fight for the Union.

Pratt carried his Winchester into battles at Nashville and Chicka-mauga—two clashes that turned into human slaughterhouses in which an estimated 41,226 soldiers lost their lives. When the war was over, he mar-ried Anna Mason and ran a hardware store in Logansport, Indiana. But he missed the military, and in March 1867 he joined the regular army and was soon dispatched to Fort Sill in the Oklahoma Territory to take charge of the Tenth U.S. Cavalry. Pratt, a second lieutenant, oversaw the Buffalo Soldiers, a unit of African Americans, and he had several Indian scouts under his command who helped the Tenth protect the white settlers who arrived in Indian Territory in their covered wagons with big dreams and little weaponry.

Shortly after Pratt galloped into Fort Sill, the situation in the area be-came extremely volatile. Native American warriors, in search of buffalo and food, stepped up their tomahawk raids on settlers, causing panic among whites to spread like an outbreak of cholera. Pratt and his Buffalo Soldiers were ordered to round up and detain leaders of the Comanches,

Kiowas, and Cheyenne. In April 1875, Pratt arrested seventy-two Indians and locked them up in the jailhouse at Fort Sill. Days later, Pratt's soldiers bound the Indians in chains and prepared to move them across the country to an old Spanish jail at Fort Marion in St. Augustine, Florida. The tribal leaders were essentially being held for ransom. The demands were this: As long as their tribal members who were left behind in Oklahoma behaved, the leaders would someday get to go home. But if the tribes continued to rebel and raid the settlements, they would be locked up—perhaps until death.

For three days, Pratt and his Buffalo Soldiers kept their rifles pointed at the prisoners as the train transporting them chugged across the wide midsection of the nation. The heavy locomotive hurtled across the plains, over the mighty Mississippi River, and through the red-clay country of Georgia. As the train neared the state line of Florida, Pratt walked with his six-year-old daughter through a car where the captives were being held. He was stopped by an Indian the whites called Gray Beard, who said through an interpreter that his only child was the same age as Pratt's little girl. He asked Pratt how he would like it if *his* legs were in chains and he were taken miles away from his wife, his home, and his little girl. Gray Beard's voice cracked with emotion as he spoke, and the question nearly brought Pratt to tears.

A few hours later, as the clock neared midnight, Gray Beard slipped out of his chains, cracked open a window, and leapt out of the train as it lumbered along at thirty miles an hour. Pratt pulled the bell rope, causing the conductor to stop the locomotive. Holding lanterns and rifles, Pratt and his men searched the thick forest for Gray Beard. When they finally found the runaway Indian, he jumped from behind a palmetto and refused to halt. A guard shot Gray Beard through the chest. Pratt's men carried Gray Beard, bleeding profusely, back to the train, where they placed him on a bed. Pratt allowed a few of the prisoners to visit the wounded Indian, and Gray Beard told them that ever since he had been taken from his home, he wanted to die. He then gave them a message that he asked to be passed along to his wife and child. Moments later, as the train rolled through the night, Gray Beard died.

The train pulled into Florida, where temperatures soared. The intense heat that gripped St. Augustine in the late spring of 1875 was too much to handle for many of the Indians, whose will to live had weakened as their distance from home increased. Within days of arriving at Fort Marion Prison several Indian leaders collapsed and died, overcome by the unrelenting weather and weariness.

While Pratt guarded the prisoners at Fort Marion, the missionary in him began asking questions: *Is it really in the best interests of the country to put Indians in chains? Is this the only answer? Is there another way to deal with Indians?*

Pratt felt a tinge of guilt every time he dead-bolted a cell at Fort Marion. These Indians were in danger of being obliterated from the planet, and Pratt believed with all of his heart that the answer to the Indian problem wasn't just to throw anyone with brown skin into a prison and look the other way, which was a sort of quiet annihilation. So Pratt became his own kind of missionary—an Indian missionary. He thought he could convert them—help them see the light that shined brightly in the white man's world—by "civilizing" the Indians and teaching them to act and behave like white men. Unlike many of his superiors, Pratt didn't think that segregation was necessarily the right course to take. He believed that Indians and whites could actually live side by side, the caveat being that Indians had to adopt a white lifestyle. They had to go to school, study English literature and American history. They had to live in houses, wear a suit and tie, and put on a felt hat. Pratt wanted to "kill the Indian and save the man," a phrase he often uttered.

In the late 1870s the Indian debate raged from the halls of Congress in Washington to church pews throughout the Northeast to saloons on the western frontier. Like Pratt, most whites believed that Indians were inferior and that the only way to save them from extinction was to turn them into God-fearing, English-speaking, short-haired people. Some thought that Indians should be used as cheap sources of labor by settlers. Others simply wanted to ignore the issue, to give the Indians a parcel of land and let them try to solve their own problems. If they starved to death, so be it.

At Fort Marion, Pratt noticed that several prisoners were as sad-eyed and withdrawn as any humans he'd ever seen—even more so than prisoners with whom he'd come in contact during the Civil War. What he witnessed touched a raw nerve, and he soon launched his great crusade. Pratt removed the chains from his Indian captives and gave them permission to walk freely inside the jail. He ordered his soldiers to cut off the Indians' flowing dark locks. He located some old army uniforms and gave them to the prisoners. Then he had his guards teach the Indians how to polish the brass buttons on their uniforms and to fold their trousers with a perfect crease.

Pratt found more comfortable sleeping quarters for the Indians within Fort Marion, and he took the amazing step of giving the prisoners their own loaded guns and allowing them to police themselves. This would have struck cavalrymen back in Indian Territory as sheer lunacy, but Pratt was building trust. Pratt then invited to the jailhouse local women, who volunteered to teach the Indians how to read English in exchange for archery lessons. The women also gave the Indians colored pencils and paper and asked them to illustrate their tribes' early days as buffalo hunters. In time the prisoners were allowed to leave the fort for a few hours, and many found work as laborers in the area. Others collected and polished sea beans—seeds of tropical plants that fall into a waterway and are typically carried into the sea—and sold them as trinkets at a souvenir store in St. Augustine. In a matter of months Pratt had become a modern-day John the Baptist, converting the prisoners to be more like the accepted, blessed ones—as he saw it.

Pratt's behavioral experiment drew the attention of many high-profile Indian reformers from New England who traveled by steamboat to St. Augustine for vacation. As he continued his work, he spent more time with Quakers and missionaries who were adamantly opposed to the government's policy of extermination. Pratt and the Quakers thought that the experiment was working, which prompted Pratt to write a letter to the secretary of the interior pleading for more assistance to train the Indians.

"The duty of the government to these Indians seems to me to be the teaching of something that will be of permanent use to them," Pratt wrote to a military superior while he was overseeing the prisoners at Fort Marion. "Teaching them to work is one thing, but St. Augustine offers practically nothing to them in this line. They have besought me repeatedly to try to get Washington to give them the opportunity to work."

Late in 1878 the imprisoned Indians in Florida were finally set free, after three years of confinement. Not all of them went back to Oklahoma. Pratt convinced seventeen of the Indians to enroll at the Hampton Normal and Agricultural Institute in Hampton, Virginia, which opened in 1868 and was one of the first schools to educate freed slaves. (The school was called "Normal" because it established "norms" or educational standards while educating future teachers.) There wasn't enough room at Hampton for all of his Indians, so Pratt continued to plead face-to-face with congressmen and bureaucrats in Washington. He told them he wanted to start an English-style military school for Indians. Pratt was an absolutist when it came to his vision: He believed that no matter how much Indians might suffer from losing their own heritage, the only thing that could save them from extinction was to become fully indoctrinated into the white man's world. He would be strict in applying this principle— even brutal, if necessary.

Slowly, Pratt won support. Several members of Congress publicly backed his idea of an Indian School, as did a few prominent journalists and philanthropists. Early in the summer of 1879, after four years of lobbying to different power brokers in Washington, the secretary of the Interior Department, Carl Schurz, granted Pratt permission to start an Indian School. He gave Pratt full use of the abandoned army barracks in Carlisle, Pennsylvania, which had been built nearly 125 years earlier when the town was being threatened by tribes of hostile Indians. But since 1871 the barracks had been shuttered and merely collecting cobwebs.

It wasn't a purely philanthropic gesture. One of the conditions set out by the interior secretary was that Pratt could recruit only Indian children who were from the most violent tribes—tribes that were causing the most trouble for the government. The secretary wanted to be able to hold these children as hostages if a full-scale battle erupted between U.S. troops and a particular tribe. Pratt agreed that the children could be valuable negotiating tools, and on September 10, 1879, he left Carlisle to recruit his first batch of students who lived in Indian camps in the Dakotas.

Pratt rode a train to Yankton, then traveled up the Missouri River on a steamboat. At Rosebud Landing he was met by a sixty-three-year-old white teacher he had hired whom he called "Miss Mather." Sarah Mather had helped Pratt educate his Indian prisoners in Florida. If Pratt succeeded in bringing back young Indian girls to Carlisle, Mather would care for them on the trip back.

Before the Civil War, Mather ran a boarding school for girls in St. Augustine. Pratt hired her to teach the Indian prisoners once he arrived at Fort Marion, and she often brought along one of her closest friends to the classroom: the author Harriet Beecher Stowe, who lived nearby in a cottage on the St. Johns River. An abolitionist, Stowe had written the novel *Uncle Tom's Cabin,* published in 1852, and the book made such an impact that when President Abraham Lincoln met Stowe at the start of the Civil War, he said only half jokingly, "So you're the little woman who wrote the book that started this great war."

After the conflict was over and Lincoln emancipated the slaves, Stowe and many other prominent abolitionists made solving the Indian problem their new cause. One of the first steps was teaching the Indians to speak English, and this was what Stowe did with Mather at Fort Marion. One afternoon the two were teaching the Indians to pronounce words ending in *th* by saying the word *teeth.* To illustrate the meaning of the word, Mather stuck her hand in her mouth and removed her dentures and placed them on a table. Stowe giggled as the Indians looked in wonder at the set of teeth. Mather made her point, and the Indians understood for the first time that the white man possessed a special gift: the power to rebuild the body.

Pratt and Mather climbed into a two-seated spring wagon that was driven by an Indian who lived at the Rosebud Indian agency, which was one hundred miles away. Pratt was determined to make the trip in two days, so he sat next to the Indian driver and constantly swatted the two mules with his black whip. When darkness fell, the Indian driver stopped the wagon. Using two blankets that he borrowed from the driver, Pratt made up a bed for Mather on the floor of the wagon. Pratt and the driver slept on a blanket underneath the wagon, but the night was so cold that Pratt couldn't stop shivering. A few wolves approached at one point in the evening, and Pratt quickly sprang to his feet with his revolver in his hand. The wolves dispersed, but until the stars finally melted into the coming light, Pratt kept his eyes open.

When Pratt and Mather reached the Indian camp at Rosebud, they tried to explain that the only way the Indians would survive as a people was if their children were given a white education. But Pratt's impassioned speeches failed to move anyone. Not one of the Indian leaders was willing to hand a child over to a cavalryman. But things changed when Pratt met with the revered chief of the Brule Sioux, a man named Spotted Tail. Speaking through an interpreter at the council house on the reservation, Pratt calmly told the chief that the government was adopting a new Indian policy. Pratt said that he believed that the Indian youth were capable of acquiring the same education as white children, and this would ultimately make them equals. He then asked Spotted Tail to trust him and send his children to Carlisle.

Spotted Tail, a stocky and physically imposing man, stood up. Speaking through the interpreter, he said, "The white people are all thieves and liars. We do not want our children to learn such things. The white man is very smart. He knew there was gold in the Black Hills and he made us agree to give up all that country and now a great many white people are getting out the gold."

"But Spotted Tail, you cannot read or write," Pratt replied. "You cannot speak the language of this country. You have no education. You claim that the government has tricked your people and placed the lines of your reservation a long way inside of where it was agreed they should be. You put your cross-mark signature on the treaty which fixed the lines of your reservation. You signed that paper, knowing only what the interpreter told you it said. If anything happened when the paper was being made up that changed its order, if you had been educated and could read or write, you could have known about it and refused to put your name on it. Spotted Tail, can you not see that if you and these with you here today had been educated as the white man is educated that you might right now have all your people out there in the Black Hills digging out the gold for your own uses? Can you not see that it is far, far better for you to have your children educated and trained as our children are so that they can speak the English language, write letters, and do the things which bring to the white man such prosperity?

"As your friend, Spotted Tail, I urge you to send your children with me to this Carlisle school and I will do everything I can to advance them in intelligence and industry in order that they may come back and help you. Spotted Tail, I hear you have a dozen children. Give me four or five and let me take them to Carlisle and show you what the right kind of education will do for them."

After Pratt spoke, Spotted Tail retreated to another area to discuss the matter with a few of his most trusted tribal members. Minutes, then hours, passed. When Spotted Tail returned, he told Pratt, "It is all right. We are going to give all the children you want. I will give you five. Two Strike will give you his two boys. Milk will give you his boy and girl, and White Thunder will give you his boy and girl. The others are going to make up the party."

Pratt's words had finally won over an Indian leader, and he felt the rush of success as he rode to the Pine Ridge agency in South Dakota to meet with Red Cloud and other tribal leaders. Pratt passed the word that Spotted Tail had given him five of his own children to take back to Carlisle, where they would receive a first-class education and learn the language and customs of the white man. He asked the Pine Ridge leaders to send their children to Carlisle so that when they became the heads of their tribes, they would be able to communicate with the white leaders. Red Cloud and the others asked a lot of questions, but finally agreed. By the time Pratt left Pine Ridge, he was given eighty-two Indian children to take back to Carlisle.

At Pine Ridge a white doctor examined the Indian children to make sure they didn't have diseases such as measles or smallpox. A few days later the Indian boys and girls gathered with their families at Rosebud Landing on the Missouri River. They ranged in age from about five to fifteen, and all of them were nearly frozen with fear. They were being separated from their families and all that was familiar to them. Many wailed and begged their mothers and fathers not to send them away. Pratt tried to reassure them. In a soothing voice, he told the children and their parents that this was for the best and that these children would one day be the leaders of all the Indian people because they were now going to attend a great school that would help them prosper. To celebrate the occasion, Pratt handed out cigarettes to many of the boys. "We will all have a good-bye smoke," Pratt announced, "and when we reach Carlisle we will all quit."

But terror seized most of the children. Many believed they were being led to a death camp. Three years earlier, Sioux and Cheyenne warriors had killed Colonel George Armstrong Custer near the Little Bighorn River in the Montana Territory, and the children were convinced that they were about to suffer an eye-for-an-eye punishment. "I could think of no rea-

son why white people wanted Indian boys and girls except to kill them," a
Sioux named Ota Kte, who was eleven years old at the time, recalled. "[I
did] not have the remotest idea of what a school was. I thought we were
going East to die."

With red, swollen eyes and slumping shoulders, the children were
herded onto a steamboat, which carried them downriver to Yankton.
There the group piled into two private cars on a train headed east. None of
the children had ever been on a "moving house," as some of them called it.
When the locomotive screamed its whistle, then lurched to start, most of
the children grabbed on to the seats for dear life. And they silently prayed
to their ancestors, begging for one thing: that their lives be spared.

Whenever the train stopped at stations, large crowds of curious onlookers
stared at the "wild" brown-skinned children in the windows. The Indian
boys and girls had long black hair—some had it braided—and frightened
dark eyes that darted about their new surroundings. They wore tan-
colored pants and shirts made of buckskin. Others had on moccasins and
buffalo-hide leggings. The older boys had feathers in their hair and their
faces were painted with streaks of black, yellow, and red. Several had
beaded necklaces draped around their necks and the boys as well as the
girls wore earrings. Every child had a wool blanket that was trimmed with
beads, and many of the children wrapped their blanket in cape fashion
around themselves to keep warm during the long, drafty nights on the
train. A handful of them knew how to speak a smattering of English, but
none was fluent.

Before the train reached Chicago, Pratt telegrammed several newspapers and informed them that he and his Indian children were approaching. His words must have been intriguing, because they set the gossip
chain moving. When the train pulled into the Chicago station, cameras
popped and flashed as several photographers and reporters greeted Pratt
and his batch of students.

After pictures were taken, Pratt took the children to a restaurant in
the station. They had never seen so many white people, and those whites
were pointing and staring and, in some cases, laughing at the brown-
skinned children. The boys and girls huddled together as they shuffled to
their table and pulled their blankets up close to their eyes, covering as

much of their bodies as possible. None of them knew how to use the cups, silverware, and plates that sat on the white linen tablecloth in front of them. The boys and girls grew so uncomfortable from the stares that they grabbed their food off their plates, wrapped it under their blankets, and returned to the train, where they ate with their hands.

The train rumbled out of Chicago and headed for Pennsylvania. The boys and girls had been on the train for about forty hours when, in the dead of night, they spotted a full moon hanging unnaturally low in the clear Pennsylvania sky. This was an ominous sign to the young Indians. A rumor had started on the train that they were going to be dumped off the end of the earth. They believed the earth was flat with four corners, and as the train headed farther and farther east, they were absolutely certain that the locomotive would soon fall into oblivion. Now the moon looked like it was directly in front of them, like they had reached the rim of the world.

To the surprise of the children, the train stopped at the depot in Carlisle at just after midnight on October 6, 1879. Several hundred locals stood on the platform in the chilly darkness. The men in their three-button frock coats and the women in their floor-length evening capes gawked and gossiped in whispered voices as they saw the strange-looking creatures called Indians. The young students cautiously walked off the train. Some were so scared they trembled; others cried. Pratt led them toward the Carlisle school grounds, and the townspeople followed. Most had never seen an Indian in the flesh, and they quietly inspected this batch of youngsters from head to toe.

Tired, hungry, and looking forward to sleep, the children slogged along behind Pratt. But when they entered the old military barracks, it was completely empty. The bedding and food that Pratt had requested were nowhere to be found. The children ran through the barracks looking for extra blankets, but they didn't find any. On the first night at the school the boys and girls spread their own blankets on the wooden floors and wondered how they would ever survive on this cold, bitter end of the earth.

The process of assimilation began soon after the Indian children popped their eyes open on their first morning at Carlisle. They were guided into a large room where a barber waited for them. One by one, the barber cut off their hair that flowed past their shoulders. Many wept as their locks fell to the ground. One Sioux Indian refused to have someone else cut his hair, and he ran outside with a knife and lopped off his braids himself. He sobbed because Siouxs cut their hair only when they were overcome with sadness or shame. In a matter of moments, other Indian children joined in the crying, just as they would have done back home.

The haircut was the first step in the purging of the Indians' heritage. A change of wardrobe was the second, as children were given Western-style clothes. The boys donned military uniforms—caps included—that were left over from the Civil War while the girls were outfitted in traditional Victorian-style cotton dresses that were high-waisted and ruffly. Once in their new clothes, the students were chaperoned into a classroom and forced to pick an English name. On the chalkboard before them were writings in the English language that were incomprehensible to virtually all the Indian children. An instructor handed each student a teacher's pointer and asked the child to aim it at one of the chalk scratchings on the board. Some of the names on the board had been pulled from history books and popular fairy tales, while others were as commonplace as Mary, Dick, and Jane. And even if the name was as peculiar as Julius Caesar, Rip Van Winkle, or Rutherford B. Hayes, it often stuck to the child for the rest of his or her life.

Just as Pratt had envisioned, the school was based on military life and discipline, and drill practices took place regularly on the school grounds. The entire system of punishment mirrored the military judicial system, with students determining the consequences of every offense. The most severe form of punishment was to be confined inside the Hessian Gunpowder Magazine, a building that was built in 1776. The building measured seventy by thirty-two feet and had six-foot-thick limestone walls and heavy iron doors. Sometimes children caught trying to escape from the school were locked up in the guardhouse for several days at a time. On a few occasions the local citizens could hear the children wailing for their parents as they were dragged into the building that served as Carlisle's prison. To eliminate the "Indian-ness" from his students, as Pratt promised he'd do, the Carlisle founder used every method he could—including incarceration, even if the child hadn't reached puberty.

Shortly after escorting his first group of students to Carlisle, Pratt traveled back west to join two of his former prisoners from St. Augustine—men named Etadleuh and Okahaton—who were recruiting Indian children to come to Pennsylvania. The students at Carlisle were left under the supervision of Pratt's wife, Anna Mason Pratt, and several teachers, including Mather. Predominantly female, the teachers at Carlisle came from smaller Indian Schools around the country and from within the town. Pratt didn't have a big budget, so the pay was minuscule. But Carlisle teachers weren't motivated by money; they saw themselves as being part of a cause, and they fully believed in Pratt's vision of civilizing the Indian. Most lived close to campus and pedaled bicycles to class every weekday morning.

The students' first textbook was called *First Lessons for the Deaf and Dumb*. Using this book, the teacher brought in items such as shirts, shoes, apples, hammers, and nails and showed them to the students. The instructor spelled out the item on the blackboard in English—A-P-P-L-E— and had the students copy it in their workbooks. The teacher walked around a room with posters that said, "Blessed is he who has found his trade and gets busy," "Try the pleasant way in your work to-day," and "Do not spit on the floor; to do so may spread disease." The teacher stopped at each small wooden desk and guided the boys' and girls' hands as they slowly printed each letter. The students then said the word out loud. This meticulous, time-consuming process was done over and over, and it served as the basic teaching method at Carlisle.

The students, who had to be at least one-quarter Indian to be eligible to study at Carlisle, had to learn how a clock worked, how to sit at a table, how to tie shoelaces. They had regular textbook study, just as in any school, and they also had industrial training in fields such as carpentry, blacksmithing, carriage and wagon making, painting, plumbing and steamfitting, tailoring, harness making, and shoemaking. The Indians also had art classes where they were encouraged to sketch scenes of what they remembered about their lives on the plains. The young students drew Indians hunting buffalo, warriors on horseback, and courting ceremonies. Soon, though, the scenes in these drawings changed. Flowers began sprouting from pages and cows were pictured in pastures— reflections of their new lives at Carlisle.

Every night, the students were expected to study for at least four hours. They weren't allowed to speak in their native tongues and they couldn't leave campus without a chaperone. To remind the students that they were under constant surveillance, Pratt became what the staff at Carlisle called "the man on the bandstand." On many days, Pratt could be found on the circular, elevated bandstand located in the middle of campus. He cut a powerful figure: Broad-shouldered and over six feet tall, Pratt stood ramrod straight in his blue military uniform. From the bandstand he could see the entire school, and the nickname emphasized that Pratt was always watching the students.

But this didn't stop two Carlisle girls, who missed home desperately, from trying to burn down their school. One afternoon the two girls stuffed a pillowcase with paper, lit it on fire, and threw it in a closet in their dormitory. The blaze was eventually put out and the girls were sent away for eighteen months to a Pennsylvania women's prison, but the episode showed how desperate some were to get out of the Carlisle Indian School.

On a fall afternoon eleven years after the doors to the Carlisle Indian School had swung open, a group of Indian boys crowded into Pratt's office and posed a question: *Could they play football?* The first college game had taken place twelve years earlier, and that initial contest between Rutgers and Princeton (Rutgers won 6–4) more resembled a street fight than a sporting event: the twenty-five players on each side punched and spit while they shoved one another around the field. But the game had become more organized and popular thanks to the innovations of Walter Camp, who in the mid-1870s had played at Yale. In 1876 Camp introduced such rules as the line of scrimmage and limiting the number of players on the field to eleven per team, bringing a sense of order to the game. Football's popularity was slowly on the rise, and the Indian boys were as intrigued by the sport as were white kids.

Dressed in their finest military uniforms, the Indian boys begged Pratt for a chance to play. Pratt agreed, and with his blessing each department in the school organized a football team. Throughout the fall of 1890, the teams challenged one another and played a series of games for the championship of Carlisle. But the style of play was crude. The school didn't have any football coaches on its staff and the Indians had only a vague understanding of the rules, so the players had to figure out how to play by themselves. The games were essentially pushing matches as the offense and defense slammed into each other. The Indians didn't know the proper techniques for blocking or tackling, and they had no idea how to organize a basic offensive play. Yet there was something magical about the game that appealed to them. The Indian boys relished the freedom they felt while scurrying around the football field, and for one of the first times since he had started his school, Pratt actually spotted many of the boys smiling as if they were with their families. Football was as physical as some of the rough-and-tumble games that the Indians had played in their villages, and the sport reminded them of home.

One afternoon in 1890 a group of Carlisle's best players were invited to nearby Dickinson College for an unofficial football game—the first ever between whites and Indians. Early in the contest one of Carlisle's players, a boy named Stacy Matlock, was knocked to the ground and twisted his right leg awkwardly. Before anyone knew what was happening, Stacy was rolling in the grass and screaming in pain as he clutched his leg. The Indian players quickly rounded up a carriage and laid Stacy in the back. Then they pulled him two miles back to the Carlisle campus, where a few of the Indian players ran into Pratt's office, their out-of-breath voices trembling with concern. "It's Stacy, sir," one of the players said to Pratt. "He's hurt."

Pratt was unaware that this unofficial game between his students and Dickinson had been scheduled, and he immediately ran to the window in his office, unsure of how Stacy could have gotten hurt. Outside Pratt saw several players huddled around Stacy, who was lying in the carriage and moaning. The players were all crying, and Pratt feared the worst. "Good Lord," Pratt said to himself. "They've killed him."

Pratt rushed outside to Stacy, his heart sinking. The boy's father had trusted him to look after his son, and now Matlock, a Pawnee who was one of the biggest boys on campus, was writhing in pain.

"What happened?" asked Pratt as soon as he reached the carriage. "Is he hurt badly?"

"It's his leg, sir," one of the boys said. "I think it's broken."

"How did it happen?" demanded Pratt.

"Well, sir, we were playing Dickinson College . . ."

"Football?" Pratt asked, his voice rising with anger.

Pratt looked down at Stacy. The Indian's leg was broken in two places, and his foot was facing backward. Pratt quickly lifted Stacy into his arms and rushed him to the campus infirmary. Before the doctor set the leg, he handed the injured boy a strap of leather and told him to bite down on it as hard as he could. Then, with several other players restraining their friend, the doctor straightened Matlock's leg. Seeing the horrified look on the wounded boy's face, Pratt made a snap decision: Football would no longer be allowed at Carlisle.

The next day he dispensed an announcement that was read in every class. "Carlisle teams will no longer be allowed to play football against other schools. Signed: Capt. R. H. Pratt, Superintendent."

Even before Stacy's leg snapped like a young cornstalk, Pratt had been worried about the physical dangers of the game. In 1890 more than a dozen football players across the nation had died as a result of injuries sustained on the gridiron. Players didn't wear helmets, which meant that head-to-head collisions often produced deep gashes, concussions, and even broken necks. Pratt felt he had no choice but to ban the sport because of its brutality (in 1904 President Theodore Roosevelt would consider doing the same) and he wanted his students to focus on education, not athletics.

The line stretched forty deep, snaking down the hallway outside of Pratt's office. It was the early fall of 1893, and nearly three years had passed since Pratt had issued his proclamation outlawing football at Carlisle. But with each passing autumn, the boys at the school had heard more about the game—how the Big Three of Yale, Harvard, and Princeton were dominating teams around the nation, how increasing numbers of eastern colleges were playing football, and how fans were turning out by the thousands to watch teams play. These forty boys wanted Pratt to reinstate football so they could experience the thrill of the game and maybe one day play teams like Yale and Harvard in front of large, screaming crowds. They nominated the student who spoke the best English to act as their lobbyist. He rapped his knuckles on Pratt's door, and Pratt invited them in.

The students, dressed in their uniforms and grasping their flimsy hats in their hands, filed into Pratt's office, occupying nearly every square foot of space. "Sir, we understand your reasons for forbidding us to play football against outside schools," said the Indian boy, speaking so clearly that it was as if he had written and memorized this speech. "We know that you have our best interests at heart. That you do not want us to be wounded on the field of battle. But sir, I speak for all of my brothers here in saying that it is far more important to us to play this game against other schools. We are not afraid of injuries. Those are just injuries to our bodies. In refusing to let us play, you have hurt something deeper. You have wounded our hearts. You see, sir—we know we are not inferior. We can play this game as good as the white man. In fact, we can play it better. You have to give us a chance to prove it."

The sincerity of the words struck Pratt, who hadn't realized his kids were so passionate to play. As the Indian boy continued to make his case to bring the sport back to Carlisle, Pratt looked into the faces of the young men. Most of the children had been away from home at least two years, and life hadn't gotten much easier for them. They were lonely and struggling to learn a new way of living, a new way of speaking, even a new way of thinking. Perhaps, Pratt thought for the first time, football could unleash something powerful in these boys.

Back in the villages where the kids were born, the young Indians had led vigorous lives, just as their fathers, grandfathers, and great-grandfathers had. They helped with outdoor chores, they played with their bows and arrows, and they walked long distances while hunting deer, antelope, and buffalo with their fathers. Most of the Indian children who lived east of the Missouri River played a game that resembled lacrosse. Using sticks that had a webbed net attached to the end, players would run up and down a field and crash into one another as they tried to put a rock in a goal. Kids also played a game called *chunkee,* which had many of the characteristics of field hockey. In all their native sports, the Indian boys were taught by their elders to be aggressive and agile—two skills that would one day suit them well on the football field.

At Carlisle, the Indian boys needed something to replace this physical lifestyle that they had left behind the moment they boarded the train with Pratt. Even sitting behind a desk was hard for these youngsters, who grew twitchy and yearned for the outdoor life. Many also needed a place where they could take out the anger of being displaced, an anger that boiled inside of them and grew hotter by the day. More than anything, they needed an outlet.

Pratt wanted to give the boys something positive in their lives, something that would help bind them together like family. White kids were playing football, and Pratt wanted the Indian boys to do everything whites did. And what if, thought Pratt, his boys actually *could* beat white kids at football? If they could accomplish that, it would do more good for their self-esteem than any success in the classroom.

The wheels in Pratt's mind turned faster. Maybe a football team, by traveling around the country and displaying graceful manners, could act as emissaries for the entire school. If white people saw how refined and civilized the football team was, then they would be more inclined to support Pratt's approach to full-scale assimilation.

Pratt spoke. "Boys, I realize that I must surrender," he said. "I will let you take up football again, but on two conditions."

The air in the room was thick. The boys waited in silence.

"First, promise me that you will never slug," said Pratt. "Because if you slug another player, the people who are watching the game will say, 'See that? That's the *Indian* in them! They're just savages and you can't get it out of them!' "

"Right," the spokesman for the players replied. "We agree to that."

"Second, I want you to promise me that in two, three, or four years, the Carlisle football team will whip the biggest team in the country!"

"Yes sir, we'll try!" said the Indian leader.

"I don't want you to try," replied Pratt. "I want you to *do it*. The man who only thinks of trying to do a thing admits to himself that he may fail. Never admit that it is possible to fail—and you'll succeed."

"Yes sir!" said several of the boys.

The boys rushed from the room. A dynasty was about to be born.

Practicing on a rocky, sloping pasture next to LeTort Springs Run, a stream that flowed next to the school, the Indian boys learned the game of football. One of Carlisle's teachers, Anna Luckenbaugh, was friends with Vance McCormick, who lived near the campus and had been an All-

American quarterback at Yale in 1892. Luckenbaugh convinced McCormick to be the volunteer coach at Carlisle. For a few months McCormick drilled the Indians on the rocky field, teaching them this complicated sport. Lining up alongside players such as Lone Wolf, Jonas Metoxen, and Bemus Pierce, McCormick taught the Indians by example and repetition. And by 1896, when another former Yale player, William O. Hickock, was coaching the team, Carlisle was already attracting national attention.

That fall the Indians traveled by rail to New York City to play Yale, a squad that most sportswriters had dubbed the top team in the country. Hickock had greased his connections to arrange the game, and though he didn't tell anyone at his alma mater, he believed his boys had a legitimate chance to shock the mighty Bulldogs. Carlisle had played so well the previous week against Princeton that a few of the Tiger coaches, upset at how the Indians were moving the ball, had stormed up and down the sideline and implored their players, "Kill the Indians!" The Princeton coaches also hurled racial insults at the Indians whenever the Carlisle players were within earshot. The Indians ignored them—they had grown used to hearing racial remarks—and played the finest game in the team's short history. Princeton wound up winning 22–6, but the Indians, for the first time, showed tantalizing potential.

In the mid-1890s, football was a game of mayhem, of brute force. Once a player had the ball, his teammates would often grab his jersey and try to pull and push him through the opposing team. Oftentimes the ball-carrier had suitcase handles sewn onto his football knickers, which enabled his teammates to get a better grip on him. The defenders, meanwhile, would push the offensive players aside to get to the man carrying the ball. If they had to, the defenders would punch and kick to break through the scrum of offensive players who surrounded the runner and make the tackle by any means necessary.

The game required raw strength and power. The players on the elite teams were big, stout athletes, capable of throwing their weight around to advance the ball down the field. Most of the Indian players were lean and short; on average, they weighed about 150 pounds and were five feet, eight inches tall. So to the three thousand fans who showed up to watch Carlisle play Yale on a cool October afternoon in 1896 at Manhattan Field in New York, it looked like the game was going to be a mismatch when the Indians lined up for the opening kickoff. The Yale players, who measured around five feet, eleven inches and tipped the scales at close to two hundred pounds, were anxious to prove the superiority of their race.

Sitting in the stands with one of his daughters was Pratt, who rarely attended Carlisle's games. But the players asked him to travel with them to New York because they believed they were going to dominate the Blue of Yale, a team that in the previous five years had lost only one game. Since 1883, Yale had achieved a record of 155 wins and 4 losses, and everyone in the crowd except Pratt was certain that Carlisle would be the next victim.

The Indians kicked off. Yale halfback Paul Miles caught the ball, then sprinted up the field thirty yards before being tackled. On the first play of the game, the two lines settled into their positions. The Yale players, trying to intimidate the smaller Carlisle players, growled and barked, spit flying out of their mouths. The Indians remained silent, simply staring at the Yale players. When the ball was snapped, the two lines collided, swiftly and violently, and Yale could advance the ball only a few yards. Soon they had to punt.

About five minutes later, Yale had the ball back. They were moving methodically down the field when Jim Rodgers, a burly lineman who had moved into the backfield for a power sweep, took a handoff from the quarterback. But as soon as Rodgers reached the line of scrimmage, two Indian defenders—Hawley Pierce and Martin Wheelock—crashed into him with startling force. The hit was so hard that Rodgers fumbled the ball as he fell.

The loose ball flopped around on the ground and was quickly scooped up by Carlisle's Frank Cayou. He dodged one lunging tackle attempt and then cut up the field. When he crossed the goal line and scored a touchdown, the crowd let loose a roar so loud that even Pratt was shocked. "Carlisle! Carlisle!" the crowd chanted. Pratt looked at his daughter and smiled. "That's one," he said.

Yale captain Fred Murphy screamed at his teammates, who were gathered around midfield: "We must score three times! Now buck up and hit these fellows!"

Yale scored two touchdowns before halftime, taking a 12–6 lead. Neither Yale nor Carlisle crossed the goal line in the third quarter, and the Indians still trailed 12–6 when Carlisle received the ball deep in their own

territory with just a few minutes left in the game. For almost the entire afternoon, Carlisle had failed to move the ball on offense against the bigger,
stronger Yale defense. Now, in the huddle, Carlisle quarterback Frank
Hudson gambled. He called a trick play, one that the team had relentlessly
practiced. Hudson knew that the only way Carlisle could score quickly
would be to deceive Yale.

The Carlisle players trotted to the line of scrimmage. The ball was
snapped to Hudson. He spun around and handed it to back Isaac Seneca,
who ran to his right. But just before Seneca was gang-tackled, he flipped
the ball to Jake Jamison—an end, who was running around to the left. Almost all of the Yale players had jumped on Seneca, and now they looked up
and saw the back of Jamison's jersey as the Indian ran up the field. Two
Yale players caught Jamison on the 35-yard line, but he broke free and
scored a touchdown.

The crowd sizzled in an emotional fever, cheering loudly for the underdog Indians. Several men threw their bowler hats into the air, while
Pratt and his daughter yelled. All that stood between a tie with mighty Yale
was a simple drop-kick through the goalposts by Frank Hudson, which
was what teams attempted after scoring a touchdown and was worth two
points. (A touchdown was worth four points at the time.) The key to the
drop-kick was the actual dropping of the ball. Once the kicker let it out of
his hands, he waited until it rebounded off the ground to boot it toward
the uprights.

(Up until 1934, the football that was used was rounder and more
rugby-shaped than the one used today, which meant it usually bounced
straight back up when the kicker dropped it onto the ground. To promote
more forward passing, the shape of the ball was redesigned in '34 to be
more pointed and oblong, which also made it more difficult to perform a
drop-kick because the new ball didn't bounce as true as the old one. This
change essentially rendered the drop-kick obsolete.)

As Hudson and his teammates celebrated the touchdown and prepared for the drop-kick, the official was seen sprinting up the field, waving his handkerchief. At this point in football history, coaches usually
volunteered to referee games. Before the Yale-Carlisle kickoff, Hickock,
the Carlisle coach, agreed to do the job. But now, as the Indians were on
the verge of completing one of the biggest upsets the sport of football had

ever seen, Hickock was pointing to the 35-yard line, the spot at which Jamison had busted out of the grasp of the two Yale players.

"What's going on, Coach?" asked Bemus Pierce, the Carlisle captain. "What's wrong?"

"I thought they stopped him," Hickock said.

"What?" yelled Pierce above the din of the crowd. "He broke away!"

"But *I* thought they stopped him!" replied Hickock.

"He blew the whistle!" the Yale captain, Fred Murphy, shouted. "That means the ball is dead right there and there is no touchdown."

Murphy was right: According to the rules, the play stopped when the referee blew his whistle, inadvertently or not. When Hickock vetoed the Indian touchdown and marked the ball at the 35-yard line, Pierce told his teammates that this wouldn't be tolerated. He told them that they were going to walk off the field, but as they marched toward the locker room, Pratt bolted out of his seat and caught up with his boys.

"Wait," Pratt said. "Listen to me for a minute."

"They stole it from us, sir!" said Pierce, who believed his own coach had sabotaged Carlisle's shot at winning the game, though Hickock had in fact merely made an honest mistake. "If that's the way they want to win, they can have it. We're leaving."

"Listen to me, all of you," Pratt insisted as the crowd fell quiet, unsure of what was happening. "You must not quit. You must fight the battle out. If you leave, you'll be called quitters. Nobody will remember this touchdown play. But everybody will remember that Carlisle quit a game."

A murmur in the stands started, then steadily grew louder. "Carlisle! Carlisle! Carlisle!"

"Can't you hear the crowd is with you?" Pratt asked. "Go back. Play this game out and do not quit for any reason."

The players followed Pratt's instructions and returned to the field. They lost the game, but now Pratt had firsthand confirmation of the spell that the Carlisle Indian School football team could cast over white fans. All he needed now was an elite coach who could mold the team into something special.

Late in the 1896 season, Pratt received an urgent telegram from the Chicago Press Club: They were inviting the Carlisle Indian football team to come to Chicago and play the University of Wisconsin under "electric lights" at the coliseum on December 19. This would be the first night game ever played in college football history. Newspapermen and fans in Chicago were curious to see the boys from Carlisle, whose reputation was growing with each game. Pratt accepted the invitation but decided he would not make the trip to Chicago. The boys would go with their coach and Carlos Montezuma, the team's doctor.

Three days before kickoff, the team traveled on the rails west to the southern shore of Lake Michigan. When they reached the main train depot in Chicago, the Indians were greeted by scores of reporters and photographers. Ever since the Yale game, the press couldn't get enough of Carlisle. The players were portrayed as the ultimate underdogs, and to reporters looking for a juicy story, every game was framed as an epic battle between wild Indians and refined white players. Some reporters took it even further, writing about how a Carlisle game was tantamount to a fight between the savages and the sophisticates, the old world versus the new world. And it was becoming less and less clear who should come out on top in these games—and who the white crowd was going to root for.

Earlier in the '96 season, Penn defeated Carlisle 21–0. *The Philadelphia Press* reported that the crowd had been thrilled by the crafty play of the Indians. "Suddenly there came a change in the howling, shrieking, color-waving masses in the stands," the *Press* wrote. "The wily aborigines had led the palefaces into ambush and as minute succeeded minute it looked as though a slaughter like unto that of [General Edward] Braddock's men over a hundred years ago was about to be witnessed. Gain after gain was made by the Indians. They squirmed and wriggled along the ground like eels, plunged into the line of the Red and Blue like mermaids, crashed into them with the force of colliding engines on a down grade, and struggled with each other for every inch of ground as desperately as ever their forefathers did centuries ago."

Pratt was seeing for himself that the Carlisle Indians were becoming crowd favorites—even when there wasn't a single Indian in the crowd. After many of the team's victories, Pratt received telegrams from local white folks in Carlisle offering congratulations and expressing their support for the Indians. At one impromptu celebration after a Carlisle victory, Pratt told a crowd of both Indians and whites, "Buffalo Bill travels all over the land parading in his Wild West Shows with what he says are the particular qualities of an Indian. He's a fraud. No man has ever put a greater lie before the public than Buffalo Bill. We're proving that the white man can love the Indian.

"People used to be scared when you'd tell them that a bunch of Indians were coming into your town. The women would have run down and locked the cellar doors and the men would have gotten their guns ready to shoot. But now it's different. Our friends and neighbors, the white people, join in our rejoicing when we succeed even though the teams we beat are of their own race."

For Pratt, this was the beauty of Carlisle Indian football.

The Carlisle-Wisconsin game started at 8 P.M. at the Chicago Coliseum. More than fifteen thousand fans filled the stands, and they were treated to a night of wizardry by Carlisle. Outrunning and outsmarting the Badgers, Carlisle used several trick plays to beat Wisconsin 18–8. One of the most impressed observers was Carlos Montezuma, who had stood on the sideline during the game. Montezuma was a powerful person on the football staff. A Mohave-Apache Indian who attended an English-style Indian School in Illinois before earning his medical degree at the Chicago Medical College, Montezuma helped fill in the communication gaps between whites and the players by translating. Montezuma was frequently on the sideline exhorting the players, and he could empathize with their struggles like no one else at Carlisle. Some of the boys even looked up to him as an Indian father. And like a parent, Montezuma was quick to punish the boys when he caught them drinking alcohol, a recurring problem at Carlisle.

The Wisconsin game had given inspiration to Montezuma's pen, and shortly after Carlisle's victory over the Badgers he wrote a letter to Pratt.

> I can give no words that will express the amount of good the awakening power of what Carlisle is doing for the rising generation of the Indians by your football team and band coming to. . . . The press club—the pulse of Chicago—has had their eyes opened and now they understand Carlisle as never before. . . . They thought at first the team was coming only for what money there was in it, but now they see different. It was only to make a way into their hearts, so that they may

realize their obligation to the Indian children for education and freedom into their enlightenment.

When Pratt read the missive from Montezuma, his mood soared. The
letter offered more evidence that his football team was his greatest asset
in spreading the gospel of his Indian School. But still he needed one
thing: a gifted coach.

Pop Warner blew through the door of the superintendent's office at
Carlisle, and strode toward Pratt. Warner was dressed in his finest Sunday suit, while Pratt wore his cavalry uniform. The two shook hands, exchanged pleasantries, and then sat down to discuss whether Warner
would be a good fit as the next football coach at Carlisle.

But Warner didn't treat this as a job interview. In his typically blunt
fashion, he told Pratt that he wouldn't haggle over salary: Warner, still an
attorney, requested $1,200 for the season, plus expenses—take it or leave
it. Pratt took it. Days earlier Walter Camp, the Yale coach, had written a
letter of recommendation for Warner and sent it to Pratt, telling the
Carlisle founder that Warner possessed one of the brightest young minds
in football. The letter gave Warner bargaining power, and Pratt quickly
submitted to his demands. The two shook hands again and it was official.
Warner would begin coaching the Carlisle Indians the following fall, in
1899.

With that handshake, the business of sport in America changed.
Though he had a limited budget, Pratt agreed to make Warner one of the
highest-paid coaches in college football. Pratt wanted Warner to be a
trailblazer, to be the first coach to barnstorm around the country and play
games in order to promote the school. Pratt also wanted Warner to become the first celebrity coach—someone who would court the press in
order to get Carlisle mentioned in the country's major daily newspapers.
Warner relished this challenge. The one thing that Warner never lacked
was self-confidence, and he believed he was the perfect person to be a
new kind of coach, one who was a whiz at X's and O's *and* PR.

Like most whites in America at the turn of the century, Warner didn't
hold a high opinion of Indians. He even admitted to his friends that he
had prejudices toward "redskins," who he believed always quit at every-

thing if they didn't immediately succeed. But Warner also believed that they could make ideal players in the new style of football that he planned to implement at Carlisle. Instead of coaching his players to try to overwhelm the opponent with force, Warner was going to teach his players how to use their natural speed and agility to beat any team they played. Warner even welcomed the size disadvantage his players would face each week because it played into his strategy for quickening the pace of the game. Pratt was working on his grand experiment of fitting Indian kids into white society; now Warner had his.

Late in the summer of 1899, Warner met his players for the first time. Standing out on the school's field, he told the boys that football offered a wonderful opportunity: the chance to beat white kids at their own game. Warner went on to lay out his vision of how he was going to build Carlisle into the nation's top power, and the players hung on his every word as if he were conveying the most important idea since man invented the wheel. Even Warner was surprised at how intently the Indian boys paid attention. He could see it in their brown eyes: These Indian players were desperate for something positive in their lives.

But as Warner spoke, he inspected his players—and he didn't like what he saw. They were far smaller than he remembered from the previous autumn when Cornell had faced Carlisle. Some of them even looked like they might be sickly. *How in the world,* he thought, *will I be able to justify my salary to Pratt when we lose every game this season?* "The squad ought to be trying out for beds in a hospital rather than places on a football team," Warner told Pratt. But Pratt just smiled and reassured Warner that everything would be fine.

"They have been on farms all summer," Pratt explained, "and these Pennsylvania farmers insist on getting their money's worth. The youngsters will soon begin to pick up weight, so don't worry."

Sure enough, in the first few days of practice, Warner became more optimistic about his team's chances for success. Unlike many of the white boys he coached, the Indian players followed his instructions without hesitation, as if he were their father and they were his children. He pushed his iron-fisted authority to the limit when he taught his players a new block that he called the "body block." Up until this time, most of the blocking on the football field was done with the shoulders and arms. But Warner wanted his boys to use a technique that would knock the opposing players off their feet. It required a dose of courage because the Indian players would have to sacrifice their bodies when executing the maneuver. Warner worried that his players would shy away from the block, but he was wrong: The Indians actually took joy in the vicious contact that went into the hit.

To make the move, which sportswriters soon dubbed the "Indian block," a player would run full speed at an opponent, then leave his feet, half turning with his hips, to hit the player just above the knees and follow through with a roll. It was devastating, and it chopped down opposing players like a machete through tall weeds. After just a few days of practicing the block, most of the Indian players had mastered the technique. Warner had never seen anything like it: These boys actually enjoyed sharpening their skills in practice. Every day on the practice field the level of energy was so high it was as if twenty thousand fans were watching the players' every move, fueling their energy tanks with motivation. But in truth, most of the boys had grown up in the wilds of the frontier, where living conditions had been harsh. Because of this, the Indians had more stamina and tolerance for pain than any of the white players Warner had coached.

The Indian boys also felt as free as birds in an open sky while on the practice field. Here the fears that haunted most of their waking hours— *Will I ever see my parents again? When will I be allowed to leave and go home? Will I be accepted by my people once I return home?*—could disappear as they concentrated on learning this new game. And during these initial practice sessions Warner was continually surprised by how quick and athletic his players were. Unlike the boys he coached at Cornell, who were muscular and plodding, the Indians possessed the speed of track stars, the flexibility of contortionists, and the tenacity of elite wrestlers. After a few weeks of drills and working on plays, Warner started to believe that his Indians had the perfect genetic makeup for football.

Yet the players did have a weakness: Emotionally, they were as fragile as pieces of fine china. When Warner saw something he didn't like in his previous coaching jobs, he'd point out the mistake using the bluest of language, letting a river of expletives pour out his mouth. But at Carlisle this kind of talk didn't sit well with the players. At one of Carlisle's first practices Warner spotted a player flubbing an assignment and the coach loudly cursed at him as he corrected his error. For the next two days, that player didn't report to practice. When he finally showed up three days later, Warner asked him where he had been. "I'm tired of coming out to practice every day and listening to your swearing every time I make a mistake," the player said. "I've had it."

Warner was speechless. He'd never considered the consequences of his harsh language, or the fact that as a white authority figure over young Indian boys he needed to carefully monitor everything he said. Warner told the player, "If you will come back to the team, I will never swear at you or anyone again." The player returned to the squad, and Warner's days of swearing on the football field abruptly ended—for the most part.

Every day after practice, Warner retreated to a small cottage located on the northern end of the Carlisle campus. He and his wife, Tibb Lorraine Smith, moved into the house shortly after Warner accepted the job from Pratt. With his hefty $1,200 contract, Warner suddenly became a man of means, and one of the first things he did was marry his sweetheart from Springville, New York, whom he had fallen for hard as a boy. The Warners would never have any children, which was one of the reasons why Pop thought of his players as an extension of his own family.

Warner was twenty-eight years old, and just a few weeks into the 1899 preseason practice he believed that he was on the cusp of something special. "This is a new kind of team," Warner told his wife one evening. "They're light but they're fast and tricky. Once they get into an open field, they're like acrobats, they're so hard to knock off their feet. And proud! It's just the kind of team that I've always dreamed of coaching."

Warner felt as if he had uncovered a secret. Even at the highest levels of the U.S. government, the prevailing opinion of Indians was that they were physically inferior and would have no chance of becoming better than America's finest white athletes in any sport, especially one as violent and physically challenging as football. "The Indian child is of lower physical organization than the white child of corresponding age," Estelle Reel, the superintendent of Indian Schools, told a newspaper reporter shortly after she was appointed to her federal position by President William McKinley in 1898. "His forearms are smaller and his fingers and hands are less flexible; the very structure of his bones and muscles will not permit so wide a variety of manual movements as are customary among Caucasian children, and his very instincts and modes of thought are adjusted to this imperfect manual development."

Reel believed what most whites did: that Indians were capable only of working in fields or as domestic hands in the homes of whites. Warner's eyes told him differently. He felt like his Indians were the embodiment of the perfect football player. And he was about to show how much one man, given the right team at the right time, could change the way a sport was played.

With a whistle draped around his neck, Warner drew up plays on a chalkboard that he hauled out onto the practice field. Most of the Indians spoke little English, so Warner taught them by mapping out the plays and by personally lining up and demonstrating how he wanted them to perform a particular run, block, or tackle. Warner didn't have a translator, and he quickly realized that the best way of coaching was to show them firsthand how he wanted them to play the game. This was the way most of the boys' fathers had taught them how to hunt and ride horses, and so the Indian players responded to Warner's style and flair for demonstration, which was always replete with grunts and groans. For all Warner cared, the Indians could have been deaf, because in his first few years at Carlisle he taught mostly by example, which had always been his preferred method of coaching.

One afternoon in the preseason of 1899, during a scrimmage between the varsity and reserve teams, Warner stopped the action and told his players to gather around the chalkboard. He had an idea.

"When you're on defense and the other team starts a play in which they all move to your right, what do you do?"

Martin Wheelock, one of the varsity linemen, answered. "Slide along to the right with them, find the ballcarrier, and drive in."

"Right," replied Warner. "It's only natural. Okay, you men," he motioned to the reserves, "line up over there."

Warner instructed his second-teamers, who were on offense, to move to the right. But before the ball was snapped, he told the player who was going to carry the ball to take a step or two to the right, then sprint left around the left end. Once the ball was hiked, the play unfolded just as Warner had anticipated: The second-teamers pushed to the right, and the varsity defense went with them. Before the varsity defense knew what had happened, the second-team halfback had run around the left end and, untouched, bounded into the end zone.

"Here's what I want you to remember," said Warner after the play. "Get the other team moving in one direction so your ballcarrier can go the other. And the best way to do it is for all of you to move that way."

For the rest of the preseason, the Indian boys practiced this play but never used it. Warner was saving it for the game with Penn, Carlisle's third scheduled opponent of 1899, on October 14.

In his first game as coach of Carlisle, which was against Gettysburg College on September 23, 1899, Warner's boys rolled, winning 21–0. The next week the Indians demolished nearby Susquehanna University, 56–0. But Warner viewed these games as merely warm-ups for the one that would tell him whether his radical ideas could work. On October 13, the team traveled to the City of Brotherly Love and checked into the Normandie Hotel on the eve of their game against the University of Pennsylvania. In their previous five years, the Quakers had compiled a record of 65-2, featuring winning streaks of 34 and 31 games.

Though Carlisle didn't have any alumni and had been playing football for only six years, more than 22,000 people paid twenty-five cents each to see the Indians play at Franklin Field. A large group of students from Carlisle had made the trip to Philadelphia via rail, and they cheered wildly when their players took the field before the opening kickoff. "Minnewa Ka, Kah Wah We!" they chanted from the stands. "Minnewa Ka, Kah Wah We! Minnewa Ka, Kah Wah We! Carlisle! Carlisle! Carlisle!" The special chant, which was a rallying cry from the stands to show support for the players, was created at the request of Warner. No detail was too small for the coach, and he wanted the Carlisle students to show as much school spirit as any college in the country.

The Indians received the ball first but were quickly forced to punt. The Penn quarterback, John Gardiner, gathered his team in a huddle. "Guards back, right!" he called. The Quakers lined up, fully expecting to blow the smaller Carlisle players backward. The "guards back" play was the hallmark of the Penn squad. In this formation, they placed three big guards in front of the halfback and three behind him. When the halfback received the ball, this mass of men would push forward in a tight scrum with all their weight. This single play epitomized how the best East Coast teams dominated the sport at the turn of the century.

In the previous weeks Warner had taught his defenders to stay low when confronted with this kind of power attack. If they kept their shoulders close to the ground, Warner insisted, they could gain leverage even on players who outweighed them by forty pounds and push them backward. Warner was like a physicist who calculated weights and angles and energy fields, and he believed his boys' smaller body sizes could actually help rather than hinder them. He also told his players to use their quickness to avoid being blocked. When a blocker approached, Warner explained to his boys, they should dart to the right or left and let the momentum of the blocker force him up the field. Then, he said, you can lunge into the backfield at the ballcarrier.

On the field, Warner's boys performed exactly the way they were taught. Over and over, linemen Martin Wheelock and Ed Rodgers sliced into the backfield to tackle the bruising Quaker tailback. Penn punted back to Carlisle, and this time the Indians moved the ball to the Penn 34-yard line. On third down—teams were only given three downs at the time to advance ten yards before being awarded a new set of downs—Carlisle attempted a drop-kick. Until 1897, teams were given more points (five) for drop-kicking the ball through the goalposts than for scoring a touchdown (four). By '99, the value of a touchdown had been increased to five points the same total awarded for a successful drop-kick. And Carlisle had one of the deadliest drop-kickers in the nation, a five feet, four inch, 133-pound Pueblo Indian named Frank Hudson.

For the past four seasons, Hudson had been the team's top kicker. On most early evenings in the spring and fall, he could be spotted alone on the Carlisle practice field. Holding the ball, he'd take a step forward with his right leg, then drop the ball onto the ground. Just as it bounced up from the surface, he'd swing his left leg forward like a giant pendulum and kick the ball. Traveling end over end, the ball would soar high into the twilight and through the crossbars. Deadly accurate from forty-five yards or closer, Hudson practiced in the winter as well. When snow covered the Carlisle campus, he moved inside to the gym, where he set up a pair of uneven bars to act as goalposts.

Now, against Penn, Hudson received the snap. He caught the ball cleanly, took one step forward, dropped the ball on the ground, and then just as it rebounded back up—*thwack*—the ball hissed into the blue sky, soaring higher and higher. It traveled through the uprights and, suddenly, Carlisle had grabbed a 5–0 lead.

Penn battled back, tying the score 5–5 at halftime after the Quakers' Truxton Hare booted a twenty-yard drop-kick just before intermission. Early in the second half, Hudson, who was also Carlisle's quarterback, called the play that Warner had taught his boys just weeks earlier. "This is the time for the new play," Hudson told his teammates in the huddle. He reminded them that everyone should move to the left, but at the last second he would give the ball to Isaac Seneca, the halfback, who would then run to the right.

With the ball at Penn's 45-yard line, Hudson received the snap. He broke toward his left. Everyone on the field surged in that direction as if the quarterback were a powerful magnet that pulled the defenders toward him. But just as he was about to leap into a great mass of players, Hudson handed the ball to Seneca, who, as planned, bolted to the right. The Penn team was clearly fooled, because no one was within ten yards of Seneca as he turned up the field. Two Quaker defenders finally caught him on the Penn five-yard line, but Seneca had gained forty yards. The Indian fans in the stands were whipped into a froth, screaming loudly.

On the next play Carlisle's Hawley Pierce bulldozed into the end zone for a touchdown. After Hudson drop-kicked the extra point, Carlisle led 11–5. The stunned Quakers would never recover from the surprise play. The Indians ended up handing Penn its third loss in six years, winning 16–5.

When the Carlisle team returned to its barracks later than night, Pratt and Warner allowed the boys to celebrate as if they'd just won a great battle—which they felt like they had. For one night, a powerful feeling of Indian pride pulsed on the Carlisle campus as players paraded through the grounds in their nightshirts and sang Indian songs. Students pulled the players in a wagon around the courtyard as the band played the school's

fight song. The Penn victory marked the first time that Carlisle had defeated an established East Coast power, and it heralded their arrival into
the football elite—the ruling class of the gridiron.

Indeed, almost overnight, the Carlisle team became a national sensa-
tion. Because it didn't have a home stadium, Carlisle played all of its key
games in 1899 on the road, and after the Indians toppled the Quakers,
newspaper writers became fascinated with the traveling shows put on by
Carlisle. Reporters called the Indians the "Gypsies of the Gridiron," and
wherever they went people who had never seen a football game before
paid cash to watch and be amazed.

By midseason, with Carlisle's record at 5–1 (they lost to mighty Harvard in Cambridge, 22–12), Warner's scarlet-and-gold-clad players had
become media darlings. Newspapermen followed them everywhere they
went. The exotic-sounding names of Little Boy, Brave Thunder, Owl,
Lone Star, and Fast Bear entered the dialogue of American sports as the
Indians received attention normally reserved for the nation's top professional baseball players—guys like slugger Honus Wagner of the Louisville
Colonels and pitcher Cy Young of the St. Louis Perfectos. The Carlisle play
ers were photographed practicing, eating lunch, studying at school, and
traveling to games. Newspapermen took hearty bites into the apple of hy-
perbole, writing sensational stories that detailed in grand language how a
band of Indians was playing the white man's game of football better than the
white man. Sports editors also used cartoons, elaborate diagrams, and dramatic sketches featuring tomahawk-chucking Indians dressed in football
uniforms to describe to the country how the Carlisle Indians were developing into a team that was capable of beating any college on any weekend.

The New York World described one pregame scene between Yale and
Carlisle: "On one side were the undergraduates of an old and great university. They represent, physically, the perfection of modern athletics,
and intellectually, the culture and refinement of the best modern American life. On the other side was the aborigine, the real son of the forest and
plain, the redskin of history, of story, of war, developed or veneered, as
the case may be, by education." The *Minneapolis Tribune* ran a cartoon of a
pipe-smoking Sitting Bull watching Carlisle play the University of Minnesota with the chief saying, "In old days pale faces whip old Injuns heap.
Now young Injuns lick pale faces."

After working with Warner for just a few months, the Indian boys were doing what a few years ago would have been unthinkable: They were firing the public's imagination.

Warner kept innovating. A few days before Carlisle traveled to upper Manhattan to play at Columbia University on Thanksgiving Day, he asked two of his players, Isaac Seneca and Thaddeus Redwater, to try something new at practice. He instructed Seneca, a halfback, to change his starting position. Normally a halfback would begin the play slightly bent over with his hands on his knees. But Warner had done some thinking: What if the halfback lined up in a three-point stance with his weight leaning forward on his fist?

Warner tossed a ball to Seneca. First he told him to run at Redwater starting from his regular stance; Redwater quickly made the tackle. Then Warner told Seneca to assume a crouching position in a three-point stance. Warner yelled, "Hup!" and Seneca surged forward like a bullet out of a gun. He fired past Redwater before the lineman could lay a finger on him.

"Good!" said Warner. "We'll try it."

As soon as Carlisle received the opening kick from Columbia, Warner told his backs to use the crouching start—a first in college football history. Warner again was playing the role of football physicist, and the small Indians blasting off the line in their crouched starts caught the Columbia players off guard. As Warner slyly grinned on the sideline, his Carlisle players pushed Columbia all over the field. The Indians scored at will, which left the small crowd of three thousand at Manhattan Field awestruck. Though Columbia had beaten Yale earlier in the season, the Ivy Leaguers were no match for Carlisle. The Indians thrashed Columbia 45–0.

That evening the team enjoyed a Thanksgiving feast back at the barracks in Carlisle. They celebrated their first year together with extra helpings of turkey, gravy, and mashed potatoes. The players, who back in their homes ate traditional Indian foods such as rabbit stew and cooked buffalo meat, sat side by side with their pale-faced coach just as Indians and Pilgrims had done in 1621 at Plymouth Rock. Pratt even had his students reenact the Thanksgiving story, as the boys and girls of Carlisle dressed up as the Pilgrims and Indians of that first feast.

Satisfied with the results of the season, Warner relaxed on this Thanksgiving afternoon with all of his players. But soon everything was going to change. He was about to receive a request to play a hastily arranged game out west on Christmas Day, and on the trip he would first come into contact with a skinny boy who was three-quarters Indian, one-quarter Irish. A boy who would become not only Warner's best recruit, but also the world's greatest athlete. A boy named James Francis Thorpe.

Whenever Carlisle hosted an opponent at Indian Field, fans lined up as many as ten deep to catch a glimpse of the agile, acrobatic team that was like no other. (Courtesy Cumberland County Historical Society)

5

WHAT AN INDIAN CAN DO

Dawn broke over the plains, spraying violet light across the snow-covered fields of corn and wheat that surrounded the cattle town of Lawrence, Kansas. As the black sky gave way to the light on January 12, 1900, one thousand Indian students at the Haskell Institute Indian School stumbled from their bunks and rushed into the freezing midwinter morning, their breath rising from their mouths in thick white puffs. Dressed in gray military uniforms, gray overcoats, and blue caps, the students lined up in formation outside a four-story dormitory. Moments later, they fastened their gaze onto the group of football players who emerged in the distance and pounded their way through the crunchy snow. Eleven-year-old James Francis Thorpe, a small, graceful boy with lively brown eyes, a square jaw, and a bowl of black hair, was one of the students shivering in front of the gray stone building at Haskell. Like everyone at the school, little Jim couldn't wait to meet the Carlisle Indians, who were quickly becoming larger-than-life figures to Indian boys and girls across the country.

The football players marched closer. Thorpe could see that they were wearing blue military uniforms with yellow-lined capes. They were led by a stocky, powerful-looking white man who exuded the aura of a leader—a general in command—who told his young men what to do, where to go. The sight of these approaching players caused Thorpe's lips to curl into an eager smile. The Carlisle football players were heroes, representing all that was possible for Indians, and now the young Indian's heart pumped with excitement as the team stepped closer.

Just twelve days into the twentieth century, the Carlisle football team was on the tail end of a historic journey: The Indians were returning to Pennsylvania after making the first cross-country trip in the history of college football. The University of California, seduced by the potential of a hefty payoff at the gate, had invited Carlisle to San Francisco for a post-season game to be played on Christmas Day, 1899. Warner let his players decide whether or not to accept the challenge. Many westerners, Warner reminded his boys, were wary of Indians. White America was pushing farther west every day, laying down railroad tracks and digging into the earth for minerals and erecting cities in the Arizona Territory and the Territory of Utah. Public attitudes toward Indians were overwhelmingly negative, as most whites—particularly those gritty cowboys on the western frontier—viewed Indians as relics who stood in the way of progress; or, worse, as dangerous forms of wildlife that needed to be hunted. In Arizona, for instance, a five-hundred-dollar reward had recently been offered for each "buck Indian's scalp."

The Carlisle players understood they were going into hostile territory, yet they voted in a landslide to take the long trip and become the first eastern team to play in the Pacific Time Zone. Warner expected the game to be bitterly contested—Cal had finished the season with a 7-0-1 record and had smashed Stanford, an elite team, 30-0—but he was anxious to see how his wide-open style of play would match up with a team from Northern California. As always, Warner was curious to test his methods in a new laboratory, and so in December 1899 he and his players each carried a duffel bag onto the train at the Carlisle depot, beginning an odyssey that would span some seven thousand miles.

Warner tried to keep life on the train as interesting and easy as possible for his boys. They passed the long hours by reading schoolbooks, telling old family stories, and simply looking out the window at America at the end of a century, seeing everything from curious faces that greeted them at nearly every depot to the skeletal remains of cattle that punctuated the plains. In the evening the Indian players ate dinner in the dining car, and later they closed their eyes in the sleeper cars and listened to the rhythmic clickety-clack of the train as it steamed west.

To keep his squad in shape while on the three-week trip, Warner often had his players jump off the back of the train and run alongside it. As the train snaked through the snowcapped Rocky Mountains, Warner was frequently found standing on the rear platform of the caboose, encouraging his boys to keep their legs pumping, to keep working, to remember that they had a bunch of white kids they needed to whip on the football field. When the train stopped, Warner usually found an open field where he could hold an impromptu practice. At one such session in a small western town—virulent anti-Indian country—he let his kids scrimmage by themselves. As Warner sat on a bench outside the train station and watched his boys, an elderly man with a long gray beard approached. The stranger looked over at the Indian players, who were outfitted in their red sweaters with a monogrammed C on the front, and wanted to know just who the hell they were and where in heavens they were going.

"This is the Carlisle football team and we're en route to San Francisco to play the University of California in a few days," replied Warner.

The man stroked his beard as if he was trying to solve a riddle, and then told Warner, "Well, they are going a darned long way to get the hell kicked out of them."

Carlisle continued westward. When their train reached Soldiers Summit—a broad valley pass that was the highest point on the Denver & Rio Grande Railroad in Utah—the players fell quiet as the locomotive struggled up the mountain. The train seemed like it could topple backward at any moment, and the players were sure that it would. But it finally reached the summit, and there it briefly stopped at a depot that was no bigger than a boxcar. A newsboy waiting near the tracks came onto the train and yelled out the elevation—7,500 feet—and informed the passengers that the temperature outside hovered around zero, but it felt much colder than that. Inside their cabins the boys pressed their faces to the window and fell into a dumbstruck silence, fascinated by the whitecapped peaks that were so tall they seemed to pierce the basement of the galaxy. None of the players—not even Warner—had seen such stunning

scenery before. These were the moments that made Carlisle's long football journeys seem worthwhile, no matter how many miles they traveled.

After twisting through the Sierra Nevada range, the Carlisle team arrived at the depot in San Francisco, where the clicks and flashes of photographers and the yellow pencils and notepads of reporters were waiting
for the Indians. In their stories the next day the journalists noted
Carlisle's immaculate military uniforms, their capes, and their pitch-
perfect behavior. One reporter even trailed the team to their hotel and
monitored the players like a zoologist in the jungle analyzing a rare animal. He had taken on the role of moral policeman to see if anyone in the
group committed the sin of blurting four-letter words, but he didn't find
any juice to report. "There is no loud talking, no smoking, no drinking,
no profanity; there is not even slang in their conversation," he noted.

A day before the game, Warner led his players on a tour of the Bay
Area. They visited the Chinatown section of San Francisco, where the
boys shopped for trinkets. At several stores the players spotted silver dollars sitting on the countertops. But when they tried to pick them up, the
dollars wouldn't budge; as a joke on children, the storekeepers had glued
the coins to the counters. To the Indian football players, this was a real
knee-slapper, one of the funniest stunts they'd ever come across.

On Christmas Day the Carlisle team jogged onto the football field at
the Berkeley campus to play Cal in what had been dubbed the "East-West
Championship" by sportswriters. An audience of 8,000 fans ringed the
field and stared at the Indian players with prying eyes as they warmed up.
The field was in terrible shape; it was covered in so much sand that
Carlisle's Frank Hudson, who had been named an All-American by Walter
Camp just days earlier, had trouble drop-kicking the ball. The shape of
the football itself also befuddled the players. It was fatter and heavier than
the ones they had used on the East Coast, prompting the Indians to name
it "the California pumpkin."

The Indians were the first team to leave their locker room. As the
eighteen players emerged from the portal under the covered western
grandstands and ran into the crisp winter air, a few of them cartwheeled
onto the field. The crowd applauded loudly in approval. After their
pregame calisthenics, the seven substitute players trotted to the sideline
and joined Warner, where they slipped on red sweaters to keep warm.

Because the field was layered with sand, footing was treacherous and neither team moved the ball consistently on offense. With the score tied o—o late in the first half, Warner reminded his boys that they hadn't traveled all these miles and spent all those nights away from their beds to lose or tie. The trip had already bonded the players, and Warner could tell that they no longer viewed themselves as individual Sioux or Lakota or Sac or Fox Indians. They were now all members of the same tribe—the Carlisle Indian tribe—and Warner implored them to win for one another and all the Indian people.

Then Carlisle caught the only break of the game. Cal had the ball on its 28-yard line when the Bears were forced to punt. After the kicker lined up in deep formation, the ball was snapped. But it sailed far over the head of the punter, who then turned and sprinted after the ball, which was bouncing around the field. When the punter, Pete Kaarsberg, reached the ball at the four-yard line, he scooped it up and just as he turned around to run back up the field, *bam!* With the force of a horse galloping at full speed, Bemus Pierce, one of the biggest players on the Carlisle team at 210 pounds, smashed into Kaarsberg. Pierce pushed Kaarsberg back, back, back into the end zone and then through it, tossing Kaarsberg into a low fence that sat a few feet behind the end line. Carlisle was awarded two points for the safety—the only score of the day. Carlisle won this unofficial East-West national championship game 2—0.

The next day the headline on the sports section in the *San Francisco Chronicle* blared: CALIFORNIA VIRTUALLY TIES CARLISLE; INDIANS SCORE TWO POINTS ON A FLUKE.

To Warner, stories like this confirmed that many white reporters wanted to see his Indians lose. The overtly biased story in the *Chronicle* barely mentioned that most of the game was played on Cal's side of the field and that the Indians had never before used a ball so big. In spite of all this, Carlisle had won—and Warner knew that wasn't a fluke.

Warner had more plans for this trip. This wasn't a one-and-done kind of deal—not for the coach. He believed that this journey gave him the chance to grow his program at Carlisle from good to great, and so instead of hopping back on a train and immediately returning to Pennsylvania, he wanted to stop at several Indian Schools along the way and check out the teams who were following the model of Carlisle—the original Indian School in the United States—and now playing the game.

Warner was a football bird dog. He could sniff gridiron talent from miles away, and he treated the return leg of Carlisle's journey as an extended recruiting trip—the first in the history of football. When the team arrived at one of the Indian Schools that were popping up all over the country, Warner and his players would teach a clinic to show the newer school how they played the game. The Carlisle coach would then watch as his Indians scrimmaged against the other teams. Warner paid close attention to the opposing players, hoping he could pinpoint his next star. When he saw a boy with potential, he gave him and his teachers the hard sell, turning on the full power of his snake-oil salesman charm to try to woo the young player into coming to Carlisle—the sooner the better.

Pratt also helped Warner on the recruiting trail. Carlisle had a network of school recruiters on reservations across the country, and Pratt frequently reminded them to keep their eyes open for potential football players who could one day don the red Carlisle jersey for Warner. Shortly after the turn of the century, Pratt penned a letter to an agent at the Sac and Fox Reservation in Oklahoma Territory—the same area where Jim Thorpe had been raised. "If you should by chance have a sturdy young man anxious for education who is especially swift of foot or qualified for athletics," Pratt wrote, "send him and help Carlisle to compete with the great universities on those lines and to now and then overcome the best."

When Warner told his team that their itinerary was taking them through Perris, many of the Indians were ecstatic. A few of them believed they were heading to France's City of Light to see the Louvre and the Arc de Triomphe. Warner swallowed his laughter and told these players that they were going to pass through Perris, California, a warm paradise full of tropical plants and orange groves. When the team reached the Sherman Indian School campus, which was located near Perris, in Riverside, the school band and several mandolin players greeted them. During the forty-eight hours that the Carlisle team was there, they were treated like royalty, which, among Indians, they were fast becoming.

The team next traveled southeast into the desert toward Phoenix.

During one train stop that lasted six hours, the players, needing to stretch their legs and burn energy, sprinted around an open field chasing jackrabbits. The team eventually arrived in Phoenix in early January and played the Phoenix Indian School in a dusty park next to their campus. In front of 6,000 Indian and white fans who sweated in 90-degree heat as they stood around the field, Carlisle pounded the Phoenix team 86–6. As the game unfolded, Warner's attention never waned. He was still looking for that one special player who could single-handedly transform a good team into an unbeatable team.

After their lopsided victory, the Carlisle team again piled back onto a train. Their next stop: the Haskell Institute, located on the flats of Kansas, just outside the town of Lawrence.

As soon as the boys at Haskell found out that the Carlisle Indian football team would be making an early morning stop at their boarding school, excitement buzzed through the campus like an electrical current. Jim Thorpe had learned how to play the game only about a year earlier, but ever since he first stepped on the field, running with a football in his hand seemed the most natural thing in the world. Out on the field he felt unencumbered, content, and, most of all, special—sensations that little Jim hadn't experienced often in his short life.

Early in the morning of May 22, 1888, Charlotte Thorpe gave birth to James and Charles Thorpe in a small one-room cabin made of cottonwood and hickory that sat a few miles south of the town of Bellemont in the Oklahoma Territory. The twin boys were big as infants, and they had greatness swirling in their blood: their great-grandfather was Black Hawk, the legendary chief of the Sac and Fox Indians, who were located in the territory that would become the state of Oklahoma in 1907.

The boys' father, Hiram Thorpe, stood just over six feet tall and weighed a muscular 225 pounds. Half Irish and half Indian, Hiram had a sociable spirit—he liked to invite neighbors over for summer picnics on his 160 acres of rich, fertile farmland, which he had received as a government grant—but he was also known around Bellemont as a volatile, rough, dangerous man whose Irish temper and thirst for booze often got the best of him. He usually walked around wearing a gun belt and a high-crowned cowboy hat over his long black hair, which fell to the small of his back and, when he was on his horse, blew around like a tumbleweed caught in a prairie wind. Hiram sold whiskey that he stored in big brown jugs, even though it was outlawed in Indian Territory at the time, and he was known to steal horses and shoot out white farmers' lanterns just for fun when out on evening horseback rides. By all accounts, Hiram was a man born with no fear in his blood. When trouble brewed, he never shied away—especially after a few belts of the brown water.

One night, as the story goes, Hiram rode his horse into a town near his cabin called Keokuk Falls, a stop on the stagecoach express. Whenever the coach pulled into Keokuk Falls—which was little more than a whore-house, a hotel, and the "Seven Deadly Saloons," as they were known—the driver would boldly predict to his passengers that a gunfight and a killing would surely take place within the half hour. Hiram liked to go to the sa-loon called the Black Dog, which had swinging doors and a bar made out of salvaged bridge planking. At some point in the evening two men started arguing inside the Black Dog. Insults were tossed back and forth, threats were made, and then one man pulled out a gun and shot the other. Every-one in the smoke-filled room fell silent. The gunman staggered and waved his gun to the crowd, daring anyone to challenge him. Hiram stepped forward. He walked over to the man who had just been killed, leaned down to him, and stuck his finger in the fatal bullet hole. Eyeing the gunman, he put his bloody finger in his mouth and slowly sucked off the blood, savoring it like honey. Then Hiram told the gunman, "Yeah, I'm ready. Let's go outside." The gunman backed away, slinking into the bar's darkness.

A subsistence farmer, Hiram fathered at least nineteen children by five women. He had four children with his first wife, Mary James, who was a Shawnee Indian. While still married to James, he had another daughter with a Creek Indian named Sarah La Blanche. One day in 1880, Hiram de-cided he'd had his fill of those women. He wanted them out of his life, so he put all five of his children, along with Mary James and Sarah La Blanche, on a wagon and sent them to live in another town in the Okla-homa Territory known as Okmulgee.

Shortly after exiling the two women in his life, Hiram met Charlotte Vieux, a devoutly religious Roman Catholic whom Hiram quickly married.

Like Hiram, Charlotte was big-boned, heavy, and fiercely independent. While Hiram hunted for antelope, squirrel, and turkeys to feed their growing family—Charlotte would give birth to eleven children, including six after Jim and Charlie were born—Charlotte worked outside in the sun. She planted corn, pumpkins, and beans and she constantly shooed away crows that were trying to nibble on her expansive garden.

Almost every week during Jim's childhood, usually on lazy Saturday afternoons, the entire village of Bellemont would gather on a lush green pasture bordering the Thorpe homestead. While the women of the village prepared a meal of cooked possum, raccoon, antelope, and squirrel, the men challenged one another in various athletic events. They competed in the running broad jump, the high jump, and a mile-long run. The last contest, which usually took place at sunset, was wrestling. A circle of howling onlookers formed the ring, and the matches were elimination. Almost every week the same man made the last pin: Hiram Thorpe. Hiram competed in all the events, and the games held Jim's eyes from dawn till dusk. Jim believed that no one was tougher or faster or more physically gifted than his father, and late in the day, as he watched him dominate the other men in the wrestling matches that featured loud grunting and groaning and plenty of spilled blood, little Jim pictured himself in the grassy ring, winning the admiration of everyone.

Like most rambunctious boys in late-nineteenth-century America, Thorpe was always on the move—playing chase with his friends and his twin brother, sprinting after jackrabbits, sneaking up on foxes, and trying to corral wild horses. Oftentimes, as he ran barefooted across the Indian Territory, Jim listened to the sound of his feet pounding over the dense, dry prairie grass, and he'd sink into a trance under their rhythm—*sha-kooo, shakooo, sha-kooo.*

His favorite running game was follow the leader. Whenever young Thorpe was in the lead, he'd swim in rivers, scale cedar trees and leap off branches, dive under horses, and sprint through fields of corn. His twin brother, Charlie, often had trouble keeping up with Jim because he didn't have as much strength or stamina, but the two were always in each other's sights. The North Canadian River flowed near the Thorpe cabin, and many afternoons Jim and Charlie splashed into the soft current or paddled for miles in the wooden canoes that they had made by hollowing out tree trunks. They also wrestled, had jumping contests, and rode horses for up to fifty miles a day from sunup to sundown. No matter the activity, it always turned into a game—a contest of wills and skills.

The boys attended the English-speaking Sac and Fox agency boarding school about twenty miles from their cabin. Whenever they came home, their mother Charlotte, who was half Potawatomi Indian and half Kickapoo, would often be standing over the stove cooking family meals such as fried squirrel with cream gravy and baking powder biscuits—Jim's favorite. The twins helped their mother in the kitchen by gathering blackberries, plums, and grapes that grew in the fields along the narrow river. The boys also fished from an old wagon that was stuck in the riverbed, sometimes snagging catfish as big as twenty pounds. They moved nonstop six days a week, but on Sunday things slowed down. On that day the twins and their brother and sisters always went with their mother to Mass in a nearby Catholic church. Charlotte and Hiram had lost three children to disease, and Charlotte had leaned on a higher power to battle through the sadness.

When Jim turned eight in May 1896, his dad put him and his brother to work on the farm. Hiram taught young Jim how to take care of the family's livestock, break colts, mend fences, and feed the chickens. That same month, Hiram agreed to take his boys hunting for the first time. An expert marksman, Hiram frequently brought home quail, deer, rabbits, raccoons, and possums. He'd cover thirty miles in a day, both walking and riding a horse as he looked for game. His twin sons had been begging him for more than a year to go on a hunt, but on the morning of their departure, Charlie, Jim's twin, fell sick with a fever. He couldn't go, so only Hiram and Jim ventured off together into the wild.

For three days father and son stalked game and camped in the woods. On the last day of the hunt, Hiram allowed Jim to take his first shot. Out in the distance, the two spied a beautiful white-tailed buck. Jim took aim with his rifle and felled the animal with a single shot. Hiram was so proud that he planned to host a torch-lit feast on his homestead for the entire village to celebrate his son's first kill, which was in accordance with Sac and Fox tradition.

Jim excitedly ran home, eager as always to share an adventure with his twin. Jim and Charlie were inseparable. Though they had strikingly different personalities—Charlie was considered "sweet" and "gentle" by his schoolteachers while Jim was the "incorrigible" one—they each lived in the other's shadow. But Jim always seemed to be a step ahead of his twin brother and already, at age nine, he looked stronger and ran faster than Charlie. Jim couldn't wait to show his kill to his brother, who for all Jim knew was already back on his feet.

But when Jim and Hiram reached their cabin, Charlotte met them with a terrified look on her face, and she gave the devastating news to Jim. Charlie was deathly ill at the makeshift hospital in Chilocco, some twenty miles away. Jim and his parents quickly hitched up their horses to their carriage, and within minutes they were charging toward Chilocco, the carriage bouncing over the dirt road as the horses kicked up choking clouds of dust.

As he sat in the carriage, Jim was as scared as he'd ever been. Charlie had been struck with pneumonia, which was not a far cry from a death warrant. Jim didn't know if he'd ever fish again with his brother in the early sunrise on the North Canadian River or if they would have a chance to hunt together. When the Thorpes reached Chilocco, they found Charlie in a room with other sick children. Charlie and Jim attended the English-speaking agency school in Chilocco, and now the school's principal, Harriet Patrick, was sitting at Charlie's bedside when the Thorpes arrived. Patrick told the family to keep wood on the fire that burned near Charlie's bed. Patrick then went to put hot packs on the chests of other sick children from the school, which had been racked with an outbreak of measles and pneumonia. At dawn the next morning Patrick returned to Charlie's bed and found Hiram, Charlotte, and Jim all asleep. The fire was nearly out and Charlie was nearly dead. A doctor was called, but there was nothing he could do. Moments later, Charlie passed away.

The sight of Charlie's limp body was too much for Jim to handle. In that instant, Jim lost his childhood.

Jim didn't seem interested in anything—not playing outside with his friends, not hunting with his father, and certainly not schoolwork. For months after Charlie's death, Jim simply wanted to go alone into the woods with his dog and hunt raccoon. These were the same thick woods in which a few years earlier, in 1892, the gun-wielding Dalton Gang hid after robbing a train of $10,000 in the Indian Territory town of Lillietta. Like the Daltons, Jim lost himself in this forest.

He was in the throes of a crisis of identity—one that would haunt him for years. He already was unlike the other full-blooded Indians in his village because he was one unique cocktail: a shot of Irish, a shot of Kickapoo and another of Potawatomi, and two shots of Sac and Fox. He was also one of the few boys in the territory who was Catholic. Now he grew even more alienated because he had lost his brother, his anchor. Hiram knew he had to do something for his boy.

For all his shortcomings and frailties, Hiram was also one of the few educated men in his county. He had attended one of the Kansas mission schools, which were subsidized by the U.S. government as early as 1810 and were precursors to the Indian Schools of the 1880s. There he had learned Catholicism and how to read and write English. Even before Charlie became sick, Hiram had sent his twin sons to the English-speaking Sac and Fox agency boarding school. Founded by Quakers in 1872, the government-run school was intended to "civilize" the Indian children. It sat on a small rural campus that featured a one-room brick schoolhouse and a three-story brick building that served as the dormitory. The students wore government-issue three-piece suits and black hats.

Many Indian families across the country tried to keep their children out of these schools, fearing that the youths would lose touch with their ancestry and forget their roots, customs, and even their language. After all, students could speak only English while in the classroom. But Hiram, because he was half white, wanted his sons to have a chance to succeed in the white-dominated society, so he sent Jim and Charlie to the boarding school, where they learned proper manners, how to make their beds; the fundamentals of reading, writing, and math; and the history of the white man's America, going all the way back to the *Mayflower* and Christopher Columbus. The students were taught agricultural skills as well; local farmers often visited the campus to show the boys how to raise certain crops, and the proper way to use farm tools.

The lessons on farming captivated Jim, but not much else at the school did. In the 1890s the Office of Indian Affairs listed the Sac and Fox among the tribes that were "most resistant" to a white education, and young Jim was an example of the worst of the worst. Unlike his brother Charlie, who was as attentive as any student in class, Jim would shoot at flies with rubber bands and impress his friends by doing somersaults when the teacher wasn't looking. The regimen of boarding school—*go to class, bell rings, go to next class, bell rings, eat lunch*—stood in stark contrast to the freewheeling life that Jim enjoyed when he was at home. Cooped up in the classroom, he thought of nothing but breaking free and sprinting outdoors through the fields of wildflowers by the river's edge.

Little Jim eventually began running away from the school. When he reached home, his father, who was adamant that Jim learn to read and write in English, would beat him with a leather strap. After Hiram made his point, he'd put Jim in the back of his wagon and return him to the school. On other occasions, Hiram convinced the Indian police to put Jim in their wagon and take him back to the boarding school. Often he screamed at the top of his lungs for most of the ride.

But everything changed after Charlie died. Saddened, Thorpe told his dad that he wanted to drop out of school. This time Hiram didn't force his boy to play by his rules. Hiram only hoped that being at home could shake his son out of his doldrums.

Instead, Jim became even more reclusive. When he went raccoon hunting with his dog, he started staying out all night—even though he was just nine years old. He sometimes sold his raccoon and skunk pelts, but that wasn't why he hunted; he simply wanted to be outside, in the wilds of the frontier, with no one telling him where to go or what to do. This was his way of grieving.

Hiram made Jim go back to the agency school the fall after Charlie's death, but Jim despised it even more. He'd become increasingly shy and introverted, and when he was in the classroom he would sit quietly in his chair and slip into reveries about trapping squirrels in the forest or spearing bluegills in the North Canadian River or trying to catch snakes with his bare hands. He grew so restless that just a few days after reenrolling in the school, Thorpe decided to return home. He ran and walked the twenty miles back home, covering the distance in half a day.

"What are you doing here?" Hiram asked Jim when he got back home.

"I want to be with you," Jim said.

"No, you need to be in school. Let's go."

Hiram hitched up his wagon and the two returned to the school. Hiram dropped his son off, but Thorpe didn't stay long. He took a short-cut home over rough terrain, which reduced the journey by five miles, and beat his father home. Hiram now knew he had only one option: he'd send his boy to the Haskell Institute, an Indian boarding school located in the northeastern corner of Kansas. Haskell was three hundred miles north of Thorpe's home—too far for Jim to run.

In September 1899, Thorpe was put in the back of a horse-drawn wagon and carried to the town of Guthrie in the Oklahoma Territory. A teacher from the Sac and Fox boarding school escorted him onto a train bound for Lawrence, Kansas. There, an official from Haskell met a grim-faced Jim at the depot. The two rode in another wagon a few miles outside of town and through the gates of Haskell, which had a thousand Indian students, ranging in age from about nine to nineteen. The Indian School sat on a lonely patch of land surrounded by fields of wheat, corn, and tall-grass that swayed in the prairie wind like undulating ocean waves. Three buildings formed the main campus—a chapel, a dormitory, and a school-house—and there were several athletic fields next to the common area.

When Jim arrived at Haskell in the wagon, he was pulled through a stone arch that stood at the entryway of the school grounds. Nearly every Indian boarding school in America had a similar arch marking its en-trance gate. It was the white man's symbol of moving from an "uncivi-lized" place to a "civilized" one. The arch at Haskell was an elaborate stone structure that rose about forty feet in the air and stretched some eighty feet across. The words "Haskell Institute" were carved in the arch like a frown, and many kids upon arriving shuddered with fear, as Jim did when the wagon jostled over the gravel road that led into the heart of the school.

As soon as Jim arrived, he was taken to the campus infirmary, where his hair was doused with kerosene and combed for lice. He was scrubbed clean in a bath, and given a western-style haircut—cropped short above the ears with a part down the middle. Jim slowly accepted his fate at the school, telling himself that he just had to make it through a few years. He began to make friends and he even started to take pride in his military uniform, which he wore like all the other students. Thorpe took great pains to make sure his brass buttons were always polished and that his black shoes, the first real pair he ever had, were as shiny as onyx. These were some of the first items he had ever personally owned, and he took pride in caring for them.

The students at Haskell typically spent four hours a day in the class-room learning five subjects: American history, arithmetic, grammar, composition, and biology. Every student also had to pick a trade to master. Jim chose electrical engineering, so he'd spend four hours a day in the engineering shop. Operated by the federal government's Indian education department, Haskell was modeled after the Carlisle Indian School, and its priorities, in order, were manual training, strong military discipline, and education.

The days were long. Reveille sounded at 5:45 every morning. In company formation, the students marched through the predawn darkness to the dining hall, where they stood behind their chairs, sang the "Doxology," then sat down at the long tables to eat such bland fare as hominy, potatoes, and unbuttered bread. Each evening just before nine, the students marched in company formation to the common area. Given the order to "uncover," they removed their hats and stood at attention as the school band played "The Star-Spangled Banner." The national anthem was followed by taps, signaling the end of yet another day at Haskell.

The school was as strict as a detention center. Students were punished for the slightest offenses, ranging from using Indian words (which sometimes meant the student got his mouth washed out with lye soap) to leaving their room in a mess, to even joking around. The authority figures weren't afraid to administer corporal punishment to keep the kids in line, and teachers were constantly rapping the knuckles, and swatting the behinds, of rebellious students with a hickory stick. There was an element of fear at Haskell and other Indian Schools that white children didn't have to confront: the fear of being away from home, of not knowing what was coming next, and of being severely punished if they did something that the authority figures deemed inappropriate.

When Jim wasn't in the classroom or the electrical engineering shop, or preparing for inspection or marching in drills, he could be found out on the school's sprawling athletic field, watching closely as the older boys played a game he'd never seen or heard of before: football. Most afternoons he would stand quietly on the sideline, fascinated by the varsity scrimmage. He was particularly taken with the team's star runner, an Indian boy named Chauncey Archiquette, a fullback who weighed more than two hundred pounds and had astonishing speed for his size. When Archiquette had the ball in his arms, tacklers bounced off him as if he were a brick wall. *One day,* Thorpe told himself, *I'm going to be as tough as Chauncey.*

After watching the eighteen-year-old Archiquette dominate the daily practice sessions, Jim would linger on the field once the players had re-treated to the locker room. As the bright orange sun spilled across the western sky, he raced back and forth over the empty field, zigging here, zagging there, trying to emulate his idol. Eventually Archiquette noticed this lone little boy. Thorpe was eleven years old and not even five feet tall or one hundred pounds. When Archiquette talked to Jim, he was shocked at how much the youngster knew about the game, its nuances and strate-gies. Besides watching, Thorpe had been listening to the big boys as they talked to one another and called out plays in the huddle. Archiquette asked Thorpe if he'd like to have a football of his own. Thorpe nodded his head excitedly, so Archiquette led him to the harness shop and sewed some leather scraps together. He stuffed the makeshift ball with rags and handed it over to a grinning Thorpe, who couldn't take his eyes off his new prize.

Now that Jim had his first football, he organized games among his friends after one of the school's instructors taught them the basics of the sport. Though he was one of the smallest boys in his class, Thorpe was able to outrun his classmates and possessed an undeniable grace. That may be why he never seemed to tire of the game. Whenever he had a free moment, Thorpe, wearing his hickory-cloth work shirt and jeans, was ei-ther watching the older kids play or practicing by himself, faking out imaginary defenders, running a hundred yards with the ball lodged firmly between his right arm and chest. In his mind, the game was freedom. It was played in an open field and you could do anything you wanted, just as long as you abided by a few simple rules. Jim often felt trapped at Haskell, unable to run freely in the outdoors and hunt and fish as he did as a boy. But not on the football field. Out there, anything was possible. As it was for many of the Carlisle Indian players, football to Thorpe was a powerful thing: escape.

The train arrived in the small hours of the morning, rolling into Lawrence even before the sun had peeked over the plains. The Carlisle players were awakened by the metallic screeching of the cars coming to a halt. By the time they arrived on the snow-covered Haskell campus, the red light of dawn was just beginning to reach across the horizon.

To welcome the Carlisle football team to its campus, the students at

Haskell proudly performed a dress parade, which in the military was a part of everyday life. The parade was a formal ceremony of troops—in this case, students—dressed in their finest uniforms and marching in a body to the beat of a drum signal. At the order of "Halt!" the marching stopped, roll call was taken, and important orders were read. The students were supposed to keep their eyes facing forward, but the young Haskell boys kept stealing glances at the towering Carlisle football players, who were now standing right next to them. Maybe, many of the Haskell boys thought, they would be one of them someday.

After breakfast in the domestic sciences room, all the students moved into the chapel, where the Haskell school band and the glee club performed for the Carlisle football team. The superintendent at Haskell, H. B. Peairs, welcomed the football team from the oldest Indian School in the nation. A few minutes later Carlos Montezuma strode to the front of the chapel and shared the story of his life: Growing up in Arizona, he was captured by a group of Pima Indians and eventually sold in 1871 to an itinerant Italian immigrant named Carlos Gentile. At the time, he was about six years old. Gentile legally adopted the boy, and he renamed him Carlos Montezuma. Gentile sent his son to school with other American immigrants who were hoping to become American citizens, and Montezuma eventually earned a medical degree from Chicago Medical College.

Now an advocate of assimilation schools like Carlisle and Haskell, Montezuma told the boys in the audience how he initially was scared of the white man and how it was odd to see himself in a mirror for the first time. So many of the white man's habits were befuddling to Montezuma at first—from the way they wore shoes, to the way they bathed, to the way they used a fork, knife, and spoon to eat. But now Montezuma said that he believed the best way for Indians to succeed in society was to play by the white man's rules. He didn't want the boys to lose their identity as Indians, but he wanted them to learn how to blend into white society, just as the Carlisle Indian football team was doing in its own unique way. When Montezuma was done speaking, the Haskell students clapped their approval.

The supervisor at Haskell, Mr. Wright, then moved to the front of the chapel. Looking at the young Indian faces, Wright began by saying, "Carlisle and Haskell . . ." Before he could utter another word, applause rattled the room, making it impossible for Wright to speak. It wasn't often that the Indian boys and girls felt proud of anything, but now they were able to cheer for one another, for all that they were enduring. For a moment, Indian pride pulsed in the room as it rarely did at the school. Finally the students grew quiet, and Wright tried again. "Carlisle and Haskell are the two best schools in the Indian service," he said. "The two best schools in the United States!" Thunderous clapping again shook the room, forcing Wright to just stand there and smile at the young Indians who were having such a good time.

After the speeches were over, the students of the two schools mingled and talked as they walked through the school hallways. Dressed in their red turtlenecks with the *C* on the front, the Carlisle players shared stories of the long trip to California and how they had beaten the boys from Cal even though they insisted on using a football that was almost as big as a watermelon. Many of the Haskell students had read about the Carlisle players, especially the ones who'd just been named to Walter Camp's 1899 All-American team. There was Isaac Seneca, the halfback who was on Camp's first string. And there was Martin Wheelock, a tackle, who made the second string. But the one player who stole everyone's attention was Thaddeus Redwater, who stood six feet, four inches and looked like he could wrestle a grizzly and come out on top. Redwater was a Cheyenne Indian from the Tongue River Reservation in Montana.

Because of his size, Redwater frightened people. One time when the Indians traveled to Princeton, New Jersey, to play the Tigers, they stayed the night at the Nassau Inn in Princeton. On the morning of the game, a maid entered Redwater's room and, seeing it unoccupied, started making the bed and cleaning the bathroom. When Redwater thrust his head out from beneath the bed, the maid let out a bloodcurdling scream and sprinted down several flights of stairs to the lobby, where she breathlessly told the manager that a big Indian was hiding in the room she had been making up. The manager went to Redwater's room, and the towering Carlisle Indian explained that he merely enjoyed sleeping on the floor and that he meant no harm.

But Redwater did possess a temper—especially after he'd been drinking. During one trip a few months earlier, Warner had to physically restrain his massive tackle after he polished off a bottle of whiskey and then, at each successive train stop, tried to find an open saloon. But Redwater had been on his best behavior on the cross-country trip to California and now the Haskell boys couldn't stop staring at the massive football player. As Redwater stomped through the hallway at the Indian School in Kansas—*whomp, whomp, whomp*—the Haskell boys swore he was the biggest, baddest, meanest-looking Indian they had ever seen.

Thorpe's eyes danced up and down at the Carlisle Indians. Here in the halls of Haskell, he was rubbing shoulders with the heroes of Carlisle. He was looking at his future, but not even Thorpe could have predicted how winding and perilous the road to Carlisle would be.

Late in the summer of 1901, about eighteen months after the Carlisle team had visited Haskell, a classmate approached Thorpe and told him that an urgent letter was waiting for him in the school office. The classmate went on to tell thirteen-year-old Jim that his father had been shot in a hunting accident and that money would soon be sent for him to catch a train home.

Without waiting for school authorities to arrange for his transportation back to Oklahoma, Thorpe walked out of Haskell, carrying only the work clothes he had on. He walked and jogged to the railroad yards in Lawrence, and quietly slipped into an empty boxcar that was about to be hitched to a departing train. But when the locomotive left the yards, it pitched east for Kansas City—not south toward Thorpe's home on the Canadian River. At least one hundred miles passed before Jim realized he was going in the wrong direction. In a panic, he hopped off the train and immediately started walking back up the tracks. It took two weeks of walking, jogging, and hitching rides on horse-drawn wagons—not to mention relying on the kindness of strangers for most of his food—but Jim eventually made it back to his cabin in the Oklahoma Territory.

Ever since he was a boy, Thorpe did what he wanted, when he wanted to do it. His relentless independence was perhaps his greatest strength, but it was also his biggest weakness. He wasn't a good listener and he didn't take orders well, which had a way of coming back to haunt him. It did now as he walked through the door of his log cabin.

Jim immediately wished he hadn't returned. Hiram had recovered from his injury, and when he saw his son blow through the door, anger coursed through the older man's veins, and it quickly sprang out of him in a frightful fit of violence. Hiram had not given his son permission to leave Haskell—no matter what Jim might have been told by a classmate. Hiram had made it clear to his boy when he sent him to the Indian School in Kansas that he was not allowed to run away. If he did, the punishment would be severe.

Jim didn't back down. He told his father that he wasn't going back, that he wanted to be here. This line of reasoning didn't sit well with Hiram, who proceeded to beat his son severely. But as Hiram whipped him with a leather strap, Jim still insisted that he wasn't going back to Haskell and that he belonged in his home in Oklahoma. His mind was made up. His father could turn him into his personal punching bag or scar every inch of his bare back with deep welts, and make a pack of threats, but Jim wasn't returning to Haskell. Thorpe's stubbornness was another one of his personality traits that was both a flaw and an asset, and now it left Hiram with no choice. He allowed Jim to stay as long as he worked on the farm and followed every order his father gave him.

For a few months, Thorpe looked after the cattle and hogs and tended to the horses. He relished the challenge of spotting a wild pony or horse that was meandering across their property, roping the beast, then riding him bareback until he was broken. To Jim and the other Indian youths in the territory, this was sport at its purest. Hiram had also been an expert horseman, and his son inherited all his gifts. With Jim's help, Hiram's herd of animals steadily grew.

After years of boarding school and feeling shackled to a system that siphoned joy out of his life, Thorpe had found contentment. He missed playing football—the other kids in the territory didn't even know the rules of the game—but as a boy all he ever wanted was to be outside on the Oklahoma range: running, jumping, chasing animals, hunting, gazing into the sky, losing himself in thought. Finally, he was happy. And then, in a heartbeat, it all changed.

Days after Charlotte Thorpe had given birth to her eleventh child, she passed away on November 17, 1901, from complications. Her death smothered Jim with grief. He sank into a reclusive depression, as he had when Charlie had died five years earlier, and he withdrew. Sometimes he disappeared for days, living off the land as he wandered the hills and creeks of the Oklahoma Territory.

When he did help his father on the farm, Jim wasn't as focused as he had been in the past. One day Hiram traveled to Shawnee on business and told Jim and his brother George to look after the livestock. But instead of obeying their father's wishes, the brothers went to one of their favorite fishing holes and whiled the afternoon away sitting in the sunshine with poles in their hands. When Hiram returned to the farm, he found his herd scattered all over his land.

Hiram exploded. When the boys returned from fishing, he told them to get ready for a brutal beating. Jim knew he had crossed a dangerous line with his father, and instead of submitting to him, he fled the cabin and didn't look back. For days Thorpe walked south, wondering what he should do next. He hitched different rides on wagons until he wound up deep in the Texas panhandle. He needed to earn money, so he did the most mature thing of his life: He landed a job.

For a few months thirteen-year-old Thorpe worked as a ranch hand in the heart of cattle country. Drifters from all over the country found work in the expanding cattle range in Texas at the turn of the century. The job was a natural fit for Jim: He'd been doing hard work his entire life—at home on the family farm, and on school farms at both the Sac and Fox School and Haskell. In Texas he spent time building and repairing fences, but during most of his waking hours he broke horses.

When Jim faced a wild horse one-on-one in a small corral, he carefully looked at the horse as if he were sizing up an opponent before a brawl. He was searching for clues, trying to figure out by the look in the horse's eyes if it was going to bolt left or right or if it was going to bay and kick. When Jim sensed he knew the horse's next move, he threw his lasso around its neck and pulled the thousand-pound horse with all his might, tying the end of the rope around a sturdy post that stood in the center of the corral. When the agitated horse was close to the post, Jim threw a sack over its head and hopped on its back.

Then the real fight began. The horse, jumping and kicking, tried to do everything in its power to buck Jim off its back. But Jim grabbed on to the mane for dear life and never let go. He was a picture of raw athleticism as he clung to the back of the angry horse. Within weeks, Jim's muscles began to thicken; his hands and arms in particular began to gain strength.

Slowly, out here in the barren high plains of Texas, the body of the man who would one day become the world's greatest athlete was being sculpted.

Several months after running away from his father, Jim reappeared at Hiram's doorstep. With the money he earned working in Texas, he had bought several horses, which were now grazing in front of Hiram's house. Jim felt like he'd proved himself to be a man, and Hiram agreed. Jim gave the horses to his father and was allowed to move back home.

But father and son continued to squabble over Jim's future. Finally, they reached a compromise: Jim agreed, reluctantly, to go with his father to visit Garden Grove, a public, one-room, non-Indian school that was about a mile away from the Thorpes' property. The school's only teacher, Walter White, greeted the two as they approached the small clapboard building one morning in the fall of 1903.

"Can you teach this boy anything?" Hiram asked White, who knew of Jim's history of running away from schools. "I take him [Jim] to the Agency School, he come back. I take him again, he come back. Five, six, ten times I take him, all the time he come back."

White turned his gaze to Thorpe. "Why did you leave the Agency School, Jim?"

"I don't like it," he replied.

"Did they do things to you, punish you?" asked White.

"No," said Jim. "Agency school not good for Indians. Indian boys, all, don't like it."

"Will you run away from this school?" White asked.

Jim agreed not to run away, and Hiram agreed that Jim could be a part-time student. Happy to be back at home with his father, Jim did go to school—occasionally—and he also started playing baseball with the kids in town. According to the 1900 census, Bellemont's population had swelled to 114, and its main dirt road featured a cotton gin, a small hotel, a general store, and a blacksmith shop. There were usually enough people around late in the afternoon to put together pickup baseball games that were played in a fallow wheat field near town. When Thorpe was at Haskell he had seen the older boys playing the sport, and he had been especially impressed with the pitchers; he marveled at how they'd rifle the ball with all their might from the elevated mound.

Thorpe and his friends in the Indian Territory didn't have proper equipment, so they improvised and created a game they called "prairie baseball." Often using a stick for a bat, flat rocks for bases, and a round rock for a ball, Thorpe and his buddies played until the last rays of sunlight faded from the sky. A barefooted Jim, wearing his work overalls, was the pitcher and he'd fire one rock after the next over the makeshift plate. He could throw harder than anyone his age, and he usually left the opposing batter swinging at nothing but the breeze. When they finally found a real bat and real ball to use, Jim became the star attraction. Swinging right-handed, he blasted moonshots that landed deep in the woods rimming the field.

Jim was also getting involved in sports at Garden Grove. The school's teacher, Walter White, encouraged his students to participate in track and field. White had laid out a track on the school grounds and used crudely constructed bars for the high jump and the pole vault. On one of the first afternoons that Thorpe attended the school White saw the youngster standing off to the side while other boys practiced the high jump. White approached him.

"Jim, why don't you try that?" asked White.

A little encouragement was all Thorpe needed. He walked toward the bars, then accelerated into the air, easily clearing the stick. The other boys raised the height of the bar, and Jim again launched himself over. Eventually, as White watched from nearby, Jim was jumping higher than anyone at the school—even kids who were a few years older than he was.

Jim also stood out in the pickup baseball games that White organized on Saturday afternoons against other local teams. Small crowds turned out to watch the contests and they were stunned by how hard the Thorpe kid could throw the ball and how far he could hit it. The locals talked glowingly of "that young Indian" who was doing magical things on the baseball diamond, and White eventually suggested to Jim that he think about attending the Carlisle Indian School, a place where his athletic ability could bloom. But Jim wasn't ready leave the Oklahoma Territory again—not yet.

On May 12, 1904, a guest speaker appeared in Jim's classroom at Gar-

den Grove. Wearing a military uniform, the man was a recruiter from
Carlisle and he described to the students what life was like at the nation's
first and largest Indian School. He told them about the trades they could
learn and that they'd be taught by some of the finest teachers in America.
He also bragged about the burgeoning athletic program at the school; its
football team was taking on—and beating—some of the biggest college
teams of the day. Just a year earlier the team had made headlines from
New York to Los Angeles when they narrowly lost to Harvard 12–11.

In fact, if Carlisle had beaten Harvard on that Halloween afternoon in
1903, it would have been the greatest upset in the history of college football. The recruiter knew the story of that game by heart.

On the eve of their most anticipated game of 1903, the Indians of Carlisle
traveled in style and comfort, riding the spacious Colonial Express from
Philadelphia to Boston. This was first-class train travel at its finest. On
board there was a barber and a beautician. There were showers available
for the passengers, and at every stop news "butchers," usually young boys,
ran up and down the aisles hawking newspapers. Cushion-layered seats
greeted the passengers, as did walls that were paneled with inlaid wood
and beveled glass. Damask curtains hung in front of the windows, which
passengers could close if they felt like dozing. The last compartment on
the train was the observation car. Here Warner and his boys could look out
the large windows on the tail end and watch the slender iron rails stream
out behind them like runaway ropes. On the other end of the observation
car was a lounge, where passengers could enjoy a bottle of Dr. Sweet's
Root Beer and watch the world pass by on the other side of the glass.

After the eight-hour train ride from Philadelphia to Boston, the team
checked into the Copley Square Hotel, which had served as President
William McKinley's election headquarters seven years earlier in 1896.
After dinner, Warner gave his players a tour of the narrow streets of Cambridge, which were dimly lit with gas lamps. As they walked through the
night, Warner discussed the special play that the team had been practicing for weeks and been waiting to use against Harvard. He emphasized
that the conditions for the play had to be perfect: The Crimson would have
to kick the ball deep into Carlisle territory, and the Indians' return man
would have to field the ball cleanly. If these two events unfolded, Warner

said, the players would be expected to execute the one-of-a-kind play. By the time Warner and his boys were back in their hotel, all of them hoped desperately that they'd have a chance to unveil their shocking strategy against the Crimson.

On game day, the first two quarters were dominated by the defenses. To begin the second half, Harvard kicked the ball to Carlisle. Realizing that the Crimson players had more size and raw skill than his boys, Warner knew he and his players needed to outwit the Ivy Leaguers. So, before the second-half kickoff, he instructed his boys to run the "hidden ball." As soon as Warner issued the directive, excitement rumbled through every Carlisle player on the sideline. This was what they had been waiting for.

Carlisle's Jimmie Johnson caught the kickoff near his goal line. Johnson took a few steps forward and then, suddenly, the other ten Carlisle players sprinted back and formed a huddle around him at the ten-yard line. As the Harvard players charged down the field, ten of the Indians quickly took off their leather helmets and slid them under the front of their jerseys. Meanwhile, Johnson slyly placed the ball under the back of Charlie Dillon's jersey. Dillon, a guard who stood six feet and weighed about 210 pounds, was designated the hunchback because the ball seemingly disappeared between his shoulders.

Just as the Harvard defenders neared the Carlisle huddle, Johnson yelled, "Go!" and all the Indians scattered like a sack of spilled marbles. Ten Carlisle players hugged their helmets to make it look like each of them was carrying the ball. Dillon, who actually had the ball, nonchalantly jogged down the middle of the field with both of his arms free. The Crimson players were perplexed. One by one, Harvard started tackling Carlisle players—only to discover that they had been carrying nothing more than a leather helmet. When Dillon reached Harvard's last line of defense, Crimson safety Carl Marshall was so sure that Dillon didn't have the ball that he actually moved out of Dillon's way, thinking that the guard was going to try to block him. The Harvard fans watching the play unfold from the stands could see that Dillon had something bulging from his back side and they screamed to alert Marshall and the other Crimson players that they were being duped.

But it was too late. Dillon jogged untouched into the end zone for a touchdown. On the sideline Warner smiled like a man who had just pulled one of the greatest con jobs in history.

Carlisle would end up losing the game 12–11, but as news of the "hidden-ball play" crept across the country, the Indians won something that was of greater value to Warner than a victory: more fans. Warner and his Carlisle players lived to "outsmart the palefaces," as Warner liked to say, and the hidden-ball play underscored why boys from reservations around the nation wanted to come to Carlisle and suit up for Warner.

Sitting in the one-room schoolhouse in the Oklahoma Territory, Thorpe listened attentively to the officer from Carlisle. As the recruiter detailed what life was like for the Indian students in the small Pennsylvania town of Carlisle, a memory stirred: Thorpe had seen the Carlisle Indians before at Haskell. Many of the older boys at Haskell had even talked dreamily of one day playing football at Carlisle. The thought of suiting up for Warner had flown into Thorpe's mind when he chatted with the Indians back at Haskell, but it left him as quickly as the details of a dream fade once the eyes peel open in the morning.

Thorpe was still searching for an identity. His father had recently re-married and was starting a new family, which heightened Thorpe's sense of isolation. Maybe he could get a fresh start at Carlisle. Maybe there he could play football. Maybe it would be for the best if he went to a place that was far away from the plains of Oklahoma Territory.

Thorpe's father, who in the spring of 1904 was ready to get on with his new life and his new family, saw Carlisle as a last hope for his son. Jim had never been the same since Charlie died, and Hiram thought his boy was dangerously close to throwing his life away if he didn't find something that interested him. Father and son clashed frequently that spring, and seven months after the fourteen-year-old Thorpe had listened to the re-cruiter from Carlisle in his classroom at Garden Grove, Hiram took matters into his own hands. He wrote a letter to W. C. Kohlenberger, the superintendent at the local Sac and Fox agency. It read:

U.S. Indian Agent
Sac & Fox Agency OT (Oklahoma Territory)

Dear Sir—I have a boy that I Wish you would Make rangements to Send of to School Some Ware Carlyle or Hampton I don't Care ware . . . I Cannot do anything with him So plese at your Earlest Convence atend to this for he is getting worse very day—and I want him to go and make something of him Self for he cannot do it hear—

Respectfully yours
Hairm Thorpe
Bellmont OT

His Name is James Thorpe.

Hiram got his wish. Shortly after Hiram penned this letter, Jim was accepted at Carlisle, the last-resort place that Thorpe's father hoped would bring out his boy's potential, which remained concealed under the surface like a pocket of oil just waiting to be tapped. Would it stay trapped forever? Hiram believed it would if he didn't put his son on a train and send him to a distant place that neither of them had ever seen—even though it meant Hiram might never see his boy's bright eyes again.

The local Sac and Fox agent made arrangements for Thorpe's transportation to Pennsylvania, and the night before he boarded a train on the Frisco Railroad to head east, Hiram had one last message for his boy.

"Son," Hiram said, "you are an Indian. I want you to show other races what an Indian can do."

With that, Jim Thorpe left home one more time, determined to find his right place in the world.

Growing up in Abilene, Kansas, Dwight Eisenhower (front center) was constantly going on camping trips with his brothers, playing games like Cowboys and Indians, and trying to stir up either trouble or an adventure during his Huck Finn–like childhood. (Courtesy the Dwight D. Eisenhower Library)

6

THERE'S JUST NO FUTURE IN THE ARMY

In the vacant lot at Third Street and Broadway, a crowd gathered in the cool of the autumn evening, forming a ring around two teenage boys who were about to square off in a bare-knuckled street fight. The anticipation for this brawl had been building all day in the halls of Garfield Middle School in Abilene, Kansas. The kids from the town's affluent Northside desperately wanted Wesley Merrifield to uphold the honor of their neighborhood. The Northsiders lived in large, two-story Victorian homes, and they were the sons and daughters of lawyers, doctors, bankers, and merchants. The kids from the working-class Southside of Abilene formed the other half of the crowd. They were the offspring of railroad workers, carpenters, laborers, and plumbers who lived in older, smaller homes that sat on near-nothing plots of land. They were cheering wildly for the fighter who hailed from their gritty, hardscrabble part of town. His name was Dwight David Eisenhower.

The combatants leered at each other like sworn enemies, their eyes squinted in rage. Each had been selected by the boys in their respective neighborhood to represent their turf in this annual north-south slugfest. To the kids in the crowd, this fight was one of the most significant local sporting events of the season. For the rest of the year, the winning side in this clash had bragging rights over the other. The children from the Northside had always looked down on the Southsiders, whom they considered inferior and crass. For Eisenhower, who lived on the southernmost edge of the Southside, this was a chance to even the score with one glorious, thunderous punch.

This test of manhood was in keeping with Abilene tradition. Three decades earlier Abilene had been the most murderous cow town in the Wild West. Justice came in the form of two gunfighters meeting in the town square at sunset with a pair of shiny six-shooters on their sides. The pistol fights were swift, elemental ways to resolve disputes, and they were glamorized in western pulp novels, which most of the boys in the sandlot at Third and Broadway read by candlelight before going to bed at night. Same as a gunfight, the rules for this scrap in Abilene's ongoing civil war were straightforward: A boy could fight only with his fists; kicking and wrestling were not allowed. If one fighter cheated, even those in the crowd rooting for him would disapprove.

Everyone—even the Southside kids—thought Eisenhower was the underdog. Merrifield, who had a reputation for being the roughest, toughest thirteen-year-old from the Northside, was bigger, faster, and stronger than Little Ike, as the five feet, six inch, 125-pound Eisenhower was known in his hometown. Slight of build, the thirteen-year-old Eisenhower was so slow that he was often told to play on the line in the sandlot football games, even though the small kids usually played in the backfield because of their quickness. Yet Little Ike was nominated to represent the Southside in this annual brawl between the two rival groups at Garfield because no one could match his intensity, which seemed to spring out of him like bolts of lightning. Whenever Little Ike grew agitated, a storm would gather in his eyes, and his tolerance for pain would shoot to the moon. Though not many in the crowd thought he'd win this fight, they also wagered in their minds that Little Ike wouldn't quit. If he lost, it would probably take four kids to carry him out of the vacant lot.

One of the first times Eisenhower's temper spiked into a fever was when he was ten. On Halloween night in 1900 his parents allowed his two older brothers to go trick-or-treating. But Dwight had to stay home. He was too little, he was told. When his brothers left the house in full costume, Dwight slipped out the back door, his emotions boiling. He ran up

to an old apple tree in the backyard and, with his bare fists, began pounding the trunk. Over and over, he thumped at the trunk, bloodying his
hands. Eventually his father grabbed him by the shoulders, marched him
upstairs to his bedroom, and flayed Dwight's back end with a hickory
stick.

Now almost the entire school followed the two fighters to the center of
Abilene, a town of 3,500. The lot at Third and Broadway was across the
dirt road from the redbrick building of City Hall, which was crowned with
a massive bell tower. To reach the fight site, the crowd walked along a
sidewalk that was made of wooden planks. They sidestepped the mule-
drawn streetcar line that was the only form of public transportation in
Abilene, and they avoided the horse-pulled buggies that rolled up and
down the town's main drag, which featured a bank, a grocery store, a fruit
stand, and a trading shop.

Ike stood toe-to-toe with Merrifield in the vacant lot. When the
fighters raised their fists, the crowd shouted like bloodthirsty Romans at
the Colosseum. Eisenhower lunged forward, swinging his fists just as his
boyhood hero Wild Bill Hickok had done in bar fights in Abilene thirty
years earlier. As twilight fell on Abilene, the rumble for neighborhood
pride was on—a fight that would be talked about for the next fifty years by
those who were there.

The stories always had the towheaded boy sitting on the edge of his seat,
spellbound, with his eyes bulging out of their sockets. When Dwight
Eisenhower was eight years old, a man named Dudley, who was one of his
oldest neighbors in Abilene, would often come over to the Eisenhowers'
white clapboard house and tell little Dwight tales of what their town had
been like in the 1870s. He'd talk of Indian battles and of a prairie so vast
and empty that it made you think you were alone in the world. Dudley
claimed that back then he'd served as deputy to the marshal of Abilene,
who went by the name Wild Bill Hickok. Dudley's words lit a fire in the
boy's imagination. Suddenly, the pint-sized Eisenhower would be transported back a quarter of a century in his hometown, back into the
tobacco-spittin' heart of the Wild Wild West.

Abilene in 1871 was ruled by one man: Hickok, who was already a
frontier legend and the gruff hero of many dime novels. In April that year,

the town council recruited Hickok to be Abilene's marshal. His help was sorely needed. Regarded as the roughest town on the high plains, Abilene was a cesspool of gambling dens, whorehouses, dance halls, and saloons. At night the streets of this devil's paradise were aglow with gaslights and populated by gunslingers, Texas cowboys, roughnecks, destitute farm-hands, prostitutes, and card sharks. Lawlessness was rampant. Tom "Bear River" Smith had been a popular marshal before Hickok, and he had made it illegal to fire a gun in Abilene during those lusty times, but he was shot and killed in an ambush in 1870.

Abilene attracted unsavory characters because it was at the end of the Texas cattle trail. In 1867, Joseph McCoy, a young livestock entrepreneur from Springfield, Illinois, built stockyards outside of Abilene on the Kansas-Pacific rail line. McCoy printed up fliers and circulated them throughout Texas, advertising his stockyards and encouraging ranchers to send their herds of cattle to Abilene. From there he would ship them east on the Union Pacific to beef packers. Within a year, thousands of Texas Longhorn cattle were driven to McCoy's Great Western Stockyards. The herds were typically shepherded by a trail boss and ten to fifteen cowboys, and by the time they reached the Abilene railhead, they were more than ready to spend their earnings on two things: liquor and ladies.

Not even McCoy expected so much debauchery to descend on Abilene. He wrote that the cowboys would frequently "imbibe too much poison whiskey and straightaway go on the warpath. Then mounting his pony, he is ready to shoot anybody or anything; or rather than not shoot at all, would fire up into the air, all the while yelling as only a semi-civilized being can. At such times it is not safe to be on the streets, or for that matter within a house, for the drunk cowboy would as soon shoot into a house as at anything else." In July 1868 a reporter noted in the Topeka newspaper, "At this writing, Hell is now in session in Abilene."

The busiest stretch of commerce in Abilene started on Texas Street, which ran parallel to the railroad tracks. Soon neighborhoods known as "Hell's Half Acre" and "Devil's Addition" sprang to life and were as sinful as any in the nation. To clean up the town, the town council hired Hickok, the most famous gunslinger of them all.

He was paid $150 a month—plus a percentage of the fines he doled out—to preside over the first booming end-of-the-trail cow town on the frontier. Standing a strapping six feet, three inches in his custom-made

boots, Hickok wore a black hat with a sweeping brim and had a silver lawman's badge on his chest. He was usually impeccably dressed in a double-
breasted Prince Albert frock coat that had knee-length skirts in the front
and back, and whenever he strolled into a room, he sucked the air right
out of it. Heads would turn to see his blue-gray eyes, his handlebar mustache, and the long dark locks that fell on his shoulders. But most striking
about Hickok were the two glistening Navy Colts that rested in a red sash
at his sides. The ivory handles were always turned forward so they'd be
ready for the twist draw, which Hickok could perform in a startlingly
quick blur.

Hickok's first well-known gunfight took place in Springfield, Missouri, on July 21, 1865. The dispute was with a man named Dave Tutt. Wild
Bill, who had fought for the Union in the Civil War, and Tutt, who took up
arms with the Confederacy, hadn't much cared for each other from the
moment they had met a few months earlier. Their mutual dislike escalated when they both became interested in the same woman, and it turned
deadly at a late-night poker game. At some point in the evening, Tutt stole
Hickok's pocket watch. He bragged to his buddies at the bar that he was
going to walk through the town square of Springfield wearing Wild Bill's
watch. When Hickok heard this, he decided to arrive at the square before
Tutt. When Tutt showed up, Hickok stared at him, arms at his sides, and
warned Tutt not to take one more step. Tutt didn't listen. He came forward
and drew his pistol. Hickok quickly unholstered his shiny Colt. Both fired
at the same time. Tutt fell. Hickok didn't.

Hickok turned to a group of Tutt's supporters who were standing
nearby and implored them not to do anything foolish, lest they want their
last breath to be taken by a bullet. No one moved. The army post commander in Springfield, Colonel Albert Barnitz, later reported that Tutt had
been "shot directly through the heart." And so was spawned the legend of
Wild Bill, who got the nickname years earlier when he broke up a mob in
Independence, Missouri, by challenging them to pistol fight, causing a
concerned woman to shout, "Good for you, Wild Bill."

When he arrived in Abilene in the spring of 1871, Hickok announced
his presence by telling lawbreakers they had three choices: "Leave town
on the eastbound train, the westbound train, or go North in the morning."
By North, Hickok meant to a cemetery north of town known as Boot Hill,
where troublemakers would be planted in their graves "with their boots

on." For several months, relative tranquillity in Abilene prevailed under Hickok's command. Even the Texas cowboys, who were the most dangerous characters in town, stayed in line. This allowed Wild Bill to turn his attention to his favorite pursuit—gambling. He told his deputies to get him if he was needed, but otherwise he would be at the card tables at the Alamo Saloon, regaling the patrons with his gunfighting tales and straight-faced (though most likely exaggerated) claims that he'd killed more than one hundred men.

But the good times in Abilene didn't last for Hickok. After a few months on the job, he fell hard for a woman named Jessie Hazel, a southern belle who ran a high-end whorehouse. According to most versions of the story, Phil Coe, a local saloon owner, also courted Hazel. Near the end of the 1871 cattle season, Coe was with several cowboys one night when they began celebrating their upcoming departure for the Lone Star State. At one point outside of the Alamo Saloon, Coe pulled out his pistol and shot a stray dog. Hickok rose from his regular seat in the saloon, ran outside, and demanded to know who fired the shot, which was a violation of the town law. Coe stepped forward, showing Hickok his smoking gun. Words were exchanged, and Coe pointed his pistol at Hickok. He pulled the trigger, missing Hickok from eight feet away.

Hickok didn't make the same mistake. He pumped two pieces of lead into Coe's stomach. When Coe fell to the ground, Hickok heard a man approaching him quickly from behind. He turned and, before he realized that the man was his trusted deputy, fired two more shots. The deputy was hit twice in the head and lay dead. For one of the few times in his life, Wild Bill cried. He carried his young deputy's body into the Alamo Saloon and placed it on a billiards table. The deputy would be the last man Hickok ever killed.

That fall the cattle trade business in Abilene died down. The railroad had been extended westward to Newton, Kansas, and the end of the cattle trail moved with the tracks as well. All the saloon owners, prostitutes, and card sharks in Abilene packed up and left for Newton. Hickok was relieved of his duties in December 1871, and by the time Dwight David Eisenhower was born on October 14, 1890, Abilene was back to what it was when it was founded as a small prairie village in 1861: a conservative, quiet, hardworking, God-fearing, Protestant town that was the seat of Dickinson County.

But the legend of Bill Hickok never left Abilene. Stories about him arose frequently, prompting people's thoughts to spin back in time. As a boy, Eisenhower played "Wild West" with his friends and they'd pretend to be Hickok, Billy the Kid, Jesse James, and Bat Masterson—guns-on-their-hips cowboys who hunted Indians and outlaws. In fact, Eisenhower would always be fascinated with the simple, frontier-style image of justice embodied by two men in cowboy hats, silhouetted against the falling late afternoon sun, standing in the town square, ready to settle their dispute with a quick draw. And Eisenhower's admiration of the Wild West and Hickok would influence the direction of his life—and, one day, the future of the free world.

The white-framed, two-story structure on 201 South East Fourth Street in Abilene sat on a three-acre, corner plot of land. In Hickok's heyday, it was likely the site of a whorehouse known as Devil's Addition. Located in a blue-collar neighborhood south of the Union Pacific tracks that bisected the town, the Eisenhower property, which didn't have electricity or indoor plumbing, did have a two-story backyard barn that was lined with stalls. Growing up, Dwight was a natural-born thrill-seeker, and he liked to scale the barn's interior skeleton to reach the roof beam. After he got his balance on the narrow strip of wood, he'd plunge—headfirst—into the air, aiming for a stack of hay. Sometimes in midair he'd flip a somersault and come down feet first—one of the first indications of the boy's coordination.

The barn was more than his jungle gym; it housed two cows and a horse that was used for plowing and pulling the family's buggy. The Eisenhowers also had dozens of chickens and ducks and a handful of pigs. Eisenhower's mother, Ida, grew all kinds of vegetables and she paid particular attention to her flower garden, especially to her beloved Madonna lilies. The lush yard, studded with cherry and pear trees, also had an apple orchard and was ringed by syrup-producing maple trees. When the family gathered food for their meals, they rarely had to venture off their property. The Eisenhowers were better off than most families on the Southside because they were rich with crops—but not with money, which their father struggled to make as a mechanic at the Belle Springs Creamery.

The cogs that kept the engine of the Eisenhowers' small farm moving were the six sons of David and Ida Eisenhower: Arthur, Edgar, Dwight, Roy, Earl, and Milton. (Paul, a seventh son, died in infancy of diphtheria.) The boys' list of chores seemed as long as the scroll of the Constitution: feed the chickens and gather their eggs; milk the cows; pick vegetables and fruits; till the garden; cure the meat in the backyard smokehouse; help Mother cook and wash dishes; do the laundry; and find wood for the morning fire. Ida, happily humming to herself with a contented half-smile on her round face, rotated the chores among her sons, who slept in double beds in a small upstairs room. Little Ike—a play on the first sylla-ble of his last name—dreaded the before-school morning chores. The worst was when he had to wake at 4:30 A.M. on winter mornings, roll out of his warm bed, get a lantern, and walk downstairs to light a fire in the kitchen stove. Often he could see his breath as he struggled to warm the house in the bitterly cold darkness.

In their free time, the Eisenhower boys liked to have ice cream at Case's Department Store, ride their father's solid-tire bicycle, swim in the nearby Smoky Hill River, go hunting and fishing, or just roam the empty plains that surrounded their town, in the hope of finding trouble or an adventure—whichever came first. Little Ike's early years could have been ripped from the pages of Twain's *The Adventures of Tom Sawyer,* which had been published fourteen years before Eisenhower was born; his boy-hood escapades and scrapes were every bit as fanciful as Tom's. When the United States went to war with Spain in 1898, an eight-year-old Ike shouted, "Remember the *Maine!*" as he pretended to be an American sol-dier. He was a Rough Rider, trying to take San Juan Hill.

In 1896 Dwight began attending Lincoln Elementary School, located near the family's home on the Southside. Like most boys, Ike found the school days excruciatingly long, but recess always provided a reprieve. Along with his friends, he played a game called "shinny," which was like ground hockey but without the rules. Using small branches they snapped off from nearby trees as their sticks, and a tin can for a puck, the boys bat-tled and shot for hastily made goals until a teacher clanged a triangle to signal the end of recess.

One summer Little Ike and his older brother Edgar, who was known throughout Abilene as "Big Ike," earned a few extra quarters by picking apples in an orchard owned by the town sheriff. When the workday was over, the sheriff, who had served as a border guard during the Civil War, delighted the young boys with stories from the old days, telling them about the bloody fights with Indians that occurred on the very ground where Abilene sat today. Little Ike and Big Ike couldn't get enough of these yarns, and in their games they soon started battling an imaginary tribe of fierce Indians.

One of Dwight's heroes was Tom Smith, the Abilene marshal who preceded Wild Bill. Killed in an ambush, Smith was buried in the Abilene cemetery. On many summer afternoons Little Ike and Edgar would seek his gravestone. On it were carved the words: THOMAS J. SMITH / MARSHAL OF ABILENE, 1870 / DEAD, A MARTYR TO DUTY, NOV. 2, 1870 / A FEARLESS HERO OF THE FRONTIER DAYS / WHO IN COWBOY CHAOS / ESTABLISHED THE SUPREMACY OF LAW.

On other afternoons in the summer, Dwight and Edgar loaded the family's spring wagon with fruits and vegetables from their backyard and, with their horse hitched up, became traveling salesmen. They crossed the railroad tracks and headed into the wealthy section of town, where the boys went door-to-door asking people if they wanted to buy their homegrown, handpicked food. Their father made only fifty dollars a month as a mechanic at the creamery, and Edgar and Dwight—budding entrepreneurs—tried to earn extra money for the family.

But it wasn't always an easy sell. Often, the housewives from the well-to-do Northside carefully pulled back the ears of corn and insisted that the boys' produce was overvalued, forcing the Eisenhowers to drop their prices. Edgar felt as lowly as a beggar, and found the whole experience humiliating. But not Little Ike, who was thrilled simply to have some change jingling in his pockets. Ike at times could have a measured nature, and in these moments he wouldn't let anything faze him. When he was even-keeled, his judgment was always sound. But on other occasions he could snap if he thought something was unjust or a wrong had been committed, and then his temper would explode like a grenade. Ike in a fury would always be hard to handle, and soon he would find a place where he could let his emotions rage all the time, a place where he could be as wild as a drunken cowboy: the football field.

In the fall of 1906, Dwight and Edgar ducked out of school for several days. The boys were as close as two brothers could be and together they darted from tree trunk to tree trunk trying to avoid detection as they made their way to a pool hall called the Smoke House. Though their father had severely beaten Edgar a few years earlier with a leather harness for cutting classes, the boys decided that the risk was worth it: They had to know what was happening in the World Series.

The fall classic in '06 pitted the Chicago White Sox against the Chicago Cubs and was billed as the Windy City Series. Over the fortnight that the games were played, the most popular man in Abilene was Cecil Brooks, the telegrapher in the stock exchange office. Brooks had always been viewed as a special man in Abilene; the townspeople were in awe of the fact that he communicated with faraway places. He was Abilene's link to the outside world, and when the Cubs and White Sox began battling in Chicago, he kept his wire open to the east until the afternoon games had ended. Along with dozens of other kids and adults, Little Ike and Edgar spent day after day in the Smoke House, where a scoreboard was set up. Brooks would relay results to the pool hall at the end of every half inning. A few times the Eisenhower boys were so anxious to get the scores that they went next door and crammed into Brooks's office, awaiting word on how the Hitless Wonders, as the White Sox were known, were doing. The boys hung on every click of information that tapped out of the telegraph, and they listened closely as the White Sox, despite hitting only .198 as a team, defeated the Cubs in six games.

As the Eisenhower boys gained height, weight, and strength they became more physical and rough—especially Little Ike, who started to have fits of searing rage. When he was twelve his oldest brother, Arthur, had angered him while the two were outside in their yard. Seeing a brick at his feet, Little Ike reached for it and threw it with all his strength at Arthur's head. Just before the brick made a mess of Arthur, he ducked. But Dwight had been ready to seriously injure his brother.

Ida Eisenhower knew that Little Ike possessed a temper that could leap up and strike as quickly as a poked python. The one time she talked to him about it was that Halloween night in 1900 when Ike wasn't allowed to go trick-or-treating with his brothers. About an hour after Ike's father beat him with a hickory stick as punishment for repeatedly punching the apple tree trunk in their backyard, Ida came into Dwight's room. She sat in the rocking chair next to his bed and put salve on his hands, but for a long time didn't say anything. Instead she merely rocked back and forth, back and forth.

After a while, in a calming voice, she told her son that he needed to control his anger. *If you don't, it will control you and ruin your life,* she softly said. Ida knew that there was an irrational monster that lived inside Little Ike and it came alive whenever he grew agitated, and now she tried to dull that beast with a homily that was as old as language itself: Hatred, she said, was futile, and there was nothing good to be gained from it.

Little Ike listened closely, and years later he would say this moment was one of the turning points of his life. His temper didn't magically disappear, but he started to control it and use it to his advantage at certain times and places, such as on the football field during games and in the sandlots when his character—and his entire neighborhood—was challenged.

The punches kept coming, one after another, striking Little Ike in the face, the stomach, and the side of the head. For the first minutes of his fight with Wesley Merrifield, Eisenhower had held his ground, trading blows with his opponent. But after ten or so minutes, Merrifield exerted his will, bloodying Little Ike's face and lips, and it seemed just a matter of time until Eisenhower would fall to the ground, defeated.

But to the delight of the Southsiders in the crowd, Eisenhower kept striding forward. After twenty minutes—far longer than most fistfights lasted—Eisenhower was still throwing punches. Merrifield's face wasn't as badly beaten as Little Ike's, but there was no mistaking that he had been in a battle. His nose was bleeding and his eyes were starting to swell.

After about thirty-five minutes had passed, the two were wearily exchanging blows. Merrifield lacked the power to land a decisive punch, and both he and Little Ike had trouble holding their arms up. After forty-five minutes, Ike was a bloody mess. One of his eyes was completely swollen shut and he had several cuts on his face. Still, the fight went on.

After nearly an hour, the two boys were so tired that they would come together, exchange a few weak slaps, then take a few steps back to try to gather their breath.

The crowd was in awe. The sun had lowered and was now a big red globe sitting on the edge of the western plains. The shadows lengthened, and it became time for the kids in the crowd to go home and eat dinner. But virtually no one left.

An hour had passed since the first punch was thrown. Merrifield and Little Ike came together in the center of the ring, and took a few swings at each other. They backed away, hunched over, putting their arms on their knees as they struggled to fill their lungs with air.

"Ike," said Merrifield. "I can't lick you."

"Wes," Ike replied, "I can't lick you."

The fight ended in a draw. Eisenhower walked groggily home, staggered up the stairs, and collapsed into his bed. His mother cared for him by placing hot towels on his puffy face, which was caked with dried blood. He missed school for the next three days, but when he finally strolled through the front doors of the Garfield Middle School his peers all looked at him a little differently. Yes, Ike had taken a severe beating, but he never fell to the ground, never stopped coming at Merrifield. It was a striking display of endurance and guts, and for a few days in the halls of Garfield, Little Ike was the Big Man on Campus.

In September 1906, Dwight entered the ninth grade at Abilene High School, which consisted of a few rooms on the first floor of City Hall. Located almost directly below the schoolrooms in the basement was the town jail. Though it rarely held any prisoners, it was a source of gossip among the students. Every kid in Abilene knew that years earlier a jailbird had let off a stick of dynamite. The blast broke open the bars, and in the confusion that followed, the prisoner was able to escape.

The city fire department was also in the building. When a blaze was reported, the fire bell would go off, and the male students of Abilene High would spring into action. They were the volunteer fire department, and they would rush out of City Hall pulling a two-wheel fire cart and run toward the smoke and flames. The town's one police officer would also race to the rescue.

The next year, 1907, Abilene High moved into a new two-story school on the north side of town. In the classroom Little Ike had a head for math but he especially enjoyed history. The ancient Greeks and Romans came alive to Eisenhower, and he couldn't read enough about the battles of Marathon and Cannae. George Washington also captivated him. Reading about Washington's exploits in the American Revolution and how he led a ragtag army against the professional British Redcoats, Eisenhower surmised that Washington was the bravest man who ever walked the planet. Maybe one day, Eisenhower thought, he too would fight for his country.

Even as a boy, Dwight had a hunger for information. By the age of twelve he had read the entire Bible; by twenty he had done it a second time. When Eisenhower unleashed his curiosity on military history, he became so obsessed with the subject that he neglected his chores. This prompted his mother to lock his books on Alexander and Caesar in the closet. Undaunted, Little Ike searched for the key, found it, and then, whenever his mother was out of the house, he would sneak into the closet and read about the long and brutal battles that shaped early civilization.

To David and Ida Eisenhower, the game of football was hazardous to one's health, every bit as dangerous as being pulled in a buggy by a horse suddenly spooked by a gunshot. The Eisenhowers, who were devoutly religious Christians, had heard that when boys played football they smacked their heads together on nearly every play, and that the violent collisions led to injuries—sometimes even death. The Eisenhowers didn't want their boys to play the game. Yet, to a large degree, they allowed all of their children to make their own decisions. For Ike, it was as simple as deciding whether to have one scoop or two at Case's Department Store: He was going to play.

When Dwight entered his junior year of high school he stood about five feet, nine inches and weighed 135 pounds. Though slow-footed, Eisenhower was considered by the coach to be one of the team's best ends for this reason: No one could match his intensity and drive. On the field Eisenhower always pushed himself to his physical limit, throwing his frame around as if he were oblivious to the consequences, not caring if he got injured. In the huddle, when he shouted out something to his teammates, power and confidence seemed to flicker in his deep blue eyes.

There was an aura about him, one that strongly suggested he was going to get the job done on the field no matter what. He was an all-effort, all-the-time player, one who acted on impulse and instinct. In the early days of football the player who most wanted to succeed—and was willing to endure the most pain—was the one who dominated the action. This was why Ike was so valuable to the Abilene head coach.

Ike was vibrantly curious on the football field, looking intently at this and that, trying to determine what the other team was going to do next. Even when he was on the sideline, he rarely stood still, always searching around for something to do, to explore, to figure out. Then when he entered the game, he approached plays as if a higher power were judging his effort level. Shouting at his teammates to work harder, Eisenhower quickly became a team leader. When Abilene won, Ike would be so overjoyed that he figured nothing in life could be sweeter. But when Abilene lost, he blamed himself, believing that he alone was responsible for his team's not coming out on top. Football was Ike's first true love, and it generated all the feelings in him that went along with a heated teenage romance—exhilaration, heartache, and, most of all, that base desire for more, more, more.

Ike first made the football squad at the beginning of his junior year, in 1908. The sport wasn't very popular at the turn of the century, and Abilene High didn't put money into supporting its team. The uniforms were as makeshift as most Halloween costumes. The players wore light-colored duck pants—a thick style of pant once worn by English longshoremen—that helped prevent grass burns. The jerseys were nothing more than sweaters with a horse's sweat pad (for under the saddle) stitched into the shoulders. A few of the players put on worn-out dress shoes that had some sort of cleat nailed to the bottom of the sole so they could get better footing. But perhaps the cleverest feature of these low-budget uniforms was what protected the players' heads. Not able to afford the leather helmets that the fancy eastern colleges were using, the boys of Abilene High normally pulled a woman's stocking over their heads and stuffed rags underneath to provide padding for their skulls.

Whenever Ike put on his improvised football uniform, he became a serious stickler for the rules. At the time, high school football games in middle America usually didn't have a referee, and if they did, there was only one. The players and coaches were charged with monitoring their own team's play, abiding by a gridiron honor code. But this didn't stop cheating. Players would often sling mud into the faces of their opponents, take a cheap shot while making a tackle, or trip a player who was nowhere near the ball. Eisenhower, who was taught at a young age by his religious parents about the fundamental need for rules and order, would always feel a tremor of disgust in his stomach whenever he saw someone not playing fair—especially if it was one of his own teammates. When that happened, he'd light into the rule breaker as if his family honor had been assaulted. But this didn't mean Ike didn't try to hurt other players. As long as it was within the rules, Ike hit viciously—as a certain Carlisle Indian School tailback would one day find out.

Ike was fourteen when he tripped over a brick on his way home from school and skinned his left knee. It seemed like a minor fall at the time— a rambunctious, energetic boy like Dwight was frequently tumbling over things—and he was most concerned about ripping his pair of pants, which he had purchased with his own money just a few days earlier. His knee wasn't even bleeding. But a few days later, Ike began to feel ill. He lay down on the couch in what his mother called "the front room" and his fever rose. Later he woke up with a throbbing pain in his left leg, and the skin was deeply bruised below the knee. Ida Eisenhower sent for the doctor and the diagnosis wrapped her heart with fear: blood poisoning. Antibiotics had not yet been developed, and blood poisoning often proved to be a death sentence if extreme measures weren't taken. "This is serious," the doctor told the Eisenhowers. "If that reaches his abdomen, he'll die. The only way I can save him is to amputate."

While his parents waited several days before deciding whether or not to amputate, Little Ike, in a fever, drifted in and out of consciousness. In one of his waking moments he heard his parents talking about cutting off his leg. He then asked his older brother Edgar to come into his room. "Look, Ed, they are talking about taking my leg off," Ike said. "I want you to see that they do not do it. I'd rather be dead than crippled and not be able to play ball."

Growing up, Edgar and Little Ike bickered, made fun of each other, and generally acted as if they'd have been perfectly content if they never saw each other again. But they were brothers, and that bond was the most

important aspect of their childhoods. When Little Ike asked for Edgar's
help, the older brother sprang into action. After promising Ike that no
one was going to touch his leg, Edgar stood at the doorway of his brother's
room and guarded him as if he were a sleeping prince. Even at night Edgar
would spread blankets on the floor and sleep in the doorway to make sure
that the doctor, who was adamant in his belief that the leg needed to be
sawed off, didn't slip in undetected. "Nobody's going to touch Dwight,"
Edgar told the doctor. "You're not going to operate on his leg."

After two weeks of lying on what could have been his deathbed and
often biting on a fork to keep from screaming, Ike began to heal and his
fever broke. He was back up on his feet two months later, and soon he was
back in the sandlots and playing football with his buddies. But the near-
death experience had touched a chord deep inside Eisenhower. He had
made a conscious decision that he would rather die than lose his leg, because to young Ike, a life without sports wasn't worth living. When he regained his health, he had an even deeper sense of purpose whenever he
played on the fields of sport. Football became an obsession, and Ike fully
intended to make the most of what he considered a second chance.

Ike grew so enraptured with sports after his leg healed that he helped
organize the Abilene High School Athletic Association, which essentially
operated as an intramural football and baseball league that featured teams
from various nearby towns. Ike was eventually elected president of the
organization, and he proved to be an adept problem solver. When he realized that the league dues (twenty-five cents per month) wouldn't cover
transportation costs, he had his team hop onto freight trains and ride
them to whatever town they needed to get to for their next game. It was
quite a sight: the young Eisenhower, carrying a uniform and equipment in
a duffel bag, clandestinely leaping onto a locomotive as it pulled out of the
Abilene depot and then disappearing into a boxcar as the train steamed
into the plains.

Writing in the school yearbook about the athletic association, Eisenhower noted, "We improved the condition of the Association itself by
drawing up the constitution, which makes the organization a permanent
one, and each year it will be simply a question of electing new officers."

Eisenhower also was a trailblazer on the field. One autumn Saturday
the boys from Abilene were preparing to play a football game when they
noticed that a black player was on the opposing team. No one on the Abi-

lene squad had ever seen a dark-skinned player before, and all of them refused to play across the line from the African American. Eisenhower stepped in. Though he played end on both defense and offense for Abilene, he agreed to move to center, where the African American player was going to line up. Before the game, Ike marched up to his opponent and shook his hand. He did the same thing after the final whistle blew. A few of the players later admitted to Eisenhower that they were ashamed they weren't as color-blind as he.

The football coach at Abilene High was Orin Snider, who had graduated from the school in 1906. Though Abilene High owned only two footballs—one of them was so round that it bore a close resemblance to a rugby ball; the other one was smoother and more oblique and was used only in games—Abilene was a state power. In the '08 season, as Ike played right end on offense and linebacker on defense, the team compiled a perfect 7-0 record, outscoring their opponents 127 to 9. The following year, in Eisenhower's senior season, several potential opponents backed out of their scheduled games with Abilene, fearing a morale-sapping defeat. Abilene played only four games in 1909, but again went undefeated.

By the time Eisenhower graduated from high school in the spring of 1909 with an A– average, he had sprouted into a lean five-foot, ten-inch, 150-pound young man. With a posture so straight he seemed to have a spine made of steel, Ike walked with an athlete's swagger, coolly striding along as if he always knew exactly where he was going and how he was going to get there. At school Ike was considered shy but popular—girls lined up hoping that he'd take them to the "picture show" at the Seelye Theater—and when he'd amble through the halls of Abilene High he'd usually have a smile on his face that gleamed like a row of piano keys. Though his sandy hair was often uncombed, when he was freshly scrubbed he parted it on the side and slicked it back with pomade.

In his high school yearbook, the *Helianthus,* Eisenhower was described as the "Best Historian and Mathematician" in the class, and it was speculated that he would one day become a history professor at Yale. The yearbook editors wrote that Edgar, who was two years older but in Ike's graduating class, would become a two-term president of the United States.

Unlike most of his classmates, who found jobs in Abilene after graduation, Ike had been plotting a way to get out of town for more than a year.

He had become friends with Joe W. Howe, the newspaper editor of the *Dickinson County News,* and after school he'd often stroll into Howe's office and read about the world outside of Abilene. Howe received copies of all the major dailies in the country—from New York, Los Angeles, Chicago—and he'd stack up the issues next to his window. Ike couldn't get enough of the printed words, and he read the yellowed papers as if they were chapters in a thrilling novel, one that described the life and times of a growing, expanding America. "I like to read what's going on outside of Kansas," he said to Howe one day. "Makes me realize that Kansas isn't the whole world."

After graduation, the Eisenhower boys made their plans. Though Arthur, the oldest of the Eisenhowers, didn't go to college, that didn't deter Ike and Edgar from continuing their educations. (Arthur moved to the big town of Kansas City and rented a room in a house. In the days he worked as a bank messenger, and at night he'd share stories with his roommates, one of whom was an ambitious young man named Harry S Truman.) Ike and Edgar enjoyed school and believed that a college degree would allow them to one day live on the better side of the railroad tracks, next door to the rich and influential. Besides, they craved to play more football, which had now invaded their bloodstreams like a virus. One of Edgar's teachers at Abilene High was a graduate of the University of Michigan, and she told Edgar that the Wolverines had a powerhouse football team. Coached by Fielding Yost, Michigan had gone 6-0-1 in 1909. Edgar hoped to be a member of the '10 team while studying to become a lawyer.

But the Eisenhower brothers had a problem: The family didn't have enough money for both Ike and Edgar to attend college at the same time. So Ike hatched a plan. "We both want to go," he said to Edgar. "But you know what you want to do and I don't. Besides, you're the oldest, so you ought to go first." For one year, Ike would get a job in Abilene and wire money via Western Union to his brother in Ann Arbor. After that, Edgar would return to Abilene to work and Ike would then spend a year at Michigan. This pattern of flipping between working in Abilene for twelve months and then attending school for twelve months would continue for eight years. After that, both brothers hoped to have degrees from Michigan.

In the summer of 1909, following the plan he had mapped out with his brother, Ike landed a job at the Belle Springs Creamery, hauling ice and heaving coal for ninety dollars a month. The labor was strenuous. Using a chain and pulley, he'd drag three-hundred-pound blocks of ice out of a tank and then place them on a chute that took them down to the ice room. The job further chiseled Eisenhower's upper body, and after eight months of work in the creamery he eagerly looked forward to the fall of 1910 when he'd move to Ann Arbor to begin his studies and put on the maize-and-blue jersey of the Michigan Wolverines.

As he was making his plans to attend Michigan, Ike became reacquainted with Everett "Swede" Hazlett, whose father was a doctor in Abilene. Swede had gone away to Wisconsin for military school and was now hoping to attend the U.S. Naval Academy in Annapolis, Maryland. He had won an appointment to the academy, but failed the entrance exam, which consisted of four subjects: algebra, geometry, English, and history. Swede was spending a year in Abilene studying for his retest.

With similar intellects and worldly curiosities, Ike and Swede quickly became good friends. Sometimes when Ike was working the late shift at the creamery, Swede would drop in. The two would crack open some eggs on the head of a clean shovel and fry them up over the fire pit in the boiler room. As they ate, Swede would entertain Ike with stories of Annapolis, describing its vast and beautiful lawns on the banks of the Severn River. Swede also mentioned that the Naval Academy had a whale of a football team. What's more, the school was free.

For weeks, Swede and Ike continued to meet and talk. When Eisenhower was appointed the night foreman at the creamery, he started inviting several of his friends—his gang—to play penny-ante poker on company time in the engine room. As the boys whiled away the long dark hours, Swede eventually threw an idea at Ike: He should try to get an appointment and join him in Annapolis. "Look, Ike," Swede said, "why don't you come with me? You'd like it there and you'd make a fine naval officer. We'd have a swell time together."

Ike admitted he liked the idea. The books he'd read as a boy about Washington and the American Revolution came back to mind, as did all the old stories about Wild Bill Hickok and the frontier justice he administered in Abilene. Ike recalled how he had to sneak into his closet when he was supposed to be doing chores and slyly crack open books about the ancient Greek battles. Ike always had a thirst for military history, and now the thought of attending the Naval Academy intrigued him. A few days later he contacted the congressman who had appointed Swede to the academy, but the news was bad: The congressman was out of appointments. However, he advised Eisenhower to write a letter to Senator Joseph Bristow, whose office was in nearby Salina, Kansas. Ike figured that was a waste of time because his family had no political connections. Swede, arguing that Ike had nothing to lose, finally convinced his friend to give it a try and see what happened.

Following Swede's instructions, Ike asked for letters of recommendation from several Abilene community leaders, including a banker, the postmaster, and the newspaper editor. In case Bristow didn't have any appointments left to the Naval Academy, Ike requested an appointment either there or the U.S. Military Academy in West Point, New York. "I would very much like to enter either the school at Annapolis, or the one at West Point," Ike wrote in his letter to Senator Bristow. "In order to do this, I must have an appointment to one of these places and so I am writing you in order to secure the same. I have graduated from high school and will be nineteen years of age this fall. If you find it possible to appoint me to one of these schools, your kindness will certainly be appreciated by me. Trusting to hear from you, concerning this matter, at your earliest convenience, I am respectfully yours, Dwight Eisenhower."

As he waited for a response from the senator, Ike studied for the entrance exam with Swede. For three hours every afternoon the two pored over history texts and geometry problems in the office of the manufacturing plant where Swede worked. Swede helped his friend as best he could. He located old copies of past examinations and gave them to Ike. They soon extended their study sessions to the evening. Swede would show up at the creamery and the two would cram deep into the night in these one-on-one sessions, quizzing and challenging each other until the sun was on its way up.

In early September of 1910, Bristow notified Ike that he had vacancies for both the military and naval academy appointments and that he should appear on October 4th and 5th in Topeka at the office of the public instruction superintendent to take the War Department's competitive examination. If Ike scored high enough, the senator explained, he would then be eligible to take the entrance exams at Annapolis and West Point.

To further prepare for the tests, Ike reenrolled at Abilene High, taking advanced courses in chemistry, math, and physics. Ike's return to Abilene High pleased one person more than any other: Orin Snider, the school's football coach. Since his last game with Abilene nearly two years earlier, Eisenhower had grown from a lanky 150-pounder into a sturdier young man. Despite the added weight, he was also faster than before, and now, as an offensive tackle, he had the speed to throw blocks and break open holes for halfback Bud Huffman far down the field from the line of scrimmage. Ike also played tackle on defense, where he faced double and sometimes triple teams. But he could handle the extra attention: Eisenhower was routinely a disruptive force because of his strength and penetrating quickness. From the sideline, it sometimes seemed like he had been dipped in oil, the way he slid through the line to wreak havoc on the offensive backs.

On November 11, 1910, Abilene hosted an undefeated team from Salina, one of their biggest rivals. The boys from Abilene were anxious to prove that they could beat a team that paid a coach a salary (which Abilene didn't), and they ransacked Salina from the opening whistle, storming to a two-touchdown lead in the first half. Late in the game, Salina still trailed by two touchdowns—and they were getting desperate. On one play in the fourth quarter, Abilene quarterback Six McDonnell faked a handoff, and then flung the ball down the field. But after McDonnell let the pass go, Salina's Forrest Ritter tackled him hard. As Ritter and McDonnell got up, Ritter bumped his head into McDonnell's jaw, causing the Abilene quarterback to crash to the ground and temporarily lose consciousness. Ike's temper exploded. Believing that his buddy had been the victim of a cheap shot, Eisenhower played like he was trying to hurt someone for the rest of the game. On defense, he continually burst through the offensive line to make tackles. On offense, he mowed over defensive players while blocking. He tried with all his strength, hoping the Salina players would regret they had ever dared to line up against him. By the time the final whistle blew and Abilene won the game 16–0, Ike had wound up "roughing" over half the Salina team, according to one account. Afterward, the Salina coach approached Snider, the Abilene coach. He said he'd "give anything" to have a player as dominating as "that Ike Eisenhower of yours."

With a mature Eisenhower leading the way, Abilene wound up with a 3-2-1 record in 1910. They outscored their opponents 82–13 and beat all of their traditional rivals—St. John's Military Academy, Enterprise, and Salina.

On October 4, in the heart of the football season, Eisenhower rode a train thirty miles west to Topeka. Over the next two days, he took the competitive examination for the senatorial appointment in the War Department's local office of public instruction. If Ike failed the test, he probably would end up at Michigan, following the plan that he had developed with Edgar soon after they had graduated from high school. If he passed the test, he'd be eligible to move on to the next step and take the entrance exams of each of the academies. One way or another, his life was about to undergo a twist.

Ike was back in Abilene when he finally received the results of the examination a few weeks later—and he was shocked. Believing he'd ace his two best subjects, history and geometry, he wound up scoring poorly in both. But he was saved by the fact that he tallied a 99 in English and had done well in algebra. When his scores were added up, he had the second-highest total of the eight candidates who had taken the test.

Days later Senator Bristow fired off a letter to Dwight explaining that he had won the appointment—to West Point, which Eisenhower had listed as his second choice behind the Naval Academy. The first-place candidate had indicated he would accept only a nomination to Annapolis, so Bristow awarded that one his Naval Academy appointment and gave his West Point nomination to Eisenhower. No one was more disappointed than Ike's buddy Swede, who was heading to Annapolis. He emphatically told Ike that he should write to another senator and try to secure a Naval Academy appointment. But Ike said he wouldn't "look a gift horse in the mouth." If he passed the school's entrance exam, Ike told Swede, he'd report to West Point.

When Dwight proudly displayed his appointment letter to his parents, his mother told him, "That's fine, Dwight. I was sure you'd do it." David and Ida Eisenhower believed that Ike's decision to pursue a military education was between himself and God, but Ida, a lifelong pacifist, was quietly terrified at the prospect of her boy becoming a soldier. After she congratulated him on winning the appointment, she walked upstairs to her bedroom, shut the door, and wept.

One of Eisenhower's closest friends, Minnie Stewart, was adamant that attending the Military Academy would be the gravest mistake of his life, one that Ike would regret as soon as he stepped onto the campus high above the Hudson River. "There's just no future in the Army," she told him. "You're just throwing your life away."

But Ike's mind was made up: If he passed the West Point entrance exam, he would attend the Military Academy, where famous soldiers like Robert E. Lee, Ulysses S. Grant, and Jefferson Davis had already made their marks. In January 1911, after several more months of intensive cramming, Ike took the train to St. Louis for the West Point exam. It was the first time he'd ever been in a big city, and his eyes lit up when he saw the throngs of people in downtown St. Louis and all the river traffic on the wide Mississippi.

Bunking at the Jefferson Barracks, Eisenhower snuck out one evening with a new friend to experience the sights and smells and sounds of bustling St. Louis. They began by walking the streets that were ablaze with lights and filled with theaters, hotels, department stores, and restaurants. Later they took a streetcar and rode it to the end of the line. They wound up on the other side of the Mississippi in East St. Louis and were told that they had been on the last streetcar of the night. Now they had no way to get back to the Jefferson Barracks and, even worse, fog had suddenly moved in from the river and shrouded much of the city, further disorienting Ike and his friend. They tried to follow the tracks back to their barracks, but the tracks split in multiple directions. Eventually they spotted a light in a nearby building. They knocked on the door, hoping to find someone who could give them directions back into the city.

The door slowly creaked open. All Ike and his buddy could see was the muzzle of a revolver. "Who are you?" a man's voice asked.

Ike replied that they were from out of town, lost, and simply looking to be pointed to a road that would take them back to the Jefferson Barracks. The man put the gun down, let the boys in, and gave them directions. After saying thank you, Ike and his buddy walked through the darkness, crossed the river, and made it back to the barracks at about 1 A.M. They knew if the guard at the main gate spotted them they would likely be barred from taking the test; they had been told that no one was allowed to leave the barracks after the playing of taps. Hiding behind tree trunks and bushes, they darted toward the concrete wall that ringed the barracks. They scaled it undetected, and quietly slinked into their beds. Straining to catch his breath, Ike's roommate lay down and said, "You know, when I looked down the barrel of that big pistol, I could see a whole funeral procession."

The next morning a sleepy-eyed Eisenhower passed the physical exam easily and then took the written test, which had a failure rate of about 25 percent. He assumed that he'd passed, but after he went home to Abilene he waited for two months and didn't receive any news from the academy. Then a letter arrived: The secretary of war ordered Eisenhower to report to the U.S. Military Academy on June 14, 1911. He was going to be a member of the Class of 1915.

A few months after Ike received the news about his future, another young man from rural America who was too poor to afford a college education spent a few nights at the Jefferson Barracks. In early July 1911, Omar Bradley, who had been working at a boiler shop in Moberly, Missouri, traveled to St. Louis to take the Military Academy's entrance examination. Bradley had received his congressional appointment only eight days earlier, and so had little time to study. He felt so ill prepared that at one point during the algebra portion of the exam he got up out of his seat and went to hand in his booklet to the proctor, ready to give up and head back to Moberly. But the proctor was busy reading a book and didn't want to be disturbed, so Bradley begrudgingly returned to his seat and filled out his booklet. *Not a chance in hell did I pass,* Bradley thought to himself as he rode the train back to Moberly, where he fully expected to spend the rest of his life.

But three weeks later he received a telegram with information that was so shocking that he had to read the words several times to believe them: He was told to report to West Point on August 15, 1911, to become a member of the Class of 1915, which, to this day, remains the most famous in the history of the Military Academy. Eisenhower and Bradley would soon become buddies at the academy, and they shared a common dream: to become Army football players.

On the early June day that Eisenhower was scheduled to leave his child-hood in Abilene behind, he looked out of his bedroom window at the blue-sky afternoon. He let the memories of his youth wash over him—the sandlot football games, the bare-knuckled fights, the wrestling matches with his brother Edgar, the hard work at the creamery. Beyond his win-dow to the south he saw a wheat field being fluffed by the warm summer wind. To the east he spotted a farmer working on his gold and green field of corn.

He glanced at the watch his grandfather Jacob had given him years earlier, and knew the time had come. With his train ticket folded in the breast pocket of his short-sleeved collared shirt, Ike grabbed his packed bag that was sitting next to his bedroom door and headed down the stairs. His mother and his youngest brother, Milton, were waiting for him on the side porch.

"You take care of yourself Dwight," his mother said, her lips trem-bling with emotion. "And be a good boy."

"Sure, Mother," he replied. "I will."

For the first time in Eisenhower's life, he saw his mother's eyes grow dewy. He hugged her tightly one more time. "I'll be back before you know it, Mother," he said. "And I'll write you often."

A moment later, Ike bent over and grabbed his bag. He told his dog Flip to "stay home," and then he walked north, quickly, along a dusty street toward the train depot. In the faraway distance, a whistle blew and echoed across the rolling, empty plain of middle America. Eisenhower picked up his pace. He didn't want to be late: The rest of his life was about to begin.

Thorpe (running in the foreground) *was the one player who Warner knew could turn a good team into a great one, and the coach summoned all of his persuasive powers to keep the restless athlete at Carlisle.* (Courtesy Cumberland County Historical Society)

7

HE IS CERTAINLY A WILD INDIAN

The boy didn't know exactly where to go. He walked off the train at the depot and looked anxiously around, unsure of what his new life in Carlisle, Pennsylvania, was going to be like. He ambled through the warm winter afternoon, passing clothing and jewelry shops along the cobblestone streets of downtown, walking past blocks of painted wooden houses. He eventually asked a local for directions to the Indian School. Carrying a small duffel bag, the skinny fifteen-year-old, who stood five feet, five inches and weighed about 115 pounds, made his way onto the campus grounds. It was February 6, 1904, and Jim Thorpe had found his new home.

When Thorpe reached the school's main gate, he took a few moments to study the well-manicured campus. Tall maple trees shaded a four-acre lawn. Two- and three-story buildings made of wood and brick surrounded the large open area of the campus, which had a tall flagpole sprouting from the center. To his right stood the old army barracks, which housed the teachers and staff of Carlisle. To his left was another matching barracks building, which served as the girls' dormitory. Close to the dormitory was a gymnasium that had been built ten years earlier. The stuffy gym had exposed brick walls, a basketball court, and a small running track suspended twenty feet above the wooden floor of the basketball court.

Thorpe looked to another part of the campus. A small graveyard with a dozen long rows of tombstones sat on the edge of the school grounds. The simple white markers revealed the names of Indian boys and girls who had died while wards of the state at the Indian School. So many dreams were buried here, including those of Ernest White Thunder, a bright-eyed boy who arrived at Carlisle in 1880. Soon after Ernest, a Sioux, was forced to attend the Indian School, he became violently homesick and withdrew from everything. When his father, White Thunder, a Sioux chief, visited the campus, Ernest begged him to take him back to his home in Rosebud, South Dakota; his father refused. Ernest tried to sneak onto the train when his father left, but he was quickly discovered and returned to school.

Days later, Ernest fell ill. "White Thunder's son is very sick and I doubt if he recovers," Superintendent Richard Pratt wrote in a letter to another official. "I consider that it is entirely his own fault, as I explained to you. He is rather obstinate—seems to rather want to die."

Ernest didn't even make it another week, which prompted Pratt to pen a letter to the boy's father. "Your son died quietly, without suffering, like a man. We have dressed him in his good clothes and tomorrow we will bury him the way white people do."

The biggest killer at Carlisle was tuberculosis, which was what probably took Ernest White Thunder's life. Tuberculosis was a highly contagious disease, and it spread quickly between the Indian youths who slept in the same rooms together, ate meals together, and studied together. Most whites had built up immunity to the disease, but Indians hadn't been exposed to it. At Carlisle, doctors and government officials didn't understand how contagious the disease was until it was too late. Of the 10,000 children who would eventually attend the school, about 1,000 would die while at Carlisle and 190 would be buried in the school cemetery.

It was a chilling experience for the Indian students to glance over at the white tombstones. Most had friends who rested there. The worst thing was, the Indian boys and girls knew they could be next.

At the main gate a school official directed Thorpe to a windowless building known as the "guardhouse." The limestone and brick structure had
been built in 1777 by Hessian soldiers who had been captured by George
Washington's Continental Army at Trenton, New Jersey, in December
1776 during the Revolutionary War. The Hessians, who were from Hessen,
Germany, had been drafted by the British to help fight Washington's
troops. Once in Washington's custody, they were held at the Carlisle army
barracks. At gunpoint, they were forced to erect a building in which
Washington planned to store gunpowder. The Hessian Powder Magazine
was one of the few buildings at the Carlisle barracks to survive after Confederate general J.E.B. Stuart torched the military post a few days before
the Civil War battle of Gettysburg in 1863.

Thorpe entered the guardhouse and handed his entrance papers to an
administrator, who told Thorpe that he needed to be examined by the
medical staff at the school's hospital. Thorpe then walked to the infirmary, where he was washed thoroughly with hot water and soap from a
basin. A school doctor gave him a physical, which he passed. His old
worn-out overalls were tossed in the garbage and he was handed a new set
of clothes: a military-style uniform that consisted of a coat and pants; a
Civil War–style wool cap with a visor; long stockings; underwear; a night-
shirt; a black dress coat; and black wool trousers.

School administrators gave Thorpe a trunk full of towels and bedding.
He was then chaperoned to the barber's chair, where his long, dark locks
were cut down to an inch in length. After all the outward signs of Thorpe's
"Indian-ness" had been purged, he was led to his quarters in the boys'
dormitory. He would share a sparse room—where he had a bed, a wash-
stand, and a small nightstand—with two other boys.

Student life was scripted to the minute at Carlisle. A bugle woke the
seven hundred boys and girls at 5:30 A.M. After dressing, they marched in
formation to the large dining hall for breakfast at 6:15. Then they spent
the morning in classes taught by white teachers, most of whom were female. In the afternoon the students were given vocational training. The
boys learned trades such as blacksmithing and carpentry while the girls
studied such topics as nursing and dressmaking. Athletic games were

played later in the day but before dinner was served promptly at 6:00 P.M. Evenings found the students with their books until a bugle sounded taps at 9:00 P.M., when it was lights out.

Thorpe quickly found his groove at Carlisle and settled into the school's structured lifestyle, just as he had at Haskell Institute in Lawrence, Kansas, where he had spent part of his childhood. Thorpe wasn't an outstanding student, but he proved capable. He wanted to become a tailor, and so every weekday afternoon he sat in the tailor shop and learned as much as he could about the making and altering of garments—an important and intricate trade in 1900s America. With each passing day, Jim grew more comfortable with his life at Carlisle. He made friends and was shedding the cocoon of shyness he had spun when his mother died. He especially enjoyed Sundays, when he and a few of the other Catholic students were escorted into town to the Roman Catholic church for Mass.

Two and a half months after arriving at school, Thorpe received some news that brought him to his knees: His father was dead. On April 24, 1904, Hiram had passed away from blood poisoning. Thorpe didn't find out about his father's death in time to return to the Oklahoma Territory for the funeral, which deepened his heartache.

Once more, Thorpe was lost. He withdrew from everything—his friends, his teachers, his schoolwork, his sports. In the days and weeks that followed, he rarely talked to anyone and drifted around campus in a melancholic daze. His twin brother, his mother, and now his father—the three people on the planet whom Jim loved more than anyone else—were all gone, disappeared into the wind. And here he was more than a thousand miles away from anything that felt familiar.

The administrators at Carlisle kept a close eye on Jim. They feared they were on the brink of losing him—he seemed a threat to run away at any moment—and so the staff had several meetings to try to figure out how best to help Thorpe navigate through his grief. They eventually decided that Jim needed to be around a family, so school officials arranged for Thorpe to go on an "outing" and live off-campus with a volunteer white family.

The "outing system" was the brainchild of Pratt, who implemented it in 1880. In this work-study program, a student would live with a white family in Pennsylvania, New Jersey, or New York and perform household chores or tasks on the land while being treated, in theory, as a member of the family—a fledgling foreign-exchange program of sorts. The student was paid a wage that was sent to Carlisle and held in a trust. All the families were screened by Carlisle officials to ensure that students wouldn't be mistreated. "It enforced participation, the supreme Americanizer," Pratt said of the outing system. "Preventing participation stops Americanization. The native Americans have been, without exception, most harshly and by many devious demoralizing devices excluded from participation in our American family."

On June 17, less than two months after his father died, Thorpe was sent to the home of A. E. Buckholz in Somerton, Pennsylvania. Though the Quaker family embraced him with open arms, Thorpe didn't enjoy his job of cooking meals for the family and cleaning the house. Like most sixteen-year-old boys, he wanted to be outside, not pinned down with a mop and bucket or a vegetable pot. He quickly grew stir crazy. Though Pratt told the students that they didn't go on their outings as "employees" but as "part of the family," Thorpe began to feel like he was nothing more than hired help, especially since he wasn't allowed to dine with the family in the evening; instead, he ate alone in the quiet of the kitchen. When Mr. Buckholz realized that Thorpe wasn't happy in his new home, he requested that Jim be transferred to another family who needed help with outdoor labor.

Thorpe landed in Dolington, Pennsylvania, at the residence of James L. Cadwallader. For three months, he worked in the Cadwalladers' garden. But it still wasn't enough. Thorpe wanted to do heavy physical labor, such as he'd done on the ranch in Texas and back home with his father in the Oklahoma Territory. On September 15, 1905, Thorpe was moved again. This time he went to Robbinsville, New Jersey, near Trenton, to work on the farm of Harby Rozarth. Acting as a foreman in charge of a team of Indian workers, Thorpe and his men planted row after row of vegetables. He spent nearly a year on the Rozarth farm, working and earning eight dollars a month. The labor was tedious, but it further molded and strengthened his body.

One day in the spring of 1907, the urge to run away gripped Thorpe. He sprinted through the woods of New Jersey, getting as far away from the farm as possible. He hitched rides in wagons and made his way back to the Carlisle campus, where he was immediately thrown into a dank, windowless, dungeon-like holding cell in the basement of the guardhouse. Runaways were always severely punished at Carlisle, and for at least a few days the eighteen-year-old Thorpe sat in the cell, alone with his thoughts, alone with all the questions that poked and pinched at his peace of mind: *Will I ever be able to play football for Carlisle? Should I go back to the Oklahoma Territory? Will I be forced to return to the farm in New Jersey?* The hours ticked by. He was unsure of what he would do once he was freed. In this way, Jim was a typical teenager—anxious and restless and without a sense of where he belonged.

In the spring of 1907, Pop Warner, like Thorpe, returned to Carlisle. Warner had briefly left the Indian School in 1904 to coach at his alma mater, Cornell, where he led the Red Men to a 21-8-2 record over three seasons. But the lure of Carlisle was strong for Warner—just as it was for Thorpe, who could have gone anywhere in the country after running away from the New Jersey farm. Warner was enticed to return to the school by Major William Mercer, who had replaced Pratt as Carlisle's superintendent in the summer of 1904. Mercer didn't believe that Bemus Pierce and Frank Hudson, two former Indian School players who shared the coaching duties during the '06 season, were up to the task of leading the football team. So before the '07 season, he offered Warner an annual salary of four thousand dollars to be the school's head football coach and athletic director. Warner accepted.

Warner and Thorpe were now together on the same ground.

Jim Thorpe sauntered across the grassy upper practice field at Carlisle, once again feeling good about the direction his life was heading. He'd served his brief sentence for running away from the farm in New Jersey and had been let out of the guardhouse. Time also helped him move on from the loss of his father, who had passed away three years earlier. Now, in late April of 1907, Thorpe was about to play in an intramural football game with some of the other students. A great secret was about to be exposed.

Thorpe was eighteen years old. He stood five feet, eleven inches and weighed 160 pounds. The many months he'd spent away from campus on his extended "outing" had made him more eager than ever to play sports again, especially football. In his first days at Carlisle before his father died, Thorpe had been a member of the tailor shop football team. Each of the shop schools—the Tailors, the Printers, the Harness Makers, the Blacksmiths—organized a football squad, and they played one another in an intramural league most afternoons at four. If a player showed potential in those games, he might get asked to try out for the varsity.

Thorpe strolled through the spring sunshine on his way to one of these games. It was scheduled to be played on the lower practice field, but before Thorpe reached his destination he spotted several varsity track members performing the high jump on the upper practice field. He stopped to watch the boys. After the high jumpers cleared one height, they raised the bar higher. A few minutes passed, a few more jumps were made, and the bar was set at five feet, nine inches. The high jumpers tried repeatedly to surmount the bar, lifting themselves as high as they possibly could into the air, but they simply couldn't clear it.

Thorpe was intrigued. Before he left for his outing, Thorpe had become so quiet and introverted that he never would have approached boys he didn't know. But that time away from school had changed his personality. When he returned to Carlisle, Thorpe was no longer afraid to be the center of attention. He was now a young man who was gaining confidence by the day, and he felt there wasn't anything he couldn't do on the athletic fields.

Thorpe approached the group of high jumpers and asked them a question: Could he give it a try? The boys tried to muzzle their laughter, but failed. Thorpe—dressed in overalls and a heavy cotton shirt, and wearing a pair of sneakers that he had found earlier in the day in the gymnasium—looked like he should be out working the crops in the fields, not attempting a leap over a bar on the track field. But the high jumpers, believing they were about to see a comedy routine unfold, told Thorpe to go for it, to give it his best shot.

Thorpe stepped back from the bar. Standing about fifteen yards away, without so much as stretching one muscle, he took off, blasting toward the mark. But just as he was about to take flight, he stopped abruptly. Thorpe was taking a practice run, just as he had seen the other boys do. He again stepped back from the bar. This time he accelerated even faster. The bar was twenty feet away, then fifteen, then five. When he reached the mark, Thorpe lifted off, leaping into the cool April air, twisting his body and arching his back. He sailed over the bar with ease, landing softly in a sandpit. Thorpe stood up, dusted himself off, and laughed as he rejoined his friends who were walking to the lower field for their football game. All the high jumpers were stunned.

They shouldn't have been. Just a few days earlier Thorpe had won the high jump by clearing a height of five feet, three inches in the Arbor Day track and field competition held at Carlisle. He also had won the 120-yard hurdles in nineteen seconds and finished runner-up in the 220-yard dash. But now Thorpe had bettered his first-place jump by six inches, which was as improbable as trimming four seconds off one's hundred-yard dash time from one day to the next. One student who saw Thorpe's giant leap in overalls, Harry Archenbald, walked into Warner's office the next day to tell him what he had witnessed. Warner, who had never talked one-on-one with Thorpe before, immediately sent for him. An hour later Thorpe was standing in front of Warner's desk.

"Do you know what you have done?" asked Warner.

"Nothing bad, I hope," replied Thorpe.

Warner explained that, if the story of his jump was true, then Thorpe had just broken the school record in practice. Warner walked around his desk and put his arm around Thorpe's shoulder, telling him that he'd get him a track uniform that afternoon because he was now on the track team, which Warner coached along with the football team. At this moment, here in Warner's office, their lives became irrevocably linked, this thirty-six-year-old man and this eighteen-year-old boy, the athletic equivalent of Socrates and Plato. For the next five years, Warner and Thorpe would constantly be by each other's side—and rarely out of each other's thoughts—as together they charged into the consciousness of America in the early days of the twentieth century.

Warner now had his hands on an exquisite specimen of athletic potential. But Thorpe was far from a finished product. He was raw, an unpainted canvas. Warner immediately placed him under the tutelage of Albert Exendine, the twenty-three-year-old former Carlisle football player who held virtually all of the school's track and field records and still had one year of eligibility remaining on both the football and track teams. Like Thorpe, Exendine was a native of Oklahoma, and the two could speak the common language of growing up on the frontier, of struggling through Indian Schools at a young age, and of the awkward search for an identity that balanced the Indian traditions with the adoption of the white man's culture. Ex, as his friends called him, was just what Thorpe needed.

Exendine felt lucky to even be at Carlisle. Eight years earlier, in June 1899, he was attending the Mautame Mission School outside of Anadarko, Oklahoma, when he spotted an advertisement that blared: "Students Wanted for the Carlisle Indian School." Outgoing, gregarious, and adventurous, Exendine was immediately intrigued with the faraway school. He applied and was accepted, but his father wouldn't let him leave home. For six months Exendine used all of his persuasive power to convince his father, a Cherokee Indian, to let him leave. He finally agreed, and on Christmas morning in 1899, he and a friend boarded a train that would take them to the soft rolling hills of the Cumberland Valley in Pennsylvania.

But his friend didn't last long. Days after arriving at the school, he was stricken with tuberculosis. The Carlisle officials immediately put him on a train back to Oklahoma. Exendine wanted to say goodbye to his buddy before he was forced to pack his suitcase, but the bighearted Ex couldn't bring himself to do it: He was afraid to look him in the eyes. Within months, his buddy was dead.

Exendine stayed at Carlisle, and he soon became one of the most popular students at the school. And he quickly developed into one of Warner's top players. Though he had never heard of football before coming to the school, Warner taught him how to play and by 1901 he was a starting tackle. At six feet, two inches and 210 pounds, Ex was a ferocious player who had the best work ethic on the team. Warner believed Exendine would be the perfect mentor for Thorpe—both on the field and off. Once again, Warner's coaching instinct was right.

In a short time Thorpe came to treat Ex like an older, wiser brother. During the spring they grew close, sharing stories of their rugged youths in the Oklahoma Territory, or wrestling each other out on the grassy athletic fields, or secretly making fun of some of their instructors at the school. When they weren't horsing around, Ex shared his experiences of suiting up for the Carlisle football squad. Walter Camp had named him to his third-string All-American team as an end in 1903, and Ex had an arsenal of anecdotes from the gridiron, which he told Thorpe with a storyteller's flourish.

A self-made athlete, Exendine taught Thorpe the virtue of practice. Warner was paying Exendine an assistant track coach's salary to transform Thorpe's immense promise into production, and Exendine didn't shy from the challenge. During every spare moment they had, the two would steal away to the athletic fields, where Ex would mentor Thorpe in running and jumping events. To teach his protégé, Ex would perform a maneuver such as the long jump and then have Thorpe mimic precisely what he did. Exendine watched Thorpe closely, analyzing his every move and pointing out his every mistake. It was rudimentary track and field coaching, and in a matter of weeks, Thorpe's form had improved so much that late in the spring Warner invited him to compete in Carlisle's last track meet of the 1907 season.

The Carlisle track team traveled eighty miles north to Lewisburg, Pennsylvania, to the campus of Bucknell University. Thorpe enrolled in the 120-yard hurdles event, but before he ran, a steamy rain fell from the spring sky. Thorpe didn't like to compete at anything when weather conditions were poor—a flaw that Warner would never be able to correct—but he still finished second in the 120-yard hurdles, which earned Thorpe his first varsity letter at Carlisle. He hoped to win his second letter in the fall—if he made the varsity football team.

As the spring of 1907 warmed into summer in the Cumberland Valley, the majority of the Carlisle students left campus, either on an "outing" or for a brief visit home. But Warner made sure that all his athletes stayed at school to train. Thorpe spent the summer working out with the track team, playing in a baseball game that pitted students against Carlisle employees, and taking part in a pickup baseball game in Hershey, Pennsylvania, where he was given chocolates from the Hershey factory after the final out was made. Warner also enjoyed himself. On many lazy afternoons he took some of the young Indian girls on rides in his newfangled motorcar. Sitting in the back of the open-air vehicle, the girls couldn't get the smiles off their faces as Warner puttered at ten miles per hour through the streets of Carlisle. For a few months, no one was more popular in the girls' dormitory than Warner, who was an avuncular figure to all of them.

Even Thorpe had some leisure time in the summer of '07. He ventured with friends into downtown Carlisle and looked around the shops. He rode the trolley to Mount Holly Springs, a burg a few miles outside Carlisle. But Thorpe's favorite moments of the summer were the one-on-one tutorials from Exendine on the art of playing football. Telling Thorpe he needed to be "mean" whenever he stepped onto the football field, Ex taught his pupil how to run with a football, how to stiff-arm, tackle, block, kick, pass, and catch. No detail was too minor for Exendine to riff on, and the two were often seen alone together on the athletic fields with a football in their hands well after the sun faded and twilight rippled across the valley.

Warner had no intention of allowing Thorpe to play football for the varsity once practice started. He believed that the young man was too inexperienced. Perhaps after a year on the junior varsity Thorpe would be ready to play in games that mattered, but not in the 1907 season. Warner didn't want to rush the boy. Moreover, he thought Thorpe had all the earmarks of a special track athlete, and he wanted Thorpe to put all his effort into track and field.

Yet, in August, Thorpe was quietly encouraged by Frank Newman, a part time assistant coach, to try out for the varsity. Newman had seen Thorpe play for the tailor-shop team and thought he could be an asset to Warner. So on the first day of practice, after picking up a red jersey and shoulder pads from the team trainer, Thorpe jogged out to the grassy practice field.

"What do you think you're doing here?" Warner asked Thorpe.

"Pop, I want to play football," replied Thorpe.

"I'm only going to tell you once, Jim, go back to the locker room and take that uniform off! You're my most valuable trackman, and I don't want you to get hurt playing football," Warner explained.

"I want to play football," Thorpe insisted, standing his ground.

Seeing Thorpe's blazing eyes, Warner knew he was serious. He indulged Thorpe and told him to practice drop-kicking the ball. Warner knew the kid wouldn't injure himself working out with the kickers, but this didn't satisfy Thorpe, who desperately wanted to scrimmage with the varsity. Every day Thorpe asked Warner if he could test himself against the regular players. Every day Warner said no. After two weeks of being pelted with the same question, Warner caved. One afternoon at practice he forcefully threw a ball at Thorpe and in an exasperated voice said, "All right, if that's the way you want it! Give the varsity some tackling practice."

Warner hoped his varsity boys would teach Thorpe a bone-crushing lesson, one that would make him turn away from football and concentrate solely on track and field. Some forty players were scattered about the practice field. They were standing in small groups about five yards apart. Warner's tackling drill called for the ballcarrier to work his way up the field through the different groups of defenders until he was tackled. The point of the exercise was to work on tackling techniques; it was a given that the runner wouldn't make it very far without any blockers. Warner fully expected Thorpe to get taken down—hard—by the first group he faced.

Ball in arm, Thorpe confidently strode onto the field. Warner, with his trademark hand-rolled cigarette pinched between his lips, watched closely, as did backfield coach Jimmie Johnson. Warner shouted the command to begin the drill and Thorpe took off on the first important run of his football life. When he confronted the initial group of defenders, he twisted, cut, and fought through several players who lunged at his legs. The same thing happened with the next group, as defenders bounced off him as if his body had been charged with high-voltage electricity. Thorpe then knifed through the third group with a combination of power, grace, and agility that left Warner slack-jawed.

It was all so sudden, so improbable to see this kid who had appeared virtually out of nowhere plow through the veteran players. To Warner it was as majestic and rare as a comet shooting across the sky. By the time Thorpe rumbled over the goal line to score a touchdown, Warner's eyes were nearly the size of footballs.

Thorpe jogged over to the sideline and tossed the ball to his coach. "I gave them some good practice, right, Pop?"

Coach Johnson, standing nearby, jokingly told Thorpe, "You're supposed to let them tackle you, Jim. You weren't supposed to run through them!"

Unaware that Johnson was kidding, Thorpe grew angry: He hadn't yet picked up on the nuances of sarcasm in the English language. "Nobody is going to tackle Jim," he said.

Warner wanted to see if Thorpe could do it again. He also felt that Thorpe, by smugly tossing the ball back at him, wasn't showing the proper respect for his coach. Warner marched over to his defenders and ordered them to huddle around him, on the double. This was their chance, Warner told his boys in an emotional voice, to teach this rookie kid Jim Thorpe what it meant to be a varsity football player at the Carlisle Indian School. Warner commanded his defenders to lay the hammer to Thorpe, to make him wish he'd never stepped on this field today. "Get mean," Warner told his defenders. "Smack him down! Hit him down so hard that he doesn't get up. Who does he think he is? This isn't a relay race! This is football. Hit! Hit! Hit!"

Warner got in Thorpe's face and shoved the ball back into his belly. Then he pushed him out onto the field. Pop gave the command to begin the drill and again Thorpe charged up the field like fire across oil-covered grass. In a blur of twists, turns, stiff-arms, and high-kicking legs, Thorpe blew through the first group of defenders . . . then the second . . . then the third . . . then the fourth . . . trotting into the end zone and making it look effortless. Standing on the sideline in silence, Warner was astounded as he considered what this kid was capable of doing on the football field, the greatness that awaited him like a birthright. In just two runs, Thorpe had displayed more speed, more strength, more agility, more vision, and more creativity when running with the ball than Warner had ever witnessed. That first run wasn't a fluke.

Thorpe circled back to his coach on the sideline. He flipped the ball back to Warner. "Nobody is going to tackle Jim," Thorpe told Warner again, matter-of-factly.

As Thorpe walked away and joined the rest of the team on the field, Warner was overwhelmed. As an avid painter, he felt he had just seen the football equivalent of spying a teenage Monet first dabbling in watercolors. Warner knew that his defenders might not have played their best in either of the practice drills, but still: Those two runs took his breath away, and showed that Thorpe was bursting with untapped potential—the one thing Warner couldn't teach. Could Thorpe be the player who was going to propel Carlisle to the next level? Could he someday lead Carlisle to an undefeated season and prompt Walter Camp, whose rankings were more influential than those of anyone else, to proclaim Carlisle national champions?

Talking with an assistant after he had a chance to take stock of what he'd just seen Thorpe do, Warner proclaimed: "My—he is certainly a wild Indian."

In the fall of 1907 football was rapidly evolving, coming out of its primordial sea and onto the land. The changes in the game came about after October 9, 1905, when President Theodore Roosevelt called representatives from Harvard, Yale, and Princeton—the Big Three—to the White House to discuss the brutality of football. That year, eighteen men had died and more than 140 were seriously injured on football fields, including Roosevelt's son, Teddy, Jr. He was a freshman at Harvard and had suffered a broken nose that fall in a game against Yale. What most troubled Roosevelt were the mass plays that featured two teams simply lining up and, with their arms interlocked, running straight at each other like dueling rams smashing their horns. Roosevelt was a firm backer of football—in 1898 ten of the Rough Riders who fought with him in Cuba listed their occupation as "football"—but he wanted the game made safer.

Officials from the Big Three agreed. After their meeting with the president, the Big Three leaders invited representatives from about a dozen schools to New York City to discuss possible rule changes. After a heated debate, the first "commissioners" of football ratified a new set of rules that they believed would make the game less hazardous to the players and, ultimately, save the sport from White House—mandated extinction. The blood-spilling mass plays were banned, and teammates could no longer lock arms and plow forward as a group. The rule-makers were trying to open up the field and allow ballcarriers a chance to run in unoccupied spaces. They also created the neutral zone: the imaginary space that ran along the line of scrimmage. (The neutral zone measured the length of the football and it separated the two teams before the play began.) The rules committee shortened the game from seventy to sixty minutes and lengthened the yardage needed to make a first down from five yards to ten. Teams had three plays to advance the ball ten yards. (A fourth down was added in 1912.)

A more drastic rule change had already been adopted in 1906, one that was designed to spread the players out on the field even more and prevent fewer mass collisions: the legalization of the forward pass. According to the rule, one forward pass on each scrimmage down was allowed so long as the pass was made behind the line of scrimmage. It had to go five yards to the left or right from where the center hiked the ball and, if the thrown ball failed to touch a player on either side before it hit the ground, possession was given to the other team, which made the forward pass a risky proposition.

At first Warner opposed the forward pass. He didn't believe that it belonged in the game. But, gradually, the notion of flinging the ball through the sky to gain yardage began to preoccupy him. Ever since his first practice at Cornell, the strategy of football had fascinated Warner. The forward pass was like a new tool in his shed that he could use to devise plays to confuse the other team. In virtually all of his conscious hours, the questions rushed at Warner: *How can I use the pass to my advantage? Will the speed of my boys make it easier to complete a pass? What's the best way to throw a football? How can the pass help me deceive the opponent?*

By the fall of 1907, Warner, who still liked to take risks the way he did when he gambled on horses as a kid, was more intrigued by the forward pass than was any coach in the nation. In preseason practice he tested a theory: Instead of having a thrower hurl the ball down the field end-over-end, or lob it, or push the ball shot-put style in the direction of the receiver—as many other teams were doing—he taught his boys how to fling a spiral. Gripping the ball on its laces, he showed them how to let it roll off their fingertips in a spiraling motion as they released the ball. This type of throw, Warner instructed, would allow the quarterback to wing the ball with accuracy thirty to forty yards down the field.

For several weeks, all of Warner's backs practiced their spirals. Frank Mt. Pleasant quickly became proficient at the deep pass. During scrimmages, Mt. Pleasant would receive the snap and run around in the backfield, dancing nimbly and avoiding tacklers. Then when Albert Exendine, who was playing end and still tutoring Thorpe, broke free thirty yards down the field, Pleasant would heave the ball with all his might. Exendine would run under the arcing rainbow of a pass and cradle it into his arms for a long gain. After each successful forward pass in practice, Warner became more convinced that no team on their 1907 schedule could stop Carlisle's potent offense.

Three days after beating Lebanon Valley College, 40–0, in an exhibition game, Carlisle hosted Villanova in its official home opener. To promote this game, Warner enlisted the assistance of Hugh Miller, a print shop owner in town. In the days leading up to kickoff, Miller, who ran advertising and promotion campaigns out of his shop, reported to papers in the area that there had been a spate of local betting on the game, and the odds were even that Villanova would be held scoreless. No visiting team had scored a touchdown at Indian Field in the previous six years, and many of the locals, Miller reported, felt strongly that Villanova wouldn't put up a single point on the scoreboard. Miller also spread leaflets in the nearby towns of Harrisburg, Steelton, Shippensburg, and Chambersburg, reminding football fans that there was ample parking room for "autos."

This was the beginning of a long and fruitful campaign for Warner and Miller. Over the next few years they would spin a first-of-its-kind, sophisticated PR web across the United States. Working out of his print shop and a booth at the Chocolate Shop in downtown Carlisle, Miller wrote puff-piece profiles and features about the Carlisle players as well as detailed, play-by-play game accounts that he sent to more than 150 newspapers in his "news syndicate." Miller also telegraphed the papers midweek with quotes from Warner, whose spiel always hit on the same theme: We have no chance in hell to win this weekend. At the request of Warner, Miller also sent out misinformation on bogus injuries. All of this was done to make Carlisle forever the underdog—in the minds of the opposing players and fans everywhere.

Miller eventually became so busy with his PR duties that Warner hired E. L. Martin, the editor of the *Carlisle Daily Herald* and a stringer for the Associated Press and the *Philadelphia Evening Telegram,* to assist Miller. Martin's primary job was to hang promotional placards around town and help Miller plant stories in major newspapers. Warner even bought Martin a box camera for $140 so he could snap portraits of the star players to accompany the pieces that Miller wrote and disseminated. The PR arm of Warner's football program quickly proved to be as strong off the field as his team was on the field, as Miller and Martin succeeded in sticking stories in major dailies in Philadelphia, Pittsburgh, New York, and Chicago. Piece by piece, step by step, Warner was pushing football out of its dark age and into the modern era.

The afternoon was sunny and cool for the Villanova game. Visitors to downtown Carlisle were greeted by a large banner strung across the main street, announcing that the Indians were about to do battle on the football field. Warner's scheme to raise interest in the game by spreading the rumor that high stakes were being wagered on the outcome had worked: Before kickoff a crowd of more than 3,000 fans ringed the field. Many sat on the grassy knoll to the east of the field; others stayed in their autos, parked higher up on the hill. As Thorpe stood on the sideline, his eyes fell over the crush of fans pressing around the field. He'd never seen a crowd so large.

The teams were evenly matched, but the Indians made the first big play of the afternoon when quarterback Frank Mt. Pleasant flung a deep pass to Exendine, who caught the ball and rambled for thirty yards before being tackled. The crowd gasped at the play. Few had seen the ball thrown so far and so high before. Mt. Pleasant's pass spiraled perfectly through the crisp blue sky, and it left the Villanova defense in a daze. A few plays later, Carlisle's Pete Hauser, a fullback, bulled over two Villanova defenders to score a touchdown. Carlisle won the game 10–0, preserving their six-year streak of not allowing an opposing team to score a single touchdown on their turf.

Over the next few weeks, Thorpe watched from the sideline as Carlisle, astounding the opposition with its use of the forward pass, dismantled one team after the next. On October 2 the Indians crushed Susquehanna University 91–0. Three days later, Carlisle topped Penn State 18–5. After every game, Warner's PR posse typed up and sent stories to news outlets from New York to Los Angeles. They detailed in grand language how the heroic Indians had whipped a team of "palefaces." News traveled through the press that Carlisle's next game, on October 12, would be played in Buffalo, New York, against Syracuse University. As soon as Indians on reservations in upstate New York and Canada learned that Carlisle was coming, they made plans to attend the contest.

After riding a train to Buffalo, the Carlisle boys walked onto the field at Olympic Park, where the Buffalo Bisons had played baseball in the National League in the late 1800s. To the Indian boys, it felt like a home game: Several thousand long-haired Indians, many dressed in traditional buckskin clothes and wrapped in blankets, circled the field to watch their first football game. Always looking to gain the upper hand on the other team, Warner made some alterations to his players' uniforms before the game. He painted the leather helmets of his ends white and his halfbacks red, hoping that the different colors would confuse the Syracuse players. Warner also stitched half-footballs onto the shirts of the halfbacks— another tactic aimed at deceiving the Syracuse defenders.

To Warner, the football field was like one of his blank canvases on the easel in his bungalow at Carlisle: The game presented him opportunities to create something majestic not with brushstrokes, but with strategies, formations, plays, even sewn-on footballs. He was still a gambler as well— he often placed bets on games—and every day he searched for ways to swindle his opponents. Part artist, part thief, Warner whipped up cunning ideas that had never been applied to football. These brazen moves defined his coaching style, and his imaginative risk-taking would reshape the fundamental way the game was played.

Warner's tricks against Syracuse were smart. Carlisle stormed to a 14–0 lead behind the play of their quarterback, Frank Mt. Pleasant, a Tuscarora Indian who grew up near Buffalo and had dozens of friends and family in the crowd. On one play, Mt. Pleasant received the snap and acted as if he were going to punt the ball. But just before he booted it skyward, he pulled the ball back and chucked it down the field. The Syracuse defenders were taken by surprise and the closest defender was several steps behind the Indians' William Gardner when he caught the ball. By the time he was tackled, Gardner had gained thirty yards, which prompted the pro-Carlisle crowd to whoop and holler like they had just been part of a successful buffalo hunt.

Late in the game, with Carlisle in control, Warner signaled for Thorpe to get on the field. A second-stringer, Thorpe had played a few downs in Carlisle's exhibition game against Lebanon Valley, but this was his first experience playing in front of Indians that he didn't personally know from school or town. As he rose from the bench, Thorpe was staggered by the energy of the crowd. The overexcited Indian fans were inching closer and closer to the field as the game progressed. With only a few minutes remaining, they stood directly on the sideline—in some spots ten deep. Every time Warner made a substitution, the player hopped off the bench, which was set back several yards from the field, and ran through a gauntlet of screaming Indian fans.

As Thorpe made his entrance onto the field, he was patted on the back and words of encouragement were thrown at him like roses. If he ever wondered whether football was more than just a game to Indians, Thorpe now discovered firsthand that it was. The Indians in the crowd rejoiced over the fact that their people—the Carlisle boys—were thumping a group of white kids at a game that was created and developed by whites. The Indians on the field were proving that they were more capable athletes than the white players. What's more, thanks to Warner's coaching, the Indians were outsmarting the Syracuse players. These copper-skinned players represented all that was possible for Indians in America, and the long-haired fans showed their approval by howling after every play as if they were trying to raise the dead.

Thorpe played tailback. He carried the ball a few plays, but never put a dent in the Syracuse defense. He was still learning the game, and Warner was bringing him along slowly. Carlisle didn't need him today: The Indians won 14–6.

As soon as the final whistle blew, the Indian fans spilled onto the field and mingled with the Carlisle Indians. From this moment forward, the players understood clearly that every time they buckled their chinstraps, they played not just for their school, but for their entire race. The players now knew they could lift the spirits of people who had little reason to smile. It was an awesome power, and the hour was drawing closer for Thorpe to exert it.

The perks for the players who made Warner's varsity squad were as juicy as a sixteen-ounce sirloin. Warner was renovating the school hospital and, at a cost of $13,000, turning it into a spacious dormitory for his players. The new space featured a game room with a pool table and a music box. There was also a reading room where, thanks to a news-clipping service that Warner hired, the boys could read about their exploits on the football field in papers like *The New York Times,* the *Boston Herald,* the *Harrisburg Patriot,* and the *Philadelphia North American.* But the biggest reasons to envy the players who lived in the football dorm were the kitchen and the special dining room—places that became as sought after as a piece of Tutti Frutti gum to the students on campus who didn't play football.

The food in the main dining hall for all the other students at Carlisle was as bland as the slate-gray walls: breakfast consisted of coffee, oatmeal, and gravy; lunch varied but usually featured soup and a dry piece of meat; and dinner was composed of bread (no butter), beans, rice, and gravy. If the students were lucky, they also got a piece of ginger cake for dessert. Many students complained about the lackluster food, but the menu rarely changed.

Not so in the football dining room. Warner was the second most powerful man at Carlisle behind Superintendent Mercer, and when he wanted something for his players, 99 percent of the time he got it. Warner was always after his players to gain weight, so he made sure that his boys were consistently fed like turkeys before Thanksgiving. Prepared by special chefs, the food for the players included ample quantities of milk, bread (with butter), beef, and potatoes. They were even served fresh fruit, one of the most prized delicacies at Carlisle and rarely available to regular students.

There were other fringe benefits to being a Warner boy. If a football player became sick or injured, he received special attention. If a player needed some extra money, Warner provided "loans." In the 1907 and '08 seasons, Warner doled out a little more than $9,000 to his players, including $500 to Thorpe. A big believer in the importance of first impressions, Warner also gave each of his players a fancy $25 suit and a $25 overcoat from Mose Blumenthal's clothing store in downtown Carlisle. Warner even gave his best players a charge account at the apparel store. Whenever the team traveled, Warner had his boys dress in either their finest military uniform or in the off-the-rack items from Blumenthal's. Warner wanted to debunk the "heathen" image that most of white America held of the Indians, and making them look as "white" as possible was one step he took. And when the team traveled on overnight rail trips,

Warner sometimes allowed his players to enjoy such indulgences as caviar—which, of course, he paid for out of the school's athletic fund.

Then there was the booze. When the players hung out at Blumenthal's, they sometimes retreated to the back room for a secret nip of alcohol supplied by one of the team's boosters. On other occasions, Carlisle employees, usually in the dark of night, would deliver beer to the football dorm. A few times Warner even invited his boys over to his new two-story cottage on the campus grounds for a tumbler or two of whiskey. Drinking alcohol was strictly prohibited at Carlisle and it was against the law for the local saloon owners to sell alcohol to Carlisle students, but Warner and other officials at the school didn't mind looking the other way now and then.

When a player had too much to drink and found trouble with the law, Warner could make the problem go away with a magic handshake. The coach issued periodic payments to the local police that ensured his players wouldn't spend any nights in jail. Warner wanted the police to keep an eye on his boys, but he wouldn't tolerate the negative impact of a news story detailing how one of his players had been arrested. Warner simply had too much to lose. The Carlisle football team cleared a profit that exceeded $50,000 in 1907. The revenue came from Carlisle gate receipts for the eleven games that they played, and it was more than the salary paid to President Theodore Roosevelt, who in 1907 took home exactly $50,000.

Warner's team, in fact, bore a resemblance to a semipro outfit. Though some of his players had already graduated from Carlisle, Warner convinced them to remain on the squad; Warner found them jobs working on campus, and he allowed them to continue to live the good life in the athletic dorm. His best players sometimes stayed on the team for more than four years, which was the loosely enforced eligibility limit on the East Coast. And if a player skipped class or was struggling with his grades, Warner exerted his powerful influence at the school to make sure that player was on the field once kickoff rolled around.

How important was the athletic fund to Carlisle? Before Warner arrived, the school consistently operated at a deficit because of the minuscule appropriation from Congress. Pratt had been able to keep the school functioning by soliciting donations from religious and charitable organizations, but money from Warner's athletic fund allowed Pratt—and then

Mercer—to renovate the campus. The old barracks were restored and several new structures were erected, including an administration building, a college hospital, a print shop with state-of-the-art equipment, and a new wing of barracks. Warner's boys were the lifeblood of the school—and the first big-business team in college football history.

Six days after the Indians defeated Syracuse in Buffalo, the Warner publicity machine was humming. Working with his press agent Miller, Warner invited photographers from all the top East Coast dailies to Indian Field at Carlisle for an event that he billed as "Photographers' Day." Here photographers could snap as many pictures of his players as they wanted. In truth, Warner knew that Bucknell, Carlisle's opponent the following afternoon, wouldn't put up much of a fight against his Indian players. Expecting the press to ignore the game, Warner enticed the media to Carlisle by dangling the photo op.

The PR stunt, like most that Warner attempted, worked just as he had hoped. Camera-wielding men from New York, Chicago, and Philadelphia showed up to shoot portraits of the players in their uniforms on Indian Field, which Warner had built with money from the athletic fund on the same rocky pasture that the Indians first practiced on in the early 1890s. The next day they all stuck around to watch Carlisle play Bucknell. The first three and a half quarters of the game were a defensive struggle; neither team was able to sustain an offensive drive. After Carlisle scored a touchdown to take a 6–0 lead in the fourth quarter, Warner inserted Thorpe and several other second-teamers into the game. According to the rules at the time, the team that scored a touchdown then received the following kickoff. Warner instructed Thorpe to line up near the goal line and prepare to return the kick. Excited, Thorpe confidently jogged onto the field.

Dusk was now dropping over the Cumberland Valley. As the players took their positions for the kickoff, their shadows stretched across the field, growing longer with each tick of the clock. For the photographers, this meant there wasn't much good light left in the day to make a decent picture. Still, a few lingered, hoping to strike gold, to capture on film that one magical image that was as rare as catching a bolt of lightning with a click of the camera.

Then, it all happened in a startling few seconds: The Bucknell kicker hammered the ball and sent it flopping through the cool autumn air. Thorpe caught it and shot forward at full speed. He reached the thirty-yard line. He cut past tacklers and ran over defenders. He was at the fifty. He sprinted by a few more Bucknell players. He was at the forty. The thirty. Thorpe brushed off another tackler as if he were nothing more than a horsefly.

From the sideline, Warner's eyes burned with intensity. This was the type of skill that Thorpe had displayed during the tackling drill in pre-season practice, and Warner had been waiting for more than a month to see him duplicate that effort in a game. Now he was doing it, the football prodigy taking his first steps toward greatness. Certainly the crowd—including the photographers—understood they were seeing something special. They roared in delight as Thorpe continued his mad dash up the field.

He reached the twenty. The ten. The five. Just before he crossed into the end zone, Thorpe slowed, believing no one was within twenty yards of him. But then right before he scored, a Bucknell player dove at Thorpe and caught one of his ankles. Thorpe tripped and fell to the ground. When he hit the grass, the ball squirted out of his hands and rolled into the end zone. Another Carlisle player, Theodore Owl, leapt onto the ball, scoring a touchdown.

Carlisle won the game 15–0. The next day Thorpe's name and picture appeared in print for the first time. With one gallop through the gloaming, a legend was launched.

Wherever Pop Warner went—to the grocery store on North Hanover Street, to his doctor's office, to his favorite saloon—his mind was on football. Lately Warner wondered how he could get his players to move faster. He had always believed that speed and deception were the keys to winning, and now he wanted to create a formation that would both confuse the opposition and put his players in the best position to advance the ball down the field. Like virtually every college football team in the nation, Carlisle used the standard T-formation on offense—a quarterback and three backs lined up five yards behind him in a line. For days Warner

sketched out different alignments on pieces of paper. Then, in one flourish, he finally hit on something that he thought might work: a formation
he called the single wing.

The single wing as devised by Warner featured four backs: a quarterback, a fullback, a tailback, and a single wingback. Instead of having the
quarterback stand directly behind the center, Warner moved the quarterback, who stood in a crouch, five yards back. The fullback crouched next
to the quarterback and another back was lined up directly behind the
tackle. The remaining back, the lone wingback, was positioned outside
the tight end's back foot.

Once the ball was snapped to the quarterback, he would usually spin
180 degrees; then he had several options. With his back to the line, he
could hand off to another back, fake a handoff and run, or turn back
toward the line of scrimmage and plow straight into the middle of the
line. What would make the offense so hard to defend—and this would
prove to be the genius of the formation—was that all the backs in the single
wing were constantly spinning, reversing, faking handoffs, making handoffs, running the ball, passing the ball, blocking, and receiving. Also, because of the single wing's unbalanced line, the opposing defense would
constantly have to fight through double-teams and trap blocks.

When Warner introduced his novel offensive alignment to his players
during preseason practice, he was surprised at how quickly they mastered
it. "These Indian kids are born lovers of the game," Warner told a reporter. "They have speed and skill in use of hands and feet. They also have
highly developed powers of observation, handed down through genera-
tions." Though most whites in the country—including the superintendent
of all the Indian Schools in the United States, Estelle Reel, who would
hold her federal position until 1910—still believed that Indians were
physically inferior to whites, Warner knew otherwise. He was ahead of his
time, as he was about to prove once again with his new quick-hitting offense.

After more than a month of practicing the single wing, Warner decided to unveil it in a game. The single wing would make its maiden voyage on October 26 against Penn, a mere seven days after Carlisle had
defeated Bucknell.

On the day before the Penn game, the Carlisle campus felt different. There was an energy in the air, a feeling of excitement that reverberated throughout the school like an unseen cosmic force. The football games were no longer just for the boys who donned the uniforms. In a matter of hours, more than 150 students as well as the school band were going to board the train for Philadelphia to cheer on the Indian players as they battled Penn. For the Carlisle students who would use the money from their summer outings to pay their own way, this was a major social event. Boys and girls talked excitedly in the hours before their journey about all they would see. They would be chaperoned by several faculty members on the Pennsylvania Railroad train. As soon as they stepped off, they would tour Philadelphia, spend the night in a hotel, and then attend the game at Franklin Field. For many of the students, this was the most exciting time of their young lives.

On the afternoon of October 26, more than 22,000 fans pushed through the turnstiles and filed into the grandstands at Franklin Field. Nine out of ten in the stadium were rooting for the Quakers, and they expected another easy game. In the six previous matchups between Carlisle and Penn, the Indians had never won. But Carlisle had never before used the single wing.

From the opening minutes after kickoff on this bright autumn day that appeared as sweet as a dream, Penn was in trouble. After Carlisle received the opening kickoff, Warner instructed Mt. Pleasant to spin and hand the ball to Hauser, his fullback, and then Hauser was to throw a deep pass to William Gardner. Warner didn't want to wait to test whether or not the single-wing formation could be effective. He wanted to shock the Quakers right away.

Mt. Pleasant received the snap. He spun and handed the ball to Hauser, who ran a few yards to his right. Then he reared back and unleashed a beautiful spiral, sending the ball traveling in a sweeping, grandiose arc. Many in the crowd had never seen a football thrown so far before; it seemed to fly through the azure sky farther than anyone could even *kick* a football. The ball came down in the arms of Gardner, who had been streaking down the middle of the field. The play ended up gaining forty yards. The pro-Penn crowd fell eerily quiet, as if they didn't believe what they had just seen. Penn players looked to the sideline at their coach, wondering how they should defend the formation. Reporters from papers

up and down the East Coast and as far west as Denver grabbed their pencils and started writing in their notebooks. The reporter from the
Philadelphia North American marveled, "Such a pass, that first trial. It will
be talked of often this year. No such puny little pass as Penn makes, but a
lordly throw."

A few plays after the long pass, Mt. Pleasant booted a field goal. The
Indians were now flush with confidence. The Carlisle defense smothered
the Penn offense, forcing a quick punt. The outcome of the game was
sealed in the second quarter shortly after Thorpe entered the game as a
tailback. Subbing for Albert Payne, who suffered a knee injury, Thorpe
was tackled for a loss the first time he touched the ball. Warner screamed
from the sideline that Thorpe had failed to follow his wall of blockers.
Warner and Exendine had been telling Thorpe for weeks that the only way
he would succeed as a tailback was to show patience and wait for his
blockers. But Thorpe, like many young backs, simply wanted to run as fast
as he could down the field. Warner emphasized that he needed to be more
disciplined and let the play unfold before cutting up the field.

Thorpe learned his lesson. The next time he received a toss from Mt.
Pleasant, he rocketed around the end as if an engine powered his legs and
sprinted past the Penn players as if their feet were nailed to the ground,
blazing seventy-five yards for a touchdown. The Quakers were flum-
moxed. Considered one of the top teams in the nation, Penn simply
didn't have the speed to compete with Carlisle—never mind an adequate
game plan. When the Quaker defense expected a running play, Carlisle
passed; when Penn anticipated a pass, the Indians ran. Carlisle won
26–6, but the game was even more lopsided than the score. Carlisle out-
gained Penn 402 yards to 26 and by the second half the Quaker players
were moping around as if they wanted to go home.

The newspapermen covering the game sensed that this was a touch-
stone moment in college football history, one that announced Carlisle
had arrived as the newest big-time program on the national scene. The
Denver Express wrote, "The Indian on the football field stands in the very
front rank. Man for man, pound for pound he has no superior. Through
all the years of 'mollycoddling' and paternalism on the part of the 'dominant race' the hereditary trait in the Indian still manifests itself."

The Philadelphia Press reported, "With racial savagery and ferocity the

Carlisle Indian eleven grabbed Penn's football scalp and dragged their victim up and down Franklin Field, not relinquishing their grip until the seventy minutes of time allotted to the practice was up and the figures 26 to 6 told the tale. Throughout the exhibition all but a few of the 22,000 spectators sat amazed and benumbed, unable to lend any assistance except to cheer now and then when a rally of the pale faces seemed imminent, but that did not have any tonic effect."

The next weekend Carlisle traveled to the Polo Grounds in New York City to play Princeton. Though the skies over Manhattan were dark and dumping rain on the stadium, a crowd of 30,000 huddled under umbrellas to watch the game. Late in the second quarter, a large contingent of Indians, wearing traditional dress of buckskin shirts, buffalo-hide leggings, and moccasins, began sidestepping through the crowd and making their way to seats in the grandstands. Quietly, a few Princeton fans clapped at the sight of the Indians. Moments later, a few more joined. Then more. Before the Indians had found their seats, a mob of white Princeton fans were welcoming the Indians to the game by loudly cheering for them. It was more evidence to Carlisle officials of the transcendent allure of the school's football team.

The rain continued to fall on the Polo Grounds. By the time the teams lined up for the second-half kickoff, the field was a large pit of mud. Dating back to Warner's first days at Carlisle, his players had rarely played well in soggy conditions. As far as Warner could tell, the Indian boys loved the game of football just as much as the white kids he had coached. But when it rained or snowed or the temperature dropped below freezing, the Indians seemed to lose their passion for the sport. Warner never could break them of that tendency.

Two years earlier, fans of the Canton Athletic Club in Ohio, realizing that Carlisle struggled on wet fields, went to the extreme measure of spending three days spraying the Canton field with a fire hose before the two teams squared off. The ploy worked: Canton won the game 9–0.

Warner prodded his boys to ramp up their effort level whenever the skies spit rain, but none of his motivational techniques worked. When Warner asked one of his players, a center named Little Boy, why he seemed to lose his urge to play hard when the weather worsened, Little Boy replied, "Football no good fun in mud and snow."

The slick playing conditions also negated Carlisle's quickness advantage over Princeton, whose roster was chock-full of big, burly, slow-footed players. The Carlisle boys had trouble with their footing and the larger Princeton squad succeeded in pushing the smaller Indians back on their heels. The Indians couldn't use their speed to run around the Princeton players on defense, and on offense Carlisle struggled to throw the waterlogged ball. The high-scoring Indians, who were so dazzling to watch that some fans paid up to seven dollars for tickets, never got on track and Princeton shut out Carlisle, 16–0.

The quest for a perfect season was over, but in the locker room after the game Warner reminded his players that they still had a chance to make history. In just seven days Carlisle was scheduled to play Harvard, one of its most bitter rivals. The Indians had never beaten the buttoned-down Ivy Leaguers in ten tries, but now Warner knew he would be bringing a different kind of team to Cambridge, one that he believed was unbeatable—as long as the playing conditions were good.

It was early in the third quarter at Soldiers Field in Cambridge, Massachusetts. Carlisle's Frank Mt. Pleasant fielded a punt on his fifteen-yard line. After securing the ball, Mt. Pleasant cut left and dodged a tackler. A Harvard player came flying through the air at Mt. Pleasant's midsection. He ducked and, in a flourish of athleticism that left the crowd of thirty thousand *ooohing* and *ahhhing*, flipped the defender over his back. He broke a few more tackles, put a stop-and-go move on another Harvard player, then sprinted into the end zone to cap an 85-yard punt return. The score was a thing of beauty—even the Harvard fans cheered Mt. Pleasant's run—and it gave Carlisle an 18–10 lead over the Crimson early in the third quarter.

Minutes later, Carlisle had the ball again. Mt. Pleasant handed the ball off on what appeared to be an ordinary running play that netted only a few yards. When the whistle blew, a pile of bodies was stacked on top of the Carlisle runner. Harvard's Waldo Pierce, a burly 205-pound tackle, was in the middle of this mound of humanity. As Pierce tried to get up, something went off inside of him. It might have been frustration; it might have been something worse, like racism. But as soon as he got on his feet, he threw a powerful punch at Carlisle's William Gardner, who never saw it coming. The left hook landed squarely on Gardner's jaw in full view of the referee.

As Gardner lay on the ground, the referee tossed Pierce out of the game. But instead of deflating the morale of the Harvard defense, Pierce's ejection made them only more determined. Moments after Pierce was sent off the field, a Crimson player smashed through the line of scrimmage and laid a devastating hit on Carlisle's Pete Hauser, who fumbled the ball. Harvard recovered. A few minutes later the Crimson scored a touchdown to pull within three points of Carlisle, 18–15.

Midway through the fourth quarter, the Indians had the ball on first-and-ten deep in their own territory. In the huddle Mt. Pleasant told his teammates that the game was theirs to win; they simply had to move the ball on this possession. "We've got to score again!" Mt. Pleasant yelled. The Indian quarterback then took over. On one play he'd receive the snap, spin, fake a handoff, and dash around the right end for five yards. On another, he'd fake a pitch to the halfback, fade back a few yards, then fire a pass to an end over the middle for ten yards. To the fans in the stands, Mt. Pleasant looked like a master of ceremonies, deftly controlling the ebb and flow of the game.

When Carlisle moved the ball to its own 35-yard line, Mt. Pleasant again took the snap, spun, faked a handoff to his tailback, drifted to his right, and then faded back to pass. He searched down the field for Exendine, but his husky end was covered by a Harvard defender. Then he flicked the ball in a perfect spiral to his back Bill Winnie, who was running down the left sideline. The ball landed in Winnie's arms and he ran all the way to Harvard's four-yard line before he was tackled. A few plays later Hauser, Carlisle's fullback, received a handoff from Mt. Pleasant and tore through the middle of the line to score a touchdown. Harvard's spirit had been broken—and so had the Crimson's winning streak over Carlisle. After the final whistle sounded and the Indians had defeated Harvard 23–15, thousands of fans—including a handful wearing Harvard's colors—jumped over a fence that separated the stands from the players and cheered wildly as they escorted the Indians off the field.

The party was just beginning. After they rode back to Carlisle in a Pullman train car, the students begged the school's superintendent, William Mercer, to hold a spur-of-the-moment victory parade. Mercer agreed. Dressed in their nightshirts and with pillowcases draped over their heads just for the fun of it, the boys of Carlisle—football players and nonplayers alike—marched through the town streets. They held torches and sang Indian songs as they reveled in their triumph. Many of the white residents in Carlisle stood and smiled from their doors and front lawns as the long procession of Indian students, which included a few boys carrying a stretcher that had on it the "remains" of a Harvard player, celebrated in the darkness. The Indian boys also poked fun at the Harvard players, doing their best imitations of the highbrow Cambridge accent in their limited English.

Thorpe had watched the entire Harvard game from the bench, but he knew his time was coming. Carlisle was becoming more dominant by the day, and as Thorpe joined his teammates in their victory march through town, he couldn't wait to become a starter and really give this town something to celebrate: a national championship.

For their last two games of the 1907 season, Carlisle traveled to the Midwest to show off their new brand of football—and to rake in bundles of money at the gates. The locomotive carrying the team first pulled into the depot at Minneapolis. They played the University of Minnesota on November 16. The interest was so intense in the matchup that the *Minneapolis Tribune* set up a booth in front of the Tribune Building on Fourth Street where fans who didn't have tickets could monitor the game. The paper arranged for a telephone line to be linked from Northrop Field to the *Tribune* offices. A play-by-play account would be given over the telephone, and then a reporter shouting into a megaphone would relay the action to ticketless fans. "The megaphone man [will be] in instant communication with the battle scene," the paper reported on the eve of the game.

Hundreds of Indians from reservations in the Dakotas and Wisconsin sat in the stands of the outdoor field on the Minnesota campus and watched as Carlisle quickly fell behind the Golden Gophers. Four plays into the game, Minnesota kicked a field goal to take the lead. But late in the first quarter, the Indians struck back. Facing a fourth-and-goal from the Minnesota five-yard line, Warner instructed Mt. Pleasant to fake a field-goal attempt. Mt. Pleasant did as ordered: After receiving the snap, he acted as if he were going to drop-kick the ball. But at the last moment, he pulled the ball back in his arm and zipped it to Captain Antonio Lubo, who was eligible to catch a pass even though he had lined up as a tackle. The deception worked. Lubo was wide open and he easily snatched the ball out of the air to score a touchdown from five yards out to give Carlisle a 6–4 lead.

Minutes later, Carlisle was again on offense. Instead of relying on a trick play to score, this time Mt. Pleasant rifled a 35-yard pass to Gardner, who scored easily. Even the Minnesota fans marveled at the style of the Indians. Few in the Midwest had seen football like this before: This was a fast-paced ballet of athleticism and grace, not the lumbering scrum to which they were accustomed. Though Mt. Pleasant—Carlisle's top player—hurt his thumb and hip late in the game and had to be helped to the sideline, the Indians beat Minnesota 12–4. No one in the crowd was more impressed than Amos Alonzo Stagg, the coach of the University of Chicago, a team that Carlisle would face in seven days.

The next morning the Carlisle team rode a train into the Windy City and checked into a downtown hotel. Warner was upset that Mt. Pleasant had been injured. But he knew that he had a bigger, faster version of Mt. Pleasant on his bench in Thorpe, and it was only a matter of time before he was going to turn him loose on the field.

That night in his room Warner wrote a letter to a friend back east.

"We had a hard fight to win from Minnesota and victory cost us dearly, in that Mt. Pleasant broke a bone in his thumb and hurt his hip so badly that he can't get into the game Saturday except for a miracle. . . . Exendine also had a bad injury to his side but may be able to play. Coach Stagg and three of his men saw us play Saturday and the game was so hard that we had to show everything we had, and we have had no time to get anything new ready. We have not seen Chicago play at all, but I hear they are one of the best teams in the West and the best Chicago ever had. They are expected to win and it will take the very best efforts on our part to win. I think the boys will win but with Frank out of the game, it looks pretty blue. Carlisle has always fallen down at the end of the season, and if the boys lose we will not finish the season in a 'Blaze of Glory,' but we have a big game to wind up the season and perhaps the size of the enemy will key the boys up to their best efforts. Nothing short of their Pennsylvania efforts will win from Chicago."

Warner had been anxiously eyeing the Chicago date on the schedule for months because he wanted to match wits with Stagg. More than any two coaches in the country, Warner and Stagg were evolving the game of football, one innovation at a time. In his workshop in Carlisle, for instance, Warner became the first to build such equipment as blocking sleds and tackling dummies. Warner also fashioned fiber padding for uniforms that helped prevent injuries and running shoes with cleats for better traction. Stagg was also coming up with imaginative ways to gain the upper hand on his opponents. He was the first coach to try the onside kick, the man in motion, and the flea-flicker. Understanding that fans needed to be able to identify one player from the next, Stagg was the first coach to put numbers on the backs of his players' uniforms. He was also the first to award his players varsity letters.

Warner knew Stagg's biography well. In 1862, as Stonewall Jackson was leading his troops on Manassas, Virginia, Stagg was born in West Orange, New Jersey, the son of a cobbler. The young Stagg was an All-American end at Yale who landed his first coaching job in 1889 at the School of Christian Workers, which eventually became Springfield College, in Massachusetts. While at Springfield he became close friends with an instructor at the school, Dr. James Naismith. After Naismith hung two peach baskets high on a pole on either side of the gym at the Springfield YMCA in 1891, thereby inventing the game of basketball, he invited Stagg to play in the first public basketball game as a faculty member. On March 11, 1892, Stagg scored his team's only point in a 5–1 loss.

In the fall of '92 Stagg moved to the shores of Lake Michigan to become Chicago's head coach. A deeply religious man who once considered attending seminary school, Stagg insisted that his boys always show sportsmanship even in the face of a loss and be as honest and hardworking as anyone in the nation. Stagg didn't drink or smoke or gamble or cuss, and he expected his players to follow his example. He saw himself as a role model and teacher whose classroom was the football field. "The [coaching] profession is one of the noblest and perhaps the most far reaching in building up the manhood of our country," Stagg said.

Before the Carlisle game, Stagg had labeled his 1907 squad, which had won the Big Ten championship and was unbeaten and untied, as his "best ever team." But Stagg had been flabbergasted by the speed and quickness the Indian players had displayed against Minnesota. He knew his only chance for victory was to slow Carlisle down, especially their ends. So he came up with a unique game plan: Whenever the ball was snapped, his defenders were supposed to immediately knock down the Carlisle ends, targeting Exendine especially, and not let them get back on their feet until the play was over. At the time, there was no rule against such a tactic, and Stagg believed that this would smother Carlisle's passing attack.

On the afternoon of the game, the air was cool and the skies were clear over Chicago's Marshall Field. More than 28,000 fans jammed into the stadium. At both ends of the field, wooden platforms had been built to accommodate hundreds of standing-room-only fans. Before kickoff, there weren't any open spaces left on either structure.

For the first three quarters of the game, Stagg's plan worked to perfection: Carlisle struggled to move the ball because its ends were tackled the moment the plays started. Warner was furious. He paced up and down the sideline, burning through one cigarette after the next while trying to figure a countermove to Stagg's scoundrelly tactic. Early in the fourth quarter, with his team clinging to an 8–4 lead over Chicago, Warner got an idea. He was about to make the boldest chess move of his coaching career.

During a stop in play when Carlisle had the ball, he called out for Exendine and Pete Hauser. Hauser was filling in for the injured Mt. Pleasant at quarterback, and he and Exendine trotted over to their coach. Warner quickly detailed his latest trick play. After telling his players what he wanted them to do, Warner told them to get back onto the field. This, he said, was their chance to stun Stagg and his Chicago squad.

The ball was snapped to Hauser. Exendine, instead of running up the field and facing the prospect of being tackled by one or more Chicago defenders, immediately sprinted for the sideline. As Hauser drifted deep behind the line of scrimmage and tried to hold the ball as long as he could, Exendine left the field of play. He ran behind the Carlisle bench, past Warner and past Thorpe, and then reentered the field some twenty-five yards from where he left it. The Chicago defenders, believing that Exendine wouldn't factor in to the play after he exited the field, all turned their attention to Hauser, who continued to patiently wait in the backfield and avoid tacklers as Exendine ran his unlikely pass route. Finally, just before a Chicago defender hit Hauser, he chucked the ball as far and high as he could. It floated through the fall sky, and Stagg and the rest of the Chicago bench quickly turned and saw Exendine, alone, thirty-five yards beyond the line of scrimmage. There wasn't a Chicago defender within twenty yards of him, and he caught the ball effortlessly and jogged thirty more yards into the end zone for a touchdown.

The Carlisle players shouted and hopped up and down in celebration; they had outsmarted the white boys, which was always one of their greatest joys. Stagg was so mad that he nearly belted out a four-letter word. At the time, there was no rule against a player leaving the field and then coming back onto it in the middle of the play, and Warner exploited this loophole to his advantage. Though such a play would be declared illegal the following season, Warner had succeeded in outwitting his greatest rival of the day. Stagg, who was an avid reader of Horatio Alger's dime novels in which men became heroes by being courageous and honest, felt that Warner had cheated. Nonetheless, the play stood and Carlisle won the game 18–4.

The victory by the Indians prompted a reporter from the *Chicago Tribune* to write that the Carlisle team had "demonstrated their superiority over the Maroons individually, collectively, and in every department of the game. They showed themselves masters of modern football and gave such an exhibition of its possibilities as will not be forgotten by anyone."

Warner and his players traveled back to Carlisle to enjoy a Thanksgiving feast. Warner, in particular, had a lot to be thankful for: The school had pocketed nearly $17,000 in gate receipts from the Chicago game alone, setting a single-game record for Carlisle. Warner's vision of creating a new type of football team had come alive. And he firmly believed that he couldn't have done it if he had been coaching white boys. "The success of the Indians has been due to the rough, hardy outdoor life that the players have been inured to since the time they were born," Warner wrote in a magazine. "In addition to this purely physical explanation, there is a psychological one; the Indians know that people regard them as an inferior race, unable to compete successfully in any line of endeavor with the white men, and as a result they are imbued with a fighting spirit, when pitted against their white brethren, that carries them a long way to victory."

The Carlisle Indian football program was growing. The team had finished the 1907 season at 10-1 and had outscored its opponents 267 to 62. Still, Warner believed that his best days at Carlisle lay ahead. He had that kid named Thorpe whom he hadn't yet fully turned loose on the football field. When he did, Warner didn't think anyone could beat his Indians. But the coach would soon have a problem, one that threatened to derail all of his goals: Jim Thorpe went *poof!*—vanishing like a ghost from the Carlisle campus.

No one in the history of the college game—before or since—was harder to take down than Jim Thorpe during his legendary season of 1912, when he scored twenty-five touchdowns and accounted for 198 points. (Courtesy Cumberland County Historical Society)

8

A COUPLE OF WELL-PAID AMATEURS

Four years after Warner outwitted Stagg in 1907 . . .

J im Thorpe sauntered down the main street of Anadarko, Oklahoma, one of the wildest Indian towns on the frontier. He had
just thrown back a few drinks in one of the saloons and was enjoying the feeling of the afternoon sunshine on his face. It was late in the
summer of 1911, and it had been two long years since Thorpe had been
enrolled at Carlisle and playing football for Pop Warner. These days, he
was planning to lead a life of farming. He'd recently purchased a horse and
buggy and was content to be home again, surrounded by childhood
friends and family.

Thorpe made his way down Anadarko's dusty main drag, passing a few
more taverns and shops. Then, in the distance, he spotted a tall, muscular
figure lumbering toward him. This man was as husky as some of his teammates back at Carlisle had been, and when Thorpe stepped closer and
squinted into the sun, he realized that this indeed *was* an old friend from
the school: his mentor and teammate Albert Exendine. Thorpe excitedly
ran up to Ex, the big brother figure who taught him more about football
than anyone and who helped him acclimate to life at Carlisle. Thorpe
smiled at his friend as the two wrapped their arms around each other.

Exendine, now the football coach at Otterbein College in Ohio, was on his summer break visiting home. As he greeted his old protégé, Ex looked Thorpe up and down, studying him closely, as if he were a piece of art. *Could this be the same skinny Jim Thorpe that I knew at Carlisle?* Exendine thought. *Could he really have gotten this . . . this . . . big?*

During the previous two years, Thorpe had spent time playing minor league baseball in the Carolinas, and he enjoyed the freedom from Warner. He didn't have to abide by any of Warner's rules when he was swatting balls in the minors, and he wasn't locked down by the structure of the school. In that time, Thorpe had bulked up and filled out, as if he'd swallowed fifty pounds of concrete. He now weighed 185 pounds and his muscles were as well proportioned as those of Michelangelo's *David.* Exendine knew that Warner's 1911 football squad could use Thorpe, and after they exchanged pleasantries, he began lobbying on Warner's behalf.

"Why don't you go back and finish at Carlisle?" Ex asked his friend.

"They wouldn't want me there now," Thorpe replied.

"You bet they would," Exendine said.

Thorpe considered the offer: football at Carlisle. Maybe, Thorpe thought, he could help Warner make one more charge at national greatness. He had come so close once before.

Three years earlier, in the fall of 1908, the chants started late in the second half against Villanova. "We want Jim," the crowd at Indian Field bellowed. "We want Jim. We want Jim . . ."

Warner stood on the sideline on this crisp September afternoon, trying to block out the noise. Out on the field his team was unexpectedly struggling against Villanova. Warner knew his current squad in 1908 would be weaker than his mighty '07 team—after all, his two best players from last season, Mt. Pleasant and Exendine, had finished their studies at Carlisle—but Warner didn't anticipate that his team would be tied 0–0 with Villanova with only a few minutes left in their game on September 26.

Warner walked over to Thorpe, sitting on the bench. He had planned to keep Thorpe on the sideline because he didn't want to risk getting him injured in what he thought was going to be an easy victory. But now he needed his star-in-the-making to flash his stuff. Tapping him on the shoulder, Warner told Thorpe to get into the game.

The Indian Field crowd exploded. In the first two games of the season, Thorpe had been spectacular. In his first game as a starter at Carlisle against Conway Hall, a prep school, on September 19, Thorpe had five touchdown runs of fifty yards or more and threw a beautiful thirty-yard touchdown strike to Pete Hauser in Carlisle's 53–0 win. The following week, Thorpe, running and throwing the ball all over the field, led the Indians to a 35–0 victory over Lebanon Valley College.

Thorpe jogged onto the field in his easy, graceful gait. With the ball at Carlisle's thirty-yard line, he lined up a few yards behind the center for his first play of the game. He received the snap, then bulled forward, charging into the cluster of players at the line of scrimmage. From the sideline, the fans heard a loud *thwack*. For a moment Thorpe disappeared into a swarm of defenders. But then, out of the mass of grunting players, he emerged, dragging a Villanova player with him. After a momentary struggle, Thorpe broke free and tore up the field as his legs pumped high. More defenders came at him. He pushed them aside, yelling, "Out of my way! Get out of my way!" He then outran the rest of the Villanova team and dashed into the end zone.

One play. That's all it took for Thorpe to shatter the will of the Villanova team—and that's how long Warner kept Thorpe in the game. After the touchdown gallop, Thorpe took his seat back on the bench. Carlisle won 10–0.

With Thorpe leading the charge, Carlisle mowed through its early season schedule. On October 3, Thorpe kicked three field goals as the Indians beat Penn State 12–5. A week later Carlisle traveled to Buffalo, New York, to face Syracuse. Always searching for any advantage he could invent, Warner told the press in the days before the game that many of his players were injured and run-down; frankly, Warner confessed to reporters, he didn't think his players had a lick of a chance to defeat those big boys at Syracuse.

Warner continued the charade on game day. When the Indians walked onto the field a few hours before kickoff to begin their pregame warm-up, many of the players had bandages wrapped around their fingers and heads. Some limped. The confidence of the Syracuse players ballooned at the sight of the wounded Indians, which was exactly what Warner hoped for. Once the game started, the Indians tore off their bandages and ran as if they'd been resting for weeks. Carlisle overwhelmed Syracuse with its speed, winning 12–0.

Just as in the previous season, reports of Carlisle's talent traveled across the country as if pushed by a relentless autumn breeze. Newspapers from New York to San Francisco ran stories that detailed the football power that Warner was building in the heart of Pennsylvania. The press attention heightened the anticipation for Carlisle's next game, on October 24 against Penn—the Indians' biggest rival, whose campus was only 120 miles away from Carlisle. Both teams were undefeated and Warner again tried to float through the newspapermen that his boys were badly injured and would likely struggle mightily against the Quakers. But the Penn squad didn't fall into the trap. One Quaker player said, "We place as much stock in the ambulance clang that comes from Carlisle as we would in the story of a woman telling how old she is."

Again as in the previous year, a swarm of students from Carlisle paid their own way to travel by train to Philly and watch their classmates take on Penn. The night before the game many of the students rode streetcars to the downtown department store Gimbels. Located at Eighth Street and Market, Gimbels—"Nobody but Nobody Undersells Gimbels"—was the primary rival to Macy's, the nation's other leading department store. The students were wide-eyed as they rode elevators for the first time in their lives, saw the finest clothes of the day on display, and carefully inspected shiny new items in the store's expansive toy department, such as dolls and model cars. When they went to eat in the cafeteria, an employee asked the female students to sing a few native songs before dinner, and they happily obliged. When their food arrived on platters carried by black waiters, the Indian boys and girls felt special, like kings and queens.

With a near sellout crowd of 26,000 looking on at Philadelphia's Franklin Field, the players from Penn ran onto the grass with an air of supreme confidence. They had outscored their opponents 104–4 over their previous seven games, and the Quakers were still seething over their 26–6 loss to Carlisle the previous year. Early on, it looked as if Penn was going to return the favor with a crushing performance. The Quakers scored first on a short touchdown run in the first quarter to take a 6–0 lead. But then both offenses began to sputter. Late in the fourth quarter the score was still 6–0 when Carlisle had the ball on its forty-yard line. As the crowd yearned for some offensive fireworks, Warner looked at his star player. It was his time to blast off.

Thorpe lined up at tailback. Taking a pitch from the quarterback, he scrambled toward the left end. Zigging and zagging, he nimbly danced around would-be tacklers. From the stands it looked as if the Penn defenders were trying to corral a ghost: Thorpe left the Quakers clawing at nothing but air as he sidestepped one defender after the next. Then, in a mesmerizing burst of speed, Thorpe broke free into the open field. The run was an arresting bit of theater, and the Indians in the stands who still had use of their vocal cords yelled wildly. But then at the five-yard line, a Penn player who had the angle on Thorpe lunged at him and grabbed him around the waist. Thorpe dove for the end zone. He came down on the chalk to complete his sixty-yard run. The referee signaled a touchdown.

On the sideline, Warner clapped his hands together and shook his head in admiration. It was at this precise moment that Warner knew with absolute certainty that Thorpe had the potential to be the greatest football player of his time. Years later, on the static-filled screen of Warner's memory, this was one image that never faded as he would be able to replay Thorpe's effort against Penn over and over again.

Thorpe kicked the extra point to tie the game at 6–6, which wound up being the final score. This was the only game in 1908 that Penn, the eventual national champion according to most writers, didn't win.

For the rest of the 1908 season, as reporters around the nation rhapsodized over Thorpe and searched for fresh adjectives and new metaphors to describe his play, fans in the grandstands closely watched the Indian tailback, eager to see what he would do next. Against Harvard on November 7, Thorpe was bothered by a sprained right ankle but he nonetheless twice hypnotized the crowd at Soldiers Field in Cambridge, Massachusetts. In the third quarter, deep in Carlisle's territory, Thorpe received a pitch from quarterback Mike Balenti. Drifting to his right, Thorpe rifled a pass twenty yards down the field that hit Fritz Hendricks in the chest. After taking a few steps, Hendricks lateraled the ball to another Carlisle end, Captain Emil Wauseka, who rumbled for thirty more yards before he was tackled. A few plays later, Thorpe's field goal attempt was blocked, but he made up for that when he took another pitch from

Balenti, sliced his way through the line, cut to the outside, then sprinted up the field. Sixty-five yards later, he was tackled at Harvard's eight-yard line. Again Carlisle didn't score—the Crimson held the Indians on downs—but Thorpe had wowed the crowd with his silky grace and jarring power. Harvard won the game 17–0 thanks to their superior size and strength—and the fact that all of Thorpe's eight field-goal attempts were either blocked or missed—but even the Crimson players were still in awe of that big Indian kid Thorpe. Many of them would talk for days about how Thorpe hammered one of his kickoffs so hard that it spun through the sunshine and flew through the goalposts. When it finally hit the ground, the ball had traveled more than fifty-five yards.

Seven days later, in a driving rainstorm in Pittsburgh against the University of Western Pennsylvania, Thorpe struggled for most of the afternoon, sliding all over the muddy field. Then, late in the game, he took over. He received a pitch and thundered over the right tackle. Breaking through the grasp of several Western Penn players, he willed his way into the end zone for the only score of the day. Carlisle won 6–0.

The plume of white vapor hissed into the sky like a snake slithering toward the sun as the fireman shoveled coal into the train's furnace. The engineer double-checked his instruments, confirming that the pressure levels of steam and water were good. Before the locomotive pushed out of the station at Philadelphia, all of the passengers' bags were tossed into several baggage cars. The mail was placed in a freight car. And the Carlisle Indian football players took their seats in their Pullman car.

The conductor bellowed, "All aboard!" and the large metal wheels slowly began to creak and grind. Steam shot out of the engine, and the locomotive picked up its pace. Eventually, it reached about sixty miles per hour as it chugged through the Pennsylvania countryside. If they wanted to, the Indian players could open their windows and stick their heads out to feel the force of the speed on their faces.

A few days after beating Western Pennsylvania and returning to their campus, Carlisle was back on the train at the Philadelphia station and heading to Minneapolis to play the University of Minnesota—the start of a punishing road trip for Warner and his boys. After they took on the Golden Gophers of Minnesota on November 21, the itinerary called for

Carlisle to travel south to play the University of St. Louis. After making a brief stop in Lawrence, Kansas, to play the Haskell Institute—Thorpe's old school—the Indians were going to move on to Lincoln and play the University of Nebraska. Carlisle was scheduled to finish their season at the University of Denver, in the shadow of the Rocky Mountains. All told, over a span of sixteen consecutive days away from Carlisle, the Indians would travel some five thousand miles by train. In the early twentieth century not even professional baseball players trekked so far in so short a time.

Warner worried like an expectant father. He never knew how his Indians were going to be affected by life on the road, and this was one of the longest road trips of his career. When the train carrying the team stopped in Chicago's Grand Central Station, the players left the train for a meal in the depot and to see the sights. The players always looked forward to these stops at the railroad stations. In every large American city the rail station was as exquisite as any structure. It was a center point of the community, a hub for news, and no expense was spared in building these cathedrals of transportation. Chicago's Grand Central, for instance, was made of brick, brownstone, and granite, and it featured marble floors, stained-glass windows, a marble fireplace, and Corinthian columns. On the northeast corner of the building stood a 247-foot bell tower that held an eleven-thousand-pound bell. When the tower's thirteen-foot clock, which at one time was the largest in the United States, struck the top of the hour, the bell would chime, sending a massive clang through the center of the Windy City.

Warner was afraid that the long trip would wear down his boys. All the time they spent on the train—it took more than twenty-four hours to finally reach Minneapolis—was exhausting, and it showed in their play against the Golden Gophers. Listless and apathetic, Carlisle was pushed around by Minnesota and lost 11–6. Five days later, the Indians regrouped and thumped the University of St. Louis, 17–0. After the game, the team climbed back aboard the Union Pacific and traveled three hundred miles to Lawrence, Kansas, where they beat Haskell in an exhibition game, 12–0. The Indians then ventured north into the middle of cattle country, to Lincoln, Nebraska.

Warner had arranged the final two games of the season at the last minute: He agreed to play Nebraska and the University of Denver only after Carlisle was guaranteed a flat fee of $2,500 for both games. In Lincoln, all eyes were again on Thorpe, whom the fans in the heartland had seen only in fuzzy black-and-white newspaper photographs. At one point against the Cornhuskers, Thorpe scooped up a fumble and ran thirty-eight yards for a touchdown. Warner used virtually every play his Indians had ever practiced in the Nebraska game: Carlisle ran reverses, fake kicks, catch-and-laterals, and several long passes. This was football as entertainment like none of the fans had ever seen, and Carlisle won 37–6. After the final whistle blew, the polite midwestern crowd roundly applauded the Indians as the players hustled back to their locker room.

The Indians boarded another train and were carried five hundred miles west across the corn- and wheat fields of Nebraska and into Colorado, finally arriving at Denver, the last stop on their marathon trip. A few hours before the game against the University of Denver, storm clouds rolled over the Rockies and unloaded heavy snow on Denver. Lacking good footing, Thorpe struggled. He fumbled a few times and frequently slipped to the ground. But Pete Hauser kicked a pair of field goals and Carlisle edged Denver 8–4.

With their final record for the 1908 season standing at 10-2-1, the players boarded their train for the long journey back to Carlisle. As the locomotive pulled away from the depot in the Mile High City, the players could finally relax. Thorpe in particular needed the rest. He'd been hit so hard in the Denver game that the referees had stopped play a few times so he could catch his breath and gather his wits. But bigger problems than a few crushing hits awaited Thorpe: His football career at Carlisle was about to come to an abrupt halt.

The blond-haired, blue-eyed young man roamed center field with quickness and determination, zeroing in on fly balls like a bee to a springtime flower. At the plate he didn't possess as much power as his thick build would suggest, but he was a good contact hitter. Once he reached base, he tormented pitchers by always threatening to steal. But what most distinguished the player everyone called "Wilson" was his passion for the game. He may not have had Big League talent, but he certainly possessed the doggedness of an all-star.

It was the beginning of summer in 1909, and Dwight Eisenhower was trying to make a little extra money. Shortly after graduating from Abilene

High, Ike reported to the local minor league team that played in the Central Kansas League. Not wanting to take any chances, Eisenhower told the manager that his name was Wilson. Ike had just become reacquainted with his old friend Swede Hazlett, and Swede was egging him on to apply to the Naval Academy in Annapolis or the Military Academy at West Point. At this point in his life Eisenhower was still deciding where he wanted to go to school, but if he made it into either of the academies, like all incoming cadets and midshipmen, he would have to sign an NCAA eligibility card that included fifteen questions about whether or not he had ever played professional sports. Eisenhower desperately wanted to be a football player and a baseball player when he reached college, and if he went to either Army or Navy, he fully intended to sign that card. But if it were ever revealed that he had earned money while playing professional sports, he would be in violation of the Honor Code at those schools and could be expelled, ending a potential career in the military even before it began.

So that summer he was "Wilson" when he strode to the plate for an at-bat or jogged to take his position in center field. For the season Wilson went 63 for 219 (a. 288 batting average), scored 43 runs, stole 20 bases, and had the time of his life as he played in front of a smattering of fans in a thin row of bleachers surrounded by an ocean of cornfields. It was no wonder that every time he put on his cotton uniform, Wilson couldn't suppress his Big League smile.

When the Indians returned to campus after their three-day trip from Denver in November 1908, they were greeted by an outbreak of measles. Several students had contracted the virus, and it caused a tremor of fear across the campus. Hundreds of students who had died of measles were buried on the school grounds, and the mere mention of the sickness was motivation for students to run away from Carlisle. To make sure that his football players didn't come in contact with any of the stricken students, Warner sequestered the players in the athletic dorm. None of his boys got sick—this time.

Thorpe soon rejoined the track team. With Warner acting as his coach and Exendine as his mentor, Thorpe further solidified his reputation as a gifted all-around athlete at each meet. Against Lafayette College in Easton, Pennsylvania, in the spring of 1909, Thorpe won six gold medals and one bronze. He was so impressive in the 100-yard dash (he finished third), the 120-yard hurdles (first), the 220-yard low hurdles (first), the broad jump (first), the high jump (first), the shot put (first), and the discus (first) that a few newspapermen reported that Thorpe had single-handedly defeated Lafayette. It was an exaggeration, but it contributed to the growing Thorpe mythology.

When the track season was over, Thorpe finished his studies for the school year at Carlisle and on June 6, 1909—very nearly the same day that Eisenhower reported to the local baseball team—he made his way to the Cumberland Valley train station. As he stood on the platform, he was full of dread. He was waiting to take the 10:05 A.M. train to his summer outing job, working on a farm. For once, Warner's munificence didn't keep Thorpe and several other football players from being assigned to participate in the summer outing program, where students worked and lived with white families. Thorpe enjoyed being outdoors, but now he wanted the independence to do what he wanted to do, when he wanted to do it.

A few minutes before the train arrived, two familiar faces approached: Joseph Libby and Jesse Young Deer. The two Carlisle students played with Thorpe on the football team, and Libby and Young Deer told Thorpe that they weren't heading out to a white man's farm or anywhere else to work in the summer outing system. Instead, they said that they were traveling to North Carolina to spend the summer playing baseball. It took Thorpe only a few moments to ask if he could tag along with them. Thorpe had never been introspective and he rarely analyzed the positives and negatives when making a decision. He was a man of action, of impulse, and when the train arrived, Thorpe didn't think twice about joining his fellow football players on their trip into the Deep South.

Libby and Young Deer had been signed by the club in Rocky Mount, a tobacco town of 7,500 located near the falls of the Tar River in North Carolina's coastal plain. The manager of the Class D minor league team was W. E. Fenner. His squad had been losing games in bunches since their season started in May. As a result, fans quit showing up at the ballpark. Believing he needed a gimmick to entice them to come back, Fenner had invited a few members of the famous Carlisle Indian football team to play for his squad over the summer months. Perhaps, Fenner hoped, the Indians would help the Rocky Mount Railroaders win a few games and also generate some local buzz.

Fenner greeted Libby, Young Deer, and Thorpe at the depot, and escorted them to the park. While Libby and Young Deer practiced with the team, Thorpe sat on a bleacher and relaxed under the midday sun. He and his friends were there only a few days before he ran out of money. Luckily, Fenner asked Thorpe if he'd like to play for fifteen to twenty-five dollars a week. Thorpe agreed. On June 15, about a week after he arrived in North Carolina, Thorpe made his debut with the Railroaders in the sixth inning of their game against the Raleigh Red Birds. He played third base. As he trotted onto the field, the public address announcer likely used a bullhorn to introduce Thorpe to the sparse crowd. *Now playing third base for the Railroaders, Jim Thorpe!*

All Thorpe cared about was stuffing his wallet with a few dollar bills. He couldn't have guessed the future ramifications of being paid to play baseball. He didn't know he was forfeiting his amateur status, probably didn't even know what "amateur status" meant. He was a poor Irish-Indian farm kid who badly needed some pocket money. More than that, he loved to play, and he thought it would be fun to make a favorable impression on his manager. As it turned out, he wouldn't be able to do that on this hot summer afternoon in the Carolinas: He struck out twice in Rocky Mount's 5–1 loss.

The next day, Fenner asked Thorpe if he could take the mound and pitch. Thorpe had a muscular right arm and Fenner wanted to see what it could do. Facing the Red Birds again, Thorpe went into his windup and fired one flaming fastball after another over the plate. The Raleigh batters mostly whiffed as Rocky Mount won 4–1.

By the time the summer was over, Thorpe had worked so hard on the mound that his arm was nearly lifeless. Playing for a team that lost far more than it won, he compiled a pitching record of 9-10. But it wasn't the baseball that Thorpe enjoyed most during this carefree, languid summer in Carolina. It was the freedom—the one thing he had been searching for since he was a little boy. As he traveled with the Railroaders to minor league towns up and down the Atlantic Coast Line Railroad, Thorpe was given the discretion to eat when he wanted, sleep when he wanted, and visit a saloon when he wanted—as long as he showed up for the games.

This was a far cry from the structure of Carlisle and the heavy hand that Warner used to discipline and protect his boys.

Thorpe also basked in the attention that the local kids showered on him. When he emerged from his room at the New Cambridge Hotel in Rocky Mount, dozens of boys would greet him, all wanting to carry his baseball glove and cleats for the six-block walk along the dirt streets to the small, shabby ballpark that had a set of bleachers down the left field line. Like most of the Rocky Mount players in the East Carolina League, Thorpe was treated like a motion picture star by the locals. When Thorpe and his entourage of kids arrived at the park, he'd sometimes sneak his "helpers" into the game for free.

When the summer was over, Thorpe made what to him was an obvious decision: Instead of traveling back to Carlisle, as his buddy Libby was planning to do, he was going to return to his homeland in Oklahoma. He was twenty-one years old and he wanted to be on his own and making his own money. The summer had teased him with independence, and now he packed up his bag and began the long journey home to Oklahoma.

In a way, it was easy for Thorpe to walk away from Carlisle. He was never concerned about fame, about being a star—something Warner could never understand. When Warner discovered that Thorpe had disappeared into the Oklahoma rough country, his mood turned dark. Without their best player—the player around whom Carlisle's offense revolved—the Indians struggled in 1909. After reeling off four straight wins over second-rate teams to begin the season, the Indians tied Penn State 8–8, narrowly beat Syracuse 14–11, and then lost to both Pittsburgh (14–3) and Pennsylvania (29–6). Bigger, stronger opponents were pushing Warner's players around, and Carlisle didn't have the electric talent of Thorpe to save them when things fell apart.

For Warner, the low point of the season came when one of his players, a Sioux named Asa Sweetcorn, showed up intoxicated at the rail depot in Carlisle. Warner refused to let Sweetcorn on the train that was about to ferry the team to its next game. This didn't sit well with Sweetcorn, a scrappy player who had an enormous scar that stretched across his chest. Sweetcorn grew so upset that the police eventually intervened and arrested him. This spawned a joke that Carlisle students told and retold for the rest of the fall:

Question: "Where's Sweetcorn?"

Answer: "Sweetcorn's in the can."

Late in the season, the Carlisle team—without Sweetcorn—traveled to Cincinnati to play the University of St. Louis on Thanksgiving in a game that featured an intriguing "Warner versus Warner" subplot. Pop's younger brother, Bill, coached the St. Louis team. Before kickoff, the two Warners stood at midfield and posed for photographers. Watching all the pregame activities unfold from his seat in the bleachers was one very interested fan: Thorpe.

For the previous three months, Thorpe had worked odd jobs at his sister's farm in Oklahoma. He detasseled corn, repaired fences, baled hay, and generally did whatever was needed to keep the farm running. In return, his sister provided him with a bunk and three hot meals a day. Hoping to lure Thorpe back to Carlisle, Warner had invited his former star player to the Indians' game against St. Louis. So there Thorpe sat, behind the Carlisle bench, his dark eyes riveted to the action as he rooted for his old teammates.

The sight of the broad-shouldered Thorpe in the stands inflated the intensity of every Carlisle player. In their best performance of the season, the Indians pummeled St. Louis 39–0, dominating every facet of the game. The victory was particularly gratifying for Warner. With his players darting around the field like mosquitoes and his quarterback flinging the ball from sideline to sideline, Warner gave his younger brother a first-hand demonstration of how he thought the game should be played. And Carlisle did it all without Thorpe, who cheered every big play the Indians made.

After the game, Thorpe enjoyed a Thanksgiving feast with Warner and the players. As they ate, Thorpe once again experienced the natural high of football camaraderie, of being one of the boys. He told everyone that he planned to return to Carlisle in January and reenroll in the school. Still, Warner was skeptical. He thought that Thorpe needed an extra dose of convincing, so the next day when the players boarded a train and traveled back to Pennsylvania, Warner went with Thorpe back west to Oklahoma. They were going on a hunting trip together, just the two of them.

Over the course of several days, Warner and Thorpe stalked deer and doves over the same expanse of rugged country on which Jim had spent much of his childhood. Alone together, they must have discussed several topics: football, baseball, track, Carlisle, even the 1912 Olympics. Warner knew that the only way his football team would become the best in the nation was if Thorpe was lining up at halfback, and Warner surely sweet-talked Thorpe as well as any suitor might as the two tramped the earth hunting for game. But trying to convince him to come back to Carlisle was not easy: Thorpe bolted like an untrained horse every chance he got, and he had a habit of saying one thing, then doing another.

Warner surely tried to get Thorpe to peek at the future. He believed that Thorpe's destiny was to become one of America's greatest athletes. When the issue of money arose—as it most certainly did—Warner must have informed Thorpe that a pot of gold awaited him if he returned to Carlisle, won a gold medal in the 1912 Olympics, then led the Indian football team to national glory. If he did all of that, Warner believed that promoters and professional sports teams—both football and baseball—would offer Thorpe a large pile of money. Fame and fortune were there for Thorpe's taking. Warner surely made it hard for Thorpe to resist—though, of course, Warner had a selfish reason for wanting Thorpe to return: Thorpe would put more fans in the stands and that meant more revenue for the athletic fund. Thorpe was good business for Carlisle.

After a few days in Oklahoma, Warner returned to the Indian School. Before Warner left, Thorpe told his old coach that he'd come back to the school by Christmas. He made good on that promise. For a few days in December, Thorpe visited Carlisle as he escorted several Sac and Fox boys and girls from Oklahoma who were going to enroll at the school. As a winter storm dumped several inches of snow on the Cumberland Valley, he was again the king of Carlisle. He attended a school Christmas party in the gym, traded boxes of candy with other students, and enjoyed a turkey dinner in the dining hall. Thorpe felt like he belonged, like he was in the place that smelled and tasted like home, and he rejoiced in being surrounded by his old friends and teammates. Warner hoped Thorpe was at school to stay.

But it wasn't in Thorpe's nature to stay put. A few days after Christmas, he went back to Oklahoma to work the fields at his sister's farm. Though he enjoyed his time back at Carlisle, he was still reluctant to follow Warner in lockstep and abide by his rules. Thorpe was fighting his approaching adulthood every step of the way, and he didn't know what he wanted out of his life. He spent four months in Oklahoma, where in the early spring he planted crops on his sister's farm. When his wallet was empty in late April, he hopped on a train and showed up in Rocky Mount on May 1, 1910, for the start of the Railroaders' season.

Once again, Thorpe was a sight to behold on the base paths. Whenever he attempted to steal second base, he'd come charging down the line at the infielder on the bag—his arms pumping hard, his prominent jaw clenched, his legs churning. Right before he reached the bag, he sometimes yelled as he leapt in the air. With his cleats held high, he'd slide feet first into the bag in a cloud of dust. If his cleats hit the infielder in the head or chest and peeled away some skin, well, that was just part of the game.

Late in the season, Thorpe, who continued to pitch and to hit around .250, was traded to the Fayetteville Highlanders, the top team in the league. In one of the last games of the summer, Thorpe was on first base when the pitcher went into his windup. As the pitcher let the ball go toward home plate, Thorpe took off for second with the power of water bursting through a cracked dam. Just before he slid, the catcher rifled the ball toward the second baseman in the hopes of becoming one of the few catchers to throw out Thorpe this summer. Thorpe slid. Just as he touched the base, the ball smacked Thorpe on the head, emitting a sickening *crack* that made the small crowd cringe. Blood oozed out of the cut on his head, but Thorpe wasn't fazed. As blood trickled down his face, he simply sat on the base and looked at the crowd with a big and crooked grin. Thorpe downplayed the injury, but after the game he was taken to a local hospital in Fayetteville, where he spent the final days of the 1910 minor league baseball season.

After his second summer of baseball was over, Thorpe returned home to Oklahoma to work on his sister's farm. He was so certain that he wasn't going to attend Carlisle ever again that he wrote a letter to the school and requested that they turn over to him all the money he'd earned while working on the outing program. The new superintendent of the school, Moses Friedman, who had replaced William Mercer in April 1908, responded angrily to Thorpe's demand. In a letter to Thorpe, Friedman wrote, "It is customary at this school, when students desert, that all funds

to their credit are held until they return or until the matter is given special consideration after their original term of enrollment has expired."

Friedman didn't release Thorpe's money, but Thorpe did scrounge up
enough to purchase a horse and buggy. As autumn cooled into winter in
1910, Thorpe worked the fields in Oklahoma while, back in Carlisle, the
Indians limped through an 8-6 season—Warner's worst record since
1901.

Thorpe made virtually no money over the winter and during the
spring of 1911. He was feeling decidedly down on his luck when, on that
warm early summer afternoon, he spotted his old buddy Albert Exendine
strolling down the street in Anadarko. Even though he hadn't played football for Warner for the last two seasons, Thorpe looked like he was in the
finest shape of his life. He might have been just a farmer, but he still possessed the hard body of an athlete in his prime. He was the kind of guy
who never had to try to stay in condition, and when Exendine shook his
hand, he couldn't believe how big Thorpe had become since he last played
football at Carlisle. Thorpe had grown about two inches and gained about
twenty pounds of muscle. It didn't take long for Ex to become Thorpe's
mentor again and tell him what he needed to do next in life.

The two longtime friends chatted as they stood in the afternoon sunlight.
They talked about old times, about Warner, and then Exendine told his
former protégé that it was time for him to get back to Carlisle. As an
older-brother figure, Ex had a certain power over Thorpe. He was able to
induce him to do things that few others could. Warner was keenly aware of
this, and it was entirely possible that Warner gave Exendine a bag full of
cash to travel to Oklahoma and convince Thorpe to return to Carlisle.

As usual, Thorpe didn't take long to make his decision. A happy-go-
lucky young man, his trade was action, not words, and the kid from the
Oklahoma Territory was still raw and relentless. His life was free-form,
spur of the moment, and he didn't put a lot of thought into where he
wanted to be tomorrow, next week, or next year. He always acted on
whims and itches, and now his attitude toward life at Carlisle had shifted
as quickly as the wind. He was going to return to Pennsylvania—if Warner
would have him.

Though Thorpe often felt restrained at the Indian School, he still viewed Carlisle as a special place. It was almost as much his home as Oklahoma was. Thorpe was proud of his Indian heritage, and he felt that he represented his entire race every time he slipped on the red Carlisle jersey and buckled his chinstrap. And there was something else drawing him back to Pennsylvania. Before he turned his back on the game—and on Warner—Thorpe was on his way to becoming the first football player in the history of the sport who had real star power, the kind of player that even people who didn't consider themselves football fans would pay money to see play. Thorpe had once been a topic of conversation on Indian reservations around the country. Now he was ready to rekindle that chatter.

Shortly after running into Exendine in Oklahoma, Thorpe wired a telegram to Warner expressing an interest in coming back to the Indian School. When Warner received the message, he greeted it as if a long-lost friend was about to reenter his life. Though Superintendent Friedman adamantly opposed granting readmission to Thorpe, Warner convinced him that the positives associated with Thorpe—namely, the money and exposure he would bring to the school—far outweighed such negatives as his lackluster attitude toward schoolwork and his weakness for liquor. A few days later, Warner telegrammed Thorpe, telling him he would be accepted with open arms. Warner then sent one of his assistant coaches to Oklahoma to fetch Thorpe and bring him back to Carlisle.

In the first week of September in 1911, Thorpe boarded a train that would take him to Carlisle. The wheel of fate was spinning again for Thorpe and Warner. But this time, for the first time in a long while, as Thorpe sat in his Pullman car and listened to every screech of the wheels, promise filled his horizon, a shining light that was pulling him forward.

Bloody lips and busted teeth were considered collateral damage whenever Warner put his players through a tough practice session. (Courtesy Cumberland County Historical Society)

9

A BRUTAL, SAVAGE, MURDEROUS SPORT

The bold-lettered headline splashed across newspapers from New York to Los Angeles: ARMY FOOTBALL PLAYER DIES. Dwight Eisenhower had recently graduated from Abilene High and was working at the Belle Creamery when the tragedy struck. Ike had not yet been accepted to West Point, and he was likely in the office of Joe W. Howe, the publisher and editor of the *Dickinson County News,* when he came across the startling story. Howe stacked papers from around the country in the corner of his office, and Ike liked to hang out at the *News* and read what was going on in the world. He especially enjoyed the sports section. In the fall of 1909, as football was becoming more violent and more popular, the story of Eugene Byrne, the captain of the Army football team, became a cautionary tale that shocked fans everywhere.

It was the day before Halloween at West Point. A biting autumn wind whipped up the Hudson River Valley, and the crowd at West Point's Cullum Field shivered as time ticked away in the fourth quarter between Army and Harvard. The entire Corps of Cadets, dressed in their long gray coats, and about five thousand fans sat in the two sets of bleachers that lined both sides of the grassy field. This was viewed as a watershed game for Army, a chance for the Cadets to finally join college football's ruling class.

For years, Harvard, Princeton, and Yale had been the nation's three dominant college football powers. (In 1909 Yale would go unbeaten and no team would even score a point on them.) Now Army was trying to elbow its way into the Big Three and rechristen the group the Big Four. Over the past two seasons the Cadets had gone 12-3-3 and their record in 1909 stood at 3-1 when Harvard traveled to the Point. This game, the Cadets believed, was going to rocket Army football into the stratosphere.

But it wasn't working out that way. In the fourth quarter, as the fans struggled to stay warm in the shadows of a darkening late afternoon, the Harvard players were manhandling the Cadets, shoving them around like heavyweight wrestlers against featherweights. With about ten minutes to play in the fourth quarter, the scoreboard read: Harvard 9, Army 0.

This didn't sit well with Eugene Byrne, Army's team captain. More than any other player on the squad, Byrne epitomized what Cadet players had been known for since football was first played at the Academy in 1893. He was tough as rawhide, undersized but scrappy, exhibited relentless determination, and he loved the game intensely.

The average Harvard player outweighed the typical Army player by about twenty pounds, so Byrne knew that the only chance his team had at beating the Crimson was to outhustle and outfight them. As the team captain who played end on offense and defense, Byrne exhorted his teammates to try harder—to play like they were in a battle for their lives.

Byrne flew around the field and hurled his body without fear of the consequences, a glutton for pain. Early in the fourth quarter Harvard had the ball. The Crimson's quarterback, Daniel O'Flaherty, received the snap and threw a short pass to Hamilton Fish, Jr. Byrne quickly zeroed in on Fish, then slammed into him. The two collided and fell to the ground in a heap. Fish lifted himself up, but Byrne stayed down, in a haze, immobile. After taking a few moments to regain his wits, Byrne groggily stood up and stumbled back to the line of scrimmage.

In the Harvard huddle O'Flaherty called a "mass play" to the left. This meant that Hamilton Fish and Robert Fisher, the Crimson's right guard, would crash as hard as they could into the left side of the line and take out as many Army players as possible. After running "interference," as Harvard coach Percy Haughton called it, the Crimson's Wayland Minot, a fullback who had the build of a garbage can, would blast through the gap created by the interference. On this play, the gap was supposed to open between Army's right tackle, Vern Purnell, and the team's left end, Byrne.

The ball was hiked to O'Flaherty. He spun and handed the ball to Minot. Fish and Fisher, the Harvard blockers, attacked the line of scrimmage, looking to smash into anyone who got in their way as Minot surged forward. Byrne, who weighed only 170 pounds and wore a thin leather helmet, lunged forward, attempting to tackle Minot. In a heartbeat Byrne became lost in a tangle of arms, legs, and torsos that all bashed together with such violence that, to the fans on the sidelines, it sounded as if three whips had been snapped in succession—*crack, crack, crack.*

One by one, the players picked themselves up after the play. But Byrne was motionless. Minot, the Harvard fullback, didn't move, either. The two players lay side by side in the patchy grass, their bodies seemingly frozen. Trainers and doctors from both teams quickly sprinted onto the field. When the Harvard medical staff reached Minot, he was unconscious and had blood on his face. Trying to wake him, a trainer tossed water into his face and poured some down his throat. Minot coughed and opened his eyes. After a few minutes, the trainers helped him to his feet. Then, with each arm wrapped around the shoulder of a trainer for support, Minot slowly shuffled to the sideline, still unsure of where he was.

Byrne remained on the ground. The Army trainer and several surgeons tried to wake him, sprinkling water on his face and gently tapping his cheeks. But Byrne's eyes stayed closed. Alarm spread throughout the crowd. Byrne's father, John, the former chief of police in Buffalo, New York, shot out of the stands and ran onto the field. As he huddled with the medical team over his son, the entire West Point Plain settled into a silence so deep that fans could hear the wind sigh.

Byrne's breathing grew weak. After ten minutes, the Army doctors called for a stretcher. The player's flaccid body was placed on it, and, to the shock of the crowd, he was carried off the field and straight to the West Point infirmary. After discussions with both coaches, the lead official announced to the crowd that the game was over. Harvard was awarded a 9–0 victory.

Once Byrne reached the infirmary, the doctors called for a chaplain to administer last rites. His condition appeared to be growing increasingly dire—he was losing color in his face and his breathing was becoming more labored. But the doctors were confounded: They weren't sure precisely what was wrong with the boy. They gave him oxygen, placed hot and cold packs all over his body, massaged his muscles, and hoped for the best. It was all they could do.

Then a sign of hope: Around midnight Byrne opened his eyes. A little later he talked to his father, who was keeping a bedside vigil. He couldn't move his hands or legs, but he wasn't in pain. He stayed awake for a while, but early in the morning he developed a head lesion, which affected his brain and caused his breathing to weaken again. He soon lapsed into a coma. Hours later, Byrne's breathing stopped and, at age twenty-one, he was pronounced dead. When tackling Minot, he had suffered a dislocation between the first and second cervical vertebrae. The hit had damaged his spine, causing his death.

A few days later, Byrne was buried with full military honors in the West Point cemetery. After taps was played and the mournful notes faded into the autumn air of the Hudson Valley, Army officials soon announced that the remainder of the 1909 season was canceled.

Two weeks later, horror struck the gridiron again. On November 13, 1909, the University of Virginia traveled to Hilltop Field to play Georgetown University in Washington, D.C. Late in the second half the Virginia Cavaliers held a 21–0 lead and were threatening to score another touchdown. With a crowd of about three thousand looking on, Virginia freshman halfback Archer Christian took a handoff and began running to his right. With one Cavalier player in front of him acting as a blocker and two more players to his left and right side, Christian plowed into the right side of the line. According to several accounts, he lost his footing and stumbled just as he was approaching the line. The two Virginia players at his side helped him regain his balance, pushing him forward. But just as Christian got his stride back, two Georgetown defenders lunged at him and forcefully knocked him backward. Christian, who most likely wasn't wearing a helmet, crumpled to the ground. A moment later, several Georgetown players jumped on him. By the time the referee blew the whistle to signal that the play was over, about a half-dozen players from both teams were piled on top of the runner.

Slowly, all the players rose to their feet—all except Christian. He was on the ground and out cold. Trainers ran onto the field from the Virginia sideline. Christian opened his eyes a few minutes later, and asked the trainers how close he had moved the ball to the Georgetown goal line. Then he closed his eyes and lost consciousness again.

Several doctors who happened to be in the crowd came to Christian's side. One of the first to reach the downed player was L. H. Glazebrook, a graduate of Virginia who was the deputy coroner of the District of Columbia. Seeing Christian's grave condition, Glazebrook asked one of the police officers at the game to summon a stretcher from the local police station so they could transport the injured boy to a hospital. The officer refused, saying he couldn't leave his post. Eventually a police wagon was driven onto the field. A few officers hoisted Christian into the back of the wagon "like a sack of potatoes," according to one eyewitness. Christian briefly opened his eyes again and looked at the Virginia trainer, Pop Lannigan. "Oh, I'm suffering, Pop," Christian said weakly. "Please do something."

Just as the police wagon began hauling Christian off the field, a Virginia player ran across the field, yelling, "That's my brother!" Andrew Christian, a freshman on the team, tried to jump on the back of the wagon. But the police told him to get off. Undeterred, Andrew grabbed on to the side of the wagon. A police officer tried to push him off, but Andrew didn't budge. Finally, the officer grabbed Andrew's head and twisted it until he dropped off the side of the wagon. At that point several spectators in the crowd intervened. In the chaos of the next few minutes, a few fans tried to hit a policeman on horseback as they shouted that Andrew should be allowed to ride in the wagon. The police finally gave in to the demand of what was rapidly becoming an angry mob, and Andrew was lifted onto the wagon.

The injured player's mother, who lived in Richmond, was in Washington at the time but chose not to attend the game. As soon as she received the news that her son had been hurt, she raced to the hospital. Shortly after she arrived, she contacted Dr. Harvey Cushing, a famous surgeon, who hurriedly traveled from his home in Baltimore to Washington. Cushing was something of a specialist when it came to treating football-related injuries. Just a month earlier he had cared for Edwin Wilson, a Navy football player who had broken his neck and been paralyzed while trying to tackle an opposing runner. (Wilson died six months later.)

A few hours after Cushing arrived in Washington, Archer was wheeled into the operating room. Cushing and the Virginia team doctor realized the player had developed several blood clots in his brain due to head trauma, and for three hours the two surgeons did their best to remove the clots. It was to no avail: At 3:40 A.M., about twelve hours after he took his final handoff, Archer Christian died.

"Does the public need any more proof that football is a brutal, savage, murderous sport?" wrote *The Washington Post* in an editorial following Christian's death. "Is it necessary to kill many more promising young men before the game is revised or stopped altogether?"

Football *was* brutal, savage, and murderous. But that was part of its allure. When you played football in the early days of the twentieth century, there was a real possibility that you could die. Like Romans watching gladiatorial battles, the crowds that grew larger by the year were seduced by the violence and viciousness of the action. The game was like America itself in 1909: raw yet developing, brutal yet beautiful, democratic yet dominated by only a few.

Ever since William Webb Ellis, a student at the Rugby School in Rugby, England, picked up the ball during a soccer match in 1823 and, according to legend, started running with it—an act that turned out to be the Immaculate Conception of both rugby and American-style football—football had been a rough game. Sixty-seven years later at West Point, New York, a young student named Dennis Michie wanted to start a team at the U.S. Military Academy. In the summer of 1890, Michie was one of the three cadets who had ever played the game before. Growing up the son of a West Point instructor, Michie was an avid reader and he followed all the top college teams in such papers as *The New York Times, The New York Herald,* and *The Evening Sun.* He had strapped on a leather helmet while attending the nearby Lawrenceville School, and now he wanted to found a team at Army. But how?

While on leave from the academy grounds in the summer of 1890 Michie bumped into a childhood friend who attended the U.S. Naval Academy. Their conversation veered onto the topic of football, and an idea crystallized in Michie's mind. He figured there was only one way that the top brass at West Point would allow him to form a team, and this is where his friend came in. If the Naval Academy, which had been playing football since 1879, challenged Army to a game, Michie believed there was no way that the movers and shakers at West Point would pass it up. The collective pride of the Military Academy would be on the line.

Just as Michie and his buddy had planned, a few weeks later a letter arrived at West Point from Annapolis issuing a formal challenge. Michie took the letter to his father, Lieutenant Colonel Peter Michie, a philosophy instructor at West Point who had fought in the Civil War. With his father backing him, Michie didn't have to ask twice to get permission from Superintendent Colonel John Wilson to accept the challenge.

Not everyone was pleased that this game was going to take place. Two months before the showdown, *The New York Times* ran a story on faculty upheaval at West Point. Many instructors argued that it made no sense for young cadets and midshipmen to hit and bloody one another on a football field, given that someday they might have to rely on one another in the field of combat. Yet in spite of these objections, Michie and his father kept lobbying the superintendent and others, arguing that the game would ultimately benefit both academies and bring them closer together. The superintendent agreed with the Michies, and refused to call off the game.

Now all young Michie had to do was assemble a twenty-one-man team, tutor the players in the essentials of the game, and whip them into playing shape. A classmate, John A. Palmer, later recalled what those first weeks of Army football were like in *The Assembly,* a West Point magazine. "Dennis now had his hands full. He was captain, coach, trainer and business manager of a non-existent team that must play a championship game at the end of eight weeks. Dennis had scant time to teach the simplest fundamentals to his raw recruits. They had no practices except for a few riotous scrimmages against an even more inexperienced second-team. There was no time for coaching except in the brief intervals between military duties.

"Only on Saturday afternoons when the weather was too bad for drill and dress parade could Dennis count on any time for continuous practice. Dennis was able to rouse his teammates at 5:30 a.m., half an hour before reveille, for a run around the Plain, down and back Flirtation Walk, over past Thayer Hall, around the Supe's headquarters, and then back to the barracks in time for reveille."

Undermanned and undertalented, Army ended up losing its first game to Navy, 24–0. It wasn't until the matchup was over—and the injuries were tallied—that everyone involved realized the savagery of the game. One Army player lost three teeth. Another Cadet had a piece of his ear bitten off, while yet another had his nose broken. The next day *The New York Times* placed its story about the game on the front page, hailing the contest as "the greatest victory the Navy has achieved since Decatur and John Paul Jones . . . The result was watched with national interest . . . It was generally regarded as the beginning of a new era in the athletic training of two institutions."

Beginning with that first-ever bloody game at the Military Academy, the Army team, more than any other in the nation, viewed football as a microcosm of war. Coaches at the Point at the turn of the century and into the first years of the 1900s believed in using football as a means to prepare players, who were mostly the sons of lifelong military men, for the battlefield. This was driven home in 1899 to a young Douglas MacArthur when he arrived at the academy as a scrawny, five feet, eleven inches, 133-pound plebe. As a boy growing up in Little Rock Barracks in Arkansas, MacArthur had dreamed of playing football for Army, but his mother, Mary MacArthur, didn't want her son to be injured in what she believed was a barbaric sport. (This was typical of his mother: Mary MacArthur was so overbearing that she moved with her son to West Point when Douglas enrolled in '99. For four years Mary MacArthur lived in the West Point Hotel, and from her window she had an unobstructed view of room 1123 in the barracks. If she didn't see young Doug with his head buried in a circle of lamplight at night, she'd talk to him the following day about why he wasn't studying.)

In the fall of his plebe year, MacArthur sat in the stands and watched the Army football team, wishing he could join them out on the field. What he saw was a squad that was experiencing growing pains. Army's coach, Herman Koehler, was in the process of trying to build his team into an East Coast power. In his first season in charge of the program, 1897, Koehler led the Cadets to a 6-1-1 record and the following season his players gutted out a 5–5 tie with Princeton, one of the top teams in the nation. In '99, with MacArthur often cheering himself hoarse in the stands, the Cadets struggled to a record of 4-5.

Finally, during his first class year (his senior year), MacArthur found a way to accommodate both his mother's desire that he not play football

and his desire to be connected to the football team: He became the equipment manager. While standing on the sideline with the players and
coaches, MacArthur watched Army cobble together its finest season of
football in history. The Cadets were led by tailback Paul Bunker, who had
been named by Walter Camp as an All-American at tackle the previous
season. Possessing a rare combination of size and speed, Bunker could
both power over defenders and sprint away from them. With Bunker running the ball out of Army's T-formation, the Cadets finished the 1902
season with a 6-1-1 record, including a 22–8 win over Navy. A few weeks
after the Navy game Walter Camp again named Bunker to his All-
American team—this time as a halfback. It was a historic honor: Bunker
became the first player ever to make Camp's first-string squad at two different positions.

No one was more impressed with the effort of the Cadet players—
especially Bunker—than young MacArthur, who the following spring
graduated at the top of his class. When MacArthur returned to West Point
in 1919 as a general to become the superintendent at the school, he
sneaked away from his desk for a few hours on many autumn afternoons
to attend football practice. There he would stomp up and down the side
line, his riding crop wedged under his arm, and encourage the young
cadets to play stronger, to run faster, to hit harder. MacArthur, who years
later during World War II would engage a determined officer named
Eisenhower in several heated discussions, always believed that there was
a strong correlation between sports and war, and before he left his post as
superintendent and headed for the Philippine Islands in 1922, his
thoughts on the subject were inscribed over the entrance to the physical
education office in the South Gym:

UPON THE FIELDS OF FRIENDLY STRIFE
ARE SOWN THE SEEDS THAT,
UPON OTHER FIELDS, ON OTHER DAYS
WILL BEAR THE FRUITS OF VICTORY

After the 1909 football season ended, the death toll for the year stood at
thirty-three. The high-profile tragedies of Army's Eugene Byrne and Virginia's Archer Christian had prompted several editorial writers at promi-

nent papers to call for the game's abolishment. One sportswriter, Bat Masterson, made it his personal cause to outlaw the game, and he employed flammable prose in his crusade. "Football is not a sport in any sense," wrote Masterson, the former frontier lawman turned sports editor, in the *New York Morning Telegraph*. "It is a brutal and savage slugging match between two reckless opposing crowds. The rougher it is and the more [players who are] killed and crippled, the more delighted are the spectators, who howl their heads off at the sight of a player stretched prone and unconscious on the hard and frozen ground."

However, most college presidents simply wanted to reform the game, not ban it. On November 19, the president of Princeton, an ambitious fifty-three-year-old named Woodrow Wilson, told a reporter, "Football is too fine a game to be abolished offhand. I do think, however, that it should be modified to some extent in order to obviate those fatal accidents as far as possible."

In the spring of 1910, a special college football committee made up of coaches, referees, and school presidents enacted several rule changes in an attempt to make the game safer. Seven men now had to be stationed on the line of scrimmage when the ball was snapped. Previously, only the center was required to be on the line, while the other players could stand back several yards and then run toward the other team just before the ball was hiked. The committee hoped by mandating seven players to be on the line at the time of the snap that the full-speed, mass collisions that often caused serious injuries would become a thing of the past. Blockers could also no longer link arms, nor could the ballcarrier be pushed or pulled by other offensive players. And once a runner's knee or elbow hit the ground, the play was over. This rule, the committee believed, would prevent defensive players from piling on the runner.

One final rule change that the committee considered was whether or not to outlaw the forward pass. After an extended debate the ballots were cast and the forward pass survived by a single vote. At the last minute the committee decided even to liberalize the passing rules. Instead of an incomplete pass being declared a fumble, the ball would now be dead once it hit the ground and returned to the spot where the pass was attempted. Also, passes no longer had to be thrown five yards to the right or left of the center of the field; a player could now fling a pass anywhere he wanted. By their decisions, the committee had just created a new age of football in America.

The rules were designed not only to eliminate injuries, but also to further open up the game, to make it more fluid, more of a ballet than a steel-cage wrestling match, and one person who was excited about the changes was Woodrow Wilson. A few weeks after the 1910 season kicked off, Wilson, then the governor-elect of New Jersey, visited the Princeton team and told the players, "The new rules are doing much to bring football to a high level as a sport, for its brutal features are being done away with and better elements retained."

About a year after the football rules were altered, Eisenhower stood at the train depot in Abilene. The tracks were laid out in front of him, a long thread across the plains, and when his train slid to a stop at the tiny station, he strode onto a Pullman car. Several weeks had passed since he was accepted to the Military Academy, and he carried a small duffel bag that held only the barest of essentials—toothbrush, razor, one change of clothes. Eisenhower took a seat. A few moments later, the train cranked up and pushed out of the station in a symphony of clacks, bangs, and huffs.

Dwight David Eisenhower was now officially on his way to West Point. Like Thorpe, who also rode the rails east on a life-altering journey in the summer of 1911, Eisenhower was aglow as he sat on the train and watched the low brick buildings of Abilene grow smaller and smaller and finally disappear into the Kansas prairie. West Point was only 1,237 miles away.

Eisenhower's formal cadet portrait, taken when he graduated in 1915—the most famous class in West Point history. (Courtesy the Dwight D. Eisenhower Library)

10

BEAST BARRACKS AND A BEAST
ON THE FIELD

Gazing through a window of the steaming locomotive, Dwight Eisenhower watched the miles and miles of rolling grasslands and flat fields flow by. He was traveling from Abilene to West Point, and as he sat in a rail car on this cross-country trip, he was a young man full of confidence. Over the previous twelve months both his mind and body had matured, and this put the sparkle of self-assurance in his pale blue eyes. He already understood that the rigors of the academy would be more challenging than anything life had yet thrown at him. But he welcomed all tests of character. He felt he could easily handle the academics of West Point, an engineering school. Ike was intellectually curious, and his favorite subjects were science and math. Ever since he could remember, numbers seemed to whisper secrets to him.

He didn't fear the physical demands either. In the two years since he had graduated from Abilene High, he had added bulk to his five feet, eleven inch, 150-pound frame. Still very much the scrappy kid who had fought Wesley Merrifield tirelessly in the vacant lot, he now had solid, muscular arms, and, much to his surprise, he had grown noticeably quicker over the last twelve months. At age twenty, he'd be one of the oldest entering plebes in the class of 1915 and he believed this gave him an advantage over his classmates. He had more life experience than the other boys who were now making their way to the Hudson Valley, and he felt that he could deal with adversity as well as anyone. Sure, he was leaving the comforts of home and no longer could he predict what the next day would bring. But as he sat on the train and catalogued his thoughts, he felt supremely ready—to leave Abilene, to see the world, to start writing the script of his adult life.

Dwight Eisenhower had never ventured farther east than his one trip to St. Louis for the entrance exam. When he stopped at the Kansas City depot to change trains, he couldn't help but marvel at how the wheels of technology were spinning all around him. Standing on the platform, his lone bag resting at his feet, he could see factory and foundry chimneys spurting dark clouds of smoke into the sky. His nostrils were attacked by the foul smells from the vast cattle yards and large packinghouses. And everywhere he looked, hordes of bustling people—more than the entire population of Abilene—seemed to be in a hurry to get somewhere.

His next train eased into the station—wheels grinding, steam engines hissing—and he climbed aboard and again took a seat by the window. From that point on, he would be seeing everything for the first time. During the three full days on the train, as it chugged along the slender iron lines, his wandering eyes would feast on the sights of rural 1911 America: endless stretches of rolling, gold-tinted fields; men dressed in overalls in the fields stopping their work and shielding their eyes from the sun so they could watch the train roll by; wooden farmhouses with rocking chairs on their front porches; and small rustic towns whose main streets featured only one country store, which also served as the post office and the place where farmers went to get the news of the day and trade prophecies about the weather.

Eisenhower's next stop was Chicago, where he visited red-haired Ruby Norman, his "girl," who was now studying violin at the Chicago Conservatory. In Abilene, the two had often gone together to moving picture shows that cost five cents a ticket. Dwight didn't have much time for girls in Abilene because he was always working, studying, or playing sports. But Ruby still had a flaming crush on the dreamy-eyed Eisenhower despite the fact she didn't see him often. During his brief visit in Chicago the couple strolled through parks, walked along the lakefront, went to a few movies, and visited the major sights. Eisenhower was sad to say good-bye, but after a few days, it was time for him to move on to his next stop. He had a schedule to keep.

Back on the train, he detoured to Ann Arbor, Michigan, to visit his brother Edgar, who was completing his second year of courses at the University of Michigan, where he was studying to become a lawyer. Edgar had hoped to play football for the Wolverines, but back home in Abilene the previous summer he had suffered appendicitis. The doctor wanted to operate and remove his appendix, but Edgar refused. He'd recently heard a story—perhaps apocryphal, he wasn't sure—that one Abilene doctor had performed the same operation on a boy who actually had only a bad case of food poisoning. The boy died, the story went, and Edgar wasn't about to put his fate in the hands of the same country doctors. For several days he lay on the floor of the Eisenhowers' parlor room and moaned in pain. Though he risked peritonitis—an inflammation of the membrane that lines the abdomen—he waited to have surgery until he returned to Ann Arbor, where the father of one of his roommates removed his appendix. But the illness took a toll on his body: he dropped from 170 to 150 pounds and much of his muscle withered away. He would never play a down of football for the mighty Wolverines.

One evening, Ike and Edgar rented a couple of canoes and took two college girls out on the winding Huron River. The brothers brought a phonograph, and the four listened to a few melodies while gazing at the stars. Ike had so much fun with his brother that he began to question what he was doing with his life: Was he making a colossal mistake by not following his brother to Michigan? But Ike stuck to his plan—just as he always did. With a pang of regret, he climbed back aboard his locomotive and waved goodbye to his brother through the window. Ike would not see Edgar again for fifteen years.

The special train left the depot in Secaucus, New Jersey, carrying more than one hundred young men who were about to enter the Military Academy. The locomotive rolled north along the Hudson River, choking out steam as it pressed forward on the West Shore Railroad. Outside the windows the bright summer sunshine bobbled and bounced off the Hudson River, and the water glittered as if studded with millions of diamonds.

The day was one of the hottest of the year in New York, but inside his rail car Eisenhower felt cool and collected on the afternoon he was to report to West Point. Scanning the faces of the other appointees on the train, Eisenhower couldn't believe how young they all looked. Many tried to bury their nervousness beneath loud bursts of laughter; others just sat quietly slumped in their seats, desperately anxious and afraid. Not Eisenhower. When he drew a mental comparison of himself to the other men sitting around him, he liked what he saw. *If they can do it,* he thought to himself, *then certainly I can do it.*

The train pulled into the West Point depot on the west bank of the Hudson. With bag in hand, Eisenhower stepped off. The young passengers were met by a detail of upperclassmen officers, who vociferously threw verbal grenades at the soon-to-be lowly plebes. Their initiation to life at West Point began immediately.

"Hold your head up!" they shouted.

"Hurry up!"

"Drag in that chin!"

Eisenhower and his future classmates were ushered away from the depot and led on a four-hundred-yard walk up the Hudson Highlands. The group fell quiet. On top of the steep hill, outlined against the sky, the men could see the gray granite stone of the administration building, also known as base headquarters. The building looked like a monstrous, impenetrable castle on a bluff, and in a way it was. The military fortress that became West Point had been established in 1775, and George Washington once called it "the key to the continent." The fort was critical in the American Revolution, preventing the powerful British navy from occupying the Hudson River Valley—and, perhaps, thwarting the revolution when it was still in its infancy. In 1802, the fort became the U.S. Military Academy.

Ike and the rest of the group continued to walk upward, passing through the stone portal that led to campus, the Plain as it was called. The group moved in silence, the only sound their footfalls clumping up the dirt road. At the top of the hill, the men were guided into the open quadrangle of the cadet barracks, where they were handed over to the Beast Detail—cadets in charge of teaching the arriving plebes the "traditions" of the academy. That was when all hell broke out.

"Pull in that chin, mister!" the Beast Detail yelled.

"Stand up straight, mister!"

"You have no chance of surviving here! You will not make it, mister!"

"You think you're tough? We'll show you tough, mister!"

"You are a disgrace, mister!"

After enduring several minutes of screaming, Eisenhower was taken to register in the administration building. In flat, unremarkable penmanship, he wrote that he had earned his own living "partially for six years and wholly for two years as a refrigeration engineer, also a fireman." He then emptied his pockets and handed his money to the treasurer, and was given a physical by a team of doctors. He passed with flying colors. Because he was measured to be five feet, ten inches tall, Eisenhower was assigned to the tallest cadet company, F company, on the left flank of the parade line.

The rest of the afternoon sped by in a blur of shouting and rapid motion. The new plebes—who were called "Beasts"—were issued gray jackets and white duck trousers and, later, uniforms. Then they were led to the barber for quick buzz cuts, and ordered into the gym for a set of push-ups. At 5 P.M., the 256 new faces on the Plain, the largest class the Military Academy had ever welcomed, stood in a line on the parade ground and watched as the entire Corps of Cadets marched by. Outfitted immaculately in full-dress uniform, the cadets moved in lockstep as the band played. Their steely faces were portraits of determination, and any doubt that Eisenhower had about his decision to attend the Point vanished as quickly as the notes of music that floated across the grassy Plain and into the valley of the glittery river. The pomp of the parade moved him, and he felt vitally connected to something larger than he ever could have imagined—his country and the Corps of Cadets.

After this majestic display, the cadets were asked to raise their right hands. Then, amid the lengthening afternoon shadows, the boy from Abilene and his fellow Beasts took an oath of allegiance to the United States of America.

For all of the Beasts, the heat was oppressive—sticking to their skin and threatening to melt it away. For the three weeks of Beast Barracks, West Point experienced record-breaking temperatures. Living in a tent city on the edge of the Plain—the vast grassy area in the heart of the campus—the new cadets were indoctrinated into the academy from dawn until dusk. In the stifling heat they were taught the basics of military drill, guard duty, inspections, and ceremonies. The Beasts did everything in double-quick time, always rushing up and down stairs (even jumping two stairs at a time), polishing their brass, cleaning their rifles, sweeping floors, making their beds, and saluting just about everybody. The cadet instructors constantly yelled at the young men, telling them in the harshest language that they were worthless, that they'd never cut it at the academy. In the rare quiet moments between the tongue-lashings and the thousands of tasks, Eisenhower would sometimes wander down to the bank of the river, look out at the water that moved at the speed of contemplation, and wonder just how in the world he had ended up at West Point. *What am I doing here?* he thought to himself. *How did I ever end up in this uniform?* As trying as the situation sometimes seemed, though, he always took comfort knowing that his education was free. Besides, even getting yelled at in the oppressive heat was better than his old job in the boiler room at the creamery in Abilene.

After their first week at the Point, plebes began to drop out in droves, unwilling, unfit, or otherwise unable to endure the mild torture that was Beast Barracks. Eisenhower's roommate, Henry Dykes, was wholly unprepared for the assault. Like Eisenhower, Dykes was from a small town in Kansas. Hours before he hopped on the train to head east and begin his education at West Point, Dykes was feted like a departing dignitary. A band played patriotic songs at the depot, the mayor gave a speech, and hundreds of people showered him with hugs and handshakes. But when Dykes arrived at the Point he quickly realized that almost everyone in the class had left their home as a town hero, and that his days of receiving special treatment were over. At night he'd slouch at the end of his cot and softly weep, wishing he were back in Kansas.

Thousands of boys have gone through this, Eisenhower would tell him, trying to lift his spirits. *It won't always be like this.*

"It's easy for you, but you haven't had all the acclaim they gave me," Eisenhower's roommate said. "What would my friends say if they could see me now?"

Dykes would be able to tell his friends all about the academy—face-to-face—soon enough. He dropped out shortly after Beast Barracks. When Dykes left, Eisenhower was assigned a new wife (West Point slang for roommate): Paul Alfred Hodgson, a native of Wichita, Kansas. Hodgson and Ike had a lot in common. Both were older than most students—P.A., as Hodgson was called, had already completed a year of college—and he and Ike were whizzes at math and physics. But what really bonded the duo from Kansas was their shared fascination with football.

When Ike and Hodgson learned in early September that tryouts were going to be held for the football team, they devoted most of their late-night bull sessions to discussing how they were going to make the varsity squad. Plebes were eligible to play varsity ball, but it rarely happened. That didn't faze Eisenhower; he was so full of swagger and confidence that he predicted to many of his friends that he'd be playing on Army's A-team in no time. Ike had played football for an extra year at Abilene High, and he believed with all of his heart that the experience he had would propel him to the varsity. He wasn't exaggerating when he told his buddies that the single most important thing in his life in the autumn of 1911 was making the varsity squad. It was, put simply, his obsession.

Yet when it came to his studies and bowing to kiss the white-gloved hands of the upperclassmen—as Plebes were expected to do—Ike had a devil-may-care attitude. One time during his plebe year, Eisenhower and another plebe named Atkins were cited by a cadet corporal for a minor infraction and were ordered to report to the corporal's room in "full-dress coats" after taps. Hazing was not as dangerous at the Point as it had been in the past—plebes once were forced to fight until someone was knocked unconscious—but mild forms still existed. Upperclassmen sometimes ordered plebes to crouch in contorted positions while they ate, and every so often one would be commanded to lie stomach down on a narrow wooden beam six feet above the ground and pretend he was "swimming to Newburgh," a town fifteen miles up the Hudson. This "swim" sometimes lasted several hours.

Now it was Eisenhower's turn to get hazed. Smiling wickedly, Ike prepared for his late-night meeting in the corporal's room, plotting to pull an old West Point stunt, the same one that a cadet named Edgar Allan Poe performed in 1830. Ike shined his buttons on his dress coat and the buckle for his snow-white cross belt until they gleamed like they were brand-new. Then he and Atkins appeared at the corporal's door at the appointed time. When the door swung open, there stood Eisenhower, his face as serious as a courtroom.

"Sir, Cadets Eisenhower and Atkins report as ordered!" Eisenhower said with a straight face.

"What's the meaning of this?" demanded the corporal as he glanced up and down at Eisenhower, who was wearing only his dress coat and was naked from the waist down.

"Nothing was said about trousers, sir!" replied Eisenhower.

Irate, the corporal punished Eisenhower and Atkins, also nude from the waist down, by ordering them to stand at rigid attention with their backs perfectly straight up against a wall—called bracing—until their chests ached. The kid from Abilene had once again tempted trouble. When Eisenhower told his classmates about what he'd done, they all shared a hearty but hushed laugh. Eisenhower's blatant disregard for authority as a plebe quickly made him popular with his classmates. At a school that demanded conformity, Eisenhower was something of a rebel. Though smoking was strictly forbidden, he puffed away on Bull Durhams, which he rolled himself. Charismatic, carefree, and typically flashing a smile, Eisenhower was magnetic, the kind of person to whom others gravitated because they didn't know what he would do or say next. Just a few months into his first year at the Point, many in his class felt so comfortable and friendly with Eisenhower that they started calling him by the one-syllable nickname he brought with him from Abilene.

Yet on the athletic fields of West Point, Ike was radically different. He viewed sports, football in particular, as the arena where he'd make a lasting impression—on his classmates, on his coaches, and on his opponents. When tryouts began for the varsity team, no one was as amped as Cadet Eisenhower. At practice, Ike was usually the first player out on the field and the last to leave. He understood that he didn't have as much raw talent as many of the players he was competing against for a roster spot, so he tried to outwork everyone else. After the final whistle of practice blew and Coach Ernest Graves would tell the team to head to the locker room and get treatment from the trainer for their aches and pains, Ike would linger behind, unwilling to call it a day. Alone, he'd practice punting the ball—over and over and over. Even when night fell, he'd often be out on the practice field, booming balls up into the sky and watching them disappear in the distant darkness. The team's trainer, Sergeant Marty Maher, eventually had enough of Eisenhower's overtime practice habits. It was Maher's responsibility to pick up all the balls after practice, and Ike's extracurricular kicks forced the trainer to perform an Easter egg hunt for footballs in the dark. He even cursed Eisenhower, telling him he needed to stop practicing so hard. But no words from Maher—or anyone else—could turn off Eisenhower's engine; his internal RPMs redlined every time he put on his pads.

Eisenhower's roommate played with similar gusto. After the tryouts were over, Ike believed that he and P.A. were shoo-ins to make the team. He was right—sort of. When the final varsity roster was posted, P.A.'s name appeared on the list; Eisenhower's didn't. "I'm fit to be tied," Ike told his friends when he discovered that he hadn't made varsity. The coaches admired Eisenhower's effort, but they thought that he'd get bulled over by other teams because he was so light. He weighed approximately 152 pounds. The coaches instructed Eisenhower to gain weight and to play for the Cullum Hall team, the school's junior varsity squad, founded in 1904. Cullum played a few local high schools and other military schools, and the varsity coaches carefully watched how the junior varsity players progressed.

Ike continued to practice hard, hoping to put the fear of Eisenhower, as he called it, into anyone who lined up against him. He also began attacking any food that he could get his mouth on. He needed to gain at least twenty pounds if he wanted to make the varsity squad in 1912, and so he ate like a bear before hibernation. But it was hard for Ike to put on weight during the fall of 1911 because he was so active. Playing linebacker and running back for Cullum, Eisenhower displayed all the characteristics that defined Army football: He was smart, hard-nosed, hard-hitting, and he maximized every drip of his talent. Even the varsity coaches liked what they saw out of this gutsy kid from Kansas. Near the end of the brief season, Ike played a starring role in leading Cullum to victory over a nearby military academy in what was considered the team's most important game of 1911. By season's end, Eisenhower was anticipating that 1912 would be the year he made the varsity squad and did things on the football field that would echo through the ages—or so he hoped.

They knew Thorpe was back. When the football team from Muhlenberg College, a small Lutheran school in Allentown, Pennsylvania, arrived at the train depot in Carlisle early in the afternoon of September 27, 1911, the players had already heard that Thorpe had returned to Carlisle. Warner had arranged for Muhlenberg to come to town to play the Indians in an early-season game that, in reality, would be little more than a practice session for Carlisle. To lure Muhlenberg to Indian Field for the slaughter, Warner promised their coach that his boys would play them again in the future in a widely promoted game, which would translate into a thick wad of cash for the Lutheran school.

Leaving the train, the Muhlenberg coaches and players climbed into a horse-drawn hack that ferried them to the main gate at Carlisle. The players silently gazed at the school they had read about in the sports pages for the last few years. Somewhere on these grounds Thorpe was looming. He was back at the school after his two-year exile in Oklahoma, and Warner planned to unleash him on the field for the first time against Muhlenberg. Four days earlier Carlisle had defeated Lebanon Valley, 53–0, but Warner didn't play Thorpe, who was slowly getting back into game shape after his long layoff. But today Warner was going to let Thorpe run wild.

The game wasn't scheduled to start for a few hours, so the Muhlenberg team was escorted to the gymnasium, where they were given a tour. Here in dramatic fashion the sixteen Muhlenberg players received an up-close look at just how mighty the Carlisle team was. Warner stored all the trophies and awards that his team had won over the previous twelve seasons in the gymnasium, and all the boys from Muhlenberg stared at the gleaming testaments to the Indian School's football prowess. Along with the trophies, there were also dozens of black-and-white photos of the Carlisle players, who looked more like mature men than developing boys. There were a few snapshots of Thorpe, and all of them captured his steely, confident, powerful gaze. The players would soon meet him in person.

When Muhlenberg finally made its way onto Indian Field, there was Thorpe warming up with his teammates, looking even bigger in person than he did in those grainy photos in the gymnasium. This was because he had added some twenty pounds to his five-eleven frame since he was last at Carlisle in the spring of '09. He now weighed 185. Not only was he one of the largest players on Carlisle's roster—Thorpe was "as big as a mule," according to Albert Exendine—but he was also the fastest. Warner couldn't wait to unleash Thorpe onto the field and see what he could do.

Thorpe had been back at Carlisle three weeks and had quickly re-adjusted to his routine at the Indian School. He was again living in the

athletic dorm and enjoying all the fruits that went along with being one of
Warner's players—better food, more free time, an expense account at Blumenthal's. Warner had also convinced several other players who were
finished with their studies to play football for another year or two at the
school. Warner's "athletic fund" covered their expenses and they lived
with Thorpe and the other players in the athletic dorm.

Thorpe roomed with Gus Welch, Carlisle's five feet, nine inch, 155-
pound quarterback who was astonishingly quick and aggressive. In the
previous two seasons he had played in the shop league at Carlisle, practicing the art of quarterbacking in the school's B-league system. But now
Warner believed Welch was ready for the varsity. The boy had a creative,
sharp mind, and his ability to improvise when a play broke down made
him one of Warner's favorite players. He was also a gifted, hardworking
student, the school's top debater, and Warner hoped his study habits
might rub off on Thorpe. Within days of rooming together, Welch and
Thorpe grew close as friends, which would only enhance their performance on the football field during the 1911 season.

Welch had grown up in the woods of northern Wisconsin. Like
Thorpe, he had Irish in his blood. His father, a logger, was Irish and his
mother was Chippewa. Also like Thorpe, Welch had endured a difficult
childhood. His father was killed in a logging accident when he was a boy
and five of his brothers and sisters died from tuberculosis. The two roommates could speak the common language of sadness, which strengthened
their bond. Welch was also in awe of Thorpe, who was the reason he was at
Carlisle in the first place. In 1907, while still living in Wisconsin, he'd
heard that Thorpe and Carlisle were playing the University of Minnesota
in Minneapolis, and he wanted to see the show. To pay for his train ticket,
he killed a wolf and sold its hide.

Welch arrived in Minneapolis early enough to watch Carlisle practice
before the game. He convinced another player to introduce him to
Warner, who was always looking for talent. Warner gave him a practice
uniform and had him work out with his boys. Impressed with Welch's
quickness, Warner encouraged him to apply to Carlisle for the start of the
1908 school year, which he did. For the 1911 and '12 seasons, Warner
roomed the ultraresponsible Welch with Thorpe; it would turn out to be
one of the deftest moves of his Carlisle coaching career.

Thorpe was twenty-three years old when he returned to the Indian

School in September 1911, and Warner treated him differently from the rest of his players. During practices Warner stomped around the field with a lit cigarette hanging from his mouth and, when he saw something he didn't like, angrily pulled the cigarette from his lips and screamed, "You goddamn bonehead!" or "You son of a bitch!" When his dander was really raised, Warner, at age forty, would line up in a three-point stance against a player and forcefully demonstrate the proper blocking technique he was trying to teach. Warner possessed a hair-trigger temper, and a few times it got away from him. Once he kicked a player and another time he punched a young Indian named John Wallette. Football was a serious business, and if he had to play rough, he did.

But Warner rarely raised his voice to Thorpe these days. The coach had been around Thorpe long enough to know that he wasn't a good practice player, so he allowed him to loaf through drills. He also let Thorpe practice kicking off to the side by himself, confident that his star player could get himself ready for a game. "What I like about Thorpe is his close observation of everything going on around him," Warner told a reporter. "He has little to say but he is always looking to see what is coming and sizing up the situation. He is the same way in all sports, always watching for a new motion which will benefit him. Then Thorpe has the marvelous concentrative power which he puts in every move he makes. It is a splendid sight to see him hurl a football thirty yards on the forward pass with merely an abrupt snap of the wrist, direct to the hands of the receiver, or to see him judge and catch a twisting spiral punt on the dead run."

Warner and Thorpe were also becoming closer off the field. Thorpe occasionally stopped by Warner's bungalow on campus, where the older man could often be found sitting in front of a canvas with a paintbrush in his hand, or in his garage taking an engine apart—his two favorite hobbies. Warner also took Thorpe and others on lazy drives through town in his Chalmers-Detroit 30 automobile. These off-the-field moments tightened the connection between Warner and his players, especially Thorpe, who Warner knew would be the engine powering his entire program for the 1911 and '12 seasons.

Thorpe trotted onto the field against Muhlenberg. If he felt rusty from his two-year layoff, it didn't show. Warner told Welch to hand the ball to

Thorpe on nearly every offensive play. Thorpe responded by punishing the Muhlenberg defense. He ran inside and outside, he sprinted away from defenders and rolled like a thunderstorm over them. Thorpe even threw several beautiful passes with that magical flick of his right wrist that Warner so admired.

Early in the second half Carlisle held a 32–0 lead when rain started spitting from the heavens and lightning popped throughout the sky like a flickering kerosene lamp. His uniform caked with mud, Thorpe continued to hammer at the Muhlenberg defense. On one of his final runs of the afternoon, Thorpe took a pitch from Welch and broke through the line. He came face-to-face with Walter Reisner, a 140-pound safety. Instead of trying to fake Reisner with a juke to the left or right, Thorpe put his head down and plowed into the smaller player. Reisner crashed to the ground, falling so hard on his right shoulder that he thought it fractured into a thousand pieces. He had to be carried to the sideline with a broken collarbone. "It was the first time I was glad to be taken out of a game," Reisner recalled years later.

A day after beating Muhlenberg, Warner led his boys on their weekly Sunday afternoon walk around campus. As the team strolled through the quiet of the school grounds, Warner wanted his players to quit thinking about what had transpired on the field on Saturday and start looking ahead to the next opponent, which in this case was Dickinson College. The walks were Warner's attempt to cleanse the palates of his players—getting rid of both the good and the bad tastes left in their mouths after games—and to begin focusing on what was coming up next.

The following day, Warner started the workweek with a Monday-morning meeting in his on-campus house. He huddled with his two scouts—F. E. "Cap" Craver and D. D. Harris—in his living room soon after breakfast. As Warner took drags on cigarettes, he'd shoot questions at his scouts, rapid-fire, about the upcoming opponent. *What kind of offense do they run? What defense? Who are their best players? What plays will work for Thorpe?*

Craver and Harris traveled around the country attending games that featured teams on the Carlisle schedule. As they sat in the stands, they took copious notes. Those jottings then helped Warner craft a game plan. Warner was one of the first coaches to employ scouts, and some of his players thought it was unfair and unsportsmanlike when he revealed an opponent's tendencies and weak spots. But Warner didn't care what his players—or anyone, for that matter—thought about his methods and tactics, especially his reliance on scouting, since it could help him win football games. The work of Craver, who had spent some time coaching at Dickinson College, and Harris, who was one of Warner's paid assistants, fed Warner with important intelligence about his opposition. After he digested it for a day or two he would map out a detailed plan that always targeted his adversary's most vulnerable spots.

Against Dickinson College on September 30, Warner played Thorpe for less than half the game, but Thorpe still put on a show for the 10,000 or so fans at Carlisle's Indian Field. At one point in the second half, Carlisle had the ball on its own fifteen-yard line when Thorpe, who was lined up at halfback, received a pitch from the quarterback. Breaking several tackles, he ran eighty-five yards for the touchdown, a scamper that *The New York Times* called "the feature of the contest" in Carlisle's 17–0 victory.

It was getting harder and harder to bring down Thorpe because of his increasing mastery of the stiff-arm. When a smaller defender would approach in the open field and attempt to bring him down, Thorpe would swing his free arm as hard as he could and hit the defender in the forehead. Often, the would-be tackler would fall to the ground like a prizefighter who had just been knocked out. Other times the defender would try to grab hold of Thorpe, and Thorpe would drag him along for five, even ten yards. And if a defender stood in Thorpe's immediate path, Thorpe wasn't afraid to come at him full speed and then attempt to run up the defender, digging his cleats into the opponent's body and bulldozing over him. Sometimes the black-and-blue cleat marks left by Thorpe on a tackler's legs and torso wouldn't go away for days.

After beating Dickinson, Carlisle hosted Mount St. Mary's College on October 7. Warner was so confident that his boys would easily steamroll St. Mary's that he dispatched his quarterback, Gus Welch, to Washington, D.C., so he could scout Georgetown, a team that Carlisle was scheduled to play on October 14. Warner's plan worked to perfection. Led by Thorpe's three first-half touchdowns, Carlisle dismissed St. Mary's 46–5. The next week, thanks largely to Welch's inside knowledge of Georgetown, the Indians again rolled, defeating Georgetown 28–5. Many government officials, including staffers from the Office of Indian Affairs, sat in the stands and watched Thorpe put on another tour-de-force performance. Though he didn't score a touchdown against Georgetown, Thorpe carried the ball about every other play on offense and several times left the crowd spellbound with his jarring stiff-arms that propelled him on a number of long, arresting runs. For Thorpe, the stiff-arm had become a lethal weapon.

A Washington newspaperman who was in attendance wrote, "Not since Custer made his last stand against Sitting Bull at the Little Big Horn has a battle between redskins and palefaces been so ferociously fought as that which was waged on Georgetown field yesterday afternoon, when the husky tribe of chiefs from Carlisle savagely forced Georgetown's weak, though gallant, cohorts to bite the dust 28 to 5."

With their record at 5-0, Warner and his boys next traveled to Forbes Field in Pittsburgh, Pennsylvania, to play the University of Pittsburgh on October 21. Over the previous week, newspapers across the East Coast had carried reports that described Thorpe's growing reputation—often inflating the factual record to artificially burnish the blossoming legend—and this helped prompt more than 12,000 fans to flock to Forbes Field to see Pittsburgh host Carlisle. Early in the game, Thorpe was as good in person as he was in print, ripping off several long runs. Then, in the second quarter, Carlisle faced a fourth down deep in its own territory. The Indians lined up in kick formation; Thorpe was the punter.

The ball was hiked back to Thorpe. He took a few steps forward and then—*wham!*—his right foot booted the ball high into the clear autumn sky. Thorpe immediately dashed up the field, untouched by any Pittsburgh defender. Because the Pitt players were blocking all the other Carlisle players, Thorpe quickly passed his teammates as he ran to cover the punt. The ball, meanwhile, was flying impossibly high. The kick ascended to such a height that it momentarily seemed to take the breath away from the crowd, and an instant hush descended over the stadium. Thorpe continued to sprint, untouched, at full speed. In front of him he could see four Pittsburgh players looking skyward at the ball. They were all trying to catch it. Under the rules of the game at the time, a player from either team could field a punt and then try to advance it. No one had ever seen a punter kick the ball and then attempt to try to field his own punt, but then, no player had ever possessed the combination of a powerful kicking foot and raw speed that would be required to pull off such a feat.

But Thorpe, seeing his chance, blasted up the field and zeroed in on the ball that he had just kicked. Pittsburgh had made a crucial mistake: No one had blocked Thorpe after the punt. Four, maybe five seconds had passed since he'd kicked the ball, and suddenly he was within a few feet of it. Thorpe leapt into the air. Three Pittsburgh players also were there jousting for the ball. Yet it was Thorpe who soared the highest and, in a stunning display of athletic grace, snatched the pigskin. When he came down, he maintained his balance, broke three tackles, and staggered twenty more yards to score a touchdown. This play was unprecedented in the history of college football, and even the partisan Pittsburgh crowd roared in awe as Thorpe's teammates congratulated him in the end zone.

Carlisle won the game 17–0, and afterward the several sportswriters declared Thorpe one of the greatest players ever to step onto a football field. "This person Thorpe was a host in himself," noted a reporter from *The Pittsburgh Dispatch.* "Tall and sinewy, as quick as a flash and as powerful as a turbine engine, he appeared impervious to injury. Kicking from 50 to 70 yards every time his shoe crashed against the ball, he seemed possessed of superhuman speed, for wherever the pigskin alighted, there he was, ready to either grab it or to down the Pitt player who secured it."

Another reporter wrote, "Jim Thorpe is [the] the most versatile athlete ever known . . . and is considered one of the best halfbacks in the history of the game."

The Carlisle publicity machine was now running in overdrive. The type-writers of E. L. Martin and Hugh Miller banged out fantastic stories that detailed the exploits of Thorpe. Warner's PR duo of Martin, now a reporter for the *Carlisle Daily Herald,* and Miller, the owner of the Letter Shop, soon struck literary gold with a new description of Thorpe. In every hyperbole-filled story that they spit out over their wire service, Warner's men always attached the same glorified description to Thorpe. These words would literally follow the Carlisle Indian to his grave, as they would one day appear in the epitaph on his headstone: "Greatest athlete in the world."

The Philadelphia Inquirer picked up a story that had originated in Carlisle with the headline, "This Indian the Athletic Marvel of the Age." The name on the byline read "Jim Nasium," which was the tongue-in-cheek nom de plume of Miller. The piece was a profile of Thorpe and it stated, "[Thorpe's] whole ambition in life is to now make the Olympic team, which ambition will no doubt be gratified, and if any old nation in the wide universe can dig up anything that can smother this redskin marvel in the all-around events all past records will be kicked into the middle of the Mediterranean Sea, that's all. . . . Thorpe is probably the most indifferent athlete we've ever had. He makes no special preparations for his efforts, and simply meanders carelessly up to his tasks and does them in an unconscious way that paralyzes the spectators. There is nothing showy or suggestive of extreme effort in his work."

Carlisle's next game was in Easton, Pennsylvania, against Lafayette College. Thorpe knifed through the defense for one touchdown, kicked a 35-yard field goal, and set up two other field goals with pile-moving rushes. But late in the game, as Carlisle was putting the finishing touches on a 19–0 victory, Thorpe carried the ball on what appeared to be a routine run and was tackled by a Lafayette defender. Right away, Thorpe knew something was wrong. One of his ankles had been severely sprained, and when he got up, he gingerly hobbled to the sideline. To Warner, the sight was sickening. All of his big dreams that were tethered to Thorpe—an undefeated 1911 season, a trip to the 1912 summer Olympics, another undefeated season in the autumn of 1912—were suddenly in jeopardy.

For the next few days, one topic of conversation dominated all others at Carlisle: Would Thorpe be able to play in Carlisle's next game against traditional rival Penn? In the past, Warner had enjoyed inflating the extent of injuries to reporters in the hope that the misinformation would reach the eyes and ears of the upcoming opponent, but now he was genuinely concerned that Thorpe might not be able to suit up against the Quakers. During the week, Thorpe stood on crutches along the sideline as Warner put his other players through various drills and scrimmages. Thorpe badly wanted to play—the majority of the Carlisle students were again going to make the trip to Philadelphia—but as he boarded the train on Friday afternoon he was still limping severely.

The students rode with the team on the locomotive into the City of Brotherly Love. The female students were dressed in wide-brimmed dark blue hats and long blue coats; the boys were outfitted in their dark blue, military-style uniforms. As they'd done in past years, the students stayed overnight at the Normandie Hotel at Fifty-sixth and Chestnut. On the morning of the game, the students held a pep rally for the team in the hotel lobby, serenading the players with songs and cheers. One of the students, Iva Miller, was there as Thorpe's special guest. A budding romance was developing between Thorpe and Miller, who was also from Oklahoma, and her voice added to the rally's chorus of cheers. But there was an undercurrent of worry in the lobby; no one, not even Warner, knew if Thorpe was fit enough to play.

Once he arrived at Franklin Field, Thorpe pulled on his red-and-gold Carlisle uniform in the locker room. Then he slowly walked out onto the field. Up in the stands, 30,000 fans were crammed into the bleachers, and nearly everyone's gaze was fastened on the limping athlete as he made his way onto the grassy field. Thorpe tried to jog and punt on the sideline, but after watching his star player for just a few moments, Warner knew that Thorpe couldn't play. His ankle was still sprained. He couldn't effectively cut when he ran and Warner could see that Thorpe grimaced in pain every time he tried to punt. Warner had no choice: He scratched Thorpe from the lineup.

Even without Thorpe, the Indians had no trouble with the nationally ranked Quakers. With quarterback Gus Welch leading Carlisle in a hurry-up offense—Welch often called the plays so fast at the line of scrimmage that the Penn defense didn't have time to line up properly—the Indians stormed to a surprisingly easy 19–0 victory. Welch also did his best Thorpe imitation when he darted up the field and broke several tackles on a punt return that he took ninety-five yards for a touchdown.

When the 8-0 Carlisle team boarded the train that would take them back to campus, Warner didn't allow himself to enjoy the victory over Penn, a squad Carlisle hadn't beaten in four years. By the time he'd taken his seat in the Pullman car, Warner was already thinking about the next opponent on the schedule: Harvard, the reigning national champions according to several writers.

Days later, Dwight Eisenhower sat in the stands at Franklin Field on November 24 with the rest of the players on the Cullum Hall football squad. Dressed in his long gray overcoat, Ike closely watched the action between the varsity teams of Army and Navy. During the 1911 season the Cadets, led by tailback Geoffrey Keyes and a bloodthirsty defense, hammered one opponent after the next. Army entered its season finale against rival Navy with a 6-0-1 record, having outscored its opponents 88 to 6.

But Eisenhower didn't like what he was seeing down on the field in Philadelphia. Navy clung to a 3–0 lead with only a few minutes remaining in the game. The Midshipmen had kicked a field goal early in the second quarter, then employed a conservative game plan. Rarely throwing the ball on offense, Navy was content to let the right leg of their punter, Jack Dalton, send booming punts deep into the Army territory. At one point in the game Dalton uncorked a 72-yard boot, which helped Navy win the bat-tle for field position—and, ultimately, the game. It ended 3–0.

As the teams walked off the field, one Cadet player was so distraught that he turned toward the Midshipmen players and, with tears in his eyes, yelled, "I'd rather be a plebe at West Point than Admiral of the whole damn Navy!"

Eisenhower was equally dejected. But as he left the stadium and made his way through the chilly November dusk, he took solace in one thing: Next year he'd have a chance to be on the varsity team. Next year he would personally make sure that the Cadets didn't lose to Navy, or any team on Army's 1912 schedule. Next year would be his time to shine.

The concrete horseshoe loomed in the distance on the morning of No-vember 11, 1911—the massive gray stadium as intimidating to the Indians as the burly Harvard players themselves. As Warner and his boys stepped off their horse-drawn carriages just hours before Carlisle's game against the Crimson, all of their eyes popped wide open as they beheld Harvard Stadium, which stretched half a dozen stories high. This was the first per-manent football structure in the history of the United States, and to the Indians it looked as monstrous as that gothic skyscraper that was being built in Manhattan, the Woolworth Building, which would be the tallest building in the world when it opened in less than two years.

Situated on the bank of the Charles River in Cambridge, Massachu-setts, Harvard Stadium was constructed in five months in 1903 at a cost of $175,000. It was the first reinforced concrete structure in the world, even though at the time many doubted that the concrete would be reliable enough to support 30,000 fans, which was the stadium's original seating capacity. But the designers were so confident in the strength of concrete that they told fans they would remain underneath the stands for the entire inaugural game, which pitted Harvard against Dartmouth. They kept their word, staying until the end; the structure held just fine.

By the time Warner and his boys walked onto the grass field on November 11, the gray stadium had already played a key role in the evolution of football. When the rule changes were being discussed in 1906, Walter Camp, who had a powerful voice in the sport, lobbied to widen the field by forty yards to make the game more open and free-flowing. But Camp overlooked the fact that Harvard Stadium had already been built and couldn't accommodate a wider field; as it stood, the bleachers were only five yards away from the sideline. (Perhaps Camp had a more nefarious reason for the proposal: As a Yale graduate, he was always looking for ways to stick it to Harvard.) Not wanting to make a relic out of Harvard Stadium, the rules committee dismissed Camp's idea. Instead, it quickened the pace of the game by adopting the forward pass.

In the fall of 1911, the stadium had recently been expanded, and more than 40,000 fans filled the bleachers to watch the one player the reporters in New England had been writing about for weeks: Thorpe. The standing-room-only crowd was the largest to attend any sporting event in 1911, and as the players warmed up on the field the air purred with excitement. Carlisle was undefeated; Harvard was 4-1-1. This was one of the showcase games of the entire college football season, but down on the field the fans saw a discouraging sight. Thorpe was limping around through the bright fall sunshine. His ankle, which was heavily taped, was still swollen, and the pain still sharp.

Even if Thorpe had been healthy, Harvard would have been the favorite. The Crimson had lost to Carlisle only once in the previous eleven clashes between the two schools, and Harvard's starting lineup had a dramatic size advantage over Carlisle's. The Crimson coach, Percy Haughton, oozed so much confidence that he didn't even bother showing up for the game. Instead, he traveled to New Haven, Connecticut, to watch Yale play that same afternoon. Haughton wanted to scout the Bulldogs, Harvard's sworn rival, whom the Crimson would face later in the season. It was rare for coaches at the elite teams to leave their teams on a football Saturday to scout an upcoming opponent, but Haughton's hatred of Yale bordered on the pathological. He was so intense in his desire to beat Yale that in 1908, according to a popular myth, he had choked a bulldog—like the Yale mascot—to death in front of his players before kickoff to get them riled up. The story was likely fictitious, but its mere existence underscored the intensity of his distaste.

A few days before Carlisle arrived in Boston, Haughton told a reporter that he "may not have to use his first team for the game," a statement that infuriated Warner. But Haughton had given Warner a wonderful gift, one that every football coach craves—a motivational tool. In the locker room before the game, against the chatter of the crowd, Warner told his boys that Harvard was overlooking them, and that even though the Indians had only sixteen players on their team while more than fifty would be standing on the Harvard sideline, there was no reason to be intimidated. This game, Warner said, presented an opportunity to beat the best program in the nation. During their practice sessions, the Carlisle coaches and players frequently talked about doing things with "Harvard style"—which meant to dominate while showing good manners and respect for the other team. The Crimson were the acknowledged kings of college football, Warner reminded his players before kickoff, and today—the eleventh day of the eleventh month of the eleventh year—was Carlisle's chance to smash the king in the mouth and give him a bloody lip.

The Indians shot out of their locker room and took the field. To the players, it was an awesome sight, seeing those 40,000 red-clad Harvard fans cheering full throat. Even the lush green grass on the field felt special as it crunched underneath the players' cleats; it was so thick that it seemed impossible for anyone to get hurt. But what made the scene even more dramatic to the Indians was what appeared on the opposite sideline. Warming up in the intense November sunshine were fifty players who all appeared to be as big as sumo wrestlers.

As Thorpe loosened up, he was gimpy, but he was determined to play. For the last few days Warner had been doing everything in his power to heal Thorpe's ankle—he massaged it, he placed liniment oil on it, and he rubbed a vibrating machine over it. Before the game, he put what was essentially a soft cast of adhesive plaster over the injured ankle. As Thorpe struggled onto the field to be Carlisle's deep back and receive the opening kickoff with his bandaged lower leg, all of his teammates saw that he was in pain, and it was more inspiring to them than any of the words that moments earlier had flowed from Warner's mouth.

Thorpe returned the opening kickoff about twenty yards before being tackled. On offense, Warner had made a difficult pregame decision: In the early part of the first half, he was going to use Thorpe merely as a blocker. Knowing that Harvard was expecting Thorpe to carry the ball on nearly every down, Warner told his players that Thorpe would be used as a decoy. Instead of relying on their superior quickness and running the ball to the outside, Warner told his boys that they were going to attack the belly of the beast—the middle of the Harvard defense—and ram the ball between the tackles like a sledgehammer through a block of concrete. Warner was counting on this element of surprise to work in his favor.

Facing Harvard's second string, Carlisle moved the ball down the field on their first drive behind the straight-ahead rushing of Possum Powell, whose lead blocker was Thorpe. Carlisle didn't score on its first drive, but on the Indians' second possession they again pushed the ball down the field. With Thorpe blocking for Powell, Carlisle advanced to Harvard's thirteen-yard line. Thorpe, sore ankle and all, booted the ball through the uprights to give the Indians an early 3–0 lead.

The Crimson responded. Exerting their superior size and strength, the Harvard offense pushed the Carlisle defense back and used straight-ahead plunges that netted four yards one play, six on another, nine on another. After marching deep into Indian territory, the drive stalled. The Crimson kicker tied the game 3–3 with a field goal.

Now it was Carlisle's turn to answer. Warner resisted putting the ball in Thorpe's hands—though the temptation was growing stronger by the play—and ordered his boys to keep pounding the ball between the tackles. Warner knew at some point he was going to open the playbook and unleash a torrent of reverses, passes, and misdirection plays on the Harvard defense, but not yet. The timing wasn't right. With Thorpe again paving the way as a blocker, Powell pushed the ball ahead snap after snap. Carlisle moved to the Crimson's 37-yard line. Thorpe then dropped back to kick a field goal and, from forty-three yards out, smashed the ball with his right foot. Tumbling end-over-end, the pigskin easily cleared the crossbar. Carlisle led 6–3.

A few minutes before halftime, the Indians had the ball back deep in their own territory. If they could put together a quick scoring drive, Carlisle could put Harvard in a hole out of which the Crimson might not be able to crawl. But then a Carlisle back took a handoff from quarterback Gus Welch and was hit hard by a Harvard defender. The ball popped out of his hands. As players from both teams scrambled to recover the loose ball, it squirted back into the end zone. A Crimson player parachuted over it and cradled the ball to score the only touchdown of the first half. The crowd of 40,000 leapt out of their seats and yelled. When the two teams retreated to their locker rooms for the halftime break, the fans stayed on their feet and clapped loudly. To them, order in the universe had just been restored; Harvard held a 9–6 lead.

With his cigarette wedged tightly into the corner of his mouth, Warner told his players that in the second half, the game plan would be different. The Indians would now run their reverses, passes, and misdirection plays. Also, Thorpe was going to touch the ball on nearly every offensive down. Thorpe still had a hitch in his gait due to the injury, but now at least he was loose and his adrenaline was flowing, which helped subdue the pain.

As soon as the Carlisle offense received the ball in the second half, the Indians awed the fans with their wide-open style. On one play, Welch handed the ball to Alex Arcasa, who sprinted around the right edge. But then Arcasa flipped the ball to Thorpe, who was running in the opposite direction. Thorpe, led by a guard and end who were acting as his blockers, blasted down the field for a sizable gain. Just as Warner had instructed, Thorpe had his hands on the ball on nearly every play. He ran between the tackles, he sprinted around the ends, and he even tossed a few passes. Midway through the third quarter, Thorpe led Carlisle on a 70-yard touchdown drive, which culminated with a short plunge up the middle by Arcasa. A few minutes later Thorpe kicked another field goal, this one into the wind from thirty-seven yards out. When the third period ended, Carlisle led 15–9.

On the Harvard sideline, the starters anxiously paced in front of the small canopy that covered the bench. Team captain Robert Fisher and All-American halfback Percy Wendell ached to enter the game, but the assistant coach had been given a strict order by Haughton: No starters were to play. During the two-minute break between the third and fourth period, Fisher passionately argued with the assistant, telling him that they were going to lose the game if the starters weren't inserted. The coach wouldn't budge. Fisher felt he had no choice: He overruled the assistant coach and led a mutiny. He told the starters to follow him out onto the field, and they did.

Now the battle was joined. As the fresh Harvard players jogged onto the grass, the crowd rose to its feet and roared its approval. Many of the Indians, who were on the sideline trying to catch their wind, turned around and saw the Crimson first-teamers in their clean red jerseys lumbering onto the field. The game had been as physically draining as any that Carlisle had played in the season, and now, as the Indians spotted the wave of new Harvard players coming at them, they realized that the struggle was just beginning. It was going to be a dogfight to maintain the lead.

It didn't take long for the Harvard starters to make an impact. Soon after they entered the game, Thorpe dropped back to punt. After he received the snap, he took a step forward and then smacked the ball with his right foot. But before it got airborne, a Harvard player who'd busted through the line blocked it. Crimson tackle Bob Storer snatched the ball off the ground and sprinted into the end zone for a touchdown. Though Harvard hadn't done much on offense all afternoon, the Crimson scored two special-teams touchdowns and now the game was tied 15–15.

On its next offensive series, Carlisle again leaned on Thorpe. Though the first-string Harvard defense did slow down Thorpe whenever the Indians ran a reverse, he was still effective when he received a pitch and ran around either end. And though he clearly wasn't at full power, Thorpe, grunting loudly, rarely fell to the ground on first contact. It usually took two, three, four, or even five Crimson defenders to haul him down. As Warner paced the sideline, even he was moved by the heart and soul that Thorpe was showing on the field.

With time running out in the game, Carlisle faced a fourth down with the ball on Harvard's 48-yard line. But instead of calling for a punt, Welch surprised everyone in the Indian huddle by saying that Thorpe was going to attempt a long field goal. "Who in the hell heard of a placekick from here?" Thorpe asked Welch. "Let's punt the ball."

Welch repeated the play call. Thorpe lined up deeper than usual for the placekick, knowing that he needed to take a longer run at the ball to give the kick as much oomph as possible. The ball was hiked to Arcasa, the holder who was crouching on the ground. Arcasa put the ball on the field, and Thorpe approached in a straight-ahead line. One step, two, three— Thorpe planted his left foot next to the ball and swung his right foot back as far as he could. Putting all of his weight and power into it, Thorpe drilled his foot through the ball. It barely cleared the cluster of Harvard hands that leapt to block the kick, but once it did the ball traveled higher and higher. The kick looked as pretty and as effortless as a majestic fairway shot by golfer Johnny McDermott, who just a few months earlier had ended the era of Scottish dominance in golf by becoming at age nineteen the first U.S.-born American to win the U.S. Open.

Not even Thorpe thought he could split the uprights from this distance. It seemed a country mile away from where he was standing, but he had underestimated himself. The ball flew through the air as if it had wings and glided through the goalposts with about ten yards to spare. The crowd was stunned into silence. Carlisle now had an 18–15 lead with just a few minutes to play.

When Harvard received the ball on offense, they were quickly forced to punt. Gus Welch handed the ball off to Thorpe a few more times. With just a few ticks left on the clock, Thorpe was tackled by a Crimson defender and fell to the ground hard on his ankle, reaggravating the injury. Thorpe had rushed for 173 yards, and now, as he was carried off the field by some of the Carlisle second-teamers, the Harvard fans gave him a standing ovation. After the final whistle blew, many of the Crimson players cried as they shook hands with the Indians, and in a final display of class, the Harvard fans cheered both teams as they walked to their respective locker rooms.

The next week the Crimson would beat Dartmouth 5–3, which would launch Harvard on a school-record thirty-three-game winning streak.

Newspapers around the country trumpeted the show that Thorpe had put on against Harvard as one of the most memorable in the short history of college football. A reporter for Boston's *American* newspaper noted, "Even the most partisan Crimson supporter will gladly admit, through their admiration for [Thorpe's] wonderful work against Harvard, that he not only upheld an already great reputation, but that he has placed his name in the Hall of Fame, not only of Carlisle but also of the entire football world. It was indeed a pleasure to see a man not only live up to a great reputation but add to it through work beautifully accomplished."

A reporter from the *Boston Sunday Post* wrote, "In an unequal conflict between the white man's brawn and the red man's cunning, the wiles of the redskin prevailed. . . . Harvard had heard of Thorpe and his great resourcefulness and skill. Today the Harvard Eleven, or what remained of the great team that Percy Haughton built up, can tell you more about him. Warned to be on guard against the bull-like rushes of the speedy Indian back, taught to beware of the unerring accuracy of the Carlisle man's toe, admonitions proved fruitless and the united power of the Harvard team was powerless to stop him."

When Haughton, Harvard's coach, read these game recaps, he felt like pounding his fist through his desk. He had dramatically underestimated the skill of Carlisle—a mistake he vowed never to make again.

Years later, when Warner was asked about Thorpe's performance against Harvard in 1911, he would call it one of the two best of Thorpe's career. The other came exactly 363 days after Harvard when Warner, Thorpe, and Carlisle traveled to West Point to take on Army.

The morning after the Harvard game, the Carlisle players and coaches traveled by train south to New York City. Warner had just collected $10,400 in gate receipts from the Harvard game, and he wanted to show his boys a good time in the big city. That evening, he escorted them to the Hippodrome Theatre on Sixth Avenue between Forty-third and Forty-fourth streets. Built in 1905, the Hippodrome boasted 5,200 seats and a grand, sparkling stage with opulent sets that featured vaudeville acts, trapeze performers, puppet shows, circus animals, and a five-hundred-member chorus. The Indian players loved trips to places like the Hippodrome, and it immersed them deeper and deeper into the white culture that was now embracing the Carlisle football team as never before.

When the Indians strolled into the Hippodrome, Warner's boys were dressed neatly in their military uniforms. As always, Warner wanted his players to project the image of the new Indian, and on this night in New York City, snooping stares tracked the players' every step and their every hand gesture. Once the players headed back to their hotel rooms on nights out in the big city like this, it wasn't uncommon for a few of the Indians to crack open a bottle of booze they had purchased and celebrate into the small hours of the morning. Warner knew what was happening, but he looked the other way, allowing his boys to blow off some steam.

When the Indians arrived back at the Carlisle train depot the following afternoon, the entire student body and more than half the town were waiting to greet them. With the band leading the way, the party turned into a parade that snaked through the streets. The procession eventually wound through the school gates. To everyone who was there, it felt like Warner's boys had just brought a national championship back to Carlisle. The giant had been slain.

This afternoon of unfettered joy would be the highlight of the 1911 season for the Indians. The next week Carlisle lost to Syracuse 12–11 in a game that was played on a muddy field, which usually portended doom for the Indians. Carlisle finished the season by beating Johns Hopkins (29–6) and Brown (12–6). Their final record for 1911 was 11-1, the best in school history, and the Indians had outscored their opponents 298 to 49. Warner had hoped to go undefeated and be recognized as the national champion by Walter Camp, but the loss to the Orangemen dashed that dream.

Yet Warner wasn't too saddened. He had already done the calculations and he believed that his 1912 squad would be the best team of his Carlisle tenure—maybe even a perfect team. There was only one problem: Thorpe would soon develop a severe case of wanderlust, and Warner would have to summon all his persuasive powers to convince him to return to Carlisle for the season that mattered most.

On the eve of their departure to Stockholm, Sweden, for the 1912 Olympics, Pop Warner provides a shoulder to lean on for his prize athletes, Lewis Tewanima (left) and Jim Thorpe (right). (Courtesy Cumberland County Historical Society)

11

A REAL AMERICAN IF THERE EVER WAS ONE

Life in America seemed to pick up pace in the spring of 1912. A dance craze was twisting and shaking across the country, provoking teenage boys and girls to move their feet to the local concert halls on Saturday nights and jiggle the fox trot, the horse trot, the chicken stretch, and the bunny hug. Model T Fords were also speeding up the way Americans lived. In 1912, for the first time, Model Ts were being mass-produced through a new concept called the assembly line, which reduced the cost of Henry Ford's signature car to six hundred dollars. This meant that the middle and working classes could now be like Pop Warner and afford the luxury of driving an auto.

In the spring of 1912 new products like Hellmann's "Blue Ribbon" mayonnaise and Morton's "pourable" salt were flying off the shelves at grocery stores. The Girl Scouts of America had just formed, as had a new company called Universal Pictures. Those who enjoyed reading had their hands on a French novel by Gaston Leroux that had recently been translated into English titled *The Phantom of the Opera*. Baseball fans were marveling at the play of the Boston Red Sox, who, led by pitcher Smoky Joe Wood, would go on to win 105 regular-season games—the most in franchise history—and beat the New York Giants four games to three in the World Series.

But as Dwight Eisenhower and Jim Thorpe went about their school years in the spring of 1912—and as their lives came steadily closer to colliding with the force of two Model Ts at full throttle—the one topic that dominated conversations in America was the sinking of a ship in the North Atlantic. At about 11:40 P.M. on April 13, the ocean liner *Titanic*, flagship of the White Star Line, was carrying 2,224 passengers on its maiden voyage when she struck an iceberg. Though the impact lasted less than ten seconds, the collision gashed the ship's hull. Thirty minutes later, after inspecting the damage that stretched 250 feet long, Captain Edward J. Smith issued the call to abandon ship. But the *Titanic* had only enough lifeboats to carry 1,200 people, and when the last lifeboat splashed into the water at 2:05 in the morning, more than half of the men, women, and children passengers were still on the sinking ship. Minutes later, *Titanic* plunged into the cold blue darkness of the North Atlantic, taking the souls of 1,523 passengers and crew with it.

The *Titanic* tragedy hit particularly close to home for Thorpe and Warner. Within weeks, they would be making their own cross-Atlantic voyage, traveling through the same choppy waters that were now *Titanic*'s graveyard. And as with the legendary liner, what Thorpe and Warner were about to do would be talked about long after they were gone.

Omar Bradley had a long, thin face and sad eyes, which earned him the distressing distinction of being known as the "ugliest man in [his] class" at West Point. One cadet poked fun at Bradley's looks by giving him the nickname "Darwin" because of his perceived likeness to an ape. But this Darwin had highly evolved hand-eye coordination skills, and once he stepped onto the baseball diamond with his buddy Dwight Eisenhower when they were plebes in the spring of 1912, the snide remarks stopped. The plebe players, the coaches, even the varsity guys all were impressed with what Bradley—the future five-star general who led the Allies to victory at the Battle of the Bulge during World War II—could do out on a baseball field. He caught everything that was hit his way in the outfield, running down fly balls as if he knew where they were going before the hitter swung his bat, and his right arm might have been the most powerful on campus.

Bradley, a pensive, slow-talking kid from Missouri who took his academy entrance exam in St. Louis a few months after Eisenhower, had been assigned to F company, just like Ike. The two became fast friends, swapping stories about their youths in the Midwest. Bradley wasn't as big a talker as Eisenhower, but he could listen as well as anyone Ike had ever come across. That was what made Cadet Bradley so unique. He was a master observer, and nothing slipped past his eyes undetected. When they played football together on the Cullum squad, Bradley would stand on the sideline and quickly be able to ascertain the strengths and weaknesses of the opposing team. This wasn't lost on Eisenhower, and years later he would recall his friend's keen eye for observation at one of the most critical junctures in American history.

Together Bradley and Eisenhower tried out for the baseball team in the spring of 1912. Ike was still hoping to be a two-sport star at the Point. He fully expected to be on the varsity squad in baseball after the final cuts were announced. Then, in the fall, he planned on making the varsity football team after his impressive first-year season on the Cullum Hall squad.

One spring afternoon, Eisenhower, Bradley, and a few dozen other plebes played a baseball game under the watchful eye of Sam Strang, West Point's baseball coach, who had been a pro player for the New York Giants. In 1905, Strang, who possessed the all-around skills to fill in at several different positions in the field, served as the Giants' utility player. That season he wound up leading the National League with eight hits that he smacked into play after he had been his manager's last-second substitute for the scheduled batter—and, according to lore, it was Strang's penchant for "coming through in the pinch" that led to the term "pinch hitter" being added to the baseball lexicon.

Now Strang, a well-known tippler who often traveled to New York City cabarets to go bingeing with his old teammates, watched the pickup game on this spring afternoon in 1912 closely. At one point a hard line drive was smashed toward Bradley, who was playing left field. Though he was positioned deep near the fence, Bradley snatched the ball off the ground, took a few steps, then reared back and fired the ball to home plate, putting all of his strength into the throw. As the ball hissed through the fresh spring air, Strang couldn't believe what he was seeing. The ball kept speeding forward until, most improbably, it reached the catcher. After the game, Strang approached Bradley and told his young player that in all his days in the big leagues he'd never seen a longer throw than the one Bradley had just uncorked. Strang scribbled Bradley's name down on a card and wrote: "Bats right, throws right, hits curve, fine arm." The coach then told him that he might one day make an excellent varsity player, which delighted Bradley and gave him a needed shot of confidence.

Ike also impressed Strang, but only with his fielding. The West Point coach cringed every time he saw Cadet Eisenhower swing a bat. At Abilene High, Ike had a reputation for being a sleek center fielder and being serviceable at the plate. He was trained by his high school coach to be a "chop hitter"—to take stabs at the ball with his swing and poke it into places where the opposing fielders weren't standing. It was an effective method at Abilene and was how he hit during the summer he played semipro ball, but Strang abhorred that style of swing. As a former Major League player, Strang liked guys who swung for the fences and tried to atomize the ball during every at-bat. He told Ike that he had a spot waiting for him on the varsity team next season if he became a proficient free swinger. "Practice hitting my way for a year and you'll be on my squad next spring," he told Eisenhower.

Those words left Ike crestfallen. For the second time in his plebe year, he was told that he would have to spend the season on the junior varsity. There was nothing left for Eisenhower to do but to train and start looking ahead to the near future. The start of summer football camp was only a few months away, and as soon as Ike learned that he wasn't on the varsity baseball team, football began to dog his thoughts as prevalently as a first crush. Day and night, the questions charged at him: *What do I need to do to make the varsity football squad? How can I become bigger? Faster? Stronger? How can I impress Coach Graves more than anyone else?*

Just before 9:00 A.M. on June 14, Jim Thorpe strode down a street in southern Manhattan, walking toward the SS *Finland,* Red Star Line, which was docked in the port of New York. Lugging a duffel bag and a small suitcase, Thorpe felt comfortable, at ease, and Pop Warner was strolling by his side, the familiar cigarette balanced between his lips.

At the fifth modern Olympiad, Thorpe was going to compete in the pentathlon and decathlon. Warner was acting as Thorpe's traveling partner, chaperone, and personal coach. James Sullivan, who ran the Amateur Athletic Union (AAU), had invited Warner to make the transatlantic journey. Sullivan knew that the U.S. trainer and coach Mike Murphy, who had been at Yale, had never worked with Indians before, and so he wanted Warner to tag along and train Thorpe and Louis Tewanima, a Hopi Indian from Arizona who was another of Warner's Carlisle Indian track stars. Tewanima was running in the 10,000-meter event and the marathon.

More than any other white man in America, Warner understood how to coach Indians. He had spent ten of the previous thirteen years training them and getting to know them. He took them to cities across the country, spent hundreds of hours shooting the bull on trains, had them over to his cottage for talks, drove them around town in his car on carefree afternoons, and led them on walks every Sunday during football season. He knew what they wanted and what they needed. Tewanima was so shy that he rarely spoke, but Warner had a penchant for connecting with him, just as he did with Thorpe, whose focus and concentration had a tendency to wander.

After spending years with Indians, Warner grew to be genuinely fond of them, especially his athletes—his boys. His attitude toward Indians had evolved ever since he arrived at Carlisle. When he first stepped onto the campus in 1899, he believed in all the prevalent Indian stereotypes: that they were lazy, that they were interested only in getting to the bottom of the bottle, that they were savages. But now he knew that they were as intelligent, as driven, and as athletically gifted as white kids. Warner sometimes lost his temper during practice and this caused many of the players to resent their coach, but Warner had real affection for his boys. He constantly told his Carlisle Indians that they had the chance to debunk all the Indian stereotypes with their performance on the athletic fields. Out there, they could show that they were equal to whites physically and mentally. In sport they could prove that they were second-class citizens to no one. It was a theme that Warner harped on virtually every day, and one he relayed frequently to Thorpe and Tewanima after he accepted Sullivan's invitation to accompany his boys to the Olympics.

The American team of 176 athletes and dozens of coaches was headed for Stockholm, Sweden, site of the 1912 summer Olympics. Once aboard the *Finland,* which was festooned with red, white, and blue bunting, the team had the rest of the day to unpack and adjust to their new surroundings. The 1912 squad was unlike the first four teams that the United States had sent to the modern Olympics, in two ways: women competed for the first time in 1912, and the athletes weren't just rich young white men from small club teams. This time the American organizers wanted to show the world that the finest athletes on the planet wore red, white, and blue across their chests. The talent bar had been set high, and the athletes were more diverse than any group the United States had ever sent. In the melting pot of star-spangled competitors were marathon runner Gaston Strobino, a young machinist's helper from New Jersey; sprinter Ralph Craig, a student from the University of Michigan; 350-pound shot-putter Pat McDonald, a cop from New York; and swimmer Duke Kahanamoku, a future sheriff from Honolulu.

When Thorpe strutted onto the 560-foot-long ship, he had trouble believing that such a massive structure could actually stay afloat. It was the biggest, most beautiful vessel he'd ever seen. The elegant dining hall, the spacious rooms, the twin smokestacks jutting skyward from the center of the ship—they all took his breath away. Six years later the *Finland* would transport nearly thirteen thousand troops to France to fight in World War I, but now, as Thorpe walked aboard carrying his bags, the ship seemed fit for royalty. Later in his life, Thorpe would recall this moment of stepping onto the *Finland* as his most precious Olympic memory.

A crowd of five thousand gathered at the pier to bid the athletes bon voyage. Waving American flags and shouting their support as the ship pulled out of port and into the foggy summer morning, the well-wishers were led by a man dressed as Uncle Sam. Fans carried tall sticks with large flags attached to the top and ribbons tied on the bottom that carried the message: "Bring Home the Bacon." Women in the crowd waved white handkerchiefs above their heads. The athletes gestured back jubilantly, thrilled to be receiving such a special patriotic sendoff. Along the back rail of the ship and away from the athletes, Warner stood by himself. He quietly watched the tall buildings of downtown Manhattan disappear into the fog as the ship sailed eastward out of New York Harbor. The Statue of Liberty melted into the horizon, and the boroughs of Brooklyn and Staten Island shrank into tiny specks of land and then faded from view altogether. When there was nothing left to look at but dark water, Warner began to plot a strategy for how he was going to make Thorpe the most famous athlete of the games.

The transatlantic trip was scheduled to take ten days, barring any unforeseen weather delays. For the athletes, this was no pleasure cruise. Starting at 10:30 every morning, they were put through a series of strenuous workouts that lasted into the evening. At noon they took thirty minutes for lunch—their only scheduled break of the day.

On the first morning of training, as the *Finland* steamed away from the United States, the ship was transformed into a gymnasium. In one corner of the vessel, high jumpers could be seen leaping over ropes and onto stacks of wrestling mats. The loud bangs of guns echoed from the riflemen who were firing at moving targets that had been launched from the ship over the sea. Tennis players swatted balls against a backboard, attempting to replicate match conditions. Swimmers plowed through water in canvas tanks. On the bow, weight lifters pumped iron, grunting and dropping their equipment on mats with a loud clang. On the eighth-of-a-mile cork-covered track that circled the ship, runners outfitted in turtlenecks, sweaters, and sweatpants jogged and sprinted in monotonous loops, hoping to keep up their wind for the games. Between workouts, the athletes could pick and choose from an impressive spread of food, but after several athletes gorged themselves on their first trip to the buffet, they became violently seasick, which would end up affecting their performance in the games.

When Thorpe wasn't working out, he would often sit alone and stare across the broad expanse of the Atlantic Ocean. One afternoon during the voyage, Francis Albertanti, a reporter for New York's *Evening Mail* who was making the trip with the team, spotted Thorpe. Many of Thorpe's teammates were busy training, but he was marooned in a corner and mentally visualizing flying through the air in the long jump—at the time called the broad jump—an event included in both the pentathlon and decathlon.

"What are you doing, Jim?" asked Albertanti.

"I'm practicing the broad jump," Thorpe replied. "I've just jumped twenty-three feet, eight inches. I think that can win it."

The pentathlon was a new event in the Olympics. Baron Pierre de

Coubertin, the founder of the modern Olympics, adopted the pentathlon for the 1912 games because he wanted a sport that tested all-around ability rather than one clearly defined skill. Three weeks earlier, during a special tryout in New York City's Celtic Park, Thorpe earned a spot on the U.S. Olympic Team in this new competition, which featured five events: javelin, running broad jump, 200-meter dash, discus, 1,500-meter race. When Thorpe showed up at Celtic Park with no bag and no equipment— "All Thorpe wanted to know is, 'When do we start?' " recalled one athlete who was there—he was as raw as any of the young men at the tryouts. In the discus, his footwork and form were so bad that it looked like he had never received any formal training in the event, even though Warner had given him a few rudimentary pointers. Shoddy form aside, Thorpe made the team.

The decathlon, Thorpe's other event in Stockholm, had been invented only two years earlier by the Swedes, and it was so new that only two other decathletes besides Thorpe showed up for the Olympic tryout in New York City. The tryouts were promptly canceled, but Warner strongly lobbied James Sullivan of the AAU to enter Thorpe in the decathlon, which featured ten events: the 100-meter dash, the running broad jump, the shot put, the high jump, the 400-meter run, the 110-meter hurdles, the discus, the pole vault, the javelin, and the 1,500-meter run. Warner argued to Sullivan that Thorpe had more all-around athletic skill than any athlete he'd ever come across, and that he had as good a chance to win gold as anyone else in the world. Sullivan eventually agreed to enter Thorpe in the competition.

Before leaving for Sweden, Warner arranged a track meet that pitted Carlisle against Lafayette College. Held in Easton, the meet took place on May 25, Lafayette's graduation day. When Warner and his boys arrived by train at the depot in Easton, the Lafayette track coach greeted them. "Where's your squad?" the coach asked.

"Right here," Warner replied, flicking his wrist at the eight Indian athletes who were stepping off the train behind him.

"You'd better call off the meet," the Lafayette coach insisted. "We have a squad of fifty. No sense in making a farce out of things."

"We'll compete in all the events except the pole vault," replied Warner, "and we'll try to make a contest out of it."

By the end of the meet, Thorpe had taken first place in six events, in-cluding the shot put, which he threw on one attempt. Lafayette did cap-ture the one event that Carlisle didn't enter—the pole vault—and Lafayette did score a lot of points for second-place and third-place finishes. But the Indians won everything else. Final score: Carlisle 71, Lafayette 41.

Soon after, Warner began counting down the hours until the opening ceremonies of the Olympics. *What will Thorpe do on the world stage?* Warner wondered.

The *Finland* first stopped in Antwerp, Belgium, where she docked along-side the main pier, and the first thing the team did was run off the ship and excitedly kiss the ground. When they looked up, they were greeted by members of the Swedish Olympic Committee, which serenaded the Americans with Swedish songs. For the next three days, Team USA camped out at the Beerschot Athletic Club, where training was scaled back and the athletes adjusted to being on firm ground again. Then they embarked on a bumpy four-day bus ride to Stockholm. Along the way, Thorpe stayed to himself and looked quietly out the window. There was such a powerful look of determination on his face that the other athletes privately remarked that Thorpe was going to have a successful Olympics; it was written all over him.

When the bus reached Stockholm, most of the athletes moved back into the *Finland*, which was docked outside of town and served as the team's living quarters. The rooms on the ship that weren't occupied by athletes were quickly rented out to the public to raise money to pay for the trip. This wasn't a glamorous way to live: To get off and on the docked ship, the athletes had to board a rowboat that was pulled ashore by a tug-boat.

Warner didn't want either of his Carlisle boys to stay on the ship, fear-ing that the distractions—and the temptations to create mischief with the other athletes—were too great. Instead, he arranged for Thorpe, Tewa-nima, and the rest of the marathon runners to stay in a spacious private residence in the town of Stocksund, which was about twenty-five miles outside of Stockholm. Before the games started, Warner kept the marathoners in shape by commanding them to go on ten-mile runs. He rode next to them in a car. As he motored down the road that led to Stock-holm, Warner constantly encouraged his runners to keep pushing them-selves. Tewanima especially needed to be prodded; he was still feeling seasick.

Every time Warner left the estate he ordered Thorpe to spend the af-ternoon training by himself in the backyard of the residence, which looked about as big as the Carlisle campus and featured a large garden and several towering oaks. On the first day that Thorpe was supposed to be practicing the long jump and high jump, he spotted a hammock that was slung between the trunks of a pair of leafy trees. He grabbed one of his schoolbooks from Carlisle and lay down. He closed his eyes and again vi-sualized how he was going to perform in the Olympics, how he was going to soar twenty-three feet in the long jump, how he was going to climb over six feet in the high jump.

In the days leading up to the games, Thorpe became very familiar with the hammock. He figured he was already in peak physical condition be-cause of all the time he spent on the football field, and he didn't believe he needed to fine-tune his body any more before the opening ceremonies.

Carrying the American flag, veteran distance runner George Bonhag led the 176 American athletes into the newly constructed, double-tiered Olympiastadion in Stockholm, which was jam-packed with 30,000 fans. Bonhag had won the gold medal in the walking race in 1896, and now he was a member of the largest-ever American Olympic team. More than 2,500 athletes from twenty-eight countries representing all five conti-nents—an Olympic first—filled the venue on July 6. They stood on the field and waved to the massive crowd. For the first time in history, the athletes were registered by their citizenship, not as individuals, giving the games a nationalistic flavor they had lacked since Baron de Coubertin organized the first modern Olympics in Athens in 1896.

When Thorpe first thought about participating in the Olympics, he believed it would be a nice vacation and that the games would be little more than a glorified track meet. But he slowly figured out how wrong he was. Looking up into the stands, which stretched up and up and seemed to kiss the clouds, he was dazzled. This stadium was even bigger than Har-

vard's and as grandiose as anything he'd ever seen. Suddenly, Thorpe realized he had underestimated the importance of the Olympic Games.

Once all the athletes were on the field, the crowd chanted an old battle cry that Swedish soldiers once uttered before drawing their weapons.
It was followed by a Swedish prayer, an English prayer, and speeches from
the Swedish Olympic Committee and the Crown Prince of Sweden. Trum-
pets blared from the four towers of the stadium and then Gustav V, the
king of Sweden, rose to his feet, grabbed the microphone, and shouted, "I
declare the Olympic Games to be on!" The crowd roared, and everyone in
attendance joined a chorus of 4,400 in singing Martin Luther's hymn
"Ein feste Burg ist unser Gott" ("A Mighty Fortress Is Our God"). All the
athletes passed by the royal box on their way out of the horseshoe-shaped
stadium, where the king elegantly doffed his black top hat as they passed.

By the time the opening ceremony was over, Thorpe, Tewanima, and
Warner were ready to find shade. A summer heat wave was washing over
Stockholm as temperatures hovered in the mid-90s. Most reporters
wrote that the thermometer spike would help the Americans, because
they were more used to the heat than their European rivals were. Certainly it favored Thorpe, the restless Indian boy who grew up running
everywhere he went on the torrid plains of the Oklahoma Territory, sunshine raining down on him like a spotlight.

Spread over two consecutive days, the pentathlon began on the second
day of competition at 1:30 in the afternoon. The first event was the running long jump—the same event that had occupied Thorpe's thoughts
while he lounged aboard the *Finland.* It was taken as an article of faith in
the press that the Europeans would dominate the pentathlon, which was
making its Olympic debut. Americans were considered excellent "specialized" athletes—meaning they were skilled in a particular event—but
most of the foreign writers believed that none of the Americans had the
all-around talent to compete for a medal in either the pentathlon or decathlon.

As the clock approached two in the afternoon on July 8, Thorpe stood
at the end of the runway, preparing to make his first jump. The athlete
who'd gone just before him, Norway's Ferdinand Bie, had taken the lead in

the competition with a jump of 22 feet, five and $\frac{7}{10}$ inches. Thorpe, sway-ing back and forth in the bronze-tinted afternoon light, looked down the runway, his dark brown eyes zeroing in on the sandpit that lay about forty feet in front of him. He was eyeing the 23-feet marker, knowing that's where he needed to land to beat Bie.

Compared to the other athletes in the competition, Thorpe did not cut an intimidating figure as he prepared to make his giant leap. At just a shade over five feet, eleven inches and weighing 181 pounds, he was shorter than most of the European pentathletes. But he didn't seem to have a trickle of fat on his frame. His body was perfectly symmetrical. His reach was 72.5 inches. His waist was 32.3 inches. His shoulders were slightly narrow—about 18 inches—but he was big-chested. A touch bow-legged, he commonly walked on the tips of his feet, which strengthened his calf muscles. He was such a marvel to behold that many of his com-petitors and Swedish fans started saying, in admiration, "Isn't he a horse!"

Wearing white shorts, running spikes, and a white cotton T-shirt that featured an American shield, Thorpe exploded down the runway, his arms and legs pumping like pistons. Nearby in the grassy infield, Warner watched anxiously. He believed that Thorpe could win this event if he put forth even half an effort, but he had no idea how his prize pupil would react to being on the world stage for the first time.

Thorpe blazed down the gravel running path. His back was as straight as a signpost and his chiseled chin was held up high. With every step he accelerated, then neared the scratch line. Warner watched as Thorpe hit the mark, then took off, ejecting into the air. With his arms winding above his head, Thorpe continued to ascend. At his highest point, his arms were pointed straight up to the heavens and his legs were bent at the knee, and then he soared farther than anyone in the stands could have imagined. When he landed in the sand, he fell forward. Warner smashed his large hands together in a joyous clap. He knew immediately that Thorpe had answered to the pressure of the moment. The jump was measured to be 23 feet, 2 and $\frac{7}{10}$ inches long. No one in the pentathlon would leap farther. After one competition, Thorpe had sent a statement to everyone else: He was the man to beat.

Next up was the javelin throw. The javelin competition dated back to the ancient Greek Olympics, but men had been casting spears at wild game and at enemy soldiers well before that. The key to the javelin throw was to heave the spear while running as fast as possible just before reaching the release line, which required training and proper coaching—neither of which Thorpe had received. Thorpe had been throwing the javelin for only a few weeks, and it showed. Displaying a form that was as raw as a caveman's, he took a few steps and chucked the wooden spear as far as he could. It swirled through the sky, sailing just under 153 feet, 3 inches, which was testament to Thorpe's natural strength. Sweden's Hugo Wieslander won the event with a toss of 162 feet, 7 and ³⁄₂₀ inches. Thorpe was visibly upset when he realized he'd finished in third place. Warner had hoped Thorpe would react this way, because it meant that his focus was dead-bolted on winning gold. Sometimes Thorpe's attention span unraveled like a child's, but not now. Warner told Thorpe to channel all of his disappointment into winning the 200-meter dash, the next event.

A few hours after the javelin throw, Thorpe toed the mark for the 200 with the other six pentathletes. Warner again stood nearby, anxiously pacing the grassy infield. The crack of the starting gun echoed through the stadium, and the runners were off, sprinting as hard as they could. Halfway through the race, five runners appeared to be in perfect line, shoulder to shoulder, their arms slicing through the warm air as they all tried to dig deep and find more speed. It looked as if Thorpe, two other Americans—James Donahue and Austin Menaul—and Canada's Frank Lukeman and Norway's Bie all had a chance to breast the tape first. With 50 meters to go, they were still even. The crowd rose to its feet. The race was only sixteen seconds old, but it was shaping up to be the most exhilarating of the games so far. As the fans exhorted the runners to go, go, go, Thorpe surged ahead with 10 meters left—barely. But it was enough: Thorpe, his arms and legs moving in perfect harmony, his head holding steady, hit the tape first. The electric timers and cameras, which were being used for the first time in Olympic history, recorded Thorpe's time as 22 and ⁹⁄₁₀ seconds. The two other Americans, Donahue and Menaul, were clocked at 23 seconds flat, while Lukeman (23 and ¹⁄₅) and Bie (23 and ¹⁄₂) came in fourth and fifth, respectively.

Thorpe went to bed that night out in the Swedish countryside rooming house with the lead in the pentathlon. The next day he and Warner returned to Olympiastadion for the final two events, the discus and the 1,500-meter race. Warner expected the discus throw to be Thorpe's weak spot in the pentathlon. The Indian's upper body wasn't as thick as many of the competitors', and several of the European writers speculated it would hinder him in the event. But Thorpe had a secret weapon: his legs. When he twirled and unleashed the discus into the air, the power of the throw was generated in his legs—the same legs that had run over hundreds of opposing football players in the last five years. When the judge yelled out Thorpe's distance after his first throw—"One hundred sixteen feet, eight and four-tenths inches"—the crowd again went wild. Thorpe won the event. His toss went nearly three feet farther than that of the second-place finisher, American Avery Brundage.

Thorpe had taken first place in three of the first four events and he held a commanding lead in the overall points. Unless he fell on his face and completely botched the 1,500-meter race, the final event in the pentathlon, he would win gold. Before the competition started, Thorpe and Warner had relished a head-to-head battle with Norway's Ferdinand Bie, a husky, blond-haired athlete who looked like a Viking and was the heavy favorite to win gold at the start of the pentathlon. Known for his closing speed and stamina, Bie was now in second place in the overall standings, and the strapping Scandinavian needed to win the 1,500-meter race to have any shot at the gold.

The seven runners hunched at the starting line. Thorpe—again dressed in white shorts, a white T-shirt bearing the stars and stripes of the American shield, and black running togs—had drawn a poor starting position. He was lined up second-farthest from the inside starting position, which was in the first lane that ran alongside the infield grass. Avery Brundage had the ideal spot, lining up first on the inside, while Bie was in the middle of the pack. The runners squinted into the sparkling sun as they eyed one another while taking their marks. The stands were only half full, as empty patches of seats dotted the grandstands. But those in attendance stared at the seven young men standing before a white chalk line, and a tremor of excitement rumbled through the stands.

The starting gun snapped. Thorpe didn't react as quickly as the other runners; it was as if his feet were momentarily stuck. When he finally burst off the start line, he was a few feet behind the leaders. For the first of the four laps, Thorpe was content to stay well behind the pack of leaders, which was being paced by Bie and Brundage. Midway through the second lap, just as Bie was pulling away from Brundage to take a commanding lead in the race, Thorpe accelerated, finding that extra gear. When the runners crossed the line that meant there was one lap remaining, Thorpe and Bie were running neck and neck.

The crowd was reborn. This was the duel they had come to see: the broad-shouldered, well-publicized Norskie versus the shorter, skinnier American who attended an Indian School in the boondocks of Pennsylvania. The two runners could feel each other's presence, and judging by their body language Thorpe had the upper hand. Bie was huffing to fill his lungs with air; Thorpe was cruising along like he was out running in the woods with his dog, trying to scare up game back home in Oklahoma. Bie didn't stand a chance. With three-quarters of a lap to go, Thorpe found yet another power surge and sprinted away from Bie. Thorpe won the event in dominating fashion with a time of 4 minutes, 44 and $^8/_{10}$ seconds. Two Americans—once again, Menaul and Donahue—came in second and third, respectively, while a fatigued Bie faded down the stretch to come in sixth.

As Warner congratulated Thorpe at the finish line, the Swedish crowd embraced Thorpe as if he were one of their own. His dominance in the pentathlon had been ruthless. He won four of the five events, and beat the runner-up, Bie, by a score of 7 to 21. (The low score won the competition; athletes were given one point for first place, two for second, three for third, and so on.) "His [Thorpe's] all around work was certainly sensational," James Sullivan, the commissioner of the AAU, told reporters on the day that Thorpe won gold. "It answers the charge that Americans specialize in athletics. It also answers the allegation that most of our runners are of foreign parentage. For Thorpe is a real American if there ever was one."

Thorpe had six days to rest and to prepare for the decathlon. He spent most of his time in the hammock at the private estate in Stocksund, on the *Finland* shooting the breeze with his teammates, or walking around the cobblestone streets of Stockholm. One day a few of the American athletes were lounging in a Stockholm bar when they came up with a wager. There was a chandelier hanging from the ceiling—about thirteen feet off the ground. Everyone put a dollar in a hat. The money would be given to the first one to jump and touch the chandelier. Alma Richards, a student from

Brigham Young who would eventually win gold in the high jump at these Olympics with a leap of 6 feet, 4 inches, took one step, two, three, then vaulted into the air. He soared as high as he could, but couldn't touch the chandelier. Then Thorpe, who was about three inches shorter than Richards, nonchalantly walked toward the chandelier. In one fluid motion, he jumped and rose into the air, then touched the chandelier with his hand. Thorpe took home the kitty.

Thorpe and his teammates enjoyed their downtime in Stockholm, which had been dressed up by its citizens. Roses were blooming on nearly every street. The waterfront was postcard perfect, bathed in ample amounts of sunshine for almost the entire duration of the games. And the dance halls were packed every night with the blond-haired, blue-eyed Swedish women who were eager to trip the light fantastic with young American boys, a fact that Thorpe discovered firsthand on several occasions.

Thorpe also penned several love letters to his girl, Iva Miller. Known as the prettiest girl at Carlisle, Miller had dozens of suitors, including Gus Welch, but her heart was wrapped around Thorpe. The two were both from Oklahoma and each had a stubborn streak. This showed when Warner, insisting that Thorpe wasn't as responsible as he needed to be, told Miller not to date Thorpe. But the Carlisle coach didn't sway Miller. She and Thorpe had fallen in love. Thorpe revealed his tender side to her, telling Miller that one day he would marry her and they would start a family together. Miller felt the same way, and she even had her own nickname for Thorpe: "Snooks."

In Sweden, Snooks missed his girlfriend dearly, and he poured his feelings into every letter he mailed back to Carlisle.

Thorpe had time to watch his good friend Louis Tewanima compete in the 10,000-meter run. Like Thorpe, Tewanima had already grown into a larger-than-life figure to the boys at Carlisle. A few months before the Olympics, Tewanima participated in the annual state collegiate meet held on the island in the Susquehanna River in Harrisburg. At five feet, six inches and 120 pounds, Tewanima seemed to possess the lung capacity of a whale and had more stamina than anyone Warner had ever seen. Growing up in Arizona, he often ran twenty miles a day while kicking a small ball all the way—a favorite pastime of Hopi boys. To prepare Tewanima for the 10,000 in Stockholm, Warner suggested that Tewanima run to Harrisburg all the way from Carlisle—about eighteen miles—and then participate in the two-mile run. Tewanima agreed. After covering the eighteen miles in about an hour and fifty minutes, Tewanima triumphantly jogged into the stadium. He then ran in the two-mile race. He didn't win, but that was beside the point. At the Carlisle campus, this act of endurance was the stuff of legend.

Tewanima came from a long line of runners. In fact, the first runners in America—the first athletes in America—were Indians. The earliest tribes of Indians had Runners, who delivered messages, brokered treaties, and offered advice to other tribes. In 1680, for instance, Pueblo Indian Runners sprinted across the high desert of what is now New Mexico carrying sticks that had messages coded into them. The Runners told other Pueblo Indians to rebel against the Spanish colonists who were taking over their land and burning their sacred religious symbols. The Runners successfully spread their message and colonists were eventually pushed back.

To prepare for their tasks, the Runners often covered thousands of miles. In 1890, Runners from South Dakota crossed almost half the nation to get to Washington, D.C., to relay to government officials the Indian version of what had transpired at Wounded Knee. The Hopi Indians were considered the most elite of the Runners; the Navajos called them "little rabbits."

By the time Tewanima was hurtling around the track in Stockholm in the 10,000-meter run, news of Thorpe's golden performance in the pentathlon had reached the halls of West Point. The Army football players read about Thorpe's accomplishment in the New York newspapers, which for the first time were giving the Olympics front-page coverage. Back in 1896, the first modern games had been barely mentioned in American newspapers. By 1906 a few U.S. reporters traveled to the games in Athens, but the stories were trumped by the great San Francisco fire. Now that an Indian was dominating the games, Jim Thorpe's name blared off the front pages of the nation's major dailies like *The New York Times* and the *New York Tribune*.

The West Point football players knew that Thorpe might be back at Carlisle when the Indian football team was scheduled to play at West Point just four months down the road. Soon the phrase "Get Thorpe!" would enter the West Point lexicon, as the Army players, very much including Eisenhower, discussed the mouthwatering possibility of facing the Olympic gold medalist on Cullum Field on November 9, 1912.

At 4:15 P.M. on July 8, Tewanima broke off the starting line for the 10,000-meter run, which covered 6.2 miles. Like Thorpe, Tewanima was a crowd favorite, and he was showered with cheers as he glided around the track on his first lap. Tewanima wanted to stay close to Finland's Hannes Kolehmainen. The Finns were known as the best long-distance runners in the world, and no one was better than Kolehmainen, a twenty-year-old bricklayer who was tagged with the nickname of "Smiling Hannes." Finnish newspapers hailed Kolehmainen as a role model for the working class, and at the closing ceremony Smiling Hannes would have three gold medals and one silver wrapped around his neck. He was the favorite to win the 10,000, and when the runners crossed the line to complete their first lap, Tewanima was right by Kolehmainen, matching the slender Finn stride for stride.

But Tewanima wasn't at his peak this day. The transatlantic voyage had given him a severe case of seasickness, and his internal compass was still a tick off. He gritted his teeth and tried to stay glued to Smiling Hannes's back, but by the second lap he began to fall off Kolehmainen's blistering pace. By the sixth lap it was all but over as the Finn had pulled away from the field. Kolehmainen crossed the finish line in 31 minutes, 20 and $\frac{8}{10}$ seconds, setting a world record. Some forty seconds later, Tewanima ran across the finish line. To the delight of the crowd, the little Carlisle Indian won the silver medal in a time of 32 minutes, 6 and $\frac{6}{10}$ seconds, a U.S. record that would stand for fifty-two years.

Six days later, on July 14, Tewanima tried to win another medal—this one in the marathon. When the runners lined up at the start line at 1:45 in the afternoon, the heat wave that had gripped Stockholm spiked. The air baked at 89 degrees, and the high humidity made it feel hotter than that. Though the course was flat and had been lightly watered to minimize the dust, the runners resisted setting a fast pace because of the scorching summer sun. By the midway point of the marathon, several runners had dropped out, suffering from symptoms of sunstroke and dehydration. Fluids weren't readily available along the route, and most runners wore handkerchiefs or white linen hats to shield their heads from the burning sun. One runner in particularly bad shape was Japan's Shizo Kanaguri. He eventually stumbled into the yard of a Swedish family enjoying a picnic. The family offered Kanaguri a drink of raspberry juice, which he accepted, and then the runner went inside to lie down on a bed. He never did rejoin the race.

Around the eighteen-mile mark, Portuguese runner Francisco Lazaro collapsed on the ground. He'd been stricken with sunstroke. The next day he died in a Swedish hospital, becoming the first fatality in Olympic history. Tewanima also struggled in the oppressive heat. He crossed the finish line in sixteenth place in a time of 2 hours, 52 minutes, 41 and $^4/_{10}$ seconds. The only runners who didn't seem to be slowed by the elements were South Africans Kenneth McArthur and Christopher Gitsham. With two miles left in the race, Gitsham, who was leading, stopped and gulped a few mouthfuls of water. McArthur blasted past his countryman and went on to breast the tape at the finish in a time of 2 hours, 36 minutes, 54 and $^8/_{10}$ seconds. "He said he would wait for me while I took a drink," Gitsham said after the race. "But he didn't."

"I went out to win or die," McArthur said.

Of the sixty-eight runners who started, only about half finished, which is why Warner wasn't disappointed in Tewanima's run. Given that his Hopi athlete was still reeling from the effects of seasickness, Warner felt Tewanima had definitely given an Olympic effort.

The ten-event decathlon took place over the final three days of the Olympics. Since winning gold in the pentathlon, Thorpe had participated in two individual events and was underwhelming in both: he finished fourth in the high jump and seventh in the long jump. Warner knew that Thorpe's Olympic legacy would be tethered to his performance in the decathlon, the most punishing competition in the games. To win gold in this trial of endurance, an athlete would need strength, speed, stamina, coordination, and, most of all, resiliency of spirit. If Thorpe was in the proper state of mind, Warner believed he couldn't be stopped. But as Warner and

Thorpe walked into the Olympic stadium for the start of the three-day decathlon, the coach feared that his Carlisle Indian might not even medal. A powerful thunderstorm had blown into Stockholm, and there were few things in life that Thorpe liked less than competing in the rain. Looking up into the gray sky, Warner could barely believe their bad luck. The sun had shone for nearly the entire duration of the games. Thorpe's worst game of Carlisle's 1911 football season had come against Syracuse in a rainstorm, and now Warner, looking at Thorpe's long face, feared that the elements might again conspire to slow down his young star.

Among the twenty-nine athletes in the decathlon, the favorite was Hugo Wieslander, who had won three decathlons in Europe in the months leading up to the Olympic Games. But the first event was one of Thorpe's strongest: the 100-meter dash. In the previous three months, both in meets and in practice, Thorpe had routinely run the 100 at slightly over 10 seconds. Warner, standing near the finish line rolling a cigarette between his fingers, believed this event would foreshadow how Thorpe would perform in the rest of the competition. If he was fast, he'd cruise to gold; if he was slow, he'd be lucky to snag the bronze.

Thorpe lined up at the start line. When the gun sounded, he exploded into the soggy morning. He wasn't as quick as he'd been in previous races, but he still crossed the finish line in a time of 11 and $^2/_{10}$ seconds, which was fast enough for second place. Warner wanted more out of his athlete, but this wasn't disastrous. Thorpe could still win the competition.

The next event was the long jump, which was held shortly after the 100. Warner was still concerned about Thorpe's mind-set, and Thorpe did little to allay Warner's fears when he became the only athlete who faulted on his first two attempts. The conditions on the runway were slick, and Thorpe appeared out of sorts. If he overstepped the takeoff board on his third and final attempt, he would finish dead last, which would likely knock him out of medal contention. Warner was as nervous as he'd been since arriving in Sweden. Thorpe, however, seemed as relaxed as ever. When he was in the hammock, his mind was on competing. But now that he was competing, it seemed as if the hammock was on his mind. Thorpe looked as calm as a monk as he prepared to make his final sprint down the runway: just another day and just another event. He carefully cruised down the runway, then hit his mark perfectly. He flew through the air and landed 22 feet, 2 and $\frac{3}{10}$ inches later in the sandpit. This wasn't Thorpe's best feat, but he still finished in second place. More important, Thorpe didn't sabotage his gold medal hopes with a disqualification.

Next up was the shot put. To give Thorpe a boost for the next competition, Warner told him to change out of his damp shirt and shorts. Warner wanted Thorpe to feel refreshed—and recharged—by a new set of dry clothes, and the ploy worked. Thorpe launched the shot 42 feet, 5 and $\frac{9}{20}$ inches, which earned him second place. At the end of the first day, Thorpe had more points than any other decathlete, even though he hadn't won a single event.

The next morning in Stockholm dawned bright and clear and the flags that ringed the top of the stadium were perfectly still—the ideal conditions that Warner had hoped for. When Thorpe lined up for his next event, the high jump, he was flush with confidence. The swagger was back, and over the next few hours, it showed in the results: he won the high jump with a leap of 6 feet, 1 and $\frac{6}{10}$ inches. Thorpe then finished second in the 400-meter run, with a time of 52 and $\frac{2}{10}$ seconds. In the last two events of the second day of the decathlon, Thorpe again proved his mettle. He won the 110-meter hurdles in a time of 15 and $\frac{6}{10}$ seconds, and he finished second in the discus with a throw that traveled 121 feet, 3 and $\frac{9}{10}$ inches. By this time, even Wieslander, the favorite to win gold, was awestruck by the exploits of Thorpe.

Heading into the final day of the competition, Thorpe held a 550.67 point lead over E.L.R. Mercer, an American. The first event of the morning was the pole vault. Clutching the pole, Thorpe stormed down the runway. He planted the stick and catapulted himself, easily clearing the hurdle, which was set at 10 feet, 3 inches. He landed fine in the sandpit, but the jump had spooked him. On liftoff it felt to him that the pole came perilously close to snapping in half. Thorpe was heavier than the other decathletes, and he feared he might seriously hurt himself if he made another attempt and the pole broke. Thorpe informed the judges that he wouldn't attempt another jump. He was satisfied with 10 feet, 3 inches. He finished third in the event.

Thorpe's weakest event in the decathlon was next: the javelin. But as he had done ten days earlier in the pentathlon, he launched the javelin with all the power he had and it barbed into the grass 149 feet, 11 and $\frac{2}{10}$

inches from where he stood. It wasn't pretty, but Thorpe's toss wound up being the fourth-longest among the twenty-nine competitors. Warner couldn't have been happier.

The final event of the decathlon—and the final event of the fifth Olympiad—was the 1,500-meter run. At the crack of the starting gun, Thorpe swiftly sprinted to the lead. These were his final minutes on the international stage, and he wanted to give the audience something they'd remember. When he surged ahead of the other runners, the capacity crowd erupted. He was the buzz of the Olympics, and now the crowd sizzled in an emotional fever as the young Indian started to put some distance between himself and his competitors.

If Thorpe had been worn down by the previous nine events of the decathlon or the five events of the pentathlon, it didn't show. He dug deep and found more speed as the gap between him and the others expanded. The cheers of the crowd seemed to propel him farther, and his long, easy, graceful stride almost made it look like he was floating. With one lap to go, he continued to pull away from the field. When he broke the tape in a time of 4 minutes, 40 and $^1/_{10}$ seconds—a little more than 4 seconds faster than his 1,500 time in the pentathlon—he raised his arms and drank in his triumph. Warner, standing in the infield, had never been more proud of his star football player.

"At no time during the competition was I worried or nervous," Thorpe said to reporters after the race. "I had trained well and hard and had confidence in my ability. I felt that I would win."

Thorpe was fibbing a little: The rain at the start of the decathlon had unsettled him a little. But admitting he was nervous wasn't Thorpe's way— never had been.

Thorpe finished nearly 700 points ahead of Sweden's Wieslander, the hometown favorite. As in the pentathlon, Thorpe's dominance was total. He won four of the ten events, and he never finished lower than fourth in any one of them. At the awards ceremony later that afternoon Thorpe watched the American flag rise over the stadium. Later he was called to the carpeted victory stand to receive his gold medal from King Gustav. Dressed in a coat and tie and clutching his Panama hat in his hand, Thorpe approached the Swedish king with a half-smile on his face. When his name was announced over the public address system for the final time and it reverberated throughout the stadium, the crowd thundered, giving Thorpe the loudest cheer of the fifth Olympiad. Over the previous fortnight, Thorpe had seduced the fans with his intoxicating blend of speed and strength, and this final ovation was the crowd's way of saying goodbye to the Carlisle Indian.

When Thorpe reached the victory stand, the tall, slender monarch rose to his feet. Wearing a black top hat and a long coat, King Gustav momentarily stopped clapping along with the crowd and bent down. He placed a laurel wreath on Thorpe's head and handed him one of his two gold medals—this one for winning the decathlon. Thorpe also received a life-sized bronze bust of the king, which stood four feet tall and was twenty-two inches wide. Then the monarch presented Thorpe with a silver chalice that was a gift from the czar of Russia. Weighing thirty pounds and shaped like a Viking ship, the chalice was lined with gold and featured assorted jewels that glistened in the sunlight. As Thorpe was about to leave the stage, the king extended his hand. Then, as he heartily clasped Thorpe's large, muscular grip, he got swept up in the moment. Normally austere and sober-minded, King Gustav suddenly grew smitten. He leaned in close to Thorpe and said, "Sir, you are the greatest athlete in the world."

Without missing a beat, Thorpe replied in a voice barely louder than a whisper, "Thanks, King."

Thorpe walked off the stage and into the growing afternoon shadows that were seeping into the stadium. For the rest of his life, Thorpe would replay this scene in his head. Years later, with his eyes closed, he'd rerun it frame by frame when telling the story to friends—or even strangers—of how he became the only man in history to win Olympic gold in both the pentathlon and the decathlon.

That night the alcohol flowed like spring water in the Stockholm pubs that Thorpe and his entourage visited. Thorpe was the toast of the town, and everyone wanted to buy him a stein of Swedish beer. Late in the evening he staggered onto the *Finland*. Writers, fans, and even Warner had called him "a horse" over the course of the Olympics, and when he got back onto the ship he walked up and down the decks saying, "Out of my way, I am a horse. I am a horse." Though a few of the ship's passengers were startled to see Thorpe so full of liquid courage, most simply got out of his way and applauded him for his transcendent performance in the games. On this evening, even Warner tolerated Thorpe's behavior, allowing his prize athlete to let go of it all and enjoy his historic victory.

In Carlisle, hundreds of locals, students, and staff members at the Indian School waited outside the town's telegraph office every day to receive the results. And when Thorpe won gold, it was front-page, top-of-the-fold news. W. J. MacBeth, a reporter for the *New York American,* wrote, "Jim Thorpe of Carlisle will go down in athletic history as the noblest redskin of them all. It is doubtful that any human being ever [before] combined the manifold athletic proclivities of this young buck of the Sac and Fox tribe. By winning the pentathlon and decathlon in Stockholm, this aborigine proved to be the greatest individual star of the games."

Overnight, Thorpe became a mythical figure. For about a week, newspapers in such places as New York and Philadelphia devoted as much space to Thorpe as they did to President William Howard Taft. After the games were over, Thorpe toured through Europe with his two medals draped around his neck. He participated in several different track meets along with other members of the U.S. Olympic Team, and he won every event he entered except one. During a hurdles race in Paris, he heard something rumble above him moments after the starting pistol blared. He looked up and saw an airplane slicing through the blue sky. Thorpe had never seen a plane before, and he couldn't take his eyes off it. He was so amazed that he failed to clear his next hurdle, and fell face-first into the track cinder. But he didn't care that he finished last in the race. Afterward, as he scraped the dirt off his face, he excitedly asked his teammates, "Did you see the plane? Did you see the plane?"

When Thorpe finally returned to the United States, he was given a hero's welcome wherever he went. Girls fawned over him, little boys were constantly asking for his autograph, and grown men were always asking to shake his hand. He was the first true sports celebrity in America, and his fame cast a shadow that extended all the way to West Point. If Thorpe decided to return to Carlisle for one more season, as every Army player was hoping, then the Olympic gold medal winner would be making a trip to West Point in less than four months for a football game. For the Cadet players, this would be the opportunity of a lifetime. With a resounding victory over Thorpe's Indians, Army could make a mammoth impression on sportswriters from New York to Los Angeles. And if they could stop Thorpe, they would one day be able to sit their grandchildren on their knees and say, *Once upon a time, I shut down the man who was known as the greatest all-around athlete in the world.*

Thorpe wasn't even home from the Olympics yet, but at West Point a plan of attack was already under way. Plays were being drawn up in the dirt and tactics were discussed. To all the Army players, kickoff against Carlisle couldn't come soon enough.

Top: *Though Eisenhower didn't possess the all-around talent of Thorpe, he had some-thing coaches couldn't teach: determination that was as relentless as a prairie wind. He frequently stayed late after practice to do everything from running extra laps, to calisthenics, to working on his punting.* (Courtesy the Dwight D. Eisenhower Library)

Bottom: *Nothing put more fear into an opposing team than the sight of Thorpe* (far right) *in his crouched position in the backfield—a stance that Pop Warner invented at the turn of the century.* (Courtesy Cumberland County Historical Society)

12

CHIEF THORPE AND THE HUGE KANSAN

Sirens blared from the fire trucks that slowly rolled through the summer sunshine in downtown Carlisle, their flashers throwing flickers of red light on all the faces in the crowd that lined the street, giving them an artificial, vibrant flush. Ahead of the fire trucks of the Mount Holly Fire Department was a horse-drawn carriage with a uniformed driver. As the horse clomped forward along the cobblestone street, the crowd's attention riveted on the young man sitting in the back of the carriage wearing a felt hat, a starched white-collar shirt, and slacks. It was Thorpe, flanked by Warner and Tewanima, and the trio was home again. After stepping off the 12:30 P.M. Cumberland Valley train at the Carlisle depot to mark the end of their Olympic journey, they were paraded around town like dignitaries. The large crowd of men, women, and children lined the streets on this sun-baked August afternoon in 1912, hoping to catch a glimpse of America's newest athletic prince.

More fire trucks, a marching band, Carlisle students in their military uniforms, and members of the Improved Order of Red Men all followed in the wake of the chariot that carried the Carlisle Olympians. The parade route took the heroes to Biddle Field at Dickinson College. When Thorpe,

Tewanima, and Warner stepped out of their carriage, they were led onto a makeshift stage that had been erected on the field. Once on the elevated platform, they looked out into an ocean of faces. More than 5,000 fans had gathered to greet their Olympians, and many held banners that read "Hail to Chief Thorpe," "A Carlisle Indian," and "The Greatest Coach in the World."

As women shielded themselves from the sun with parasols and men in bowler hats sweated in the heat, the superintendent of Carlisle, Moses Friedman, strolled up to a microphone. "This is an occasion for celebration," he said, his voice echoing across the field. "It is a national occasion. The things we celebrate here and the heroes whom we welcome to Carlisle concern the whole country. All America is proud of their record and achievement. We have here real Americans, known as Indians, but whose forefathers were on the reception committee which welcomed to this soil the famed first settlers who arrived on the *Mayflower*."

"We welcome you, James Thorpe, to this town and back to your school. You have covered yourself with glory. By your achievements, you have inspired your people to live a cleaner, healthier, more vigorous life." Friedman then spoke about Tewanima, saying the Hopi runner had arrived at Carlisle with other Indians as a "pagan" with tattered clothes, flowing dark hair, and earrings. But all of that had passed, gone the way of the tomahawk. Tewanima was now civilized, Friedman said, and a gold-standard example of how Indians can assimilate.

Before leaving the stage, Friedman unfurled a letter from President Taft and read it to the crowd. Addressed to Mr. James Thorpe, the missive stated, "Your victory will serve as an incentive to all to improve those qualities which characterize the best type of American citizen. It is my earnest wish that the future will bring you success in your chosen field of endeavor. With heartiest congratulations, I am, Sincerely yours, William H. Taft."

After a few local leaders spoke, Warner strode to the podium. For most of the last year, Warner and Thorpe had rarely been out of each other's sight. They had grown almost as close as father and son, but like all father-son relationships, theirs was complicated, layered. Thorpe often felt smothered by Warner, while Warner believed that Thorpe needed more heavy-handed guidance to reach his potential. It was as if the two endured a silent power struggle, and this tug-of-war for control was constantly being waged. Thorpe always wanted more freedom to do as he pleased; Warner wanted Thorpe to live within the boundary of his rules and his words. Despite this, the two were genuinely fond of each other, and they both understood that they were much more formidable when united than if they had never met. Their fateful collaboration had taken them to places they had never dreamed they'd go, and if they both remained at Carlisle for one more year, there was no telling what kind of magic they could produce.

When Warner reached the microphone, he thanked everyone for coming. Then he turned his eyes to Thorpe, who was sitting behind him. This wasn't the time or place to spell out his feelings to the famous Indian from Oklahoma, so he kept things to the point, simple. "I thank you for all you have done" was all he said.

Thorpe had hoped he wouldn't have to speak, but the crowd loudly encouraged him to. He stood up in front of the microphone and, while looking at Warner, told his coach, "All I can say is that you showed me a good time."

The spotlight continued to burn on Thorpe. A few days after the celebration in Carlisle, he traveled to New York City for the biggest party of his life. All the Olympians rode in the back of separate open-air cars down Fifth Avenue for a parade that was attended by more than one million people. The massive crowd along the avenue was eight, nine, in some places ten persons deep as they cheered and threw confetti in the air. Thorpe was nervous and uncomfortable sitting in the back of the twenty-second automobile in the procession. The convertible directly in front of Thorpe carried his trophies from the king and czar and Thorpe received the loudest cheers of the day as he was carried through the concrete canyon of midtown Manhattan. But Thorpe was embarrassed by all the attention. As his convertible motored down the slick pavement, he kept pulling his Panama hat down to shield his eyes.

He was toasted at yet another parade in Philadelphia a few days later. Finally, he returned to Carlisle to begin again. The future, of course, seemed bright. Several professional baseball teams tried to lure him onto their rosters by dangling hefty contracts in front of him. A boxing promoter wanted him to step into the ring at Madison Square Garden. A horse-racing promoter offered Thorpe a chance to race a Thoroughbred. A slew of professional football teams wanted him to line up as their starting tailback. Promoter C. C. Pyle—known as "Cash and Carry" Pyle—promised Thorpe ten thousand dollars if he would go on a nationwide barnstorming tour with his baseball team. And several track coaches encouraged Thorpe to compete in events across the nation for the next year.

It was a dizzying time for Thorpe as he tried to make sense of all that was happening to him. There was only one person to whom Thorpe felt he could turn for advice on how the next act in his life should play out, and that was Warner. As soon as he was back on American soil, Warner turned his attention to the 1912 football season. He believed with a religious ferocity that his team would be considered the national champion at season's end—as long as he could convince Thorpe to give him one more season. When Warner talked to Thorpe about playing one more year of ball, he told his player that his value on the open market would be higher if he stuck around and led Carlisle to the national title. Warner also said that large crowds would watch him each weekend—larger than any in the 1911 season—and newspapermen would monitor Thorpe's every step on the gridiron as if he were a Hollywood leading man. *Carlisle's your home*, Warner told Thorpe. And to sweeten the pot a little bit more, Warner promised to give Thorpe a longer leash than in years past. He'd be allowed to wander outside of the rules that governed the rest of Warner's players.

The deal was just too irresistible, and Thorpe agreed to stay. Football fascinated him like no other sport. It fired his creativity, and playing it left him feeling like he was doing what he was born to do. Thorpe had also become more self-aware in the last twelve months, and he knew that when he stepped between the chalk sidelines he wasn't just representing his school. He accepted that he was a symbol, a role model even, for Indians all over the United States who were struggling to find their place in the America of 1912. Thorpe gave Indians hope for a better future, a better life, and if he could lead Carlisle to a national championship, it might lift the spirits of downtrodden Indians everywhere. This was the power that Thorpe now wielded whenever he laced up his cleats and trotted onto a football field.

In early September, a few weeks after returning from Sweden, Thorpe strolled back out onto the Indians' practice field, determined to make his last season at Carlisle his most memorable. It had been a fruitful summer for him; now he hoped his last verse at Carlisle would sound as sweet as the Shakespearean sonnets that the Indian students read when they opened their books in English literature class.

The silhouette of the solitary figure could often be seen on summer evenings out on the track at West Point. There in the gloaming a blond-haired young man dressed in shorts and a T-shirt stood at an imaginary starting line. He crouched in a sprinter's stance and then, in his mind, he'd hear the blast of the starter's pistol. The cadet would then bolt off the mark in a frenzy of churning legs and pumping arms. He'd sprint a few yards and then stop, turn around, repeat the drill.

Throughout the summer of 1912, Dwight Eisenhower worked as hard as anyone at West Point to improve his quickness. He had run track over the winter and was selected to play on the intramural medicine ball team, which consisted of the eight cadets who were judged to be the fastest out of the dozens who tried out for the squad. Once football camp opened in August, Eisenhower hoped to earn a position on the varsity as a halfback and linebacker, but the coaches had told him that the only way he'd make the squad was if he improved his foot speed. So whenever he had a few spare moments over the summer, he headed to the track, alone. There he practiced what he called "fast starts." If Ike didn't make the football team, it wasn't going to be from lack of effort.

The coaches also wanted Eisenhower to add some muscle to his frame, a request that further stoked his midwestern work ethic. To strengthen his arms and legs, Ike met with the gymnastics coach and practiced tumbles on the mat and other muscle-building exercises. He knew he didn't have a lot of time to harden his body, so he attacked every session with a sense of urgency. Football was the number one priority in his life, and he was going to do everything in his power to be on the varsity squad for the first game of the season against the Stevens Institute of Technology on October 5.

Eisenhower's chance to impress the coaches in game conditions arrived in early September when the Cadets scrimmaged a squad of soldiers on the parade grounds. Ike, who was buried on the depth chart because of his junior varsity status, sat on the sidelines for the first half, fidgeting for his chance. Then, early in the third quarter, Ernest Graves, Army's coach, pointed at him and told him to get out on the field.

Ever since Eisenhower had read his letter of acceptance to West Point, this was the moment that he had been waiting for. The thought of running free and wild and reckless on the football field while wearing the Army colors had sustained him through his darkest, hardest hours in his first year at the Point—through the hazing, the all-nighters of pulling guard duty, the stress of being away from Abilene—and this was his opportunity to turn his hope of making the team into a reality. Graves valued athletes who played as if they had something to prove—long the hallmarks of the archetypal Army football player—and in these next few minutes Ike planned to put on a show, going full-throttle to raise as much hell as was humanly possible on that grass with white stripes on it.

Graves, who was starting his second tour of duty as Army's coach, had a discerning eye for talent. In 1904, while a cadet at West Point, he was a lineman who served as the team's captain. Two years later he coached the Army team with Henry Smither. (That year, one of Graves's players was George S. Patton, who ultimately was sidelined for the season with two broken arms that he suffered while playing end.) Graves specialized in coaching line play, and his reputation quickly grew after his one season of tutoring the players at the Point. In 1908, Lieutenant Graves was serving in the Corps of Engineers when he received an offer from Harvard coach Percy Haughton to be the Crimson's line coach. Haughton was so desperate to get Graves on his staff that he sent a message to President Theodore Roosevelt asking that Graves be detached from his duty in Washington. Roosevelt, a Harvard graduate, then fired off a note to Graves's superior, Secretary of War William Howard Taft, a Yale alum. The president told Taft, "I was a Harvard man before I was a politician. Please do what these gentlemen want."

Graves, who opted not to coach at Harvard in spite of the presidential arm-twisting, now stood on the sideline and watched Eisenhower jog onto the field. For the next thirty minutes, Ike let go of any fears or nervousness he may have had and played as if it were the most important football game of his young life. Whenever he carried the ball on offense, he'd barrel into the line and push the pile forward, inch by grueling inch. When he cut to the outside, he flashed surprising speed and was able to outrun most of the defenders. His weight was now up to 174 pounds, and his chest had grown thicker. All the running on the track and in his regular cadet training had paid off as well. He was now one of the quickest cadets at the Point—a fact that would have amazed his former teammates in Abilene. Eisenhower wasn't as impressive at tailback as Geoffrey Keyes, the starter, but Graves liked what he saw whenever this Kansan got his hands on the ball.

Ike also made an impact on defense. From his linebacker position, he made sturdy, sure-handed tackles. He wasn't flawless, but Graves thought Ike had the perfect temperament for an Army football player. From snap to whistle on every play, he gritted his teeth and gave it his all, hustling even when he had no chance to make the play. At the end of the scrimmage, Eisenhower, his uniform covered with dirt and grass stains, pulled off his leather helmet. It wasn't in his nature to be satisfied, but he knew he couldn't have tried any harder.

Though practice was over, Eisenhower wasn't ready to head for the showers. He still had a few gallons of energy to burn, so he started jogging around the field. He ran his cool-down laps as the coaches stood nearby and compared notes on the scrimmage. After Ike completed several laps, he jogged toward the gymnasium that housed the locker room. He passed the coaches, who were walking toward the gym. When he was about twenty yards in front of Graves, he heard someone yell his name.

"Eisenhower!"

Ike turned around and saw that Graves was calling for him to come back. Ike sprinted to his coach, stopped, saluted Captain Graves, and bellowed, "Yessir!"

"Where did you get those pants?" Graves asked.

As was the case for many of the nonvarsity players, Eisenhower's uniform didn't fit. Before the scrimmage he was issued a pair of pants by the football manager that was about two sizes too big. While the varsity players had pants that fit snugly around their waists and legs, Eisenhower's were baggy and he was constantly pulling them up.

"From the manager, sir," Eisenhower replied to Graves.

"Look at those shoes," Graves said. "Can't you get anything better than that?"

Eisenhower froze. He didn't know what to say. As with the uniform, he had been given his old pair of scuffed cleats from the team's equipment

manager. Eisenhower meekly told his coach, "I'm wearing what I was issued."

Graves turned his attention to the Cadet manager, who was standing
nearby. Then he uttered words that Eisenhower would never forget. "Get
this man completely outfitted with new and properly fitting equipment."
Graves continued to needle Eisenhower about his sloppy appearance, but
Ike was in such a state of ecstasy that he could barely hear what Graves
was saying. Cadet Eisenhower immediately understood the implication of
what his coach was telling him: He needed a new uniform because he had
just made the varsity.

For the next few moments, Ike was in a dreamlike daze, as if everything was happening in slow motion. All the long hours spent alone on
the track, all the somersaults and flips that he'd done in the gymnasium,
all the force-feedings in the mess hall so he could gain weight—it was all
done so he could experience this moment, standing here in the sunshine
in front of his coach. *A varsity football player.* The thought strummed at
Ike's heartstrings, and as soon as Graves dismissed him Ike bounded into
the locker room like a kid who had just snagged an autograph from Ty
Cobb, the most famous baseball player of the day. Ike had waited an entire
year to put on a varsity uniform, and now the wait was almost over.

The equipment manager eventually joined Eisenhower in the locker
room. He handed Ike a freshly washed varsity practice uniform, one that
fit perfectly. When Cadet Eisenhower left the locker room and strolled
back to his bunk in Thayer Hall, he felt that he had just turned a corner in
his life. What was around the bend? Eisenhower couldn't wait to find out.

Late in the evening of September 17, Thorpe sat in his room at Carlisle
writing a letter to his brother Frank. "Well, Bud, I'm right in the game
again, playing football," Thorpe wrote. "We have our first game next Saturday. . . . Frank, I have a chance to make a bunch of dough after leaving
this school. Just started going today. God but it's hard to be back again, but
it is for my own good, so I will make the best of things. . . . Frank, it is getting late and I must close, hoping to hear from you real soon. Your
brother, James Thorpe."

After the final game of the 1911 season, as the Indian players rode a train from Providence, Rhode Island, back to Carlisle, the team voted for its captain of the '12 season. The vote wasn't close; Thorpe won the honor in a landslide. When he rejoined the team for practice just six days before Carlisle's first game of the 1912 season against Albright College on September 21, the players looked at him differently. Thorpe was no longer just one of the guys. Now he was the legend of the Olympic Games, an athlete who was known around the world, an Indian who was the pride of his people. The players had been reading about Thorpe in the newspapers, and now here he was, in the flesh, strolling onto the football field with them. Even though Thorpe was their buddy, many of the players— especially the younger ones—were starstruck when he first pressed his cleats into the crunchy grass field in the fall of 1912.

During the first days of practice, Warner wanted to scrape the rust off Thorpe's game, so he worked his tailback hard. In scrimmages Thorpe carried the ball on nearly every play. With his knees kicking high—his knees would become weapons in '12 whenever anyone tried to tackle him head-on—Thorpe sliced through the defense with such ease it was as if he hadn't missed any practice time. And the linemen who were blocking for him were already throwing their bodies around trying to protect him as if he were president of the United States—though to Indians everywhere, Thorpe was more important than that.

Carlisle opened its season by beating Albright College 50–7 on September 21. Four days later, the Indians demolished Lebanon Valley, 45–0. To the disappointment of the crowd, Thorpe remained on the sideline for the games, watching the action along with everyone else.

Away from football, Thorpe tried to adapt to his post-Olympic celebrity life at Carlisle. But the pressure of being famous weighed on him. Everywhere he went—to a pool hall in town, to a watering hole, to a fruit stand to pick up an apple or a plum—he could sense that the eyes of John Q. Public were following his every move. To get away from it all, he sometimes convinced his roommate and closest confidant, Gus Welch, to come with him and have a few beers behind one of the buildings located on the school farm. Welch had been charged by Warner to keep an eye on Thorpe and keep him in line, and Welch took the responsibility seriously. Whenever they tossed back a few suds, Welch made sure that he and Thorpe returned to their room without causing a commotion.

Thorpe's fellow Olympian Tewanima left school for his old home on the reservation in Arizona. All the soft-spoken Hopi ever wanted in life was to tend his herd of sheep, and before he stepped on the train to head west, he gave most of his track medals away as presents. A few girls at Carlisle promptly used them as shoe buckles.

Thorpe finally made his football debut in 1912 against Carlisle's crosstown rival Dickinson College on September 28. The last time Thorpe had been at Dickinson he had been feted as an Olympic champion, and now, as he jogged around Biddle Field during pregame warm-ups, the 10,000 fans in attendance were already on the edge of their seats, anxious to see if the local wonder boy was going to be as dominating as he had been the previous year.

Playing on a hot, humid afternoon, Carlisle started the game sluggish. After the first period the score was tied 0–0, but then, in an instant early in the second quarter, it all changed. Thorpe took a handoff at Dickinson's 29-yard line and darted straight ahead. Seeing a hole that his offensive linemen had ripped open, Thorpe blasted through. With his feet flying, he made a few impossibly quick cuts in the secondary that caused defenders to trip over their own feet. Then he charged into the end zone to score his first touchdown of the season.

Carlisle's defense held Dickinson and so forced a punt. The Dickinson defense stiffened. The Indians, deep in their own territory, lined up to punt. Thorpe was standing near his own goal line when the snap went back to him. But right away, he could see something was wrong. The center, Joe Bergie, was normally pinpoint accurate when he made the twelve-yard snap to the punter, but now the ball sailed over Thorpe's outstretched arms. Thorpe immediately sprinted after the ball, which was flopping around near the back of the end zone. When he reached the pigskin, he looked up and saw a half-dozen Dickinson defenders barreling toward him.

From the sideline, Warner yelled for Thorpe to merely fall on the ball and take a safety, which would give Dickinson two points. This would be better, Warner instantly knew, than if Thorpe advanced just a few yards and was tackled near the Carlisle goal line. If that happened, Dickinson would be awarded the ball and be within easy striking distance of scoring a touchdown, worth six points.

But for Thorpe it was a matter of instinct. He snatched the ball and immediately turned up the field. He quickly sprinted to the outside, faked a handful of defenders with a few ankle-breaking cuts here and there, busted through a few arm tackles with ease, then broke into the open field and turned on the afterburners. He outran everyone else for about 105 yards for the touchdown. The effort offered a stunning display of Thorpe's world-class speed and raw power, and the fans were still screaming wildly when Thorpe booted the extra point through the uprights. Carlisle won the game 34–0.

Over the next several days in practice Warner began experimenting with a new formation that he hoped to use at some point later in the season—perhaps, he thought, on November 9 against Army, a team that he was already fretting about because of their superior size. In this new formation, which Warner had scribbled on a piece of notebook paper days earlier, he moved his two tailbacks in the T-formation and lined them just to the outside of the defensive ends. The backs were set a few yards behind the line of scrimmage. In Warner's vision of this new offense, these two wingbacks—as he called them—would give him greater flexibility to throw the ball to the outside and run reverses. The wingbacks could be pass receivers, they could run the ball on reverses, and they could be blockers. Eventually Warner coined a name for the formation—the double wing.

Knowing that advance scouts from schools such as Army would be sitting in the bleachers for Carlisle's game against Villanova in Harrisburg, Pennsylvania, on October 2, Warner didn't unveil his new offense. Instead, he instructed quarterback Gus Welch to pitch the ball to Thorpe on nearly every play. Before it was even halftime, Thorpe had scored three touchdowns and kicked seven extra points. The rout was on and Warner removed Thorpe from the game. In the second half, as Carlisle was marching toward a 65–0 victory, Thorpe approached Warner on the sideline and asked if he could leave the area to join a group of friends. The coach reluctantly agreed. But as Thorpe walked away from the field, a horde of fans rushed him and followed him to the cluster of cars that were parked nearby. Thorpe signed autographs and shook hands with the Villanova fans, leaving many of them speechless.

In four games, Carlisle had outscored its opponents 194 to 7. As

Warner and his boys traveled back to campus after pummeling Villanova, Warner could almost see the faint outline of something in the faraway distance that he craved more than anything: a national championship.

Dwight Eisenhower walked onto the football field at West Point on October 5 with dreams the size of Kansas. The Cadets were about to play Stevens Institute in their season opener, which was taking place four days after Carlisle beat Villanova, and no player was happier to be strapped into a leather helmet than Ike. Now a starter on the varsity squad, Eisenhower was thrilled, for the pregame scene at the Point was just as he had imagined it during his endless summer of conditioning. A few thousand fans were sitting in the grandstands, including the Corps of Cadets. The Army band played, and the music filled the Hudson River Valley.

Ever since Eisenhower had caught the eye of Army coach Ernest Graves during a preseason scrimmage against a team of soldiers, Ike never let up trying to improve as a football player. At every practice he was the first player out on the field. While other Cadets were in the locker room still pulling on their football knickers and practice jerseys, Ike would be running warm-up laps around the field. At the end of practice, he would do the same thing. When the coaches looked over their shoulders as they walked toward the locker room, they would see Cadet Eisenhower still running loops around the field, out there alone as the day's last beams of light sprinkled through the maples and oaks on campus.

But it was how Eisenhower played during scrimmages that caused his status to skyrocket in the minds of the coaches. On offense, he played left halfback, and when he was handed the ball, he ran with the determination of someone who needed to gain ten yards or face the firing squad. Clutching the ball tightly, Ike slammed his body into opposing defenders who were trying to tackle him. If you weren't watching closely, it was hard to tell if he was on offense or defense—he was forever administering blows. Even Marty Maher, Army's team trainer, who'd seen a lot of aggressive play in his many years of working with the team, noted that Eisenhower was "mighty rough" during these preseason practice sessions.

Maher didn't think many athletes at West Point ever fulfilled their potential—especially football players. He chalked it up to the relentlessness of the academy lifestyle: the younger cadets were challenged in the classroom by instructors, in the mess hall by other cadets, even in their dorm rooms by the upperclassmen. They rarely got a chance to goof off, to be kids, and it was hard to relax and regenerate both the mind and the body. Maher, who would spend fifty-five years at West Point, believed this was why football players at the Military Academy never seemed to develop as fully as players at other schools.

Eisenhower was different. He was always gunning for an opportunity to play a prank and lighten the mood of everyone around him. When he was up to his high jinks, he'd wear a mischievous grin and be just as determined to get a laugh as he was to gain yards on the football field. One time he hurled a piece of meat at another cadet in the mess hall, hitting him in the back of the head. When the cadet turned around and saw Eisenhower trying to conceal a giggle, he tossed a potato in Eisenhower's direction. Before it hit him, though, another cadet stood up in the line of fire and was struck in the eye.

Another time he was busted and given five demerits—a serious infraction—for "smiling in ranks at drill after being corrected." Ike had a soft spot for silliness and he told his buddies that, some nights, boys just need to be boys. On a few occasions Ike and his friends would walk to the bathroom in their barracks and, when no one was looking, crawl out through the window. They'd meet a few more classmates and they'd silently sneak past the sentry post and walk down to the Hudson River. There they'd pile into a boat and paddle fifteen miles to Newburgh for a late-night sandwich. If Eisenhower and his buddies had ever been caught off the academy grounds, they could have been tossed out. But these small acts of rebellion made life at West Point bearable to a fun-loving character like Eisenhower, and he and his buddies always stayed in the shadows when they were on these midnight excursions.

A few days before Army's first game against Stevens, the Cadets' starting left halfback, Geoffrey Keyes, the team's top player, hurt his knee in practice. The coaches elevated Eisenhower to the first string for the season opener.

Without Keyes, Army's 1912 season got off to a lethargic start against Stevens, a technological school in Hoboken, New Jersey, that had little football tradition. But slowly, with Eisenhower getting a few carries on offense, Army moved the ball late in the second quarter. Ike didn't possess shifty feet; he preferred to bull over tacklers rather than try to dance and cut around them. By the third quarter, his bruising style of running between the tackles helped the Cadets wear down the smaller Stevens defense. Scoring twenty points in the second half, the Cadets rolled to a 27–0 victory.

After the final whistle blew, Ike and his teammates celebrated the win with their fans. But the party was tempered with caution. The Army players knew that their team was a work-in-progress. The game against the intimidating Jim Thorpe and the Carlisle Indians was only thirty-five days away. For the Cadets to have a chance to pull off the upset, they had to improve—and fast.

As the Indians warmed up for their game against Washington & Jefferson College in Washington, Pennsylvania, Warner strolled up and down the sideline. The weather in western Pennsylvania was unseasonably hot on October 5 and Warner worried that the heat would sap his team's energy. Moreover, Washington & Jefferson was a regional power. If the Indian players overlooked W&J, their dream of a perfect season would melt like a GooGoo Cluster candy bar under the scorching Pennsylvania sun.

Once the ball was kicked off in front of 10,000 fans at the W&J stadium, it didn't take long for Warner to realize that his boys were flat, their rhythm off. On offense the Indians fumbled several times on reverses when one Carlisle player tried to flip the ball to another. Thorpe was also uncharacteristically amateurish. He did break off a few spectacular runs—he was always good for that—but he never pushed the ball over the goal line. His famous right toe also failed him, as he missed field goal attempts from 27, 40, and 45 yards. After nearly two hours of back-and-forth action, neither team had scored and the game ended 0–0. Carlisle surely would have been beaten if Thorpe hadn't intercepted four Washington & Jefferson passes.

After the game Warner consoled his players. They could still win a national championship, he told them, if they steamrolled through the rest of their schedule. But Warner's words didn't soothe the Indians. When the team arrived at the Pittsburgh rail station on their journey back to

Carlisle, they had a stopover of three hours before their next train arrived. Most of the team walked to a nearby diner for a bite to eat, but
Thorpe and Gus Welch lit out to a nearby bar to drink away their disappointment. When the team gathered to catch their train to Carlisle,
Thorpe and Welch were nowhere to be found. Warner asked his boys if
they knew where they were; someone pointed to the saloon down the
street. Furious, Warner marched into the bar and ordered his two offensive stars to return to the station immediately. An argument between
Warner and Thorpe erupted. With every set of eyes in the bar trained on
Warner and his tipsy tailback, Warner and Thorpe traded verbal punches
and dialed up the decibel level of their voices. Warner eventually convinced Thorpe, who adamantly wanted to stay in the bar, to walk to a
nearby hotel. There, in the lobby, the argument kept raging. A crowd of
onlookers gathered outside the lobby window; it looked like fists were
about to be thrown between coach and player.

Warner eventually calmed Thorpe down. The bulls unlocked horns
and Warner escorted Thorpe out of the hotel's back door. With a few
Carlisle players pulling Thorpe along, Warner got him onto the train. In
all the years they had spent together, Warner had never been so deeply
disappointed in Thorpe. He felt like he had been betrayed, that everything he had taught Thorpe had been forgotten in a boozy haze. Warner's
anger rose to an unprecedented level when an article in one of the Pittsburgh newspapers reported that Warner had knocked Thorpe out in a
drunken street brawl. As soon as Warner read the story, he called Thorpe
into his office.

"Thorpe," Warner said. "You've got to behave yourself. You owe it to
the public as well as to your school. The Olympic Games have made you
into a public figure and you've got to shoulder the responsibility." Warner
also told his player that he had disgraced himself, that he had succeeded
in living up to the very worst of all the Indian stereotypes, and that he
needed to apologize to the rest of the team.

That afternoon before practice, Thorpe, as demanded, stood in the
athletic dorm in front of his teammates and said in a low, barely audible
voice that he was sorry for his drunken behavior and that it wouldn't happen again. The half-hearted apology did little to mollify Warner's anger.
Warner had always been a master communicator when it came to con-

necting with his Indian athletes. But now not even he knew if Thorpe—the Olympic gold medal winner, the hero to an entire nation of Indians—fully understood how much he had messed up.

The picture of his boyhood friend from Abilene caused Swede Hazlett to take a second look, as if he could hardly believe what he was seeing. There was Ike for all the world to see in black and white in *The New York Times,* decked out in his football knickers and punting a ball. Hazlett was a mid-shipman at the Naval Academy when he spotted the two-column picture of Eisenhower in the Old Gray Lady, and he quickly read all about how his friend had led the Cadets to a 19–0 victory over Rutgers on October 12— the same day that Thorpe led Carlisle to a 33–0 win over Syracuse. Unlike every other midshipman, Hazlett felt a surge of pride wash over him as he learned that Eisenhower was powering the Army football team. He care-fully clipped out the article and tacked it on his wall.

After just two games in the 1912 season, the *Times* was already calling Eisenhower "one of the most promising backs in Eastern football." An-other publication dubbed him the "huge Kansan." Against Rutgers, Ike made several notable runs, consistently dragging tacklers along with him as he plowed up the field. His tough running style made him a fan fa-vorite, and his popularity soared among the Corps of Cadets.

When the edition of *The New York Times* that carried Eisenhower's pic-ture finally arrived in Abilene, the native son quickly became the talk of the town. His former teammates and coaches marveled at how his frame had filled out in the fifteen months since he'd left the Kansas prairie. They were also surprised to learn that he'd developed into one of the quicker players on the Army team. When he had played at Abilene High, foot speed certainly hadn't been his forte. Everyone in Abilene—the Northsiders and the Southsiders alike—was proud of Ike. The local boy was making good on college football's biggest stage.

The day after Army's 19–0 victory over Rutgers, the coaches at Yale gath-ered at the Hotel Taft in New Haven, Connecticut, for a late-night meeting with "advisors" to the program, such as Walter Camp. Yale's next oppo-nent was Army, and the Bulldog leaders were trying to figure out how they could end the Cadets' two-year winning streak over them. They also crafted a plan to stymie the Cadets' power running game and slow down that relatively unknown kid named Eisenhower.

Before traveling to West Point for the game against Army, Yale coach Arthur Howe banned newspapermen from attending Yale's practices. He was paranoid that Cadet-friendly spies would gather important intelligence on the Bulldogs' game plan. Howe considered winning the Army game this season almost as important as beating archrival Harvard, and he had a security guard patrol the practice field to bar anyone not affiliated with Yale football from the area. The Bulldogs hadn't scored a single point on the Cadets in two years, and Howe suspected that the Army defense may have known what plays the Yale offense was going to run, thanks to the work of spies.

That same week Warner was in his office reading a paper when his eyes stumbled onto a few words that caused a grin to stretch across his face like a rubber band. In one of the local Pittsburgh papers, someone affiliated with the Pittsburgh football team, which was hosting Carlisle on October 19, was quoted as saying, "Thorpe will never run through us . . . we've got him figured."

Warner couldn't have asked for a better pregame treat than this. He showed the quote to Thorpe, and it torched a fire deep inside of him. Nothing motivated Thorpe like being told he couldn't do something, and as soon as the ball was kicked off against Pittsburgh, Thorpe crashed through the line and barreled into defensive players as if each one of them had personally insulted him. A few minutes into the first quarter, Thorpe caught a short pass from Welch and, in front of an awestruck crowd of 15,000, gave everyone a memory that would not fade for years.

After cradling the ball in his arms, Thorpe turned up the field. He bulled over one defender, then another Pitt player bounced off his legs as if he'd been electrocuted at the touch of Thorpe's football knickers. Thorpe turned on his Olympic speed and began sprinting down the field. After twenty yards, he pulled one of his signature moves—the stop-start—to juke another Pittsburgh player, who overran Thorpe and plunged headfirst into the air. As Thorpe neared the goal line, he stiff-armed a defender, dropping the player to the ground. He then glided into the end zone. And Thorpe wasn't done. By the time the game was over, he had ripped off another long touchdown run and had scored thirty-two total points. Carlisle beat Pittsburgh 45–8.

After the final whistle blew, the fans gave Thorpe and the rest of the Indians thunderous applause. Thirty-three years after the founding of Carlisle, the school's football team had helped transform the public's attitude toward Indians. No longer feared and reviled, the Carlisle Indians had become almost mythological figures in Warner's eleventh year at the school, symbolizing a last charge at greatness for a dying race. Thorpe's Sac and Fox tribe in Oklahoma, for instance, had only six hundred members left, and every time Thorpe touched the ball it was as if time had been turned back and the Indian people were again flourishing. This was the myth they were creating, and white fans couldn't turn their eyes away from the Carlisle boys, the ultimate underdogs. There were never more than a few dozen students at the Indian School who Warner felt were big enough to play the game, but seven games into the 1912 season, the undermanned Indians were starting to look unbeatable. They were peaking at the perfect time.

Earlier that afternoon, several thousand fans took their seats in the grandstands at Army's Cullum Field. A cold rain had fallen most of the morning, but at 2:30 in the afternoon—some thirty minutes before kick-off between the Cadets and Yale—the sun was out and drying the grass.

Earlier in the week, Army coach Ernest Graves told Eisenhower that he would be the second-string left halfback for the game against the Bulldogs. After missing the first two games of the season with a knee injury, Geoffrey Keyes was now healthy enough to play, which meant that Ike would begin the game on the bench. But this didn't diminish Eisenhower's enthusiasm. He still knew he might have a chance to sub for Keyes late in the game and make a difference when it mattered most.

For the entire first quarter the defenses dominated, but with a few minutes left in the first and Yale in possession of the ball, Leland Devore, Army's captain and best player, tackled the Yale halfback on what appeared to be a routine running play. After the pile of players was untangled, Devore stayed on the ground, grabbing his right knee.

At six feet, four inches, 225 pounds, Devore could control the line of scrimmage from his defensive tackle position like few in the nation. In 1911, he had been selected to Walter Camp's first-string All-American team. What made him so special on the football field was his athleticism. He lettered in baseball, basketball, and football. He also was the school's heavyweight boxing champion and silver medalist in the heavyweight wrestling division. On the football field, he was Army's best tackler, best blocker, and best drop-kicker, and he played with a streak so mean that his teammates were careful not to incur his wrath. When angered, Devore was capable of cruelty—as the Carlisle Indians would soon find out.

As Devore limped off the field against Yale, the Corps of Cadets in the stands gave him a standing ovation. The Army trainer wanted to take him to the hospital immediately, but Devore insisted on staying on the sideline. Reluctantly, the trainer brought him a folding chair, and Devore planted himself in it. But with Devore no longer in the game, Yale's game plan became so simple it could have been diagrammed in the dirt before every play: Run the ball straight at the new left tackle who had replaced Devore in the lineup.

Yale quickly moved the ball. Ten yards one play, six the next, eight the next. Early in the second quarter the Bulldogs' Jesse Philbin took a hand-off and plowed over Devore's substitute to score a touchdown from three yards out. As the smattering of Yale fans clapped and watched Philbin miss the extra point, Eisenhower stood in the growing late afternoon shadows with a long gray coat hanging over his shoulder pads. He itched to strap on his leather helmet and enter the game. Like every other Cadet player, Ike knew that the possibility of a perfect season was now in jeopardy. If he could put the "fear of Eisenhower" into Yale, maybe he could lead his team on a comeback.

Early in the fourth quarter, with Yale still up 6–0, Ike got his chance when Keyes aggravated his knee injury after being thrown to the ground by a Yale tackler. Snorting fire, Eisenhower trotted onto the field. With the ball on its own 22-yard line, Army began its best offensive series of the game. Running the ball between the tackles, Ike gritted the ball forward. None of his runs were spectacular or caused the crowd to rise to its feet, but as darkness began to fall over the Hudson Highlands, Eisenhower was finding holes in the line of scrimmage and gaining yards. After using several minutes of the clock, Army had the ball, first-and-ten, at Yale's twenty-yard line.

In the huddle, Cadet quarterback Vernon Prichard called for a pass play. Army had struggled the entire game with the forward pass, but Prichard thought he could catch the Yale defense off guard. After receiving the snap, though, Prichard overshot his end on a pass and the ball fell incomplete. On second down the Cadets made the most critical mistake of the game: They were penalized ten yards for holding. A running play on third down netted only a few yards, and Army punted on fourth down. Eisenhower wouldn't carry the ball again as Yale held on for a 6–0 win.

Afterward, Ike and his teammates shook the hands of all the Yale players, including Theodore York, a guard. York walked gingerly along as he pressed the flesh with the Cadets. Every step was a struggle for York because, though he didn't yet know it, he'd fractured two ribs during the game. A few days after the game, York was back in New Haven when he checked into the college infirmary. He felt ill, and doctors soon found that an abscess had formed near his abdomen.

A tragic series of events had been set in motion. A short time after the abscess was discovered, blood poisoning developed, which caused pneumonia to set in. On Halloween eve, just ten days after shaking the hand of Eisenhower and the other Cadets following Yale's 6–0 win, the twenty-year-old York, one of the most popular players on the team, became the first Yale football player to die as a result of an on-the-field incident since 1885.

The line of parked Model Ts stretched for blocks along the road that led to the main gate of Georgetown University in Washington, D.C. As happened everywhere Carlisle traveled, a capacity crowd awaited the Indians when they walked onto the field at Georgetown on October 26. More than 5,000 fans filled the bleachers and crammed around the sidelines to get a glimpse of Carlisle and, specifically, of that big, elegant Indian who had won two gold medals in the Olympic Games three months earlier.

Before kickoff, an impeccably dressed guest visited the Indians' locker room: Pennsylvania senator Boies Penrose. The senator told the Indians that the Carlisle Indian School Appropriation Bill was currently being debated in Congress, and that a victory today would help get the bill passed and thus allow the school to survive for another year. The senator also joked that whoever played a great game would earn citizenship to the United States. The one-liner reminded players that, as native Indians, they weren't considered American citizens, though this didn't seem to matter to a player named Big Bear, who recoiled at the thought of becoming a citizen. When the senator asked the player why he didn't want citizenship, Big Bear responded, "They tell me if I become a citizen, I will have to pay taxes."

With twenty minutes to go before kickoff, Thorpe strutted confidently out of the locker room and into the sunny and pleasant autumn afternoon. A refreshing breeze from the Potomac palisades ruffled the orange and brown leaves on the oaks that stood close to the field, and as the Indians made their way to the sideline for their final pregame talk from Warner, leaves blew through the air and floated onto the playing surface. The weather was perfect, which put Thorpe in a perfect mood. As he lined up to receive the opening kickoff, he felt ready to put on a show.

Early in the first quarter, Thorpe had several runs that featured him dragging three, four, even five players as he advanced the ball. Carlisle scored thirty-four points in the first half. Through it all, a big grin lighted Thorpe's face, like a kid who had just received a lollipop—even when he was viciously tackled. Every time he was stopped, Thorpe quickly popped up and congratulated the Georgetown defender on his fine play, sometimes giving him a pat on the shoulder. This display of sportsmanship brought a feeling of pride to Oklahoma congressman Charles Carter, who was sitting in the stands. Carter was the first congressman to be elected from the former Indian Territory, which had been granted statehood in 1907, and he beamed as he watched the twenty-four-year-old from the Oklahoma plains shred the Georgetown defense.

Carlisle beat Georgetown 34–20 to raise their record to 7-0-1. Warner was inching closer to his first national championship, but he didn't have much time to bask in the glow of the Georgetown victory. The next morning he hurried his team to Washington's Union Station. The Indians needed to catch a train to Toronto, where in one day Carlisle would play in an event that was a promoter's dream: the first-ever football game that featured one team from Canada and one from the United States.

———————

Eisenhower anxiously stood on the sideline at West Point, his concerned eyes watching the action on the field. Every Cadet football player had been deeply stung by their loss to Yale a week earlier, and now, just three minutes into their game against Colgate, being played on the same day that Carlisle beat Georgetown, the Cadets had already fallen behind 7–0. Colgate had received the opening kickoff and marched swiftly down the field for the opening touchdown.

But Army stormed back. With Keyes in the lineup at halfback, the Cadets took control of the line of scrimmage. By the end of the third quarter Army had built an 18–7 lead. In the final quarter Eisenhower subbed for Keyes. Realizing he wasn't going to have many opportunities to impress his coaches as long as Keyes was healthy, Ike ran with a sense of purpose every time he touched the ball.

Late in the game, as the temperature fell and daylight faded, Eisenhower gashed through the line to make significant gains. No one on the field was putting out more effort than Ike, and he was stamping a lasting impression on the coaches, fans, and newspapermen. The reporter for the *Howitzer,* Army's yearbook that would be published at the end of the school year, noted that "Eisenhower in the fourth quarter could not be stopped." And a reporter from the *New York Tribune* gushed that "the work of Eisenhower brought joy to the Army rooters."

Army defeated Colgate 18–7. Next up on the schedule was Holy Cross. Then, a week later, the quarry that the Cadets had been talking about ever since the end of the summer Olympics: Carlisle.

Warner followed the money. The University of Toronto promised him about three thousand dollars that he could put in his athletic fund if he would bring his Indians to Canada for a game that would celebrate the hundredth anniversary of the War of 1812. Even though the travel would strain his players, the deal was too sweet to pass up. Warner agreed to the game, which would consist of two halves: the first would use the rules of American football; the second would be governed by the rules of Canadian rugby.

Warner promoted the game by saying it would show once and for all the superiority of American football over Canadian rugby, which made for good copy in the Toronto newspapers. The Indians then backed up Warner's bravado. After the ball was kicked off to the Indians, it didn't take long for Thorpe to spin a little magic. On the second play from scrimmage, he took a handoff from Welch, broke through the line, nimbly sidestepped a few bewildered rugby players, then easily raced the length of the field for a touchdown. To put a final flourish on his run, he planted the ball between the goalposts as he jogged by. The ten thousand Canadian fans exploded. Thorpe was everything they'd read about and more.

Behind Thorpe's running and kicking—one of his tight-spiral punts went on a 75-yard voyage—Carlisle won the game 49–1. Immediately afterward, the Indians boarded a train to head back to Pennsylvania. Warner wanted his players to get back to the business of winning a national championship as soon as possible. In just five days, Carlisle had to play Lehigh, a team with a 5-1 record that included a 14–0 win over Navy.

President William Howard Taft was enjoying dinner at the Brooklyn Navy Yard some forty-eight hours after Carlisle had overwhelmed the Toronto rugby team when he received some fork-dropping news: James Sherman, his vice president, was dead. The vice president had succumbed to a kidney ailment, and it was a devastating blow to Taft and his reelection hopes. Because the general election was only weeks away, Taft didn't have time to select a new vice president, which meant that Sherman's name would be on the ballot on that second Tuesday in November. Taft wound up losing to Democrat Woodrow Wilson, who just five years earlier was one of football's strongest advocates while serving as the president of Princeton.

Out of respect for Sherman, officials at the Military Academy canceled Army's November 2 game against Holy Cross. But out of the sadness of Sherman's passing came an opportunity for the Cadet football players of West Point: Now they had a few extra days to prepare to take down the Indians of Carlisle.

As soon as Warner and his boys returned to Carlisle from Canada, Warner had one urgent message for his players: Do not take Lehigh lightly. It was natural for the Indians to look past Lehigh and gaze at the contest that was two weeks away. To every Indian player, the game against the Cadets wasn't just the most important game of their season, it was the most significant of their lives. The matchup was so rich in symbolism—the Indians, wards of the state, playing against the young men who one day would likely run that state—that it was hard for the Carlisle players to concentrate on Lehigh in the days following their triumph in Toronto. Even Warner had one eye on the Army game during practice sessions before the Lehigh game, as he repeatedly had his players run the special formation that he planned to unveil for the first time in history in the game against the Cadets. The new formation was going to be Warner's secret weapon, and his players were becoming more deadly at running the double wing by the practice.

Warner was tempted to use the formation on November 2 in Bethlehem, Pennsylvania, but he resisted. Instead, he called Thorpe's number—over and over. As the superior Carlisle team pulled away from Lehigh in the second half, Thorpe had some fun with the Lehigh players. After Carlisle lined up in its offensive formation, Thorpe often yelled such questions as, "How about through left tackle this time?" Seconds later, Thorpe carried the ball over the left tackle for a long gain, just as he had called out. On another play Thorpe yelled to the Lehigh defense, "Right end, huh?" And then Thorpe barreled around the right end for another big run. Lehigh eventually started stacking its defense over the spot where Thorpe said he was going to run, but it rarely slowed the Carlisle halfback. The Indians won 34–14, with Thorpe scoring twenty-eight points.

On the short train ride back to Carlisle, Warner was already a bundle of nerves as he peered ahead seven days on the calendar. The Army game, for Warner, was personal. Years earlier, when he was still a young man, Warner had taken the West Point entrance exam, hoping that one day he could become a cadet and have a career in the armed forces. But he didn't score high enough on the exam, and now he was about to come face-to-face with the Army football team for the first time in his career. Warner had been pushed away by the Military Academy as a teenager; he didn't plan on getting bowled over by Army again as a forty-one-year-old.

There was one other issue weighing on Warner's mind as the train chugged back toward Carlisle: He'd never been so close to a national championship. As he gazed out the window at the rolling brown hills of the Pennsylvania countryside, he silently began planning how his boys were going to crush the Cadets. With all his heart, Warner believed that a lot of wrongs were going to be made right in just seven days.

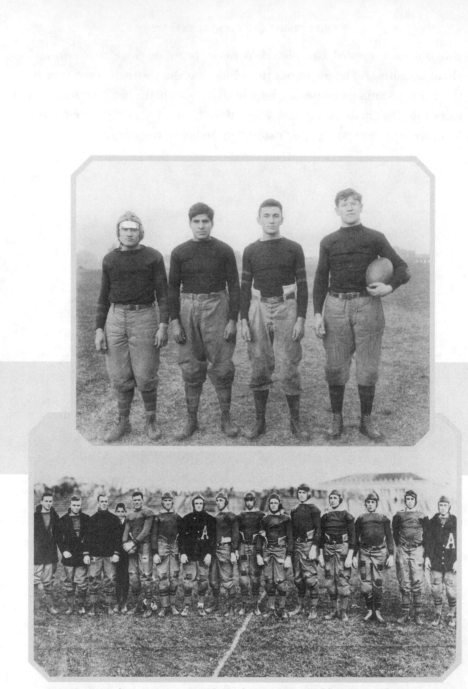

Top: *Carlisle's famed starting backfield of 1912 consisted of* (left to right) *Alex Arcasa, Possum Powell, Gus Welch, and Jim Thorpe.* (Courtesy Cumberland County Historical Society)

Bottom: *A few weeks before the Carlisle game, Eisenhower* (second from left) *and his teammates, who included Omar Bradley* (second from right), *posed for a camera.* (Courtesy the Dwight D. Eisenhower Library)

13

THE CLASH OF HEROES

The two teams stood on opposite sidelines of Cullum Field at West Point, studying each other closely as whites and Indians once did from opposite sides of frontier battlefields. Kickoff between the Carlisle Indian School and Army was minutes away. The cold November air at West Point was thick with tension. This was it, the game James Francis Thorpe, Dwight David Eisenhower, and Glenn Scobey Warner had been waiting to play all their lives.

For Thorpe and the other Indian players, this was their chance to prove once and for all that they could play the game of football better than the white man—and better than the sons of the military men who shared the same blood as the soldiers who pulled the triggers at Wounded Knee. This was the Indian's chance to avenge, in some small way, that massacre of twenty-two years ago. A victory would also amount to further justification of the Carlisle Indian School: a good showing could prove that Indians were every bit as competent and powerful as their white contemporaries.

For Eisenhower, this was his chance to create his West Point legacy. Football was the single most important thing in Ike's life, and his reputation as a player who was as relentless as the wind had grown each week of the 1912 season. If he could stop Thorpe—or, better yet, if he could knock Thorpe out of the game with a blockbuster hit—Ike didn't believe there was any way his team would lose. Ike always loved challenges, and no challenge in his sporting life was greater than taking on an Olympic legend and the other Indians who were as swift as antelopes. Before kickoff, a fever arose in him.

For Warner, this was the chance to prove that his new style of football was superior to the power game that Army played. Warner's players had wowed crowds all over the country with their speed and agility, with their deception and their cunning, and in this game Warner was going to use all his tricks to confuse the bigger Cadet players. And Warner, who understood what made Indian athletes tick better than any white man in America, knew exactly how to fire up his boys before the game. He reminded them that it was the fathers and grandfathers of these Army players who had killed their fathers and grandfathers in the Indian Wars. They were the ones who murdered innocent women and children at Wounded Knee. They were the ones who spilled Indian blood all over the plains.

Now, Warner told his boys, it was the Indians' time to fight back. It was time to make their ancestors proud. It was time to beat the living daylights out of Army.

The ball tumbled end-over-end through the gray November sky, plummeting toward the earth like a zeppelin stripped of its power. Jim Thorpe cradled the ball in his arms, then started to run. He was a bull suddenly released from the gate, and he charged forward with knees kicking high. The five thousand fans who encased the West Point field belted out an ear-splitting cheer, and the most anticipated game of the 1912 college football season was finally rolling.

In the west stands sat the Corps of Cadets in long gray coats over their dress uniforms. The temperature hovered around freezing at three in the afternoon at West Point, and storm clouds rolled over the Hudson River Valley. A touch of moisture hung in the cold autumn air. A stiff breeze blew from the west and swirled around the Point, shaking the red and gold leaves off the maples and oaks that rose like giant umbrellas across campus.

Before the game the Corps paraded on the Plain and marched past the Carlisle players, who marveled at their second-by-second precision. They all seemed to move as one large, commanding mass of energy. The Cadets were just as taken aback by the Indian players: They were far smaller than they had expected. For months everyone at West Point had been reading newspaper accounts of the barnstorming Indians and their domination of every team they played, which explained why Carlisle was considered a slight favorite over Army. But now here they were, and aside from the five-foot, eleven-inch Thorpe and a handful of players, to the cadets in the bleachers the Indians looked like a high school team. On average the Army players who wore their black-and-gold uniforms were about four inches taller and twenty-five pounds heavier than the Indians. In the south stands the throng of enlisted men, outfitted in their olive fatigues, also were surprised at the diminutive stature of the Indians, who stood on the sideline with red Carlisle blankets wrapped around their shoulders. The Indians were quiet before taking the field—as always—and their expressionless faces masked the full-scale ferocity that was about to explode out of them like thunder.

Thorpe received the kickoff at the fifteen-yard line. He rumbled for thirteen yards before being taken down by an Army defender. In the huddle, Gus Welch told the Indians that they were finally going to use their secret weapon. Carlisle broke the huddle. At first the Indians settled into their standard power formation with two halfbacks and a fullback lined up behind the quarterback. But then Welch called out a signal, prompting the players to shift into the double-wing formation. Thorpe, who was at left halfback, moved closer to the line and crouched in a three-point stance to the outside of the left offensive tackle. The right halfback, Alex Arcasa, did the same thing and aligned himself to the outside of the right offensive tackle. A nervous chatter rose from the crowd as the Indian players shifted into new positions. No one was sure what Carlisle was doing or what Warner, the great football magician, was up to.

As Army defenders tried to figure out what was going on, the ball was snapped to Welch, who immediately flipped it to Arcasa. Running around the right end, Arcasa cut up the field and plowed forward fifteen yards and got a first down. On the next play the real tricks began: After receiving the hike, Welch tossed the ball to Arcasa, who was running from his right to left. Arcasa took a few steps and then flipped the ball to Thorpe, who was running from left to right. Thorpe then bolted around the right end for fifteen more yards and another first down. Three snaps later, the exact play worked again; Thorpe galloped around the right end and sprinted into an open field. The Army defense was again caught off guard. They pursued Arcasa until they realized that Thorpe was breaking for the end zone. Thorpe ran ten, then fifteen yards. Eisenhower, from his line-backer position, and another Army defender had the angle on Thorpe as he blazed down the sideline. The two Army players lunged at the Indian ballcarrier.

This was the instant, the moment, that Eisenhower had been fanta-sizing about for months. This was his chance to take out the great Thorpe and remove Carlisle's most valuable player from the game. Ike and the other Army defender threw themselves at Thorpe as hard as they could. The three collided. The hit was so jarring that the ball popped out of Thorpe's hands as he fell to the ground. Another Army defender quickly leapt on the ball to recover the fumble. Realizing the hard tackle had forced a turnover, Eisenhower popped up and celebrated with his team-mates as the crowd went wild. Behind him Thorpe was still on the ground, writhing in pain and grasping at his right shoulder. Maybe the hit had done it. Maybe it had knocked Thorpe out of the game and onto a stretcher.

On the sideline, Warner's heart sank. A minute passed and Thorpe was still on the ground. Warner lit a cigarette and nervously sucked the tobacco and paper away into a red-gray line of ash. Two minutes passed. A group of Carlisle players now stood around their fallen star. Warner fi-nally ran out onto the field and took a knee next to Thorpe. He quickly re-moved Thorpe's shoulder pads. The coach ran his fingers over Thorpe's shoulder, feeling to see if his collarbone was fractured. The referee looked at his watch. He told Warner that Thorpe needed to get off the field and the game needed to be restarted. But then Army's team captain, Le-land Devore, interrupted.

"Hell's bells, Mr. Referee," Devore said in a loud voice. "We don't stand on technicalities at West Point. Give him all the time he wants."

Hearing Devore's words, Thorpe immediately popped up like he'd bounced on a trampoline. To Thorpe, Devore's plea to the referee was belittling, and it infuriated the Indian tailback. Though his shoulder was sore, Thorpe was cursing under his breath as he walked back to the huddle. The last thing he wanted was pity—especially from a player whose grandfather might have tried to kill his ancestors, for all Thorpe knew. Warner's biggest complaint about Thorpe was that he sometimes wasn't as motivated as he needed to be; thanks to Devore, that wouldn't be a problem for the rest of the game.

After holding Army on downs and forcing the Cadets to punt, Carlisle had the ball first-and-ten near midfield. Out of their new double-wing set, Welch handed the ball to Thorpe, who wanted to flatten Devore. Thorpe plowed through the line, dodging a few tacklers before being dragged down after running for twenty yards. Carlisle again threatened to score, but then the Indians were called for holding and eventually turned the ball over on downs.

Starting on its own 49-yard line, Army took control of the game. Relying on their superior strength and size, the Cadets ran straight at the Indians. Every time the ball was snapped, the Army offensive line pushed the Carlisle linemen back on their heels and tore open holes for Eisenhower and Keyes—who for this game moved to fullback to allow Ike to play at right halfback—and Leland Hobbs, who was in as left halfback. After a series of pile-driving runs—eight on one play, twenty on another, six on another—Army moved to the Carlisle four-yard line, where they had the ball first-and-goal. The crowd was riled, believing that their Army boys were about to draw first blood in this fight. But just when it looked as if the Cadets would roll into the end zone, the Carlisle defense suddenly blinked to life, holding the Cadets to no gains on first and second down.

Now it was third and goal. In the Carlisle huddle the Indians, breathing hard, understood that if they stopped the Cadets on this play, Army would be forced to attempt a field goal. In the Cadet huddle quarterback Vernon Prichard called the play: a sweep around the right end. Hobbs would carry the ball; Eisenhower would be the lead blocker.

The ball was snapped to Prichard, who lateraled it to Hobbs. Running to his right, Hobbs followed directly behind Eisenhower, who was looking to paste the first Indian who closed in on Hobbs. The Army duo sprinted around the end, and then *wham*—Ike threw a block that rocked one of the Indian defenders with the force of a grenade. With his path cleared, Hobbs pushed into the end zone, scoring the first points of the game.

Behind the south end zone, the air thundered and the ground vibrated when a cannon boomed. A puff of smoke billowed from the tube and drifted in the cool autumn air. Up in the stands the crowd celebrated as if the New Year's Eve ball had just been dropped in Times Square, a tradition that began only a few years earlier in 1907. Suddenly, Army was in control—which didn't sit well with Warner. He stood on the sidelines with a look of disgust on his face.

The Cadets lined up for the extra point. The ball was snapped back to the holder, and Army's kicker on extra points, Prichard, approached the ball. He swung his right leg back and whipped it forward, connecting solidly with the ball. It flew over the outstretched arms of the onrushing Carlisle players, but then veered wide of the goalposts. Yet this didn't dampen the energy of the home crowd. About ten minutes into the first quarter, the big white numbers on the scoreboard at the north end of the field, updated manually by a scorekeeper who stood nearby, read: Army 6, Carlisle 0.

Devore kicked off for Army, sending the ball deep into Carlisle territory. After a short return by the Indian deep man, Warner instructed his offense to again operate out of the double-wing formation. But this time the Army defenders were ready: Three running plays by Carlisle netted only a few yards, forcing a punt. Thorpe lined up twelve yards behind the center, received the snap, took two steps, and put the full force of his right foot into the ball, launching it into orbit. The ball climbed high, sailing over the heads of the two Army deep backs, which sent them scrambling backward. The ball landed on the ground and bounded toward the Army goal line. A Cadet finally fell on it about seventy yards from where Thorpe had punted the ball, and now Army was pinned deep in its own territory. On the strength of Thorpe's golden right foot, the battle for field position had flipped in Carlisle's favor.

Army coach Graves instructed his offensive players to keep attacking the belly of the Indians' defense, to keep pounding the ball between the tackles. Even if the Cadets didn't make a first down on this series, Graves's plan was to wear down the Indians by being as physical as possible, by consistently running straight at them. Carlisle would eventually tire, Graves believed, then late in the second half Army would dominate the play with its bigger players and win the game.

But now Carlisle had the momentum because of Thorpe's sky-scraping punt. It was as if that boot had infused every Indian player with added strength. On Army's first offensive play of the series, the smaller Indian defenders knifed through the Cadets' offensive line to throw the Army back for a loss. On second down, a Cadet was called for holding, which pushed Army back even farther toward their own goal line. And on third down, the Carlisle defense, playing with a sense of urgency, slammed the Cadet ballcarrier to the grass as he tried to push his way through the line. Army then punted the ball, which was fair-caught by Thorpe on West Point's 44-yard line.

From the sideline, Warner implored Welch to confuse the Cadet defense by running reverses out of the double-wing formation. Following orders, Welch on first down took the snap and flipped the ball to Arcasa, the right wingback, who was running behind the line of scrimmage from his right to left. As Arcasa blasted around the left end, he tossed the ball to Thorpe, the left wingback, as he ran from left to right. Thorpe burst around the right end, broke a tackle, then bulldozed his way for seventeen yards. Three downs later Thorpe took another handoff from Arcasa on the same "crisscross play" and bolted up the field for fifteen yards, pushing the ball to the Army six-yard line.

On the next play the Indians surprised the Cadets by running straight up the middle with Joe Bergie, who was normally a center but for this play lined up at fullback. Bergie easily stormed through the Army defense and bolted into the end zone. In front of a suddenly silent crowd, Thorpe kicked the extra point, which glided through the uprights. Near the end of the first quarter, Carlisle held a 7–6 lead—the difference being the missed extra point by Army's Prichard.

After receiving the ensuing kickoff, the Cadets again tried to run the ball between the tackles. But Carlisle's collective quickness foiled this plan. The Indian defenders sidestepped the bigger Army players as the Cadet linemen tried to engage their blocks. Three straight runs gained only a few yards and Army was forced to punt the ball back to Carlisle.

On offense, the Indians kept attacking the Cadet defense with reverses and fake reverses out of the double wing. To the fans, the game that

Carlisle was playing didn't look like football; it was more like gymnastics or basketball on grass, the way the Indians darted back and forth across the field and flipped the ball around as if there were a rule that at least three players had to touch the pigskin on every play. Few in the stands had ever seen a circus act like this. As Thorpe gashed the defense and ripped off long runs on Carlisle's offensive possessions, even Walter Camp, who was standing on the sideline, was dazzled by Warner's Carlisle Indians, like they were sweet-talking him on every play.

The Indians moved the ball to the West Point five-yard line, where they had first and goal. The crowd came to a boil, yelling for the Cadets to stop the Indians and keep them out of the end zone. On first down, Eisenhower, Keyes, and Devore gang-tackled Thorpe for a short gain. On second down, the Army defenders nailed Arcasa at the line of scrimmage. On third down, the Cadets made another big play, tackling the Carlisle runner for no gain. On fourth down, Warner decided to go for the touchdown, which was a mistake: Eisenhower and the rest of the Army defense stuffed Thorpe, holding him to no gain. It was Army's finest goal-line stand of the season—perhaps, considering the opponent, of the century.

Not wanting to risk a safety or a fumble with the ball at their own five-yard line, Graves ordered his team to punt on first down—a common practice at the time when the offense had the ball deep in its own territory. As Keyes lined up in punt formation, Thorpe trotted back to midfield to field the kick. The most dangerous sight in all of college football was Thorpe in the open field, and there he was, standing alone at the fifty-yard line in his red Carlisle jersey, polka-dotted with grass and dirt stains.

Catching the ball from his deep position, Army's Keyes took a few steps and slammed his right foot into the ball, which rocketed off his laces and climbed up, up, and up into the chilly late afternoon air. Thorpe took a few steps forward, stopping at the Cadets' 45-yard line, waiting for the ball to come down into his arms. The Army players all sprinted down the field, charging full-speed at Thorpe. Thorpe waited. Keyes knew that Thorpe was a lethal return man, and so Keyes purposely kicked it as high as he could to give his teammates a chance to surround Thorpe before he caught the ball. As the ball started to fall from the sky, Thorpe was surrounded by Cadets in their black jerseys and gold pants.

Finally, the ball landed with a thud in Thorpe's arms. The semicircle of Cadets lunged at Thorpe the instant he fielded the ball. Thorpe twisted, backpedaled, stiff-armed, then cut to the outside. In one breathtaking second, he had broken out of four potential tackles. He sliced up the field. He juked one defender with his stop-start move, causing the player to fly helplessly past him. He broke another tackle. Then another. Suddenly he was in the open field again, galloping toward the end zone. The noise level of the crowd rose, as if a volume knob were being turned up with every step that Thorpe took. Thorpe punished another defender with his stiff-arm, causing the Army player to drop to the ground. Thorpe was at the twenty. He cut again, making two more defenders miss, then bolted toward the end zone. An Army player tried to yank Thorpe to the ground by tugging on his jersey, but Thorpe pulled out of the tackle and sprinted across the goal line, leaving the field littered with Eisenhower and the rest of the Army players. Touchdown Carlisle.

Immediately, fans in the stands and the reporters on the sideline were telling one another that this was the most magnificent and stunning run they'd ever seen. Every Army defender on the field had put a hand on Thorpe, and he had slithered away. This one play eloquently summed up Thorpe's gridiron brilliance, showing his speed, his grace, his agility, his strength, his instincts. This was Thorpe at the zenith of his powers, and even the Cadets in the stands gave him a standing ovation.

But wait. As Thorpe celebrated with his Indian teammates, a referee came running down the field waving his arms. He had thrown a flag and now he was signaling that there was a penalty on Carlisle, nullifying the once-in-a-lifetime return. An angry Thorpe approached the referee, demanding to know who committed the holding penalty. The referee then scanned the faces of the Indians, who were all giving him looks that said "No, sir, I'm not guilty of any crime." But the referee pointed at Cotton Vetternack, an end. Thorpe asked Vetternack if he had done anything wrong, and Vetternack admitted that he might have accidentally hooked an Army player. Incensed, Thorpe ordered Vetternack to stand on the sidelines for a few plays. As team captain, Thorpe had the right to make that call.

Army punted again and this time the ball landed in the arms of Welch, who was held to a short gain. The penalty on Vetternack had shifted the momentum of the game back to the Army side, and now the Cadet defense held Carlisle to three short gains and forced the Indians to punt. Thorpe dropped back deep in kick formation. Instead of trying to loft the ball high into the air as Keyes had done, Thorpe smashed a low line drive; the ball never rose more than twenty feet in the air. It traveled some fifty-five yards before an Army player scooped it up and returned to the Cadets' thirty-yard line. The second period was nearly half over.

Early in Army's offensive series, Eisenhower took a handoff from Prichard and barreled into the line. Twisting and turning and pushing forward, Eisenhower ran over one, two, three Indian players before being tackled with a twelve-yard gain. It had been almost a half hour in real time since Army's last first down, and the fans all loudly cheered as Eisenhower lifted himself up from the ground. The Cadets were smitten with this kid from Kansas who never quit, who never seemed to be tackled by just one player. The first twenty minutes of the game had proved that the Indians were the superior athletes, but the Cadets still had a fighting chance because their roster was filled with players such as Ike, whose intensity raged. The scrappy toughness that was forged in the sandlots of Abilene was now helping Army stay in the game against Carlisle, and Ike hoped he could carry the ball—and his team—on every single play.

But as Eisenhower ran back to the huddle, a fight broke out between Carlisle's Possum Powell, a linebacker, and West Point's Charles Herrick. Powell thought that Herrick was playing dirty and administering cheap shots when the referees weren't looking. Powell tightened his hand into a fist and swung at the Cadet, violating the fundamental rule of Carlisle football that Pratt had laid out back in 1893. "Promise me that you'll never slug," the founder of Carlisle had said back then. But Powell's emotions got the best of him, and then Herrick swung back. It took several players from both teams to break them up. A referee had seen Powell throw the first punch and so he immediately kicked him out of the game, which was turning more tumultuous by the second.

The Indians were assessed a 25-yard penalty for Powell's poor judgment, and Army had the ball on Carlisle's 32-yard line. But for the Indians there was an unspoken advantage to having Powell ejected from the game: It angered the Carlisle players, and gusts of rage blew through their huddle as they prepared for the next play. The Carlisle defense then held its ground for the next three plays and forced an Army punt. Soon after the Indians had the ball on offense, the referee blew his whistle, signaling halftime. Carlisle still led, 7–6.

The two teams jogged to their respective locker rooms. Now that the Army players had been up close and personal with Thorpe, they thought he was better in real life than his newspaper write-ups suggested, that if God were ever to create the perfect football player, it would come pretty darn close to the image of Thorpe. The Cadets knew they had to do something to slow Thorpe if they were going to have any chance of outplaying the Indians in the second half. Eisenhower had a plan.

In the locker room, Ike huddled with Leland Hobbs, who also played linebacker on defense. Eisenhower and Hobbs had spent the previous two quarters chasing Thorpe from sideline to sideline, and each had experienced the full impact of his devastating stiff-arm and his high-kicking knees that clubbed defenders who tried to tackle him. Now Eisenhower wanted to turn the tables. With one spectacular hit—a hit with the maximum level of violence and power and ruthlessness—Ike believed they could take Thorpe out of the game. The hit would have to be within the boundaries of the rules—that went unspoken between the teammates—but that didn't mean they couldn't try to plaster Carlisle's best player.

To pull this off, Eisenhower proposed to Hobbs that they give "that Indian" Thorpe the "one-two" early in the second half. The "one-two" meant that Eisenhower, with all the ferocity he could stockpile, would smash into Thorpe's chest while Hobbs plowed into Thorpe's legs as hard as he could. They hoped that the shattering blow would send Thorpe to the sideline—if not the hospital. As the Army players drank cups of water in the locker room, Hobbs and Ike finalized the precisely orchestrated plan. The two Cadets then ran back onto the field. There the growing darkness of the early evening shrouded them and their hearts thumped with anticipation. This play on Thorpe, they imagined, might be the one that everybody would talk about for years to come.

Army received the second-half kickoff, but failed to move the ball and punted to Carlisle. Devore, the Army punter, angled his kick away from Thorpe, who didn't get a chance to return the punt. Thorpe was still feeling the sting of the called-back touchdown in the second quarter and, as he lined up in the backfield, he was determined to take over the game once and for all. On first down Welch pitched the ball to Thorpe, who for the first time in the game flung a pass down the field—this to one of his ends for a long gain. On the next several plays, Welch flipped the ball over to Thorpe, who ran outside and inside and tossed more passes as Carlisle quickly marched down the field.

Frustration mounted for Eisenhower and Hobbs: They couldn't get a clean lick on the shifty Thorpe. Later on the drive Welch took the snap, pivoted, then tossed the ball to Arcasa, the right wingback who was running around the left end. Arcasa's lead blockers were Thorpe and tackle Joe Guyon. Running full-speed into the left side of the line, Thorpe and Guyon rammed simultaneously into Army's star tackle, Leland Devore, at the same time. The Army captain wasn't prepared to take on the blocks of two flying Indians—Thorpe and Guyon had left their feet, just as Warner had taught them to do—and Devore crumpled to the ground. With the left edge of the line sealed by the blocks of Thorpe and Guyon, Arcasa strolled into the end zone as effortlessly as if he were on one of Warner's Sunday walks across the green lawns of Carlisle. Thorpe kicked the extra point. About midway through the third quarter, the Indians gripped a 14–6 lead.

As the two teams lined up for the ensuing kickoff, the 240-pound Devore, Army's team captain, was seething. Army was losing control of the game, but what really ignited his fuse was being steamrolled by Thorpe and Guyon on the previous play. Gasping for breath, nostrils flaring, Devore was set to detonate.

Thorpe booted the ball, sending it deep into Army territory. As it flew toward the Army goal line, the Indian defenders, including the 180-pound Guyon, sprinted down the field. Almost all of the Army blockers also drifted back and formed a wall in front of the return man, Keyes. But not Devore. His eyes turned cold, and once Thorpe kicked off the ball, he beelined it in the direction of Guyon, whose attention was focused down the field on Keyes. As Guyon continued to run—bam!—he was blindsided by Devore. Guyon flew through the air as if a runaway train had just plowed into him.

Keyes was tackled, but all eyes in the stadium quickly shifted to Devore, who was farther up the field and standing over the nearly unconscious Guyon like a heavyweight prizefighter who'd just bloodied a lightweight. The referee immediately threw Devore out of the game, citing "rough play." Army's captain pleaded his case while Warner screamed at Devore from the Carlisle sideline. Though Devore claimed he didn't do anything wrong, the referee was adamant: Army's captain was ejected.

With Devore headed to the showers, it was now up to Eisenhower, Keyes, and Hobbs to save the hour for Army. But without Devore, the team's best blocker on offense, Ike and Keyes couldn't find any running room on three straight plays, and the Cadets were forced to punt. Keyes kicked the ball away from Thorpe and in the direction of Arcasa, who was quickly tackled at the Carlisle 25-yard line. The third quarter was almost over.

On first down, the Indians lined up in their double-wing formation. Thorpe had carried the ball on the majority of the first-and-ten plays throughout the game, and now Eisenhower and Hobbs expected Thorpe to be handed the ball again. The two Army linebackers gave each other a knowing look. This would be their chance.

The ball was snapped. Welch handed the pigskin to Thorpe, who was now rumbling up the middle. This was it, the moment when Ike could seize his athletic destiny. Thorpe burst through the line. Eisenhower and Hobbs closed in on the Olympic champion. Thorpe accelerated straight ahead in the middle of the field. Eisenhower and Hobbs rushed toward him. Ike left his feet and threw the full force of his body into Thorpe's chest. Hobbs also acted according to plan, diving at Thorpe's knees.

From the stands, the collision sounded like a pair of two-by-fours being thwacked together, and all three players fell to the ground in a heap. A few silent ticks of the clock passed. Then, slowly, Hobbs regained his senses and staggered to his feet. A few seconds later, Eisenhower lifted himself up. But Thorpe was still on the ground, in a fog, trying to shake off the blow. Looking at Thorpe as he was sprawled out on the cold West Point grass, Eisenhower thought he and Hobbs had done it, that they had knocked the so-called greatest athlete in the world out of the game. But a few moments later the big Carlisle Indian rose to his feet and slowly ambled back to the huddle. The hit hadn't really fazed him at all.

Eisenhower was shocked. He believed he had just personally proved that Thorpe was "as human as any one of them," as he later recalled, but still Thorpe was in the game. Upon seeing Thorpe rebound so quickly from the jarring tackle, Ike became even more determined to hammer him. This was becoming personal to Eisenhower, his own one-on-one battle, and a few plays later Ike again told Hobbs that, if Thorpe was handed the ball, they should put the "one-two" on the Carlisle halfback. This time they would crash into him even harder, hit him with a vengeance.

The ball was hiked to Welch, who flipped it to Thorpe. The Carlisle offensive line ripped open a hole for Thorpe, who blew through it with the power of a freight train. Thorpe was blasting at full speed up the center of the field when Eisenhower charged at him from one side while Hobbs sprinted at him from the other. This was another chance to wipe out Thorpe—maybe Ike's last chance—and he dove at the Indian runner with all the force he could muster. Hobbs did the same thing, lunging through the air. But Thorpe, flashing his intuitive feel for the game, stopped the instant before the two Army linebackers were set to collide with him. This was Thorpe's famed "stop-start" move, and he went from a full sprint to standing still in an eye-blink.

Eisenhower and Hobbs smashed into each other violently. As Thorpe gained a few more yards before being tackled by another Cadet, the two Army linebackers were on the ground on the verge of unconsciousness. After a minute or so, Eisenhower blinked his blue eyes and was alert. But right away he felt as if someone was prodding his right knee with a fire poker. He slowly got up and, grabbing his knee, limped around the field, trying to make the pain go away. As Eisenhower was hobbling around the field, Hobbs was equally dazed. Hobbs eventually staggered to the sideline to seek medical help.

Eisenhower desperately wanted to stay in the game and try to give Thorpe a lick he would remember, but Graves could see that he was injured. Graves ordered him onto the sideline. Begrudgingly, Ike limped toward the bench. The crowd, realizing that Eisenhower was hurt, clapped as he gingerly made his way to the sideline. There the Army trainer put a pack of ice on Eisenhower's aching knee. Omar Bradley, a backup center, looked at his friend with concern as Ike shook his head in disappointment.

Thorpe continued to carve up the Army defense, further sapping the morale of the Cadets with every run and every flick of the wrist that led to a completed pass. Without Devore, Hobbs, and Eisenhower on the field, Carlisle quickly moved the ball to Army's five-yard line, where Arcasa took a handoff from Welch and burst into the end zone for his second touchdown of the day. Thorpe again split the uprights with his extra-point kick, and Carlisle led 21–6 with about eleven minutes remaining in the game.

Twilight was now falling on West Point. There were no electric lights around the field, and the fans had trouble making out who the different players were. After Thorpe kicked off, Army's deep back managed to catch the ball after it fell from the dusky sky, and returned it to near the Cadets' thirty-yard line.

Eisenhower was so upset that he couldn't bear to watch any more of the game. Carrying his leather helmet in one hand and a bag of ice in the other, he limped to the locker room while bitter disappointment raged inside of him. As Ike trudged away from what was supposed to be the game of his life, his despair deepened. Army failed to move the ball and punted it to the Indians. With Thorpe knifing through the defense, Carlisle marched quickly down the field as Thorpe ripped off one sizable gain after the next. Thorpe was pure magic out there. He was just as capable of powering through the middle as he was of sprinting to the outside, and the fatigued Army players looked ready to submit. But then Carlisle had the ball first and goal, and the Cadets got a second wind. Army defenders stonewalled Thorpe and the other Carlisle backs on four straight plays, forcing the Indians to turn the ball over on downs. About five minutes remained in the game.

With the ball on their one-yard line, the Cadets tried three straight plunges into the line, but could gain only a few yards. They were forced to punt, so Keyes lined up deep in his own end zone. He received the snap, took three steps forward, then launched the ball upward with his right foot. But just as the ball was arcing into the pink sky, it clanked off one of the wooden goalposts, which sprouted out of the ground at the goal line. The Indians recovered the ball at the twelve-yard line. Four plays later, Arcasa scored his third touchdown of the game from two yards out. Thorpe, making his only mistake of the day, botched and missed the extra point. About two minutes remained in the game.

After Thorpe kicked off, Army hit the Carlisle wall again and couldn't move the ball. Keyes punted back to Carlisle, and Thorpe returned the ball a few yards before being tackled at midfield. A few plays later, the referee blew his whistle. The game was over. Carlisle 27, Army 6.

In the weakening light, Thorpe was swarmed. The Cadets—many with tears flowing from their eyes—surrounded the Indian star and shook his hand after the game. Thorpe had rushed for nearly two hundred yards on two dozen carries, and Warner told any reporter who would listen afterward that this had likely been Thorpe's finest game as a Carlisle Indian.

"That Indian is the greatest player I have ever stacked up against in my five years of experience," the Army team captain Devore told reporters in the locker room. "He is super-human, that is all. There is no stopping him. . . . There is nothing he can't do."

As Devore talked to reporters, Eisenhower shuffled around the locker room with an ice pack on his knee. Through his frustration and sadness, Ike couldn't possibly have seen what was coming, but that fraction-of-a-second injury was about to threaten his military career. The day he tried to tackle Jim Thorpe would haunt him for years—and would mark a turning point in his young life.

Pop Warner (in the background, wearing a stocking cap) *watches his Indians players practice late in the season. The Carlisle Indians had a history of wearing down late in the year, but Warner was determined to make 1912 different.* (Courtesy Cumberland County Historical Society)

14

THE DEAD INDIAN AND ANOTHER
WOUNDED KNEE

The locomotive steamed south along the Hudson River Valley, its engines burping out plumes of black smoke, invisible against the dark sky. Inside a dimly lit Pullman car, a group of Carlisle Indian football players surrounded a white-haired man with a salt-and-pepper mustache; they were telling him all about what it had been like earlier that afternoon on the football field against the Cadets of West Point. Walter Camp listened attentively, enchanted by the firsthand accounts that described the sights, sounds, and scents of the game between Indians and soldiers, a game that was unlike any other in college football history.

A few hours after beating Army 27–6, the Indians rode with Camp to New York City, where the team would spend the evening in a Manhattan hotel. As the train plowed through the cold autumn night, Camp told the players—who had changed into their blue military uniforms and caps after the game—that Carlisle was one of the finest teams in the nation, maybe the best. He also fawned over Thorpe, searching for words to describe his on-the-field brilliance. But Camp saved his most effusive compliments for Warner, who had surprised Army with his novel double-wing alignment. With that new formation, Warner had given the game a mighty evolutionary push forward, and even Camp's mind raced with the possibilities that the double wing could offer offensive coaches everywhere. Warner had injected his DNA into the genetic makeup of football, and Camp was one of the first to realize that the sport would never again be the same.

That night, Eisenhower went to bed in his cramped dorm room knowing that he'd never have another chance to face Thorpe on the football field. Ike's knee still hurt and, as he closed his blue eyes and tried to slip into dreamland, the disappointment of the day still stung like a pain that no drug could dull. Football meant everything to Eisenhower at this juncture, and nothing bothered him more than losing. He felt personally responsible for all that had gone wrong against Carlisle, and felt that he had let down his teammates, his coaches, and his entire school. Now, as he struggled to slide into sleep on this bitterly cold November night, Eisenhower's spirits were as low as they'd ever been at West Point.

After enjoying the night in cozy Manhattan hotel rooms, the Indians boarded a morning train back to central Pennsylvania. At the Carlisle train depot, they were greeted like conquering heroes by the student body and locals alike. The news of the Indians' victory over Army twenty hours earlier, which had been relayed to Carlisle on a telegraph machine, filled the students with joy. As one, they celebrated the symbolism of Indians beating soldiers on the football field as a small triumph of their people over their former oppressors.

The Indian players now stood at the summit of the sport, and from this view they could see the road that led to the national championship. If Carlisle finished the season by beating Penn, the YMCA College (formerly the School of Christian Workers, where Stagg had coached) in Springfield, Massachusetts, and Brown, the Indians and Warner would claim their first national championship, which Camp awarded at the end of each season. Warner had never cobbled together an undefeated season in his eleven years at Carlisle. His roster of small players had a history of wearing down as the season progressed. They typically started stacking losses during the months of November and December. But Warner also had never had a team quite like this—and he never had a player quite like Thorpe.

A few hours after arriving back at Carlisle, Warner led his players on their traditional Sunday walk. Through the crisp autumn air, the team wandered around the campus, tramping over the brown grass to reach places such as the secluded wooded area on the north end of the Indian School. Out here in the solitude of the Cumberland Valley, amid the trees that had shed their leaves and were now as bare as newborns, Warner gave his boys one last chance to savor their win over Army. It had been a beautiful game for the Indians, one that Warner would tell children about three decades later, and he was as proud of his players' effort against the Cadets as of anything they had ever done. The Indians had stood toe-to-toe with America's finest future soldiers in the most intimidating environment imaginable, and they had slain their Goliath with their own kind of slingshot: cunning plays mixed with agility and speed. Warner had his players visualize all that they had done against Army as they continued to meander through the Pennsylvania countryside. Now was their time to enjoy the magnitude of the moment, he told them, to realize what their victory meant to downtrodden Indians as far west as Arizona, as far north as the Dakotas, as far south as Florida, and as far east as New York City—all of whom were just now hearing by word of mouth the news of Carlisle's victory.

But the reverie was not to be basked in for long, and Warner fired a verbal warning at his players. Penn, which was next up on the schedule, was a dangerous team, even though the Quakers had fallen on hard times. Penn would enter the game with a 4-5 record, having suffered embarrassing losses to Swarthmore, Brown, Lafayette, and Penn State. As the Carlisle players trailed around campus, Warner told them to start focusing on the Quakers. The Army game was ancient history. If Carlisle was going to win the national championship—which was something that would *really* give Indians throughout America cause to rejoice—the players couldn't afford to spend another moment looking backward.

Thorpe walked by himself onto Franklin Field in Philadelphia at 2:25 on November 16. Clutching his leather helmet and adorned in his red Carlisle jersey that had the team's trademark *C* emblazoned on the chest, he was greeted by booming applause from the 25,000 fans in attendance. Thorpe's big brown eyes looked over the crowd, and eventually he spotted the Indian students in the stands. They broke into their familiar chant: "Minnewa Ka, Kah Wah We! Minnewa Ka, Kah Wah We! Minnewa Ka, Kah Wah We!" Moments later Thorpe met the Quakers' team captain underneath one of the goalposts for the coin flip. Carlisle won the toss. Penn would kick off.

The twenty-one other Indian football players ran onto the field. Warner, watching his players go through their last pregame warm-up drills, feared an emotional letdown. A week earlier, Warner had given the most poignant pregame speech of his career in the locker room at West Point when he reminded his boys of all the Indian killers who were related to the Cadet players, and the Indians responded by playing their best game of the season. But now he worried that his boys weren't mentally prepared to take on Penn, a formidable team despite its lackluster record. Warner had learned over his eleven previous seasons at Carlisle that two things often caused the Indians to play poorly: bad weather and slipping into an emotional valley a week after peaking on the football field. This game seemed like a trap for his Indians.

After receiving the opening kick, Carlisle lined up on offense. On first down, the Indians ran the ball for a short gain. On second down, the quarterback Arcasa, who was subbing for Welch, again handed the ball off to a back, who pushed ahead a few yards. On third down Arcasa dropped into a shotgun formation, setting up seven yards behind center. The ball was hiked back to Arcasa, but it flew over his head. Arcasa sprinted after the loose ball as it rolled into the end zone, but couldn't gather control of it. The pigskin squirted out of his fingers and a Penn defender smothered it. Touchdown Quakers. Less than two minutes into the game, Warner's worst fear was confirmed. His boys weren't ready to play.

Carlisle made careless mistakes: Possum Powell fumbled the ball on their next possession, setting up another Penn touchdown. Thorpe later flubbed a field-goal attempt from point-blank range. Soon after that miss, Thorpe was covering a Penn end who was running a deep route when the Quaker quarterback launched a bomb in the end's direction. Thorpe was running stride-for-stride with the Penn player and, when he glanced upward and saw the ball in the air, he judged that the Quaker wasn't fast enough to catch up to the pass and the ball would be overthrown. Thorpe slowed, gambling that the pass would fall incomplete, but the Penn player kept sprinting. He didn't stop until he caught the ball in the back of the end zone to score another touchdown for the Quakers. Warner stomped and cursed on the sideline. This, Warner thought, was the single worst play of Thorpe's career.

Trailing 20–6 with time running out in the second period, the Indians had the ball on their own twenty-yard line when Thorpe took a pitch from Arcasa. Running with a sense of desperation, he tore through the line, hitting would-be tacklers with vicious force. Thorpe then cut to the outside, sprinting away from the Penn defenders. Quaker defensive back Tubby Green grabbed the back of Thorpe's jersey when he reached mid-field, but Thorpe pushed Green back with his right arm and then blazed into the end zone. Thorpe kicked the extra point to trim the deficit to seven at halftime, 20–13.

In the locker room Warner's temper got the better of him. How could his boys let go of everything so easily? How could they be so careless? How could they forget everything they'd worked on all season? Warner told his Indians that they still had a chance to come back, but they needed to play smart and poised football. They needed to play Carlisle football.

For the first few minutes of the third quarter, it looked like Warner's words had stirred something deep in his boys. After forcing the Quakers to punt on their first possession of the second half, the Indians took control by putting the ball in the hands of Thorpe. He busted through the line for ten yards, then twelve, then six, then thirty-two, then eight. Near the end of the period Carlisle had scored two touchdowns to seize the lead, 26–20. Warner, smoking vigorously, was starting to feel better.

But Carlisle was tiring. At the start of the fourth quarter, the bigger Penn players appeared to catch a second wind. The Quakers moved the ball steadily down the field and scored a touchdown to retake the lead, 27–26. With about six minutes to play, Carlisle got the ball back. Needing a score to keep their undefeated season alive, Warner again told his quarterback Arcasa to give the ball to Thorpe and let him either win or lose the game.

With the ball deep in Carlisle's own territory, Arcasa took the snap from center, but instead of pitching the ball to Thorpe, he dropped back to pass. He spotted Thorpe, and rifled him the ball. Thorpe caught it cleanly, but then was hit hard by a Penn defender. As Thorpe was falling to the ground, the ball came loose. A Penn player pounced on it, causing the home crowd to cheer as if they'd just witnessed the upset of the century. Thorpe was inconsolable. Penn quickly scored another touchdown to go up 34–26 with just minutes to play. When Thorpe touched the ball again on offense, he was so frustrated that he took a swing at a few of the Quaker players after he was tackled. Time dripped away. Exactly one year after Carlisle had lost their only game of the '11 season to Syracuse, the final whistle blew and the scoreboard froze: Penn 34, Carlisle 26.

Dozens of Penn students stormed the field, dancing and shouting wildly. When a few of the students noticed Thorpe walking off the field, they rushed at him, hoping to shake his hand. But Thorpe, who had been booed for the first time all season when he had tried to punch the Penn players, blew past the extended hands as if he never saw them. He had just fumbled away the national championship, and he was in no mood to give a cheap thrill to anyone wearing a Penn sweatshirt.

In the locker room Warner was so upset he was at a loss for words. But he did ask Thorpe about the long touchdown pass he had surrendered in the first half. From Warner's perspective, it looked like Thorpe could have knocked the ball down if he'd given a full effort. Thorpe didn't disagree. "Sure, I could have batted it down easy," Thorpe told his coach. "I didn't try because I never thought the receiver had any chance to reach the ball." Hearing Thorpe's excuse, Warner exploded. This error, he felt, revealed Thorpe's only weakness: The level of his effort didn't always match the level of his talent.

For a long time, Thorpe sat in front of his locker, staring blankly ahead and wondering how everything he had worked so hard for could evaporate so quickly.

One hundred and fifty miles to the northeast of Philadelphia, Dwight Eisenhower limped onto the field at West Point. Ever since he went down in the game against Carlisle trying to bull-rush Thorpe, Ike had worked diligently with Army trainer Marty Maher, trying to heal his twisted and swollen right knee. For six days he iced it, wrapped it, and even put a rudimentary brace on it while he practiced with the starters forty-eight hours before Army hosted Tufts. Though the knee throbbed with pain, Eisenhower convinced Army coach Ernest Graves that he was healthy

enough to play against Tufts on the same day that Penn had upset the Indians.

Eisenhower trotted onto Cullum Field for the opening kickoff. The
Tufts kicker lifted the ball to Army's Leland Hobbs, who blasted up the
field. Like the Indians against the Quakers, the Cadets were emotionally
flat against Tufts. Just two minutes into the game, Army's quarterback,
Vernon Prichard, fumbled the ball in the backfield at his own ten-yard
line. Prichard slipped to the ground and a Tufts defender scooped it up
and ran into the end zone to give Tufts an early 6–0 lead.

Midway through the third period, with the scored tied 6–6, Eisenhower took a handoff from Prichard. Though his knee was still aching, Ike
had made several tough runs on this gray afternoon, bringing the crowd of
3,000 to its feet. Blocking out the pain, he attacked the Tufts defense with
the kind of determination that had made him a fan favorite. When Ike ran
with the ball, he always had a scowl on his face, as if he put on a mask when
he played, and the intense look in his eyes was enough to make the other
team nervous. Earlier in the season, one opposing player, upon seeing
Ike's icy glare as he prepared to line up, ran to the referee, pointed at
Eisenhower, and anxiously pleaded, "Watch that man!"

"Why?" replied the referee. "Has he slugged you or roughed you in
any way?"

"No," said the player. "But he's going to."

Now Ike gripped the ball tightly as he slammed into the line. He
gained one yard, two, three. As he pushed forward for more yards, a Tufts
defender shot forward. He grabbed the ankle on Eisenhower's injured
leg. Undaunted, Ike forged ahead, trying to gain a few more yards. The
Tufts defender didn't let go. Then he twisted Eisenhower's leg as hard as
he could.

Ike immediately went down. Clutching his knee, he writhed on the
field in agony, flopping like a fish on dry land. Ike had felt a pop in his leg,
and he knew this injury could be bad. He tried to get up and walk but
couldn't. He stayed down, shrieking in pain. After a few minutes, the
medical personnel carried him off the field and laid him on the sideline
grass, where Army's chief surgeon, Dr. Charles Keller, examined the
knee. The Cadets' next opponent was Navy, their archrival, and all Ike
wanted to know was: Would he be able to strap on his helmet and play
against the Midshipmen?

"Not the Navy game," the surgeon told Eisenhower, noting that his knee was swelling rapidly. "Not this year . . . You'll have to spend several weeks in the hospital flat on your back. By the time you leave we'll be able to tell you more."

Ike was despondent. Football was everything. It was his escape, the place where the tough-minded, quarrelsome boy in him got to play. As he was carried on a stretcher across the campus to the infirmary, he could hear the rise and fall of the crowd noise. The Cadets would win the game 15–6, but Ike was in no mood to celebrate as he lay in his hospital bed. Eisenhower, for the first time since he left Abilene, felt like crying. A few days later he was told he might never be able to play football again.

On November 22, six days after losing to Penn, Warner led his players onto a train for the team's final road trip of the season—and of Thorpe's Carlisle career. The Indians were traveling to Springfield, Massachusetts, for a game against the YMCA College. Five days after that, Carlisle would play Brown in Providence, Rhode Island, on Thanksgiving Day.

The hurt of the Penn defeat hadn't dulled. It was the first time that Thorpe had lost in anything since he returned with two gold medals from Stockholm, and he didn't take it well. Now, as he sat in his Pullman car heading north to New England on the final train journey of his Carlisle career, he simply wanted to get back out on the field.

Like all the Indian players, Thorpe had grown accustomed to the rhythms of football seasons: Travel on Friday morning, stay in a hotel on Friday night, play a game on Saturday, stay in a hotel on Saturday night, make the return trip to Carlisle on Sunday or Monday. The destinations changed every weekend, but the travel schedule rarely varied. The Indians would log some twenty thousand miles on the rails in 1912 and spend a total of four weeks sleeping in strange beds in unfamiliar cities. It was the price of being a part of college football's wildly popular traveling circus.

Warner didn't expect the YMCA team to put up much of a fight, but the physical education majors from Springfield who comprised the team, playing in front of 10,000 curious fans, jumped to an early 14–0 lead. Six Indian starters had to sit out the game with injuries, and in the first twenty minutes the Indians appeared disinterested in playing. But then, in a flash, Thorpe took control of the game, bounding around the field like some mythical beast of Greek lore. In the third period he received a pitch from Arcasa, broke through the line, cut to the outside, stiff-armed one YMCA player, then another, then galloped fifty-seven yards for a touchdown. Thorpe was a running machine. By the time the fourth quarter was over, Thorpe had scored all the Indians' points in Carlisle's 30–24 victory. The arresting performance astounded the crowd, which gave Thorpe a standing ovation as he walked off the field.

For a few days Dwight Eisenhower stared at the ceiling in the infirmary, wondering if he'd ever make it out on the football field again. His roommate, P. A. Hodgson, frequently stopped by to check in on him, and to keep his friend up-to-date on West Point gossip. The doctor caring for Ike had some good news: He expected a full recovery. The knee wasn't as severely damaged as Dr. Keller first thought, and Keller told Ike that he could resume football next season "provided you don't do anything foolish."

"That knee has been badly hurt, and joint injuries take a long time to heal," Keller told Eisenhower on the day he was released from the hospital. "The knee's weak. It'll remain weak for months to come. Don't put any more weight on it than you have to."

On the same afternoon that Thorpe had run wild against the YMCA in Springfield, Eisenhower stood on the sideline at West Point and watched Army beat Syracuse 23–7. Though he still walked gingerly, Ike fully expected to be in the lineup in seven days on November 30, in the season finale against Navy at Philadelphia's Franklin Field, the site of Thorpe's worst afternoon as a college football player.

Two days after watching the Cadets top Syracuse, Ike hobbled into the vast Riding Hall at the academy, which had been completed only months before, and reported for cavalry riding drill. His knee was feeling better, but Ike knew he had to be careful and not do anything too taxing. Dr. Keller had warned him not to take part in cavalry training; mounting and dismounting would put too much stress on his knee.

The horses at West Point were notoriously volatile. Most were former army polo ponies with hair-trigger tempers. Many Cadets suffered broken jaws and broken bones after being bucked off a horse during "monkey drill," which consisted of mounting and dismounting a horse while it was galloping. What made the drill even more dangerous was that the cadets often jumped off the rear of the horse when they attempted to dismount.

The senior riding instructor was Julian R. Lindsey, a cavalry major who had a clear dislike for Cadet Eisenhower. Lindsey interpreted Ike's supreme self-assurance as arrogance. And so when Ike limped into the Riding Hall on this November afternoon, Lindsey didn't think twice about accusing him of malingering. In a raised, angry voice, he charged that Cadet Eisenhower was faking his injury to get out of riding drill.

The accusation sparked an internal hailstorm in Eisenhower. He could have told the instructor that he'd been ordered by the doctor not to participate in the monkey drill, and the issue would have died. But Ike had been challenged, just as he'd been challenged by Wesley Merrifield to a school fight back in Abilene years earlier, and now the heat of the moment caused his determination to boil. He strode toward a horse, the same way his boyhood hero Wild Bill Hickok had done so many times after a gunfight. His roommate P. A. Hodgson frantically whispered for him to stop and collect his thoughts and think about his knee, but Ike's pride had been challenged. Glassy-eyed with anger, Ike climbed atop a horse.

In an instant, the horse took off, neighed, and gained speed. Lindsey issued the command to dismount and Ike jumped—falling through the air like a bag of rocks.

To prepare his boys for their Thanksgiving Day game against Brown, Warner took his team to the Leicester Inn, located in the woods outside of Worcester, Massachusetts. He led his Indians on long hikes over the hills of central Massachusetts, encouraging them to visualize making plays against Brown. Warner also held a few light practices in the grassy field behind the inn. When word spread through the local community that the famous Carlisle Indians were staging practices in the area, curious fans and newspapermen wandered by, wanting to be dazzled by the show.

The day before Carlisle left for Providence, Charley Glancy, a former baseball manager, decided to travel to the hotel and check out the practice. Glancy, who lived in nearby Southbridge, was standing off to the side of the field and chatting with a reporter from the *Worcester Telegram* when

Thorpe jogged by. Glancy did a double take, then said aloud, "Why, I know that guy. He played for me a couple of years ago."

Glancy went on to explain to the reporter, Roy Johnson, that Thorpe had been a pitcher on the Fayetteville team he managed in 1910. *Yes, Glancy told the reporter when asked, Thorpe had been paid a salary for being on the team.*

It took Johnson only a split second to realize he had the sports scoop of the year. Thorpe wasn't an amateur when he had won Olympic gold, which meant he shouldn't have been eligible to compete in the games in the first place. For the next two months, Johnson would fact-check the story, keeping his uncovered secret hush-hush until he was triple-sure of his facts.

Thorpe was oblivious to what was happening on the sideline on this cool November afternoon in Massachusetts. This was his final practice as a Carlisle Indian, and he innocently lumbered around with nothing apparently wrong.

The pain was electric, rolling through his nerves like a jagged shard of glass. It was the most complete, fully formed rush of pain that Dwight Eisenhower had ever experienced. The instant his right foot planted in the ground after he had leapt off the horse during the monkey drill, Ike felt a surge of white-hot torture grip his right leg. The ligaments in his right knee were shredded the instant it was forced to support the weight of his 180 pounds.

Hodgson rushed over to Ike, who was fighting back tears. P.A. helped him up, but the knee Ike first hurt when trying to tackle Thorpe was so weak that he couldn't support himself. Hodgson put his arm around his roommate, and then tried to act like a crutch for him. But Ike still couldn't walk. Then Hodgson cradled his buddy into his arms and carried him back to the infirmary. As they walked, Hodgson couldn't hold his tongue. He told Ike that this could have been avoided if he'd simply followed the doctor's orders.

When they reached the hospital and Hodgson laid Ike on a table, Dr. Keller came into the room. He was irate. As he looked at the knee, which was already red and swelling badly, the doctor let the expletives fly, telling Eisenhower just how foolish he was for ignoring his advice. The doctor was also upset with the drillmaster who had essentially challenged Eisenhower's manhood—something that a boy raised on the American frontier would react to even if it put him in harm's way. Ike's strength of character proved a weakness: He never gave in to anyone.

When Army coach Ernest Graves learned of Eisenhower's injury, he felt like sticking his fist through a wall. "Here I come up with the best line plunger and linebacker I've ever seen at West Point," Graves told the messenger, "and he busts his knee in the riding hall."

A foot-to-groin cast was put on Eisenhower's leg. For the next four days, he wouldn't be allowed to leave the infirmary. And for the first time in his life, as he lay in his cold hospital bed, he was overcome by the darkness of depression.

The snow fell in thick clumps on the Providence campus on November 28, and threw a white blanket over Andrews Field. Minutes before kickoff, Jim Thorpe, wearing a red cape that he wrapped around his uniform, jogged onto the field. His teammates followed in his wake. This was Thorpe's final appearance before the curtain closed on his Carlisle career, and nearly everyone at Brown's home stadium—the eight thousand fans, the other Carlisle players, even some of the Brown players—wanted to see one last astounding performance before he exited the stage.

The week before, Brown had beaten Penn—the same squad that had upset Carlisle—by the score of 30–7, so Warner knew his team would be in for a fight. On top of that, the storm that spit chunks of ice and snow down from the cold sky wouldn't play in the Indians' favor; bad weather never did.

After receiving the opening kick, quarterback Arcasa handed the ball to Thorpe, who ran between the tackles for seven yards. On the next play Thorpe again hammered the pigskin between the tackles, this time for six yards. First down. The Indians quickly snapped the ball again. Arcasa pitched it to Thorpe, who now sprinted to the outside. Though the footing was poor, Thorpe kept his balance as many of the defenders slipped to the ground. As he ran up the field, it looked so effortless, as if he were moving in slow motion. But in reality, he was sprinting past defenders, one after the next, and the crowd rose to its feet. Thorpe was finally tackled thirty yards downfield. First down.

At halftime, with the Indians leading 12–0, Warner felt the momentum was swinging in Brown's favor. To motivate his boys, he reminded them that this was Thorpe's last game and that Thorpe deserved to finish his career on a high note with a win. *You owe him a victory for the many times he has won for you,* he told them. As the coach spoke, he noticed that all the players had perked up, as if they'd each just taken a shot of adrenaline.

Early in the second half, Warner called one of his favorite trick plays: "The Dead Indian." After a Brown defender had tackled an Indian back, the Carlisle player tried to rise to his feet. But then he staggered like he was drunk and fell back to the ground. The Brown defense relaxed, believing that the Carlisle back was injured. But then the "injured" Carlisle player quickly hunched over the ball and snapped it over to Thorpe, who was standing almost halfway across the field about ten yards behind the line of scrimmage. The rest of the Carlisle offensive line was in front of Thorpe, and as soon as he received the ball he easily ran sixty-five yards for a touchdown. The Brown coach loudly protested that the Indians had cheated, but the official said the play, which Warner had transferred from his imagination onto the gridiron with surprising ease, was perfectly legal.

Thorpe finished his career with a flourish. In the last quarter of the game he made several bone-jarring hits on defense. He threw a twenty-yard dart to one of his ends on offense. And when he had the ball in his arms and sliced through the Brown defense, he was as graceful as a ballet dancer and as powerful as a lumberjack. On the final touchdown of his Carlisle career, he took a direct snap at the Brown eighteen-yard line, squirted through an opening in the line, turned on the speed, then glided into the end zone to score his twenty-fifth touchdown and 198th point of the season—both college football records.

After crossing the goal line on his final touchdown run, Thorpe continued to jog through the end zone, then looped back and planted the ball in the snow beneath the goalposts. He then trotted to take his position as the kicker on the extra-point team. A few minutes later the final whistle blew. Indians 32, Brown 0. Carlisle's season—along with Thorpe's college career—was over. In his final game, Thorpe had rushed for close to 250 yards in the snowstorm.

Two days later Eisenhower stood with the aid of crutches in the balmy December sunshine on the sideline at Franklin Field in Philadelphia. Ike and a crowd of thirty thousand watched Army lose to Navy, 6–0.

When Eisenhower returned to the academy with the rest of the Cadets, his morale and outlook on life were as low as they'd ever been. The realization that he'd never play football again because of the knee injury he first sustained when trying to tackle Thorpe sank in deeper with every passing day. Football was like a first love to Eisenhower, and now that it was gone, his heart was as broken as his knee.

Ike started to smoke frequently (a habit he wouldn't break until 1949), his grades slipped, and he started contemplating dropping out of the Point. Nothing seemed to matter to him anymore—not the notions of Duty, Honor, or Country, not his schoolwork, not his potential future in the army. All he could focus on was his busted knee and its severely torn cartilage and tendons.

"Seems like I'm never cheerful anymore," Eisenhower wrote in a letter to Ruby Norman. "The fellows that used to call me 'Sunny Jim' call me 'Gloomy Face' now. . . . I sure hate to be so helpless and worthless. Anyway, I'm getting to be such a confirmed grouch you'd hardly know me."

Carlisle finished the season 12-1-1 and outscored their opponents 504–114. Walter Camp didn't name the Indians as the national champions—that honor went to Harvard, which finished with a record of 9-0—but he did put Thorpe on his first-team All-American squad. "Thorpe showed again the greatest individual prowess of any back on the gridiron," wrote Camp.

Shortly after the season was over, Thorpe returned to Oklahoma for the Christmas holiday. There he again tramped over the land of his youth, visiting relatives and walking side by side with his older brother Frank to check out the land the Thorpe family owned. When he stopped in to greet old friends and acquaintances, it wasn't uncommon for Thorpe to see yellowed newspaper clippings that were stored in scrapbooks that detailed his rise to Olympic and gridiron glory. These were good days for Thorpe, maybe his best, because he couldn't yet see the storm clouds gathering on the horizon.

The train pulled into Abilene in the small hours of the morning. The depot was vacant when the West Point cadet, dressed in his uniform, stepped off the locomotive and into the warm prairie air. With his duffel bag in hand, Dwight Eisenhower walked along the dusty streets of Abilene, happy to be back home.

In the summer of 1913, seven months after playing in the last organized football game of his life, Eisenhower was given a thirty-day furlough from the Point. He hadn't told anyone he was coming back, and when the wooden planks creaked on his front porch as he entered the house, his mother was surprised and overcome with joy. She hugged her boy tightly, like she never wanted to let go.

A lot had changed for Eisenhower in the seven months since he had tried to flatten Jim Thorpe on the football field. In the weeks after he hurt his knee, he grew so unhappy that he considered dropping out of West Point—a decision that might have dramatically changed the future of America. If Ike had chosen to abandon a military career, he never would have become a general, never would have issued the command to launch Operation Overlord on what became known as D-Day, and never would have become president of the United States. If he had left West Point, Ike likely would have returned to Kansas and lived a quiet life on the lonely prairie.

But a few months after his injury, Eisenhower's smile slowly began to return. He started to think of life beyond sports and of a career in the military and serving his country. When Ike returned home in the summer of 1913—his only "vacation" from West Point in his four years at the academy—the gleam in his blue eyes was back.

But Eisenhower wasn't the same person who left Abilene twenty-four months earlier. Ike was different now—that's what everyone in town said. He was bigger, stood up straighter, talked more directly. But there was something else, something indescribable yet palpable. Was it an air of destiny? No one could precisely pinpoint it, but years later many in town swore they sensed that Ike was on the path to greatness when he visited home in the summer of 1913.

Though the emotional scar of the knee injury was healing, Ike still missed the game like it was a best friend he could no longer locate. But it helped to tell stories. And so one summer afternoon Eisenhower asked his brothers Earl and Milton to gather around. He had a tale to tell about the day he tried to take out the great Jim Thorpe.

"Carlisle had the ball," Ike excitedly told his brothers, who were hanging on his every syllable. "We knew Thorpe would take it on the next play and we knew he'd come through the line because the line had never stopped him before. Well, we timed it just right. We gave him the old high-low, the old one-two, just like that."

His brothers were silent, their eyes wide as the plains, bright as the high-noon sun.

"He'd made a big gain before we stopped him, but we really stopped him. Hard. When we got up he was still lying on the ground. We were sure we'd laid him out for good. But he managed to stagger to his feet in a minute or two and take his place behind the line. Even then we weren't worried because we were sure we'd ruined him for the rest of the day. But do you know what that Indian did? On the very next play he took the ball and went right through us for ten yards!"

Ike went on to describe all that transpired on that gray afternoon at West Point when he came face-to-face with Thorpe and the rest of the Carlisle Indians, and his brothers couldn't hear enough about that day. It wasn't often that Indians beat up on cowboys, and the story was as riveting to the brothers as a ghost tale told around the campfire.

For Eisenhower, Thorpe was now a memory. But when Ike left Abilene at the end of the summer to return to West Point, Thorpe and that game occupied a small corner of his thoughts. Then again, that's what Thorpe and the Indians did to you: mesmerized you with their grace, dazzled you with their speed, and always left you wishing for more, long after the show of Carlisle Indian football had moved on to the next town.

The image of Thorpe thundering down the field with the ball in his hands would stick with Dwight Eisenhower for years, staying vivid in his mind even after he completed his second term as president of the United States, in 1961. (Courtesy Cumberland County Historical Society)

EPILOGUE

THE GHOSTS OF CARLISLE

He paced in his trailer, strolling back and forth like a philosopher deep in thought. Outside the windows a gale-force wind was blowing through the town of Portsmouth, located on the southern coast of England. Rain poured down from the black sky in a dark curtain. It was just past 3:30 A.M. on June 6, 1944, and now Dwight Eisenhower, the boy from Abilene, the teenager who'd always been captivated by the tales of Wild Bill Hickok, the adolescent who threw his body at Jim Thorpe with reckless abandon, had a decision to make—a momentous decision.

Eisenhower left his trailer that sat on an estate known as Southwick House, ducked his head in the rain, hopped in a jeep, and drove down a muddy road. After a mile he reached the main Southwick House. Inside, he walked to the mess hall, poured a cup of steaming coffee, and once again started pacing, back and forth, back and forth, across the mess hall. Ike was the supreme commander of the Allied forces in World War II, and he stood on the precipice of history: If he gave the green light, Operation Overlord, the largest invasion in human history, would be launched. The Allies called it D-Day.

More than 500,000 Allied troops stood ready, but the weather conditions were so poor that Eisenhower was considering postponing the operation. What should he do? He continued to pace, to think, to weigh the options. At this moment he was the most powerful man in the world—perhaps the most powerful in the history of the world. Hundreds of millions of people would be affected by his decision. Governments would fall, the world map would be redrawn, and blood would be shed in dozens of countries.

Finally, Dwight David Eisenhower quit pacing. In a quiet yet steady voice, he said, "OK, let's go."

Before he became a full-time soldier, Ike still had to finish his studies at West Point. After spending the summer of 1913 in Abilene, he returned to the Military Academy. Though his knee injury prevented him from playing football, he couldn't turn his back on the game, so he did the next best thing to putting on the pads: He became a cheerleader. On Friday nights before games, Cadet Eisenhower would whip the Corp of Cadets into a froth at pep rallies, excitedly beseeching—almost commanding—his classmates to cheer like their lives depended on it. This was Eisenhower's first extended experience as a public speaker, and he quickly proved to have a way with words in front of a crowd.

That fall Eisenhower also volunteered to be an assistant coach for the Cullum Hall football team, which was made up solely of plebes. Coaching with the same tenacity with which he played, Ike always lingered on the field with a few plebe players well after practice had ended, teaching them the finer points of the game. The players responded to Ike. They followed his words as if he were their father, and they worked tirelessly to please him. Slowly, the DNA of a once-in-a-generation leader was beginning to form.

Late in the season, on November 25, Ike nervously walked along the sideline at the West Point football field as he watched his players go head-to-head against the New York Military Academy, which was the plebes' version of the Army-Navy game. With the entire Corps of Cadets sitting in the grandstands, Cullum Hall kicked a field goal late in the fourth quarter to win the game 3–0. Ike was overjoyed.

In June 1915, Eisenhower ambled into the office of Dr. Keller, the

West Point physician, for his final physical examination before graduation. When the doctor again examined Ike's knee, he was inclined to fail Cadet Eisenhower, which would have meant the end of his military career. But Keller decided to look the other way and passed the future five-star general and thirty-fourth president of the United States.

After taking a brief trip home to Abilene after graduation, Eisenhower was told to report to the Nineteenth Infantry Regiment at Fort Sam Houston, outside San Antonio. As he rode the train to Texas in mid-September 1915 to begin his career as a military officer, Ike made a simple promise to himself: He was going to try his hardest to be the best he could be. This was the fundamental approach he took in football; he would attack the rest of his life the same way.

Years after Eisenhower had played his last football game, Jim Thorpe was asked if he remembered the day he came face-to-face with Ike at West Point's Cullum Field. Thorpe nodded his head and said in a deep, powerful voice, "Good linebacker."

The date was February 24, 1943, and the two former West Point football players sat in a private suite at the sprawling St. Georges Hotel in Algiers, Africa. The hotel sat atop a hill and from their vantage point, Dwight Eisenhower and Omar Bradley, then a two-star general, could see the bustling city and harbor, which was packed with ships. Eisenhower, who soon would become the supreme commander of the Allied forces in World War II, had summoned his old teammate to North Africa. He needed his help.

Eisenhower was worried that American troops were being outperformed in the North African theater by the older, more experienced Germans. Ike asked Bradley—the most observant cadet he ever came across on the playing fields of West Point—to go to the Tunisian front and act as his "eyes and ears." Bradley followed the order, and based on his reports, Eisenhower made several personnel and tactical changes. He eventually tapped his West Point buddy to command the First Army and then, later, the Twelfth Army. By the summer of 1943, Bradley had 900,000 men obeying his orders—the largest group of American soldiers ever to be under the command of a single general.

"Throughout the war Omar Bradley was not only an outstanding commander, but he was my warm friend and close advisor," Eisenhower said after the war. "Bradley was the master tactician of our forces and in my opinion will eventually come to be recognized as America's foremost battle leader."

Wearing a fedora hat and a tailored blue suit, Jim Thorpe marched into the Fifth Avenue office of John McGraw, the manager of the New York Giants baseball team, and took a seat in front of McGraw's expansive desk. It was February 1, 1913. Newspaper photographers lined the walls around them. Thorpe grabbed a pen and, under the glare of camera flash powder, signed one of the most lucrative contracts in all of baseball, one that would pay Thorpe about six thousand dollars in his first year.

"It has been my ambition to become a big-time ball player since my school days were over," Thorpe told reporters. "And now I have a chance to have the ambition of my life realized."

So began Thorpe's career as a professional baseball player, which was already fraught with controversy. A few weeks earlier the *Worcester* (Mass.) *Telegram* finally ran the article with the sports scoop of the decade: Thorpe had been paid while playing baseball in 1909 and 1910, thus negating his amateur standing, which would have made him ineligible to compete in the 1912 summer Olympics. Soon after the story broke, the Amateur Athletic Union voted to "secure the return of prizes and readjustment of points won by [Thorpe], and will immediately eliminate his records from the books." Thorpe, reluctantly, returned his Olympic gold medals. The controversy caused his fall from grace as one of the nation's top athletes in history.

Without Warner to goad and guide him, Thorpe never became a baseball star. He was a serviceable player—in six career seasons in the bigs as an outfielder his batting average was .252 and he hit seven home runs—but by no means a spectacular one. His heart just wasn't in it; his favorite part of the game was the paycheck.

Football was different. In between baseball games Thorpe still strapped on the leather helmet whenever he could. In 1915 he suited up for the Canton (Ohio) Bulldogs, where he played against the likes of Knute Rockne and George Halas as the Bulldogs toured the country and played at any stadium where they could make some money. Playing halfback,

Thorpe led the Bulldogs to championships in 1916, '17, and '19. The next year, 1920, he became president of a loosely organized association that would one day evolve into the National Football League.

Thorpe wouldn't quit playing until 1928. He was forty-two and his spirit was still willing, but his body, which had been ravaged by hard hits and alcohol abuse, simply gave out. After Thorpe limped away from the game, he could never again find the happiness and contentment in life that he had experienced on the field. Thorpe married three times and had four children. (Thorpe had wedded his girlfriend at Carlisle, Iva Miller, in a ceremony at the school on October 14, 1913, and the marriage lasted a decade.) When the Depression hit in the 1930s, Thorpe struggled to find a consistent paycheck. At different times, he worked as a ditch digger, security guard, nightclub bouncer, and painter. He served a stint in the merchant marines in World War II and later went to Hollywood to try to make it in films, but he landed only a few bit roles—usually playing an Indian chief. Through it all, he maintained contact with Warner, whom he considered a true friend.

Thorpe sold the rights to his biography to Warner Bros. for $1,500, and in 1951 a movie based on Thorpe's life hit the silver screen. Starring Burt Lancaster, the film highlighted Thorpe's struggles with racism and alcoholism as he rose to become the greatest athlete in the first half of the twentieth century, which was what an Associated Press poll of sportswriters determined in 1950. Thorpe (who scored 875 points in the poll) beat out Babe Ruth (539), boxing icon Jack Dempsey (246), and baseball legend Ty Cobb (148).

One of Thorpe's four children, Grace Thorpe, last saw her father in 1951, shortly after the motion picture on his life was released. They were in Pearl River, New York, and Jim needed a ride to the bus stop. He was heading to New York City, and was dressed in a suede jacket and a broad-brimmed hat and was carrying the same beat-up suitcase he'd been lugging around for years. When they reached the bus stop, Jim kissed his daughter goodbye, stepped out of the car, and waited. As Grace drove away, she looked in the rearview mirror and saw that the bus stop was located in front of the Pearl River Theater. Up on the marquee in big letters was the title of the film that was playing in the movie house: *JIM THORPE— ALL AMERICAN.*

Thorpe stood there alone under the marquee. There was something profoundly heartbreaking about this moment to Grace, and this scene dramatically underscored the two worlds of Jim Thorpe's life. On the athletic field no one in the history of the United States has ever had more all-around natural gifts than Thorpe. But away from sport, Thorpe was like many Indians in the first half of the twentieth century: He struggled to discover his true identity and true place in America.

Two years later, Thorpe was eating dinner with his third wife, Patricia, in their mobile home in Lomita, California, when he felt a pain in his chest. It was his third heart attack, and his last. Thorpe died that evening at the age of sixty-four. A few days later the sitting president of the United States, Dwight David Eisenhower, sent a telegram to Thorpe's family expressing condolences.

Nearly thirty years after his funeral, Thorpe's two gold medals he won in the 1912 Olympics were restored and returned to his family. In 1987 the United States Olympic Committee finally determined that Thorpe didn't knowingly violate any rules when he accepted money to play minor league baseball with his Carlisle buddies in the summers of 1909 and '10. It was long overdue, but finally Jim Thorpe was a champion again.

Pop Warner stayed at the Carlisle Indian School through the 1914 season and continued to use the double wing—a formation that would soon revolutionize the sport and ultimately be the forerunner of the modern football offense. On February 25, 1915, a group of Warner's former players gave him a going-away party in the athletic dorm at Carlisle. He had coached 164 games at Carlisle, compiling a record of 114-42-8, and now he was taking the head coaching position at the University of Pittsburgh. Warner sensed that the doors at Carlisle would soon be boarded up. The negative PR generated by Thorpe's Olympic scandal and accusations of embezzlement by school officials had prompted Congress to take a long look at the school. A joint investigation by Congress found problems everywhere at Carlisle, from the dining hall conditions to classroom truancy to the consumption of alcohol by football players.

Warner also was tarred during the investigation. One player accused him of selling tickets that had been allotted to the school and keeping the money himself. Other players testified that Warner allowed them to drink alcohol in their dorm, that he had called the players profane names, and that he had physically harmed a few of the boys. Warner downplayed the allegations. Later in his life he wrote, "To my dying day I will maintain that Carlisle was a great and helpful institution. . . . From its very inception, however, the school was fought by a type of politician who sees the Indian only as an opportunity for exploitation and plunder."

Still using his double-wing formation at Pittsburgh, Warner won his first twenty-nine games and led the school to national titles in 1915, '16, and '18. He moved on to Stanford in 1924. Two years later, he guided the Cardinal to a 10-0-1 record and the national title. But it wouldn't be until 1934 that Warner's football legacy was finally cemented.

Warner was in the winter of his career. He was the head coach at Temple University in Philadelphia, the final stop in his coaching odyssey. On April 19, 1934, a five-year-old local youth football league called the Junior Football Conference held a banquet for its players and coaches. A dozen college coaches committed to speak to the boys and parents, but on the afternoon of the event, a spring snowstorm fell on Philadelphia. Trains at Broad Street and Thirtieth Street stations were delayed, and the roads were icy. Eleven of the college coaches phoned and told the league director that they had to cancel their appearance. But no one from the league heard from Warner.

Held in an auditorium at Philadelphia Junior High School, the banquet started at 7:30 P.M. A few speeches were given. An hour passed—still no word from Warner. But then, just after 8:30, the back door creaked open and there stood the sixty-three-year-old Warner. Using a cane, he shuffled to the stage as the youngsters and adults clapped in approval. Warner had braved the elements and driven across town to the banquet. Once on the stage, Warner scanned the crowd through his round eyeglasses and then, without notes, began talking about his career in coaching. For more than an hour, he enchanted the crowd with tales about his days at Carlisle, about Thorpe, and about beating teams such as Army. He was a living repository of college football history, and by the time he exited the stage, everyone was awestruck. Afterward, as he made his way through the crowd and back into the chilly Philadelphia night, he signed dozens of autographs and encouraged every boy to keep playing the game he loved so dearly.

Warner's generosity and off-the-cuff speech deeply touched the league officials. A few weeks later, they made a decision: Their league would no longer be called the Junior Football Conference. Instead, from here on, it would be known as the Pop Warner Football Conference. As soon as Warner's name was attached to the organization, it acquired instant and widespread credibility. Young boys all over the country began begging their way onto teams. Today, more than seven decades later, nearly 500,000 kids across forty-two states—and in several countries—play youth football each autumn in the Pop Warner league. Warner, who never had any children, wasn't paid a cent for his affiliation with the organization. He died from throat cancer on September 7, 1954. He was eighty-three.

On September 1, 1918, the War Department, needing a place to treat the wounded soldiers who were coming back from the World War I battle-fields in France, seized control of the Carlisle Indian School and turned it into a base hospital. The great experiment of the Carlisle Indian School officially ended when a Pueblo Indian named Jacob F. Duran, a Carlisle student, yanked down the American flag at Carlisle and handed it over to a major in the army.

Yet long after the Carlisle Indian School football program became a memory, the ghost of Thorpe still stirred in the mind of one of his old adversaries. "Thorpe was able to do everything that anyone else could," Dwight Eisenhower said late in his life. "But he could do it better."

ACKNOWLEDGMENTS

One of the wonderful things that you discover when you write books—and this is my fourth—is how frequently people are willing to lend you a hand simply because you want to tell a story. Over the last two years this generosity has come in many forms, from a stranger helping me for hours at a library, to an acquaintance spending countless hours fine-tuning my manuscript, to a fellow writer passing along to me the very idea for this book.

The genesis of this work can be traced to Jeremy Schaap, a reporter for ESPN and author, who mentioned Carlisle's 1912 victory over Army to Scott Waxman, my agent. My editor at Random House, Mark Tavani, is simply one of the most skilled pros in the business; Mark's fingerprints are all over this work. My wife, Sara Anderson, who's the Homes editor at *Southern Living* magazine, edited two drafts of the manuscript and stamped her literary flourishes onto nearly every page. (Thanks once again, S.P.) Karen Lingo, who's a senior writer at *Southern Living*, also read a version of the manuscript, and her deft touches and pitch-perfect changes improved the final product immensely. My stepfather, Gordy Bratz, a retired army colonel, did an outstanding and thorough edit and always pointed me in the right direction whenever I had a military question. Joey Goldstein, a sports publicity legend in New York, assisted me with my research by traveling to different libraries around the country and combing their archives. Barb Landis, Rob Schwartz, and Richard Tritt of the Cumberland County Historical Society in Carlisle, Pennsylvania, all patiently answered all of my questions and helped fill in many historical blanks. Nita Ogg, a librarian at the Fultondale, Alabama, public library, made sure that my two tons of checked-out books were never overdue.

And Scott Waxman strongly encouraged me to pursue this project and helped develop the idea. Without Scott's guidance and persistence, what you now hold in your hands never would have been possible.

A final thanks goes to Terry McDonell, David Bauer, Rich O'Brien, and the rest of the crew at *Sports Illustrated*.

A NOTE ON SOURCES

In the process of researching this work I consulted hundreds of books, reference volumes, magazines, newspaper articles, online databases, correspondence, yearbooks, and scrapbooks. I interviewed dozens of historians as well. At times I was confronted with contradictory information. In these instances, I weighed all the available evidence and went with what I believed was the most accurate source.

I also want to especially acknowledge four authors whose works I leaned on particularly hard: Bill Crawford's *All American: The Rise and Fall of Jim Thorpe*, Kenneth S. Davis's *Dwight D. Eisenhower: Soldier of Democracy*, Jack Newcombe's *The Best of the Athletic Boys*, and Robert W. Wheeler's *Jim Thorpe: World's Greatest Athlete*.

When piecing together the narrative of this book, I re-created scenes that, in some instances, took place over one hundred years ago. In doing so, my research assistant and I painstakingly pored over all of our material to try to reconstruct characters and events as factually as possible. To paint the fullest possible picture, I strung together my research as best I could and tried to fill in the blanks to the best of my ability. I wish I could have been on the sideline for that epic game in 1912—and had the chance to chat face-to-face with Thorpe, Eisenhower, and Warner (who, it turns out, was born one hundred years to the day before me, on April 5, 1871)— but instead these men talked to me through the words they left behind and through the writers who chronicled their lives. It is my sincere hope that I have done them all justice.

NOTES

1 THE THRILL OF POSSIBILITY

3 nervously paced through the locker room: Robert W. Wheeler, *Jim Thorpe: World's Greatest Athlete* (Norman: University of Oklahoma Press, 1979), p. 128.

3 five thousand fans: *New York Times,* Nov. 10, 1912.

3 he planned to unveil his latest: Pop Warner, *Football's Greatest Teacher: The Epic Autobiography of College Football's Winningest Coach,* edited by Mike Bynum (Langhorne, Pa.: Pop Warner Little Scholars, 1993), p. 141.

4 he explained that this was a chance: Wheeler, *Jim Thorpe,* p. 128.

6 The paper ran a two-column photo: Stephen E. Ambrose, *Eisenhower: Soldier, General of the Army, President-Elect, 1890–1952* (New York: Simon & Schuster, 1983), p. 49.

6 from his linebacker position: Kenneth S. Davis, *Dwight D. Eisenhower: Soldier of Democracy* (New York: Smithmark, 1995), p. 137.

7 Walter Camp, the former Yale player: Jack Newcombe, *The Best of the Athletic Boys* (Garden City, N.Y.: Doubleday, 1975), p. 202.

2 SHOT LIKE BUFFALO

9 The colonel of the cavalry troops: Renée Sansom Flood, *Lost Bird of Wounded Knee: Spirit of the Lakota* (New York: Scribner, 1995), p. 28.

10 "Indians are dancing in the snow": Charles Phillips, "Wounded Knee Massacre: United States Versus the Plains Indians," *American History Magazine,* December 2005.

11 "What do you want here?": Alan Axelrod, *Chronicle of the Indian Wars* (New York: Prentice Hall General Reference, 1993), pp. 252–55.

12 Many local newspapermen applauded: Roger L. Di Silvestro, *In the Shadow of Wounded Knee: The Untold Final Chapter of the Indian Wars* (New York: Walker, 2005), pp. 84–85.

13 Yellow Bird began dancing the Ghost Dance: Flood, *Lost Bird of Wounded Knee,* pp. 27–28.

13 One young Indian, Black Coyote: Axelrod, *Chronicle of the Indian Wars,* pp. 254–55.

13 Lieutenant James Mann yelled: *Lost Bird of Wounded Knee,* p. 29.

14 "They had four troops dismounted": Flood, *Lost Bird of Wounded Knee*, p. 41.

14 "Everyone was shouting and shooting": Flood, *Lost Bird of Wounded Knee*, pp. 41–42.

14 "We tried to run": Axelrod, *Chronicle of the Indian Wars*, p. 255.

15 She was wearing a cap: Di Silvestro, *In the Shadow of Wounded Knee*, p. 91.

15 "It was a thing to melt": Frederick E. Hoxie, *Encyclopedia of North American Indians* (New York: Houghton Mifflin, 1996), p. 696.

15 "Fully three miles from the scene": Di Silvestro, *In the Shadow of Wounded Knee*, p. 91.

15 Corporal Paul H. Weinert: Flood, *Lost Bird of Wounded Knee*, p. 41.

15 Plenty Horses looked like a classic Sioux warrior: Robert M. Utley, "The Ordeal of Plenty Horses," *American Heritage*, December 1974, www.americanheritage.com/articles/magazine/ah/1974/1/1974_1_15.shtml.

16 On the morning of January 7, 1891: Di Silvestro, *In the Shadow of Wounded Knee*, pp. 97–101.

16 *"Hau, kola"*: Di Silvestro, *In the Shadow of Wounded Knee*, p. 98.

16 this death would mark an end: Di Silvestro, *In the Shadow of Wounded Knee*, p. 101.

3 POP LEARNS FROM MA

19 The kids teased Warner by calling him "Butter": Warner, *Football's Greatest Teacher*, p. 37.

19 He taunted Glenn with a few words: Warner, *Football's Greatest Teacher*, p. 37.

20 Warner's father, William: Bill Crawford, *All American: The Rise and Fall of Jim Thorpe* (Hoboken, N.J.: Wiley, 2005), p. 23.

20 One of the most popular games: Warner, *Football's Greatest Teacher*, p. 38.

21 a teacher persuaded him to take the entrance exam: Warner, *Football's Greatest Teacher*, p. 38.

22 To make matters interesting: Crawford, *All American*, p. 24.

23 Over the next two years: Warner, *Football's Greatest Teacher*, p. 39.

23 In June 1892, Warner rode the train: Glenn S. Warner, "Battles of Brawn," *Collier's*, November 7, 1931.

24 He decided to write his father a letter: Warner, "Battles of Brawn."

24 The buddy mentioned that there was someone else on board: Warner, *Football's Greatest Teacher*, pp. 43–44.

25 he asked Warner if he'd be interested: Warner, *Football's Greatest Teacher*, p. 44.

25 "Get on your stuff right away": Warner, "Battles of Brawn."

26 Johanson informed Warner: Warner, *Football's Greatest Teacher*, p. 45.

27 on one of the first days of practice Johanson: Warner, "Battles of Brawn."

28 The team was so popular that Campbell's: Julie Moran Alterio, "Campbell's Cooking Up New Ideas," *White Plains* (N.Y.) *Journal News*, January 29, 2006.

28 In his spare time: Warner, "Battles of Brawn."

28 On Sunday afternoons: Crawford, *All American*, p. 30.

29 Warner diagrammed play "Number 39": Warner, *Football's Greatest Teacher*, pp. 54–55.

31 The business manager: Warner, *Football's Greatest Teacher*, pp. 58–60.

33 Warner eventually bet: Warner, *Football's Greatest Teacher*, pp. 60–62.

33 Many of the cowboys in the crowd: Mike Bynum, Introduction to *Football's Greatest Teacher*, p. 25.

35 he would review weekly accounts: Warner, *Football's Greatest Teacher*, p. 32.

36 Warner compared the undefeated Princeton: Warner, *Football's Greatest Teacher*, p. 76.

36 When the final whistle blew: Warner, *Football's Greatest Teacher*, pp. 76–77.

37 "We outscored 'em but": Crawford, *All American*, p. 35.

38 But soon after the team's final game: Warner, *Football's Greatest Teacher*, pp. 81–82.

4 THE TRICKIEST PLAY

42 When he was a young boy: Robert M. Utley, Introduction to Richard Henry Pratt, *Battlefield & Classroom: An Autobiography by Richard Henry Pratt*, edited by Robert M. Utley (Norman: University of Oklahoma Press, 1964), pp. xvii–xxiv.

42 When the war was over: David Wallace Adams, *Education for Extinction: American Indians and the Boarding School Experience 1875–1928* (Lawrence: University Press of Kansas, 1995), pp. 38–39.

43 Pratt walked with his six-year-old daughter: Pratt, *Battlefield & Classroom*, pp. 113–14.

43 he jumped from behind a palmetto: Adams, *Education for Extinction*, p. 39.

44 Like Pratt, most whites believed: Robert Lipsyte, *Jim Thorpe: 20th-Century Jock* (New York: HarperCollins, 1993), p. 17.

45 "The duty of the government": Pratt, *Battlefield & Classroom*, p. 167.

47 Pratt hired her to teach the Indian prisoners: Pratt, *Battlefield & Classroom*, pp. 154–55.

47 Pratt and Mather climbed into: Pratt, *Battlefield & Classroom*, pp. 220–29.

48 the government was adopting a new Indian policy: Pratt, *Battlefield & Classroom*, pp. 221–24.

49 "We will all have a good-bye smoke": Newcombe, *The Best of the Athletic Boys*, pp. 68–69.

49 "I could think of no reason why white people": Michael L. Cooper, *Indian School: Teaching the White Man's Way* (New York: Clarion, 1999), pp. 1–5.

51 The boys and girls grew so uncomfortable: Cooper, *Indian School*, p. 7.

51 they spotted a full moon: Cooper, *Indian School*, pp. 7–10.

51 The process of assimilation began: Adams, *Education for Extinction*, pp. 100–103.

52 Some of the names on the board: Cooper, *Indian School*, p. 40.

53 the teacher brought in items such as shirts, shoes: Cooper, *Indian School*, pp. 51–52.

54 To remind the students: Stephanie Anderson, "On Sacred Ground," *Central Pennsylvania*, May 2000, available at http://www.wordsasweapons.com/indianschool.html.

54 One afternoon the two girls stuffed: Cooper, *Indian School,* p. 48.

55 "It's Stacy, sir": Moss Hall, *Go, Indians! Stories of the Great Indian Athletes of the Carlisle School* (Los Angeles: Ward Ritchie, 1971), pp. 7–15.

57 "Sir, we understand your reasons": Hall, *Go, Indians!,* pp. 13–15.

58 Practicing on a rocky, sloping pasture: Robert Cantwell, "The Poet, the Bums, and the Legendary Red Men," *Sports Illustrated,* February 15, 1960, pp. 77–83.

59 Carlisle had played so well: Newcombe, *The Best of the Athletic Boys,* p. 81.

60 Sitting in the stands: Hall, *Go, Indians!,* pp. 20–27.

63 Earlier in the '96 season: John S. Steckbeck, *Fabulous Redmen: The Carlisle Indians and Their Famous Football Teams* (Harrisburg, Pa.: J. Horace McFarland, 1951), p. 20.

63 At one impromptu celebration: David Wallace Adams, "More Than a Game: The Carlisle Indians Take to the Gridiron, 1893–1917," *Western Historical Quarterly* (Spring 2001), pp. 26–27.

64 "I can give no words that will express": John Bloom, " 'Show What an Indian Can Do': Sports, Memory, and Ethnic Identity at Federal Indian Boarding Schools," *Journal of American Indian Education* 35, no. 3 (Spring 1996), http://jaie.asu.edu/ v35/V35S3sh.htm.

65 Warner, still an attorney: Warner, *Football's Greatest Teacher,* p. 83.

65 Warner didn't hold a high opinion: Warner, "Heap Big Run-Most-Fast," *Collier's,* October 24, 1931.

66 "The squad ought to be trying out": Warner, "The Indian Massacres," *Collier's,* October 17, 1931.

68 When he finally showed up: Wheeler, *Jim Thorpe,* pp. 46–47.

68 "This is a new kind of team": Hall, *Go, Indians!,* p. 30.

68 Even at the highest levels: Margaret L. Archuleta, Brenda J. Child, and K. Tsianina Lomawaima, *Away from Home: American Indian Boarding School Experiences* (Phoenix: Heard Museum, 2000), p. 31.

69 "When you're on defense": Hall, *Go, Indians!,* pp. 30–39.

70 checked into the Normandie Hotel: Steckbeck, *Fabulous Redmen,* p. 29.

71 On most early evenings: Hall, *Go, Indians!,* pp. 28–32.

73 *The New York World* described: Adams, "More Than a Game," p. 31.

74 A few days before Carlisle traveled: Hall, *Go, Indians!,* pp. 35–37.

75 Pratt even had his students: Anderson, "On Sacred Ground."

5 WHAT AN INDIAN CAN DO

78 Just twelve days into the twentieth century: Newcombe, *The Best of the Athletic Boys,* p. 55.

78 Public attitudes toward Indians: Lipsyte, *Jim Thorpe,* p. 15.

79 As the train snaked through: Newcombe, *The Best of the Athletic Boys,* p. 56.

79 As Warner sat on a bench outside: Warner, *Football's Greatest Teacher,* p. 87.

79 the windchill factor outside: *Indian Helper,* January 17, 1900.

80 "There is no loud talking": Adams, "More Than a Game," p. 37.

80 At several stores the players spotted: *Indian Helper,* January 17, 1900.

80 It was fatter and heavier: Newcombe, *The Best of the Athletic Boys,* p. 56.

80 As the eighteen players emerged: *San Francisco Chronicle,* December 26, 1899.

82 Shortly after the turn of the century: Newcombe, *The Best of the Athletic Boys,* p. 64.

82 A few of the players believed: *Indian Helper,* January 17, 1900.

84 Whenever the coach pulled into Keokuk Falls: Brad Steiger and Charlotte Thorpe, *Thorpe's Gold: The Inspiring Untold True Story of Jim Thorpe—World's Greatest Athlete* (New York: Quicksilver, 1984), pp. 43–44.

84 At some point in the evening two men: Crawford, *All American,* p. 15.

84 One day in 1880: Steiger and Thorpe, *Thorpe's Gold,* p. 18.

85 They also wrestled: Wheeler, *Jim Thorpe,* p. 9.

86 but on the morning of their departure: Wheeler, *Jim Thorpe,* p. 8.

86 Charlie was considered "sweet" and "gentle": Newcombe, *The Best of the Athletic Boys,* p. 44.

87 At dawn the next morning: Steiger and Thorpe, *Thorpe's Gold,* p. 42.

88 He had attended one of the Kansas mission schools: Crawford, *All American,* p. 16.

88 In the 1890s the Office: Newcombe, *The Best of the Athletic Boys,* p. 38.

88 Jim would shoot at flies: Lipsyte, *Jim Thorpe,* p. 21.

89 When he went raccoon hunting: Crawford, *All American,* p. 20.

90 It was the white man's symbol: Archuleta, *Away from Home,* pp. 24 and 50.

90 Every student also had to pick a trade: Wheeler, *Jim Thorpe,* p. 15.

91 Operated by the federal government's: Newcombe, *The Best of the Athletic Boys,* pp. 53–54.

92 he organized games among his friends: Crawford, *All American,* p. 41.

93 A few minutes later Carlos Montezuma: *Indian Helper,* January 17, 1900.

94 On the morning of the game: Steckbeck, *Fabulous Redmen,* p. 64.

95 a classmate approached Thorpe: Newcombe, *The Best of the Athletic Boys,* p. 57.

98 its main dirt road featured: Newcombe, *The Best of the Athletic Boys,* p. 58.

99 "Jim, why don't you try that?": Crawford, *All American,* p. 49.

99 The locals talked glowingly: Crawford, *All American,* p. 50.

102 Many of the older boys at Haskell: Wheeler, *Jim Thorpe,* p. 20.

103 "Son," Hiram said, "you are an Indian": Wheeler, *Jim Thorpe,* p. 20.

6 THERE'S JUST NO FUTURE IN THE ARMY

105 forming a ring around two teenage boys: Davis, *Dwight D. Eisenhower,* pp. 77–78.

106 On Halloween night in 1900: Michael R. Beschloss, *Eisenhower: A Centennial Life* (New York: HarperCollins, 1990), pp. 18–19.

107   a man named Dudley: Peter Lyon, *Eisenhower: Portrait of the Hero* (Boston: Little, Brown, 1974), p. 37.

108   Not even McCoy expected: Lyon, *Eisenhower*, p. 37.

108   Soon neighborhoods known: Carlo D'Este, *Eisenhower: A Soldier's Life* (New York: Henry Holt, 2002), p. 12.

111   In Hickok's heyday: Lyon, *Eisenhower*, p. 39.

111   he liked to scale the barn's interior skeleton: Geoffrey Perret, *Eisenhower* (New York: Random House, 1999), p. 29.

112   The worst was when he had to wake: Perret, *Eisenhower*, p. 18.

112   In their free time, the Eisenhower boys: D'Este, *Eisenhower*, p. 23.

112   When the United States went to war: Perret, *Eisenhower*, pp. 21–22.

112   he played a game called "shinny": D'Este, *Eisenhower*, p. 38.

112   When the workday was over: Davis, *Dwight D. Eisenhower*, pp. 72–73.

114   the most popular man in Abilene: Dwight D. Eisenhower, *At Ease: Stories I Tell to Friends* (New York: Doubleday, 1967), p. 80.

114   Seeing a brick at his feet: Davis, *Dwight D. Eisenhower*, p. 68.

115   she tried to dull that beast with a homily: Dwight D. Eisenhower, *In Review: Pictures I've Kept* (New York: Doubleday, 1969), p. 4.

115   The punches kept coming: Davis, *Dwight D. Eisenhower*, pp. 76–79.

116   The fight ended in a draw: Ambrose, *Eisenhower*, p. 29.

116   years earlier a jailbird had let off: Perret, *Eisenhower*, p. 28.

117   By the age of twelve he had read: D'Este, *Eisenhower*, p. 33.

118   when Abilene lost, he blamed himself: Ambrose, *Eisenhower*, p. 34.

118   The players wore light-colored duck pants: Perret, *Eisenhower*, p. 29.

119   taught at a young age by his religious parents: Ambrose, *Eisenhower*, p. 34.

119   a few days later, Ike began to feel ill: Eisenhower, *In Review*, p. 8.

119   "This is serious": Davis, *Dwight D. Eisenhower*, p. 47.

119   "Look, Ed, they are talking about": Eisenhower, *In Review*, p. 8.

120   When he realized that the league dues: Ambrose, *Eisenhower*, p. 35.

120   "We improved the condition of the Association": Ambrose, *Eisenhower*, p. 35.

122   "I like to read what's going on": Perret, *Eisenhower*, p. 33.

122   "We both want to go": Perret, *Eisenhower*, p. 36.

123   Ike landed a job: Eisenhower, *In Review*, p. 9.

123   Swede also mentioned: Ambrose, *Eisenhower*, pp. 38–39.

123   "Look, Ike": Davis, *Dwight D. Eisenhower*, p. 106.

124   Swede, arguing that Ike had nothing to lose: Ambrose, *Eisenhower*, p. 39.

125   after McDonnell let the pass go: Davis, *Dwight D. Eisenhower*, pp. 115–16.

126   "look a gift horse in the mouth": Davis, *Dwight D. Eisenhower*, pp. 113–14.

127   The door slowly creaked open: Eisenhower, *At Ease*, p. 107.

128 Bradley had received his congressional appointment: Omar Bradley, *A General's Life* (New York: Simon & Schuster, 1983), pp. 27–29.

129 On the early June day: Davis, *Dwight D. Eisenhower*, pp. 117–18.

7 HE IS CERTAINLY A WILD INDIAN

132 So many dreams were buried here: Cooper, *Indian School*, pp. 43–46.

133 Thorpe entered the guardhouse: Crawford, *All American*, p. 55.

134 He especially enjoyed Sundays: Newcombe, *The Best of the Athletic Boys*, p. 78.

134 They eventually decided: Wheeler, *Jim Thorpe*, pp. 48–49.

137 Thorpe approached the group: Wheeler, *Jim Thorpe*, pp. 50–52.

138 Thorpe had won the high jump: Newcombe, *The Best of the Athletic Boys*, p. 97.

138 Warner explained: Warner, *Football's Greatest Teacher*, p. 120.

139 he spotted an advertisement that blared: Newcombe, *The Best of the Athletic Boys*, p. 65.

139 But his friend didn't last long: Newcombe, *The Best of the Athletic Boys*, pp. 65–66.

140 But Warner made sure: Newcombe, *The Best of the Athletic Boys*, pp. 98–101.

141 Thorpe was quietly encouraged: Wheeler, *Jim Thorpe*, pp. 52–55.

142 Thorpe jogged over to the sideline: Warner, *Football's Greatest Teacher*, pp. 121–22.

146 Warner enlisted the assistance of Hugh Miller: Newcombe, *The Best of the Athletic Boys*, pp. 112–13.

149 Warner was renovating the school hospital: Newcombe, *The Best of the Athletic Boys*, pp. 111–12.

150 There were other fringe benefits: Crawford, *All American*, pp. 87–89.

151 Warner found them jobs working on campus: Newcombe, *The Best of the Athletic Boys*, p. 112.

151 Pratt had been able to keep: Cantwell, "The Poet, the Bums and the Legendary Redmen," p. 78.

152 Warner invited photographers: Newcombe, *The Best of the Athletic Boys*, p. 114.

155 For the Carlisle students: Newcombe, *The Best of the Athletic Boys*, pp. 115–17.

156 Subbing for Albert Payne: Crawford, *All American*, pp. 79–80.

157 Two years earlier: Wheeler, *Jim Thorpe*, p. 59.

157 Little Boy replied: Warner, *Football's Greatest Teacher*, p. 123.

159 As Gardner lay on the ground: Steckbeck, *Fabulous Redmen*, p. 50.

160 a few boys carrying a stretcher: Newcombe, *The Best of the Athletic Boys*, p. 118.

160 The Indian boys also poked fun: Warner, "Heap Big Run-Most-Fast."

161 "We had a hard fight": Steckbeck, *Fabulous Redmen*, p. 73.

162 "The (coaching) profession": Michael Richman, *Investor's Business Daily*, March 16, 2001.

162 Stagg had labeled his 1907 squad: Warner, *Football's Greatest Teacher*, p. 123.

163 At both ends of the field: Crawford, *All American*, p. 82.

164 "The success of the Indians": Glenn S. Warner, "Athletics at the Carlisle Indian School," *The Indian Craftsman: A Magazine Not Only About Indians But Mainly by Indians,* February 1909.

8 A COUPLE OF WELL-PAID AMATEURS

168 "Why don't you go back": Newcombe, *The Best of the Athletic Boys,* pp. 147–48.

168 the chants started late: Wheeler, *Jim Thorpe,* p. 67.

170 "We place as much stock": Newcombe, *The Best of the Athletic Boys,* p. 132.

170 sing a few native songs before dinner: Newcombe, *The Best of the Athletic Boys,* p. 133.

171 It was at this precise moment: Warner, *Football's Greatest Teacher,* p. 124.

173 Warner had arranged the final two games: Newcombe, *The Best of the Athletic Boys,* p. 134.

174 Shortly after graduating: *Sporting News,* June 28, 1945; Associated Press, June 29, 1945.

176 He was waiting to take: Wheeler, *Jim Thorpe,* pp. 78–80.

177 On June 15, about a week: Crawford, *All American,* pp. 122–24.

178 Sweetcorn grew so upset: Newcombe, *The Best of the Athletic Boys,* p. 143.

181 the ball smacked Thorpe on the head: Crawford, *All American,* p. 130.

181 In a letter to Thorpe: Newcombe, *The Best of the Athletic Boys,* p. 143.

183 Warner then sent one of his assistant coaches: Steiger and Thorpe, *Thorpe's Gold,* p. 139.

9 A BRUTAL, SAVAGE, MURDEROUS SPORT

186 Early in the fourth quarter: Joel Stashenko, Associated Press, October 20, 1989.

188 Two weeks later, horror struck: John S. Watterson, "The Death of Archer Christian: College Presidents and the Reform of College Football," *Journal of Sports History* 22, no. 2 (Summer 1995), pp. 149–167.

190 "Does the public need any more proof": John S. Watterson, "Inventing Modern Football," *American Heritage,* September/October 1988, www.americanheritage.com.

190 a young student named Dennis Michie: Jack Clary, *Army vs. Navy: Seventy Years of Football Rivalry* (New York: Ronald, 1965), pp. 9–11.

191 If the Naval Academy, which had been playing: Gene Schoor, *100 Years of Army-Navy Football* (New York: Henry Holt, 1989), pp. 2–6.

10 BEAST BARRACKS AND A BEAST ON THE FIELD

198 Dwight Eisenhower had never ventured: Davis, *Dwight D. Eisenhower,* p. 121.

198 Eisenhower's next stop was Chicago: D'Este, *Eisenhower,* p. 59.

199 The doctor wanted to operate: Davis, *Dwight D. Eisenhower,* p. 111.

199 But the illness took a toll: Eisenhower, *At Ease,* p. 3.

199 Ike would not see Edgar again for fifteen years: D'Este, *Eisenhower,* p. 59.

200   Scanning the faces of the other appointees: Davis, *Dwight D. Eisenhower*, p. 124.

200   "Hold your head up!": Ambrose, *Eisenhower*, p. 43.

200   The fort was critical in the American Revolution: D'Este, *Eisenhower*, p. 60.

201   For the three weeks of Beast Barracks: Davis, *Dwight D. Eisenhower*, p. 127.

202   *What am I doing here?:* D'Este, *Eisenhower*, p. 62.

202   A band played patriotic songs: D'Este, *Eisenhower*, pp. 63–64.

202   *It won't always be like this:* Perret, *Eisenhower*, p. 47.

202   "It's easy for you": Eisenhower, *At Ease*, p. 5.

203   he predicted to many of his friends: D'Este, *Eisenhower*, p. 65.

203   Hazing was not as dangerous: Perret, *Eisenhower*, p. 46.

203   a cadet named Edgar Allan Poe: Ambrose, *Eisenhower*, p. 48.

204   "Sir, Cadets Eisenhower and Atkins": Eisenhower, *In Review*, p. 13.

204   "What's the meaning of this?": Davis, *Dwight D. Eisenhower*, p. 132.

204   When Eisenhower told his classmates: D'Este, *Eisenhower*, p. 65.

204   Though smoking was strictly forbidden: Ambrose, *Eisenhower*, p. 47.

204   Just a few months into his first year: D'Este, *Eisenhower*, p. 65.

204   Even when night fell: D'Este, *Eisenhower*, p. 67.

205   "I'm fit to be tied": D'Este, *Eisenhower*, p. 67.

205   He also began attacking any food: Ambrose, *Eisenhower*, p. 48.

205   Ike played a starring role: D'Este, *Eisenhower*, p. 67.

206   To lure Muhlenberg to Indian Field: Newcombe, *The Best of the Athletic Boys*, p. 149.

207   Warner had also convinced: Steiger, "Thorpe's Gold," p. 143.

207   His father was killed: Crawford, *All American*, p. 134.

208   Warner possessed a hair-trigger temper: Newcombe, *The Best of the Athletic Boys*, p. 157.

208   "What I like about Thorpe": Wheeler, *Jim Thorpe*, p. 82.

208   Warner also took Thorpe and others: Crawford, *All American*, p. 137.

209   He came face-to-face with Walter Reisner: Newcombe, *The Best of the Athletic Boys*, pp. 149–50.

209   Warner was one of the first: Newcombe, *The Best of the Athletic Boys*, p. 155.

210   Sometimes the black-and-blue cleat marks: Crawford, *All American*, p. 138.

211   Thorpe immediately dashed up the field: Wheeler, *Jim Thorpe*, p. 87.

212   These words would literally follow: Newcombe, *The Best of the Athletic Boys*, p. 162.

215   As the teams walked off the field: Clary, *Army vs. Navy*, p. 49.

216   The Crimson coach, Percy Haughton: Crawford, *All American*, p. 140.

216   he had choked a bulldog: *Orlando Sentinel*, May 30, 2004.

217   A few days before Carlisle arrived: Warner, *Football's Greatest Teacher*, p. 128.

220   But instead of calling for a punt: Newcombe, *The Best of the Athletic Boys*, p. 167.

222   he escorted them to the Hippodrome: Newcombe, *The Best of the Athletic Boys*, p. 169.

11   A REAL AMERICAN IF THERE EVER WAS ONE

225   In 1912, for the first time: David Blanke, *The 1910s: American Popular Culture
      Through History* (Westport, Conn.: Greenwood, 2002), p. 131.

226   At about 11:40 P.M. on April 13: Blanke, *The 1910s*, pp. 242–45.

226   One cadet poked fun at Bradley's looks: Davis, *Dwight D. Eisenhower*, p. 134.

228   Strang scribbled Bradley's name down: Bradley, *A General's Life*, p. 32.

228   "Practice hitting my way": Eisenhower, *At Ease*, p. 7.

229   he wanted Warner to tag along: Crawford, *All American*, p. 166.

230   The talent bar had been set high: Dick Schaap, *The History of the Olympics* (New
      York: Knopf, 1975), pp. 130–33.

230   the well-wishers were led: Gregory Richards, *Jim Thorpe: World's Greatest Athlete*
      (Chicago: Children's, 1984), pp. 61–62.

230   Along the back rail of the ship: Arthur Mann, "Thorpe—The Poor Indian," *Street
      and Smith's Sport Story Magazine*, December 1935.

231   On the first morning of training: Wheeler, *Jim Thorpe*, pp. 99–102.

232   he wanted a sport that tested: Crawford, *All American*, p. 165.

232   "All Thorpe wanted to know is": Steiger and Thorpe, *Thorpe's Gold*, p. 167.

232   When Warner and his boys arrived: Warner, *Football's Greatest Teacher*, pp. 132–33.

233   When they looked up: Richards, *Jim Thorpe*, p. 63.

233   There was such a powerful look: Steiger and Thorpe, *Thorpe's Gold*, p. 173.

233   he arranged for Thorpe, Tewanima: Mann, "Thorpe—The Poor Indian."

235   Once all the athletes were on the field: Crawford, *All American*, p. 170.

236   At just a shade over five feet, eleven inches: Newcombe, *The Best of the Athletic
      Boys*, p. 184.

239   There was a chandelier hanging: Douglas Collins, *Olympic Dreams: 100 Years of
      Excellence* (New York: Universe, 1996), pp. 86–87.

240   But the Carlisle coach didn't sway Miller: Crawford, *All American*, pp. 210–11.

240   Growing up in Arizona: Steiger and Thorpe, *Thorpe's Gold*, p. 119.

241   After covering the eighteen miles: Newcombe, *The Best of the Athletic Boys*, p. 181.

241   The earliest tribes of Indians had Runners: Lipsyte, *Jim Thorpe*, pp. 1–4.

241   Navajos called them "little rabbits": Hampton Sides, *Blood and Thunder: An Epic of
      the American West* (New York: Doubleday, 2006), p. 66.

241   Back in 1896, the first modern games: John Kieran and Arthur Daley, *The Story of
      the Olympic Games* (New York: Lippincott, 1952), p. 76.

243   "He said he would wait for me": Schaap, *The Olympics*, p. 131.

244   Among the twenty-nine athletes: Crawford, *All American*, p. 174.

247 when he got back onto the ship: Warner, *Football's Greatest Teacher*, p. 135.

248 He was so fascinated: Steiger and Thorpe, *Thorpe's Gold*, p. 185.

12 CHIEF THORPE AND THE HUGE KANSAN

252 "This is an occasion for celebration": Wheeler, *Jim Thorpe*, p. 114.

253 "I thank you for all you have done": Crawford, *All American*, p. 180.

255 He had run track over the winter: D'Este, *Eisenhower*, p. 67.

255 So whenever he had a few spare moments: Eisenhower, *At Ease*, p. 13.

256 "I was a Harvard man": *Sports Illustrated*, November 5, 1990.

257 He ran his cool-down laps: Eisenhower, *At Ease*, pp. 13–14.

259 he sometimes convinced his roommate: Crawford, *All American*, p. 183.

260 All the soft-spoken Hopi ever wanted: Crawford, *All American*, p. 181.

261 In Warner's vision of this new offense: Newcombe, *The Best of the Athletic Boys*, p. 197.

262 Even Marty Maher: Davis, *Dwight D. Eisenhower*, p. 135.

263 One time he hurled a piece of meat: D'Este, *Eisenhower*, pp. 65–66.

265 "You've got to behave yourself": Warner, *Football's Greatest Teacher*, pp. 138–39.

265 said in a low, barely audible voice: Newcombe, *The Best of the Athletic Boys*, p. 198.

266 The picture of his boyhood friend: Davis, *Dwight D. Eisenhower*, p. 135.

266 He carefully clipped: Ambrose, *Eisenhower*, p. 49.

267 "Thorpe will never run through us": Crawford, *All American*, p. 185.

268 Thorpe's Sac and Fox tribe: Cantwell, "The Poet, the Bums, and the Legendary Red Men," p. 80.

270 On Halloween eve, just ten days: *New York Times*, October 31, 1912.

271 When the senator asked the player: Crawford, *All American*, p. 186.

272 The reporter for the *Howitzer:* D'Este, *Eisenhower*, p. 67.

272 The University of Toronto promised him: Newcombe, *The Best of the Athletic Boys*, p. 187.

274 Thorpe had some fun: Wheeler, *Jim Thorpe*, p. 127.

13 THE CLASH OF HEROES

278 storm clouds rolled over: *New York Times*, November 10, 1912.

279 He rumbled for thirteen yards: Play-by-play sheet of Army's 1912 football season from the original files of the United States Military Academy, West Point, N.Y.

279 Arcasa cut up the field: Crawford, *All American*, pp. 191–92.

285 Thorpe approached the referee: Newcombe, *The Best of the Athletic Boys*, pp. 201–202.

287 To pull this off, Eisenhower: Davis, *Dwight D. Eisenhower*, p. 137.

289 Eisenhower and Hobbs closed in: Davis, *Dwight D. Eisenhower*, p. 137.

289 "as human as any one of them": D'Este, *Eisenhower*, p. 68.

290 stopped the instant before: D'Este, *Eisenhower*, p. 68.

292 "That Indian is the greatest player": Wheeler, *Jim Thorpe*, p. 132.

14 THE DEAD INDIAN AND ANOTHER WOUNDED KNEE

295 Walter Camp listened attentively: Wheeler, *Jim Thorpe*, p. 132.

295 But Camp saved his most effusive compliments: Newcombe, *The Best of the Athletic Boys*, p. 202.

298 Thorpe was covering a Penn end: Warner, *Football's Greatest Teacher*, pp. 139–40.

300 When Thorpe touched the ball again: Newcombe, *The Best of the Athletic Boys*, p. 203.

300 "Sure, I could have batted it down easy": Warner, *Football's Greatest Teacher*, pp. 139–40.

301 Earlier in the season: Perret, *Eisenhower*, p. 49.

301 As he pushed forward: D'Este, *Eisenhower*, pp. 68–69.

301 Would he be able to strap on: Davis, *Dwight D. Eisenhower*, p. 138.

305 "Why, I know that guy": Newcombe, *The Best of the Athletic Boys*, pp. 204–5.

306 "Here I come up with the best line plunger": D'Este, *Eisenhower*, p. 69.

307 Warner called one of his favorite: Crawford, *All American*, p. 194.

308 Ike started to smoke frequently: Ambrose, *Eisenhower*, p. 50.

310 "He'd made a big gain": Davis, *Dwight D. Eisenhower*, p. 137.

EPILOGUE: THE GHOSTS OF CARLISLE

313 He paced in his trailer: Ambrose, *Eisenhower*, pp. 303–8.

314 On Friday nights before games: Ambrose, *Eisenhower*, p. 50.

314 Ike nervously walked along the sideline: Davis, *Dwight D. Eisenhower*, p. 145.

315 Ike made a simple promise to himself: Ambrose, *Eisenhower*, p. 56.

315 Jim Thorpe was asked: D'Este, *Eisenhower*, p. 68.

315 the two former West Point: Bradley, *A General's Life*, pp. 131–33.

315 "Throughout the war Omar Bradley": Bradley, *A General's Life*, p. 13.

316 Jim Thorpe marched into the Fifth Avenue office: Crawford, *All American*, p. 213.

317 They were in Pearl River, New York: Bob Greene, "The Man in Front of the Movie House," *Chicago Tribune*, August 11, 1992.

319 On April 19, 1934: Joel D. Balthaser, *Pop Warner Little Scholars* (Portsmouth, N.H.: Arcadia, 2004), p. 13.

320 The great experiment: Crawford, *All American*, p. 223.

INDEX

ABOUT THE AUTHOR

LARS ANDERSON is a *Sports Illustrated* staff writer and a graduate of the Columbia University Graduate School of Journalism. He is also the author of *The All Americans*. He lives with his wife in Birmingham, Alabama.

ABOUT THE TYPE

The text of this book was set in Filosofia. It was designed in 1996 by Zuzana Licko, who created it for digital typesetting as an interpretation of the sixteenth-century typeface Bodoni. Filosofia, an example of Licko's unusual font designs, has classical proportions with a strong vertical feeling, softened by rounded droplike serifs. She has designed many typefaces and is the cofounder of *Emigre* magazine, where many of them first appeared. Born in Bratislava, Czechoslovakia, Licko came to the United States in 1968. She studied graphic communications at the University of California at Berkeley, graduating in 1984.